Rediscovering Economic Policy as a Discipline

Government interventions in market failures can encounter objections from those who doubt their efficacy. Acocella, a leading expert on economic policy, counters these unfounded criticisms, making the convincing case for the foundation, coordination and reach of government action through economic policy. Arguing for the governmental potential to devise democratic, fair and effective institutions and policies, this book also demonstrates the validity of the principles outlined by Frisch and Tinbergen, amongst others, for controlling the economy, in a strategic context, equivalent to the rational expectations assumption. Demonstrating how unconventional monetary policies and other policies (such as macroprudential regulation, new fiscal rules and new forms of international policy coordination) can offer an effective response to the multiplicity of current economic issues, the recent financial crisis arguably indicates that economic policy must once again take centre stage as the applied complement to mainstream economic theory.

Nicola Acocella is Emeritus Professor of Economic Policy, Sapienza University, Rome. His fields of specialisation include welfare economics, theory of economic policy, policy games, and monetary and fiscal policy, amongst others. He has published in prominent journals and authored a number of books, including *Economic Policy in the Age of Globalisation* (2005), and, with Giovanni di Bartolomeo and Andrew Hughes Hallett, *Macroeconomic Paradigms and Economic Policy* (Cambridge, 2016).

T0323682

Federico Caffè Lectures

This series of annual lectures was initiated to honour the memory of Federico Caffè. They are jointly sponsored by the Department of Public Economics at the University of Rome, where Caffè held a chair from 1959 to 1987, and the Bank of Italy, where he served for many years as an advisor. The publication of the lectures will provide a vehicle for leading scholars in the economics profession, and for the interested general reader, to reflect on the pressing economic and social issues of the times.

Rediscovering Economic Policy as a Discipline

Nicola Acocella

Sapienza University of Rome

CAMBRIDGE
UNIVERSITY PRESS

CAMBRIDGE
UNIVERSITY PRESS

University Printing House, Cambridge CB2 8BS, United Kingdom

One Liberty Plaza, 20th Floor, New York, NY 10006, USA

477 Williamstown Road, Port Melbourne, VIC 3207, Australia

314–321, 3rd Floor, Plot 3, Splendor Forum, Jasola District Centre,
New Delhi – 110025, India

79 Anson Road, #06–04/06, Singapore 079906

Cambridge University Press is part of the University of Cambridge.

It furthers the University's mission by disseminating knowledge in
the pursuit of education, learning, and research at the highest
international levels of excellence.

www.cambridge.org
Information on this title: www.cambridge.org/9781108470490
DOI: 10.1017/9781108556705

© Nicola Acocella 2018

First published 2018

Printed and bound in Great Britain by Clays Ltd, Elcograf S.p.A.

A catalogue record for this publication is available from the British Library.

Library of Congress Cataloging-in-Publication Data
Names: Acocella, Nicola, 1939– author.
Title: Rediscovering economic policy as a discipline / Nicola Acocella,
Sapienza Universita di Roma.
Description: Cambridge, United Kingdom; New York, NY: Cambridge
University Press, 2018. | Includes bibliographical references and index.
Identifiers: LCCN 2017061451 | ISBN 9781108470490 (hardback)
Subjects: LCSH: Economic policy. | Economics.
Classification: LCC HD87 .A2856 2018 | DDC 338.9–dc23
LC record available at https://lccn.loc.gov/2017061451

ISBN 978-1-108-47049-0 Hardback
ISBN 978-1-108-45491-9 Paperback

To Federico Caffè, anticipator of economic policy as a discipline, educator of thousands of students and my mentor

Contents

Figures

Tables

Tables

Preface

In the process to specialisation of the unitary economic science that had developed since Adam Smith's *Wealth of Nations* (1776), at least three economic disciplines have arisen over time, each with some degree of autonomy, albeit linked one to the other. Adam Smith's analysis contained the seeds for all future developments. First, it was economic analysis, which progressively proceeded towards a highly abstract set of principles, after other economic disciplines had developed. Then, public finance emerged as a necessary step for designing the main task of a modern state, i.e. to levy taxes to meet public expenditures. This discipline arose by the end of the nineteenth century, but some bricks were laid well before. Economic policy – which had a limited role for Adam Smith and other classical writers – arose only later, as we will see.

What differentiates the various disciplines is their different degree of abstraction or remoteness from reality, economic analysis being the most theoretical one, followed by economic policy, encompassing the action of government in all economic areas and, then, public finance, confined to the action of government for taxes and expenditures.

The seeds of economic policy were laid from the end of the nineteenth century to World War II, but the discipline can be said to have been 'officially' established only by the end of the 1950s. Market failures were first identified through a microeconomic lens only, by what is now termed 'social choice and welfare theory', and then, by Kalecki, Frisch, Keynes and others, also in macroeconomic terms. As I will say, market failures represent the 'logic of economic policy', which justifies the existence of government action in many areas to correct or substitute the market for its failures. It constitutes what I call the 'first pillar' of the discipline.

Facing the numerous government tasks arising from market failures – and thus the rise of multiple targets – requires a number of effective policy tools as well as a coordination of their use to guarantee the attainment of goals. This is done in the 'theory of economic policy', which constitutes my 'second pillar' of the discipline of economic policy.

Economic policy has also a third branch, applying the concepts of its two pillars to given historical and institutional contexts. I call it 'applied economic policy'.

This book is organised as follows: Chapter 1 traces the development of economic policy as a discipline, which concluded in the 1950s. Chapter 2 deals with the progressive dismantling and the demise of this conception of economic policy for a long time. Specifically, the discipline as sketched in Chapter 1 became obsolete as a result of many critiques addressed to it. Some of these critiques were 'minor', as they could rather easily be incorporated in the realm of the classical version of economic policy.

'Vital' critiques, instead, referred to the central aspects of the two pillars and threatened their foundations and, thus, their validity. If they are unaddressed, the whole discipline – or at least a part of it – collapses. The first such vital critique was advanced by Arrow in 1950–51 and concerned the impossibility of defining social targets starting from individuals' preferences (Arrow's critique). This critique threatened the possibility of tying government goals to the preferences of the citizens and, thus, the possibility of their democratic derivation.

The second vital critique referred to the ineffectiveness of macroeconomic policy action and derived from the introduction of 'rational expectations' in the 1970s. Rational expectations implied that any government action could be foreseen and neutralised by the private sector. This deprived government action of a set of relevant macroeconomic policies, even if it retained some degree of acceptance of microeconomic policy intervention as a way to influence the structure of the economy.

These critiques were not addressed for too long, which led to the demise of the discipline. Chapter 3 investigates the long process of rehabilitation of economic policy as a discipline. After a couple of decades, the first critique was overcome, which required an appeal to the need for a theory of justice. The rehabilitation of the second pillar needed even longer. It passed through a silent and slow revolution, laying down various pieces that contributed to clarifying the rationale – and conditions – for the effectiveness of public policy. Around a decade ago, this finally led to a statement of the theory of economic policy in a strategic setting, rather than in a parametric context, as in the classical theory.

Chapter 4 describes the content and methodology of the theory of economic policy in a strategic context. It indicates static and dynamic conditions for the controllability and stabilisability of an economy that go back to the well-known Tinbergen rule of the existence of at least so many instruments as targets. The theory also states the conditions for the existence of an equilibrium or multiple equilibria when more than one agent satisfies the rule. It can therefore be depicted as a theory of conflicts among agents having competing targets or target values and their resolution – thus a 'theory of conflicts' and a 'theory of consent'. It is thus useful for model and institution building, i.e. it can help both researchers – in devising suitable models – and policymakers – in successfully coping with real problems, which imply total or partial convergence of interests and/or conflicts. It also deals with announcements that can help in finding one equilibrium out of many.

Chapters 5 and 6 apply the tools developed by the theory of economic policy in a strategic context. Chapter 5 provides several practical examples on how the theory works. It applies the theory of economic policy to a number of fields, in particular, to the main current problems, the economic crisis, inequality, stagnation and globalisation. Chapter 6 reveals the helpfulness of the new theory of economic policy in laying down signals that provide sufficient information for pointing out economic conditions in general and imbalances in particular that can be useful for preventing crises. The chapter also discusses the realistic assumptions and the political economy concepts that should be incorporated into economic policy for effective policy action.

Finally, Chapter 7 explains the crucial role of institutions when conceiving economic policy as an autonomous discipline. In fact, institutions underlie and link together the two pillars of economic policy, as well as the third part of the discipline, applied economic policy. Institutions thus constitute the glue of the three parts of economic policy, the logic of economic policy (notably social choice and welfare theory), the theory of economic policy and the applications of these two pillars to a given situation.

Acknowledgements

In preparing this book, I was greatly assisted by the advice and criticism of many friends and colleagues. Some parts of this book draw on the results of my previous research, such as many of my papers and books, sometimes jointly authored with others. I therefore thank the co-authors with whom I wrote: Giovanni Di Bartolomeo, Douglas A. Hibbs, Andrew Hughes Hallett, Giovanni Paolo Piacquadio and Patrizio Tirelli. Giovanni Di Bartolomeo and I first devised the new theory of economic policy that overcame radical objections to the classical theory, reestablishing what I call the 'second pillar' of economic policy as a discipline. I still remember how excited we were when we realised the innovative character and deep implications of the new theory.

Joint works are all cited in the relevant parts of this book where they are used and are included in the References. In some cases, the parts drawn from these papers are rather long, and I have asked permission from the co-authors to reproduce them. Anyway, the sources of these parts are not only quoted, as usually, but explicit mention of them is made at the beginnings of the relevant sections.

I must thank the friends and colleagues who have read the whole manuscript or parts of it and suggested a number of changes, in some case of perspective. Among them I must recall Alberto Baffigi, Guido Candela, Giovanni Di

Bartolomeo, Andrew Hughes Hallett, Reinhard Neck, Michele Raitano, Roberto Schiattarella, Mario Tiberi and Ignazio Visco.

I am grateful to the members of the committee selecting the contributors to the Federico Caffè Lectures and the Bank of Italy for supporting the initiative. Cambridge University Press did a great job in preparing this book to be published. I am grateful, in particular, to Phil Good, who took over the editorship of the Federico Caffè Lectures from Chris Harrison, who first supported the initiative of a dedicated series. As in the past, Veronica Fedeli helped me in carefully checking and editing the whole manuscript.

Finally, I am mostly grateful to Federico Caffè, my mentor, whose memory this book intends to honour. He first introduced me to the wonderful world of economic policy as a discipline.

Part I

Economic Policy As a Discipline

Part I

Economic Policy As a Discipline

1

Introduction

1.1 The Core of Economic Policy and Its Two Pillars: The 'Logic' and the 'Theory' of Economic Policy

This chapter provides an overview of the process through which the discipline of economic policy, to some extent autonomous from economic analysis, emerged in Scandinavian countries and the Netherlands. Such a discipline had, first, to justify (on democratic grounds) the action of a public institution after Adam Smith's statement about the virtues of competitive markets. In other words, there should have been a part of it to justify policy activity, what Federico Caffè called the 'logic' of economic policy (Caffè 1966a: 86). In addition, it should have prescribed a set of rules for consistent and effective public action. In other words, it should also have contained a 'theory' of economic policy (Tinbergen 1952: 3, again in the words of Caffè 1966a). These two branches would constitute the two 'pillars' of the discipline, to be applied to real situations of specific countries or regions according to their historical and institutional backgrounds.

This chapter briefly deals also with some factors that brought the discipline to a decline – in particular, as an effect of the destructive critique of a part of its 'core' (by moving to what we will call 'vital' objections, in addition to minor ones) – and with some recent theoretical advances that could or should contribute to its resurgence. Finally, this chapter devotes some space to how the discipline developed in Italy, as some such advances have recently appeared there.[1]

Section 1.2 offers an overview of how the discipline developed. Section 1.3 defines the exact contents of positions to resist in order to provide contents to the core, such as those of the 'invisible hand' and the 'night-watchman' state. Section 1.4 takes account of the long accumulation of elements for the definition of the logic of economic policy, beginning in the last quarter of the nineteenth century through the interwar period and after World War II. Section 1.5 deals instead with the shorter (though decades long) gestation of the theory of economic policy. Section 1.6 tries to explain why this discipline flourished in some countries of Continental Europe mainly and in Australia. Section 1.7 deals with developments of the discipline which occurred in Italy in the 1960s. Box 1.1 underlines the role of Federico Caffè in anticipating economic policy as a discipline. Section 1.8 concludes and hints at the critiques moved to its core as a possible explanation of both the limited extension and impact of the discipline outside Europe and its demise after the 1970s in most countries where it had first developed.

Subsequent chapters will continue to analyse the possible explanations, first, for the limited impact of the discipline and its setback in the 1970s and the following decades and then not only for rehabilitating the two pillars of the discipline in more recent years but also for keeping them together in a unitary discipline, the link being provided by a theory of institutions.

1.2   Overview of the Development of the Discipline

Adam Smith first suggested a theory of institutions and a role for the state, claiming that the action of individuals

---

[1] This chapter draws on Acocella (2017).

motivated by self-interest would ensure, as led by an 'invisible hand', some kind of social benefit, thus limiting government action to a few essential actions (Smith 1776). After Smith, in the course of the nineteenth century, a stiffer line of reasoning had developed in the economic discipline, asserting the reasons for a 'night-watchman' state (*Nachtwächterstaat*).

Over the years, the night-watchman position became an exception, as most classical and marginalist economists tended to state a number of specific or general cases, in addition to those claimed by Smith and supporters of the night-watchman argument, where government intervention was in order. All the same, until the 1930s, there were only some 'general' principles, stated mainly by Pigou, justifying microeconomic government intervention in a market economy, due to divergences between the marginal private and social net product. However, in most cases, only a set of practical rules was stated, aiming at asserting technical procedures of government intervention in the realm of microeconomics (in particular, customs policy, price controls and taxation) and banking and monetary theory. Theoretical contributions on the theory of international trade and the balance-of-payments adjustment were considered as specific parts of the economic discipline. In Italy, the analyses of Pareto's 'Manual' (1906) and Barone (1908) had left only limited (but significant, as we will see) seeds on the side of mathematical economics.

A more general setting for market failures and government intervention had to wait for a number of innovations. These were (1) the foundations of macroeconomic government intervention introduced by Michał Kalecki, Ragnar Frisch and John Maynard Keynes (pertaining to the logic of economic policy),[2] (2) a number of other developments in the 1930s, and more importantly and (3) the statement in the

---

[2] This does not imply an absence of any kinds of macroeconomic interventions in previous years. To be true, these were generally 'negative' (tending e.g. to balanced budgets) rather than 'active' or 'positive' actions.

1950s of the principles for coordinated and consistent policy action (the so-called theory of economic policy developed by Jan Tinbergen). Our understanding of economic policy completely changed after the above-mentioned additions. Economic policy as a discipline had a core including a complete logic of government interventions from both microeconomic and macroeconomic perspectives and a full guide for consistent and effective policy action.

Until the 1950s, public finance had a higher status than economic policy worldwide, as it had developed a theory of public goods and a conception of the role of the state, with important contributions by Italian and Scandinavian scholars (Pantaleoni 1883; De Viti De Marco 1888; Mazzola 1890; Wicksell 1896; Lindahl 1919). According to Einaudi (1934), Italian economists' contributions made it possible for public finance to acquire a scientific status. A similar appreciation came later by Musgrave and Peacock (1958) and Buchanan (1960). Scandinavian contributions were well known in other countries, as Lindahl (1919) was originally published in German and soon reviewed in an English-speaking journal (Peck 1921).

A subject such as macroeconomic analysis and policy barely existed, as these only started with Kalecki's (1933)[3] and Keynes' (1936) contributions, which, however, were not easily accepted in Italy and some other European countries. In the 1930s and following decades, further essential theoretical seeds were added, partly following the emergence of new pressing practical requirements. On the side of the logic for government intervention in market economies, a debate began involving some leading economists of the time. This concerned the principles of government intervention, the

---

An exception was interventions of the Bank of England reacting to deficits of the UK balance of payments.

[3] Kalecki's contributions remained practically unknown in Western countries, at least until 1935, when they appeared in *Econometrica* and *Revue d'Economie Politique* (see Kalecki 1935a, 1935b).

role of distributive considerations vis-à-vis those of efficiency, the need for effective or potential compensation and the possibility of taking both efficiency and distributional aspects into consideration in order to maximise a society's economic welfare starting from individual preferences. The concept of macroeconomic market failures also emerged in addition to the microeconomic ones already stated by Sidgwick, Marshall, Pigou and others. On the other side, the possibility of empirical testing of theoretical propositions as a consequence of the birth of econometrics offered the opportunity to take into account the multiple interrelations that exist in an economic system for coordinating government interventions directed at a set of different targets.

These advances made it possible for an autonomous discipline to finally sprout in Scandinavian countries and the Netherlands in the 1950s. The geographical location of the fathers of the discipline was the product of a number of circumstances: not only the political trends and social substrate prevailing in those countries but also their full participation in – or even anticipation of – the wave of theoretical innovations that had produced the slow but steady developments of the essential seeds of the discipline. Italy had been rather isolated from such developments – at least those in which we are interested – during the Fascist phase, but in the 1950s it was ready to import theoretical advances from abroad as a result of the concurrence of specific circumstances rather different, however, from those operating in Scandinavian countries and the Netherlands. Starting late did not prevent theorists in this country from soon borrowing the new discipline in the early 1960s. Moreover, they offered – in the years after 2005, together with other theorists well trained in the original, classical theory – possibly decisive advances for its re-emergence, after a long decline starting in the 1970s, as an effect of what seemed to be a fatal critique of part of its core, i.e. the theory of economic policy.

1.3   The 'Invisible Hand' and the 'Night-Watchman' State

Obviously, economic policy as a discipline could not have emerged in the absence of a diffuse position of economists in favour of state intervention to correct or substitute markets. The birth of the economic science – if we date it back to Adam Smith – was characterised by a position opposed to such a wide involvement of the state in economic and social activity.[4] This was expressed by the founder of the discipline and can be indicated synthetically by the term 'invisible hand' to refer to the unintended social benefits accruing from the actions of individuals pursuing their personal interest in a market.

The term was first employed by Smith with respect to income distribution in his *The Theory of Moral Sentiments* (Smith 1759). Here he claims that increased wealth of the rich 'trickles down' to the poor (a concept also used after World War II in the theory of development to sustain a line of action of the World Bank). Use of the term with reference to production is made in *The Wealth of Nations* (Smith 1776). The exact expression – but not the concept that it encapsulates – is used just three times in

---

[4] In doing this we are conscious that, in giving primacy to the birth of economic policy vis-à-vis economic analysis, positions such as bullionism and neomercantilism were common before Smith. These had developed arguments in favour of state intervention and studied proper policies to this end. Our historical account of the development of the different economic disciplines within economic science would change if we dated their birth back to other periods or authors before Smith. We think we are justified in our choice for two reasons. On the one side, Smith is usually believed to be the founder of the discipline of economic analysis. On the other, we would anchor – whenever possible and being conscious of a number of cases where this is not true – the development of economic disciplines with economic history. Bullionism and neomercantilism are typical of periods of very active state intervention, whereas Smith marks the triumph of a free-trade attitude and capitalism. On the links between the evolution of economic ideas and economic reality, see e.g. Screpanti and Zamagni (1989).

Smith's writings. The concept might have been borrowed from Richard Cantillon, who developed both economic applications (Cantillon 1755).

We are conscious that the prevailing interpretation of the meaning of Smith's 'invisible hand', as a naive idea of Smith's fully pro-market position, is unfounded in his works. This interpretation has been criticised by a number of authors (e.g. Grampp 2000; Rothschild 2001; Roncaglia 2005; Marglin 2008). These critiques refer, first, to the inappropriateness of the use of the term 'invisible hand'. This with respect to either the letter of Smith's work (particularly in *The Wealth of Nations*) or the context where Smith makes use of this term to argue in favour of the virtues of the market (typical is the case of the home bias in Smith 1776: book IV, chap. 2). Moreover, according to these critiques, the term is not fully representative of Smith's thought. From a substantive point of view, undoubtedly Smith gives a positive assessment of the market, whose operation – in his opinion – usually tends to pursue the public good in a number of ways, especially by favouring the division of labour. However, he also believes that governments play an important role not only in defence but also in fields that can be labelled as being more directly relevant to economic activity, such as infrastructure and education. In any case, for the sake of brevity, we will use the term 'invisible hand' as a metaphor of the Smithian position as well as of later theories, in particular, neoclassical thinking, that have then prevailed, even if the latter are deprived of some social aspects of the working of the market that certainly were in the work of Adam Smith.

The 'night-watchman' position is advocacy of a minimal role for the state, which should be limited to ensuring defence of the members of a community from external assault and internal violence, theft, breach of contract and fraud. This position is also called 'minarchism', a form of libertarianism, as it advocates for the state only the minimal protection needed to avoid chaos. This is indeed different from 'anarchy', which, apart from its many possible interpretations, we intend in essence as a community which is governed by members basing their action on 'we rationality' (with a *homo reciprocans*), where then a true state becomes useless, as cooperative behaviour arises and conflicts tend to disappear (see e.g. Smerilli 2007).

This position was inaugurated by Bastiat (1850) and Spencer (1850) and was later resumed by Pareto's *Cours d'Economie Politique* (Pareto 1896–97), leading more recently to the economic and philosophical schools of evolutionists such as Hayek (1960) and Nozick (1974) and contractualists such as Buchanan (1975) and Tullock (1976). In Italy, the 'minimal state' doctrine had a number of followers, starting with Ferrara (e.g. 1859) and, as already mentioned, Pareto.

The rationales for the night-watchman position may be numerous: defence of power relations, protection from the pressure of lobbies and parties, an attempt to reconcile laissez-faire with democracy, moral limitations on the use of state force and belief in the superior performance of institutions based on a market economy, with few external constraints. The practical issues behind some of these positions and the different arguments put forward in support of some minimal state doctrines are reconstructed by Romani (2015). According to Screpanti and Zamagni (1989: chap. 11), the post–World War II contributions having this same orientation can be considered as reappraisals of Smith's project in favour of a minimal state as a consequence of comparing different institutions. After World War II this orientation reacted, on the one hand, to the negative experience of planned economies and, on the other, to the tendency of welfare economics to confine analysis of institutions to that branch of the economic discipline and in terms of efficiency only.

1.4   The Seeds for the Birth of the Logic of Economic Policy

1.4.1   Economic Policy in the Early 1930s: A Little More Than a Collection of Examples of Empirical Policy

Most classical writers and the marginalists had suggested cases where public intervention was in order, in particular in the case of taxation. This had been so for Smith (1776), Ricardo (1817), Malthus (1820), Mill (1848) and Walras (1874–77, 1898). We have already described the essentials of Smith's position vis-à-vis government intervention in social life. Ricardo's relevance from the point of view of the construction of economic policy as a discipline lies not in an explanation of some positive role of government in the economy but on the fact that he introduced a concept, that of growth, as an important viewpoint of economic policy action. However, such an objective would be pursued in the United Kingdom simply by prescribing abolition of impediments to trade, in particular, the 'corn laws' (Ricardo 1817, but his previous writing on this topic was dated 1815). These laws – by establishing protection of home granary production in Britain – were indeed an obstacle to industrialisation and, thus, growth.

The relevance of Malthus' analysis of arguments in favour of state intervention is along similar lines. He did not explicitly develop any specific role for public policy, but he introduced concepts that proved to be very useful for later analyses, having an immense impact on the foundations of the first pillar of economic policy as a discipline. In fact, some of these concepts were developed by Frisch, Kalecki and Keynes more than a century later. Keynes largely recognised his intellectual debt to Malthus, who had shifted the focus of analysis towards the short-run changes in economic activity and its monetary aspects. Inflationary and deflationary tendencies were determined by 'effective demand', i.e. demand sustained by purchasing power.

The feeble position of the economic discipline in favour of government intervention evolved slightly with the conclusions of the classical school. In conjunction with a positivist turn in the orientation of analysis, Mill introduced a distinction between productive and distributive actions. The former obey the laws of an objective nature, not allowing for any discretionary behaviour; the latter, instead, leave room for voluntary choices, as they depend on the opinions and sentiments of a society.

The cases for policy intervention indicated so far were largely what Walras called 'examples of empirical policy' rather than a broad-ranging and consistent set. They were certainly dictated on the basis of an analytical evaluation of the circumstances suggesting them but were not part of a systematic assessment of the foundations and articulation of public policy.

A systematic investigation of the foundations of government intervention only began to emerge towards the end of the nineteenth century. We can refer to it as the 'logic of economic policy', or what was initially called 'welfare economics' and later became a part, first, of social-choice theory and, more recently, of implementation theory.[5]

The first attempts to develop such a theory were those of Sidgwick (1883), whose treatise had economic policy as an object in its third part. Henry Sidgwick introduced qualifications to the proposition according to which Adam Smith's system of natural liberty was able to pursue the public interest only up to some point going beyond the issues arising from distribution. There are, in fact, cases – not to be relegated to imperfections, which could be omitted in a theoretical analysis – where the self-interest of people diverges from social interest. Typical is the case of production of what later will be called 'public goods' and of goods that favour future

---

[5] Sen (1999b) traces the origins of social-choice theory back to the fourth century BC, when books by Aristotle in Greece and Kautilya in India were written, entitled, respectively, *Politics* and *Economics* (see Section 7.4).

generations. Individuals produce a scarce quantity of the former, as they cannot get sufficient revenue now. The same thing happens for the latter, whose revenue will accrue only in the future (Sidgwick 1883). This conclusion derives from recourse to an impartiality argument, according to which 'the time at which a man exists cannot affect the value of his happiness from a universal point of view; and ... the interests of posterity must concern a Utilitarian as much as those of his contemporaries' (Sidgwick 1874: 414).[6]

Along a line similar to Sidgwick's – possibly reflecting some negative consequences deriving from the triumphant industrial revolution – Marshall (1890) and Pigou (1912, 1920) also laid down essential principles for state intervention, partly connecting it to the preferences of citizens. These writings had not been produced only as an almost occasional and case-by-case by-product of analytical investigations (as it was for the 'classics' and Walras) but derived from a systematic corpus of principles that could justify a number of microeconomic policy interventions.

Pigou offers the first general and systematic account of the divergences between the marginal private and social net product, which justify public intervention due to 'the fact that, in some occupations, a part of the product of a unit of resources consists of something, which, instead of coming in the first instance to the person who invests the unit, comes instead, in the first instance (i.e. prior to sale if sale takes place), as a positive or negative item, to other people'. These people may be (1) the owners of durable instruments of production, of which the investor is a tenant, (2) persons

---

[6] The same point of view is held by Pigou – on different grounds, that of rationality (instead of impartiality) – when he speaks of the defective telescopic faculty of people. Pigou draws this principle from Jevons (1871), who claimed that the factor expressing the effect of remoteness should play no role in our decisions, allowance being made for uncertainty. The different positions of Sidgwick, on the one side, and Pigou and Jevons, on the other, are certainly determined by their different formulations, philosophical in one case and economic in the other.

who are not producers of the commodity in which the investor is investing and (3) persons who are producers of this commodity (Pigou 1920: 174).

In fact, in the first case, there is the tendency for the tenant to intensify the use of the instruments when the end of the tenancy is approaching. In the second case, one person may render uncompensated services or disservices to other persons not involved in the exchange, as in case of lighthouses, afforestation and so on. The latter case refers to industries that could produce at increasing returns due to external economies internal to the industries that they could earn as an effect of their growth but are prevented from doing so in a competitive market because expansion is not similarly profitable for each firm.

Apart from these authors and the cases of market failure they indicated, generally speaking, the principles of state intervention advocated by Pigou were condemned to dormancy until the 1930s, when they were criticised by Robbins (1932) and the new welfare economics. Supporting the virtue of markets was the commonly held view inspiring political parties and governments, and this view was not contradicted by the rather satisfying evolution of the economy in most developed countries – also as an effect of a number of favourable economic circumstances – until the end of World War I and the postwar recovery. But a number of factual and theoretical developments were looming that sprouted in the 1930s, making a stronger case in favour of government intervention, due in particular to the insurgence of macroeconomic failures.

1.4.2 Developments of the 1930s and after World War II

The most important factual changes in economic performance were related to the difficult adaptation to the postwar economic and social situation of some economic systems (e.g. the United Kingdom), especially if the new situation was approached with the old pro-market lens and policies; the emergence of the prolonged Great Depression; and the progressive contraction of international economic exchanges of goods and capital.

Two notable developments in the theory and a semantic novelty emerged in the 1930s[7] that laid the ground for the take-off of the discipline after World War II. First was the development of the 'new welfare economics', which began with Robbins' (1932) rejection of the axioms of interpersonal comparisons and equality of utility perceptions on which Pigou had based his welfare economics. This rejection was the starting point, if not the 'manifesto', of the new welfare economics, which really threw new light on a possible range of economic policies open when accepting the Pareto criterion. In particular, a large debate (continuing after the war) arose on the application of the basic principles of policy intervention in a way that enlarges the cases of government action as envisaged by this criterion. This allowed for only a partial ordering of the various possible situations and was conservative in nature, thus imposing the tyranny of the status quo (Acocella 1994). The debate discussed the compensation principle (Harrod 1938; Hotelling 1938; Kaldor 1939; Hicks 1939; Scitovsky 1941; Little 1949) to complement the Pareto principle and enlarge its scope of application, along non-utilitarian bases. Harrod's argument was that, without some kind of interpersonal comparison of utility, economists would be condemned to suggest no indication of policy action. In particular, they could not have recommended the Repeal of the Corn Laws, as Ricardo (1817) had made. The final position of Little (1949) is of

---

[7] In the previous decade, there was practically no relevant contribution to the theory, with the exception of Sraffa's contribution leading to the conclusion that it was 'necessary ... to abandon the path of free competition and turn in the opposite direction, namely, towards monopoly' (Sraffa 1926: 542).

specific interest, as it underlines the impossibility of separating the distributional from the productive aspects of a change and thus evaluate it in terms of pure efficiency, excluding equity considerations. The Pareto principle and optimum are thus undressed of their supposed objective nature, therefore justifying the final consideration of Sen (1970a: 22) that a social state can be Pareto optimal but still be 'perfectly disgusting'. In addition, Bergson (1938) introduced the notion of a social-welfare function (SWF), offering a new conceptual tool that would prove to be useful after World War II.

Second was the advent of Keynesian thought, tied to a change of paradigm as well as of the historical contingencies (Jesperson 2015), which rather soon developed as the new orthodoxy (but see Asso 1990). This introduced a new important case of market failure – unemployment, the first of a macroeconomic type of failures – and the need for suitable government action. This innovation is already in Keynes (1930), and, more notable from a practical point of view, can be found in Frisch (1933, 1934), Kalecki (1933) and Keynes (1936).

Frisch (1933: 236) clearly expounds the paradox of thrift when he says, '[t]he fact that we "save" therefore means at this juncture that we destroy our productive forces'.[8] Frisch (1934) clearly expounds the intrinsic tendencies towards contraction and expansion in an exchange system and the essence of the multiplier. Frisch called these tendencies an 'encapsulating phenomenon', an absolutely meaningful term for the expression 'macroeconomic market failure'. This term was first used in the 1980s by Stiglitz (1986: chap. 4), even

---

[8] The first author to attract attention to this contribution of Frisch's was Klein (1998). He also recalls that Frisch had given three radio lectures in a university series that were published in Norwegian only in 1947 and 'had some of the same ideas as Keynes for policies to help to pull an economy out of depression' (p. 495). On the relevance of Frisch's 1933 pamphlet, see also Bjerkholt and Qvigstad (2007).

though not only unemployment but also inflation, low (or excessive, unsustainable) growth and external imbalances were already well known causes of market failures during or after World War II.[9] For an explanation of the reasons for use of the term 'macroeconomic', see Acocella (1994). Kalecki (1933) built a dynamic model containing all the ingredients of later models of Keynes due to Lange and Hicks. The contribution by Keynes (1936) is well known and does not require many details at this point.

The semantic novelty worth noting is that certainly by the mid-1930s the term 'economic policy' had been forged for the new discipline to appear, even if – at least in the Italian case – much of the old wine was in a new bottle. In Italy, the expression used by Fontana Russo (1935) was *politica economica*, although the content of his new book remained pretty much the same as before in referring mainly to trade treaties and policy (Fontana Russo 1902).

1.5 The Theory of Economic Policy and the Link between the Two Pillars

1.5.1 Developments after World War II and Extensive State Intervention

After World War II, a number of the actual features of the economic and social systems in advanced countries had changed or the changes looming before the war became evident with clarity (Thomas 1994: chap. 4). In particular, new social groups had emerged or had become more powerful, and growth of big business had brought with it growth of big

---

[9] The use of this term by Stiglitz deserves some comment. He had suggested a cause for unemployment, in terms of efficiency wages (Shapiro and Stiglitz 1984), and thus he is certainly justified in using the term 'macroeconomic failures'. We must, however, be careful in accepting this justification, as critiques have been moved to it and alternative explanations have been suggested. To date, we can say that involuntary unemployment is still a problem in search of a satisfying explanation.

labour, which was to acquire greater voice and power as conditions for full employment were progressively restored after reconstruction of factories and infrastructure.

Government intervention was much more widespread and penetrating. To a large extent, it started from the Keynesian precepts aiming first at full employment. Since fears of stagnation were very diffuse, following the World War II experience, a new policy target emerged – growth. For the most open economies, another issue – the balance of payments – began raising concern before the Marshall Plan and when the relief of American aid ended. The international economic institutions created at Bretton Woods in 1944 had devised proper rules to avoid excessive capital movement, ensure symmetric adjustment by 'creditor' and 'debtor' countries, regulate free trade in a way so as not to impair the welfare state provisions and ensure international liquidity. In practice, domestic policy adjustments were necessary only for debtor countries. For those countries, equilibrium of the balance of payments and, with it, the need to ensure a proper evolution of internal prices – which had soared just after the war as a result of a lack of supply and again rose in the 1950s as a consequence of sustained growth – became part of the set of macroeconomic targets. The four targets – unemployment, inflation, growth and balance of payments – made up the 'magic square' later introduced by Kaldor (1971).

Keynes had insisted on the use of different policy instruments (both monetary and fiscal policy), and the war experience had shown the possibility of adding price and income controls to these, while the International Monetary Fund (IMF), even within a fixed exchange rate system, allowed for parity adjustment.

The need then arose for (1) managing the different policy tools in a way that took account of the multiple interrelations between macroeconomic targets and policy instruments, aided by input-output analysis, national accountancy and econometrics, and (2) preparing a programme (a plan), possibly covering more than one year, as the Marshall Plan itself required.

Some conceptual tools that had been devised in the inter-war period were useful for empirical analysis and policy. These were the use of national accounting (including intro-duction of the concept of gross domestic product (GDP), improving on that of national dividend used by Pigou) as an instrument for practical implementation of Keynesian policies, the discipline of econometrics as a development of mathematical economics that permits empirically assess-ment of interrelations and the values of the system's parameters[10] (Tinbergen 1935). Construction of formal mod-els to be tested against reality introduced the idea of the need for consistency of different public policies and the possibi-lity to check their real effectiveness. This factor played an essential role in the development of the theory of economic policy. It then appears not so strange that the authors who first contributed to this theory (e.g. Tinbergen and Frisch) were among the founders of the Econometric Society and the journal *Econometrica* in the early 1930s. Finally, input-output analysis was introduced by W. Leontief (1941), who later adapted it to a very versatile policy analysis tool, espe-cially useful for disaggregating macroeconomic models.

In addition to these developments, a contribution to the idea that governments could be successful in ruling eco-nomic systems – possibly even more than markets, which had been hit by the Great Depression – came from planned economies. Such economies, in fact, had experienced high growth rates in the 1930s and following decades, which had an influence on the economic thought of many economists. Frisch, the first economist to devise the theory of economic policy, and his follower, L. Johansen, thought that national economic planning managed by well-trained economists

---

[10] However, Keynes criticised Tinbergen's econometric work on the basis of his concept of 'inductive probability logic' (on this, see Bray 1977).

was clearly superior to the market (Kærgård, Sandelin and Sæther 2008), while being suspicious of the political architecture of Soviet society.

Thus, after the war, the theoretical advances of the 1930s and the changes in the economic and social conditions, as well as in policy aspirations, prompted radical innovations. These changes occurred in the way that policymakers conceived their goals and scholars looked at economic policy, and in due time they resulted in the generation of a theory capable of dealing with these new issues, thus conceiving of economic policy as an autonomous discipline.

The first step in formulating economic policy as an autonomous discipline was the statement of the 'theory of economic policy'. In the second step of this intellectual process, the theory of economic policy was associated with the existence of market failures. Each step will be detailed in the next two subsections.

1.5.2   Devising the Theory of Economic Policy

Frisch (1949, 1950, 1957) first formulated this theory.[11] He had laid down some of its ingredients before World War II in participating in the debate on the economic feasibility of a planning scheme for socialist countries.[12] His approach was in terms of 'flexible targets'. The policymaker, in the

---

[11] Bjerkholt (2008) notes the ambivalence of Frischian scientific economics in its crossing of positive and normative orientations, based on structural modelling, before World War II, and constructing planning tools and models, after the war, possibly due to the consequences of the Great Depression that affected his sense of social responsibility.

[12] The debate was originated by the sceptical view of von Mises (1920), later followed by Hayek (1935) along the same line, to which Dickinson (1933), Lerner (1934) and Lange (1936, 1937) had reacted. Frisch suggested use of linear programming to organise exchanges in an economic system and detected the fundamental problem of planning in mediating between two objectives: on the one side, 'to utilize more fully the existing productive capacity'; on the other, 'to conform as much as possible with the particular desires of the individuals and groups involved' (Frisch 1934: 260–61). These were really the seeds of his post-war contributions.

same vein as a householder, should make a plan tending to maximise his or her preferences under the constraint of a set of equations describing the given behaviour of the economic system on the basis of technical, behavioural and – a later stage – institutional constraints. These constraints depend also on the value of the instruments that can be set by the policymaker. Thus, the government's targets would be expressed in terms of 'flexible targets', as the values that could really be reached would depend on the constraints. The initial formulation of Frisch's conception of the theory also was rather complicated because the constraints were expressed in terms of a system of input-output relations à la Leontief, with some devices that should allow overcoming non-substitutability between inputs.

Tinbergen – who had built the first econometric models of the Dutch and US economies in 1936 and 1939, respectively (Hughes Hallett 1989) – drew inspiration from Frisch, as he recognised (see Tinbergen 1952: introduction) but followed a different approach. In fact, Tinbergen (1952, 1956) developed the theory in terms of 'fixed targets', suggesting that a number of instruments at least equal to that of targets should be available to the policymaker in order for him or her to be able to exactly reach the preferred set of target values (Tinbergen's 'golden rule of economic policy').

Frisch's route was instead followed more closely by Theil (1956, 1964), who generalised Frisch's formulation while making it simpler and more workable. The objective of the policymaker would be to minimise a loss function in terms of quadratic deviations from a set of target values for the variables of interest.[13] Minimisation would be under the constraint of the relations between targets and instruments expressing the behaviour of the economic system.

---

[13] Obviously, this was not different from introducing a preference function, as maximising preferences and minimising a loss function are equivalent.

A plan of action for the policymaker can be drawn from this process of minimisation (or maximisation). In summary, a plan (or programme) is formed of three elements: targets, instruments and the model of the economy. Targets, goals or objectives have already been defined. The policymaker, perhaps with the help of an economist, as suggested by Frisch, constructs a map of 'social' indifference curves reflecting the preferences of society (a SWF defined over a set of 'goods' or a loss function defined over 'bads'). The policymaker 'superimposes' the map on the 'transformation curve' between the variables that are arguments of his or her utility function derived from the model of the economy, thus determining the optimal choice of objectives. The reason for calling this the 'optimising' approach to planning should be clear: the values of the targets are not predetermined; rather, they are defined by the optimisation process (by way of maximisation or minimisation according to whether the policymaker is using a SWF or a loss function), the constraint being given by the 'transformation' curve or, more generally, by the model of the economy. The value to assign to instruments – which are usually assumed to have no value per se[14] – can be derived from the optimal values of targets to pursue by inverting the matrix of multipliers, which relates targets to instruments. In contrast to the optimising approach, the values assigned to the objectives in the fixed-target approach are simply satisfactory, not optimal.[15] Obviously, preparing and optimising a programme are much more complex in practice. It was even more complex when there were no computers and matrix inversion had to be done by hand or when the first available computers required days or weeks to do the

---

[14] Generalisations are possible where instruments also have an intrinsic value.
[15] For a more detailed description of the contents of a programme, see Acocella (1994).

same job that requires a few minutes nowadays.[16] In any case, it was shown that this approach could improve on the previous ways to implement policy programmes, in particular, in terms of correction of the errors derived from making forecasts and choosing policies that would make the forecast look acceptable (Bray 1975).

This became the general way of setting a policy problem in a 'parametric context'. In the case where the policymaker has a sufficient number of instruments – as indicated by Tinbergen's 'golden rule' – the loss function is minimised, and the set of fixed target values is consistently reached by using appropriate values of instruments. In other words, under this condition of (at least) equality of the numbers of instruments and targets, the policymaker would control the economic system and direct it to reach his or her goals. Otherwise, the solutions that can be obtained are only a second best, what can realistically be obtained with the existing instruments. The only possibility of achieving a better solution requires devising new instruments to add to them. The solution that could be obtained by dropping some targets in order to satisfy conditions for controllability would not be comparable with the previous one where controllability is not possible.

Scandinavian and Dutch contributions to the theory of economic policy were not limited to Frisch, Tinbergen, Theil and other economists directly following their route. In fact, the Norwegian school of the theory of economic policy, founded by Frisch, had also other economists following his route (O. Aukrust, H. J. Kreyberg, B. Thalberg and, most importantly, Trygve Haavelmo and Leif Johansen) (Johansen 1977, 1978). Haavelmo was at the forefront of econometrics and macroeconomic models (see Anundsen et al. 2014) and had worked with the Cowles Commission.

---

[16] For a description of the first attempts to prepare national plans in Norway, see Bjerkholt (2005).

His works relevant to our topic are, unfortunately, mainly in Norwegian (such as Haavelmo 1966, but see Haavelmo 1965). To our knowledge, the most important contribution for tracing the roots and development of the Norwegian school is that of Bjerkholt (2005).

Lawrence Klein, who had worked with Cowles Commission from 1944 to 1947 with Haavelmo and many others under the direction of Jacob Marschack to build a model of the American economy, visited the Oslo Institute in 1947–48 to work with Frisch and Haavelmo (Visco 2014). He had published a very popular book on the Keynesian revolution, 'had constructed the first macroeconomic model in [the] USA and demonstrated that the model, indeed, did better in forecasting than the experts in Washington' (Bjerkholt 2005: 15).

Bent Hansen – a Danish-born economist who had graduated from Uppsala University – became an influential advisor to the Swedish government and a professor at the University of Stockholm (and the University of California at Berkeley) and offered an independent contribution to the goals/means theory of economic policy (see Hansen 1955; Erixon 2011). For a rather exhaustive review of the contributions to the theory of economic policy especially by Scandinavian and Dutch authors, refer also to Rey (1967), Hughes Hallett (1989), Jonung (1991), Kærgård, Sandelin and Sæther (2008) and Acocella, Di Bartolomeo and Hughes Hallett (2013).

1.6   The Classical Theory of Economic Policy with Fixed and Flexible Targets

This section largely draws on Acocella, Di Bartolomeo and Hughes Hallett (2013: chap. 2).

1.6.1   The Fixed-Target Approach

The static economic relationships between variables are defined by the following general linear algebraic system:

(1.1) $Ay = Bu + k$ (structural form)

where $y \in R^q$ is the vector of relevant economic variables (the government's target variables) whose generic entry is denoted by $y(i)$, extracted from Y; $u \in R^m$ is the vector of the government's policy instruments, whose generic element is denoted by $u(j)$, extracted from Z; A and B are appropriately parameterised target and instrument coefficient matrices, and k is an appropriate vector of constants, each component of which is a linear combination of constants, exogenous variables and white-noise shocks.

We assume – without loss of generality – that A and B are full-rank matrices; i.e. all targets and instrument variables are linearly independent of each other. There are q distinct targets and m distinct instruments to be chosen and set, respectively, by the government.

The linear 'reduced-form' model can be derived from (1.1) as follows:

(1.2) $y = A^{-1}Bu + A^{-1}k = Cu + \bar{c}$ (reduced form)

provided that A is nonsingular, as it is from our rank assumptions. Matrix C is a matrix of multipliers and is sometimes called the 'Jacobian matrix'. Element $C(i,j)$ indicates the effect on target i of changes in instrument j; i.e. $\partial y(i)/\partial u(j)$. Policy effectiveness and policy neutrality can be defined in terms of (1.2).

Policy Effectiveness. An instrument, e.g. instrument $u(j)$, is ineffective with respect to target $y(i)$ if changes in that instrument determine no changes in the target variable. In this case, $C(i,j) = 0$. Otherwise, it is effective.

(Exogenous) Policy Neutrality. Economic policy is neutral with respect to a target variable if *all* the instruments are ineffective with respect to that target variable. In this case, the row entries of matrix C are all zeros.

The aim of the government is to control the economic system (1.2). This will involve finding values of the instruments that enable it to reach any desired values of the target variables $\bar{y} \in R^q$ ('target values') in their economy; i.e. the vector u that solves the equation $\bar{y} = Cu$ can always be found for all possible desired values of $\bar{y}$. The system is weakly controllable if a *given* (specific) vector of target values can be reached. Controllability clearly implies weak controllability, but not conversely. Moreover, it should be noticed that controllability is in fact an existence condition for suitable policy instrument values ('existence problem'). However, controllability ensures neither the uniqueness of the policy ('uniqueness problem') nor how best to determine it ('policy design problem'). Notice also that controllability clearly implies policy non-neutrality, but the converse is not true.

Existence conditions for a solution are easily found by applying standard mathematical techniques. Usually these are rank conditions on certain coefficient matrices or transformations of those matrices.

Theorem 1.1   (*controllability*). The system $y = Cu + \bar{c}$ is controllable for any vector of desired targets if and only if $r[C] = q$. It is weakly controllable, for a given vector of targets values $\bar{y}$, if and only if $r[C : \bar{y}] = r[C]$.

Having $r[C] \le min\{q, m\}$, $r[C] = q$ implies that $q \le m$. Thus, controllability embodies the famous Tinbergen precepts about the number of instruments and targets.

Theorem 1.2   (*Tinbergen theorem or static controllability*). The government can achieve any vector of independent targets by an appropriate vector of instruments if and only if the number of independent instruments is equal to or greater than the number of targets.

Formally, the Tinbergen theorem comprises two conditions (Preston and Pagan 1982):

1. A counting rule, according to which the number of instruments should be greater than or equal to the number of targets, i.e. $q \leq m$; and
2. An independence rule stating that the (linearly) independent instruments are at least q in number if this is the number of independent targets.

The theorem can be qualified to impose uniqueness. This requires $r[C] = q = m$; the number of independent targets must be equal to that of the independent instruments. In such a case, the optimal policies for the original system are

$$(1.3) \quad u = B^{-1}(A\bar{y} - k)$$

because $C = A^{-1}B$ and the inverses are unique. Henceforth, we will say that an equation system is controllable (statically controllable or controllable in the sense of Tinbergen and Theil) if the number of independent instruments equals that of independent targets.

This result must be qualified. In fact, if some of the instruments have value of their own (e.g. as they might imply distortions, causing losses), their number can be lower than that of targets, which include some of the instruments.

Assuming that the policy model fails to satisfy the appropriate weak or strong existence criterion of controllability, the first best policy cannot be achieved. The failure to find a solution for the fixed-target problem in those cases generates the need for some alternative, which we discuss in Section 1.6.2.

1.6.2   The Flexible-Target Approach

The flexible-target approach is based on the minimisation of a 'loss function'. A useful formalisation of the government's cost for deviations of the relevant variables from their target values is the following quadratic form:

(1.4) $L = (y - \bar{y})' Q(y - \bar{y}),$

where Q is an appropriate symmetric, positive-definite matrix of relative priorities between the target variables. In (1.4) we do not explicitly consider instrument costs. We refer to $\bar{y}$ and Q as the parameters of the government's preferences.

Quadratic functions are used not only for their mathematical tractability but also for their useful economic properties. In fact, deviations from the target in either direction are associated with increasing costs. The marginal rate of substitution between any couple of target variables is therefore never constant but depends on the values of the two variables at the point at which they are computed. In addition, quadratic forms can be obtained as second-order Taylor approximations of more complex functions.

The flexible-target policy is obtained by minimising (1.4) with respect to the vector of instruments, subject to (1.2). The corresponding first-order condition is

(1.5) $C' Q C u = C' Q(\bar{y} - \bar{c})$

where $\bar{c} = A^{-1} k$ and $C = A^{-1} B$ were defined in (1.2).

As in the preceding case, existence of a solution is ensured if $r[\Phi : k_\Phi] = r[\Phi]$; that is, if Φ is left-invertible, where $\Phi = C' Q C \in R^{m \times m}$ and $k_\Phi = C' Q(\bar{y} - \bar{c}) \in R^m$. Uniqueness, however, requires, in addition, the non-singularity of Φ. It is worth noticing that as Q is positive definite, $r[\Phi] = r[C]$. Thus, C being full column rank, $r[\Phi] = m$, meaning that Φ is of full rank too.[17] It follows that (1.5) has a unique solution.

The policy design problem therefore implies the following *optimal* policies:

---

[17] If Q is a positive-definite matrix, then $r[C'QC] = r[C]$ for any conformable matrix C.

(1.6) $u = \Phi^{-1}k_\Phi = \left(C'QC\right)^{-1}C'Q(\bar{y} - A^{-1}k)$

If $q = m$, the preceding policy selection reduces to $u = B^{-1}(A\bar{y} - k)$ – the same expression found in the fixed-target case (1.2) – which implies that $y = \bar{y}$ when inserted in (1.1).

When considering the flexible-target approach, any policy is endogenous and depends on the policymaker's preferences. For this reason, we find it convenient to redefine neutrality as follows.

(Endogenous) Policy Neutrality. Economic policy is neutral with respect to a target variable if the optimal value of such a variable is not affected by any change in the policymaker's preferences.

This definition generalises that of exogenous neutrality in the same way as the flexible-target approach to policy-making nests the fixed-target approach. In the chapters that follow, we focus on strategic contexts where policies are always endogenous, and when speaking of neutrality, we will always refer to the concept of endogenous policy neutrality instead of the concept of exogenous neutrality.

A geometric representation of the cases of fixed and flexible targets can be useful. We can now give an example of the geometric representation of the problem of fixed targets. Consider an aggregate demand–aggregate supply (AD-AS) representation of the economy, as taken from Hansen (1968) and reproduced by Preston and Pagan (1982):

(1.7) $\begin{cases} AD : p = bq + au_1 & \text{with } b < 0 \\ AS : p = dq + cu_2 & \text{with } d > 0 \end{cases}$

The reduced form of system is

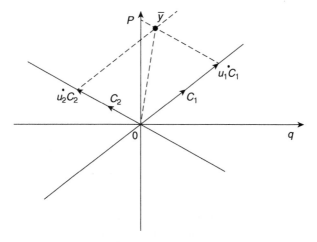

Figure 1.1 *Fixed-target approach.*
(Source: Acocella, Di Bartolomeo and Hughes Hallett 2013)

$$(1.8) \quad \begin{bmatrix} p \\ q \end{bmatrix} = \begin{bmatrix} -\dfrac{ad}{b-d} \\ -\dfrac{a}{b-d} \end{bmatrix} u_1 + \begin{bmatrix} \dfrac{bc}{b-d} \\ \dfrac{c}{b-d} \end{bmatrix} u_2$$

or, more generally, $y = C_1 u_1 + C_2 u_2$.

We can say that, in their reduced form, these targets can be expressed in terms of the column vectors C_1 and C_2, weighted by the values of instruments u_1 and u_2, respectively. Differentiating (1.8) with respect to u_1, we get the per-unit impact (multipliers) of the first instrument on the two targets (p and q). Similarly, differentiating the equation with respect to u_2, we get the multipliers of the second instrument with respect to the two targets.

In Figure (1.1), $[\overline{p}, \overline{q}]' = \overline{y}$ indicates the policymaker's desired targets. Let us consider the same problem as earlier, except for the fact that the government now wants to minimise (1.4), where $y = [p, q]'$, subject to (1.8), but having only a single instrument available. Let us say it uses u_1, with u_2 set at zero. In this case, only the C_1 line appears in (q, p) space.

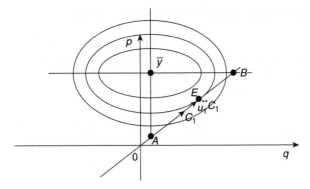

Figure 1.2 *Flexible-target approach.*
(Source: Acocella, Di Bartolomeo and Hughes Hallett 2013)

We can still represent the targets in the same space. Figure 1.2 shows concentric ellipses around the first best point and indicates a sequence of loss levels which diminish as we go towards the centre of the ellipses. If $Q = I$, these ellipses will become concentric circles.

Of course, to reach the centre of the ellipses or circles would represent the solution in the case where the system is actually Tinbergen controllable. In contrast, we need to consider the case where only one instrument is available, as described in Figure 1.2.

If only one instrument is available, the policymaker cannot achieve his or her first best target value $\bar{y}$. But this instrument can still be set to achieve either the desired value for the quantity (point A), or prices (point B), or for a range of points in between. Clearly both A and B are suboptimal since they fail to find the lowest possible loss, given the constraint. The optimal policy, marked as u_1^{**} here, corresponds to the point of tangency between the innermost reachable ellipse and the line defined by slope C_1. At point E, the marginal rate of substitution is equal to the policy multiplier (in substance, the marginal rate of transformation of q into p), and thus the policy-maker's marginal benefit equals his or her marginal cost.

1.6.3   Uncertainty and Certainty Equivalence

In examining the impact of uncertainty on policy choice, consider first the case of a source of uncertainty that can be expressed as the additive error vector ('additive uncertainty') only and then the more difficult one where it leads to 'multiplicative uncertainty'. The first case takes place when the government is not sure about the transmission of the effect of its instruments (u) on its targets (y) as uncertainty about the non-controllable variables is present. Formally,

$$(1.9) \quad y = Cu + \bar{c} + \varepsilon$$

where ε_t is a vector of stochastic terms, with $E[\varepsilon] = 0$ and $E[\varepsilon\varepsilon'] = \Sigma$. In this situation, the government will minimise the following expected loss:

$$(1.10) \quad E[L] = E[(y - \bar{y})' Q(y - \bar{y})]$$

In terms of expectations, the condition that solves the government's problem does not differ from the optimal policy under certainty. Thus, we can state that if the only source of uncertainty is additive, then the optimal policy of the government is to behave 'as if' everything was known with certainty given the expectation ('certainty-equivalence principle').[18]

Certainty-equivalent decisions require no knowledge of the distribution functions of the random variables beyond their conditional means. However, the larger the dispersion of stochastic terms for a given mean, the greater are the risks about the realised target values. Hence, certainty-equivalent decisions reflect a risk-neutral attitude; they are unaffected by risk aversion or indeed by any term reflecting the *degree* of uncertainty. This is their chief disadvantage: they do not react to risk or the degree, skew or possibility of catastrophic outcomes (fat tails) in the random variables. However,

---

[18] The result was first proposed by Tinbergen (1952) and then Theil (1958).

different 'risk-sensitive' or robust decision rules have been suggested (see Holly and Hughes Hallett 1989 and references therein).

'Multiplicative uncertainty' takes place when there is uncertainty about the parameters of the model. In this case. the policymaker cannot behave as if uncertainty does not exist. As a result, under multiplicative uncertainty, policymakers will usually tend to be more cautious in the exercise of policy and express a less vigorous response to disturbances. The decisions that minimise $E[L]$ would actually be

$$(1.11) \quad u^* = [E(C'QC)]^{-1}E[C'Q(\bar{y} - \bar{c})]$$

which in general gives values for the instruments that are very different from those offered by the 'first-order certainty-equivalence solution' unless variances and co-variances of the uncertain parameters (and the co-variances of those parameters with exogenous shocks) are small (for indications on how to deal with multiplicative uncertainty, see Acocella, Di Bartolomeo and Hughes Hallett 2013).

For brevity, we omit consideration of controllability in a dynamic setting, possibly in situations of uncertainty, instrument costs and linear quadratic preferences, referring the reader to Acocella, Di Bartolomeo and Hughes Hallett (2013: chap. 3).

1.7 Linking the Two Pillars

The second step in the process of formulating economic policy as an autonomous discipline is associating the theory of economic policy with the existence of market failures. As underlined earlier, a set of microeconomic failures had already been indicated around 1900. After World War II, they were investigated in a systematic manner and codified (e.g. by Kapp 1950 and Bator 1958). Asymmetric information as a cause of market failures came much later (Akerlof 1970), even though the great Italian probabilist Bruno de Finetti had anticipated this concept in an article in a little known Italian journal (de Finetti 1938). However, more relevant from the point of view of computation and the definition of policy programmes were the macroeconomic failures introduced since the 1930s. Market failures as the logic of economic policy, together with the theory of economic policy as a tool for ensuring consistency and effectiveness of policy actions, thus became the ingredients of the core of the discipline.

A difficulty soon emerged (Arrow 1950, 1951) due to the impossibility of starting from individual values to define goal choices of the SWF. In order to bridge the gap between individual preferences and policy goals, Frisch devised the expedient of referring the SWF to politicians' preferences, thus adopting the perspective offered by Bergson's (1938) formulation of the SWF, to which Paul Samuelson (1947) also had added. From a practical point of view, this was enough. SWFs should be derived from official documents and statements or interviews with policymakers (Frisch 1957, 1970 and van Eijk and Sandee 1959 contain a specific example of how this might be done in practice using revealed-preference techniques). The democratic process would ensure consistency between the government's preferences and those of the constituency. In his Nobel lecture, Frisch stated some of the rules to be followed for deriving such a function – as a first stage in the process of cooperation between experts and politicians – and added that he had a number of tests in favour of their practical effectiveness.

Zeuthen (1958), whose book had a large diffusion in Scandinavian countries and was translated into Italian in 1961, was the first (and successful) author to offer a systematic and consistent summary of developments in both welfare economics and the theory of economic policy as cornerstones of economic policy as an autonomous discipline.

The discipline entered the curricula of master degrees in Scandinavian universities in the 1960s and 1970s via textbooks by Tinbergen (1956), Zeuthen (1958), Johansen (1977, 1978) and others.

The meaning of the term 'autonomous discipline' must be clarified at this point. We conceive it along a tradition starting with Frank Knight (1952: 48) and passing through Gustavo Del Vecchio and Federico Caffè. According to Knight, the ultimate aims of economic disciplines (as any social science) are twofold: 'first, to understand or explain some set of phenomena; and second, to use knowledge for the guidance of action'. Accordingly, economic disciplines develop at different levels of abstraction: economic policy as the second step in the progression of economic discipline from more abstraction towards more realism: general economics, economic policy, public finance.

1.8   Why Did Economic Policy As a Discipline First Develop in Scandinavia and the Netherlands – And How Did It Develop Elsewhere?

This is a very difficult issue to deal with. A number of circumstances certainly contributed to explaining why both pillars of the core of economic policy could be built in Scandinavian countries, thus locating there the conception of economic policy as a discipline. I will try to indicate some of the relevant factors, but a more accurate map of the rise of the discipline and the factors favouring or hindering it in each country should be drawn on a country-specific basis.

The first such factor is certainly the openness of the Scandinavian and Dutch world to the theoretical innovations introduced elsewhere since the beginning of the century, in particular, as far as the theory of microeconomic failures is concerned. Section 1.5 referred in particular to the role of the openness of the Norwegian school to progress in macroeconomic analysis through the contributions of Haavelmo and Klein. In some cases, scholars of those countries even anticipated macroeconomic failures. In fact, the most notable members of the Stockholm school, Knut Wicksell, Gunnar Myrdal and Bertil Ohlin, offered important contributions on the dynamics of a market economy and macroeconomic market failures. Especially relevant were the influence of Wicksell on Keynes (Wicksell 1898, 1934, 1935) in integrating the monetary and real sectors and the demonstration by the Stockholm school of how employment can be stimulated by economic policy, which originally appeared before Keynes (Ohlin 1937). When Swedish economists first read the general theory, they thought that 'Keynes' ideas were tracking the views already developed in Sweden', and in their opinion, Keynes was too 'classical' and not innovative enough, which made them increasingly irritated (Jonung 2013: 2). Indeed, Carlson and Jonung (2013) show that there seems to have been an interaction between Keynes' and Ohlin's ideas.

In general, the main characteristic of the Scandinavian (and possibly the Dutch) economic community is its relatively asymmetric openness to international intellectual circuits. Living in small countries, Scandinavian economists learnt and could speak foreign languages, really more German than English, up to World War II. Even if they often wrote in their native languages, exchanges among the scholars of the different Scandinavian (and also Nordic, i.e. including Finland) countries were guaranteed by regular conferences and a 'Marstrand Meeting' – the most important meeting forum – for economic researchers from 1936 to 1985 (Kærgård, Sandelin and Sæther 2008). Thus, policy thinking became similar. This made it possible for developments abroad to penetrate each Scandinavian country and to spread in the region, but it also might have delayed or made it difficult for some ideas introduced there to be absorbed abroad, thus impairing future developments of the discipline.[19]

In addition, one might argue that the development of economic policy as an autonomous normative discipline was natural for countries adopting (indicative) planning for their economies. Thus, even if Zeuthen had warned that the theory of economic policy was not only necessary for planned economies but potentially useful for less interventionist societies, because of the need to ensure mutual consistency of their policy choices, in fact, 'economic policy action changing according to moods can be extremely harmful' (Zeuthen 1958: 133 Italian trans.).

Undoubtedly, complexity of economic policy and the need for coordinating the various fields of action are more acute where policy goals to correct markets are more ambitious and widespread. This could rather easily explain why such a theory never developed in the United States, where the dominant credo was one of scarce public interventions, with the exception of unemployment and anti-inflationary policies. Important contributions to optimal control theory and the theory of economic policy were those of Kendrick (1976, 2000), Chow (especially 1973, 1976) and Ando and Palash (1976). The few textbooks on economic policy published in the United States usually lacked systematic treatment of the general ends of public economic action, dealing mainly with more or less technical notions of the economic policy instruments that can be used to further specific ends (e.g. see Boulding 1958; Norton 1966). A partial exception is Watson (1960), whose book has many features of a complete textbook on economic policy, including a (short) discussion

---

[19] In addition, easy penetration of foreign ideas and theories into these countries could have been one of the causes of the almost sudden disappearance of the theory of economic policy and the whole conception of economic policy as an autonomous discipline (see Section 2.2).

of welfare economics and market failures, but lacks any reference to the theory of economic policy.

In a similar vein, one could say that this was also the case for Germany, where the Keynesian precepts penetrated with difficulty, and the principles held of an economy largely based on market forces within a set of rules (*Ordoliberalism*). This was especially during the Ehrard era (Ehrard was a firm believer in economic liberalism and a supporter of the market) until the second half of the 1960s. At that time, the new minister of the economy, Karl Schiller, provided for coordination of federal, land and local budget plans in order to give economic policy a stronger impact. In 1967, under the pressure of an economic slowdown, the Bundestag passed the Law for Promoting Stability and Growth, known there as the 'Magna Charta of Medium-Term Economic Policy Management', trying to pursue the targets of the Kaldor magic square (*magisches Viereck* is the German expression) and thus adopting an approach of 'global guidance' (*Globalsteuerung*). The case of Austria differs from that of Germany, since in Austria, which was characterised by a larger role of the public sector, there was at least one economist, Reinhard Neck, who cultivated the theory of economic policy and ancillary techniques (see e.g. Neck 1976).

This explanation, which links the development of economic policy as a discipline in a country to the extent of government intervention in the economy of that country, would also fit the case of the United Kingdom. In this country, there was a vast array of public actions, including – in addition to macroeconomic policy – extensive recourse to public enterprises and the welfare state. The theory of economic policy and the whole discipline of economic policy did not pervade the profession, but there were some interesting cases of scholars cultivating them, especially the former. There were rather isolated cases of direct or indirect contributions to the theory. Stone and Croft-Murray (1959) and others offered systematic studies of national accounting.

Meade (1951, 1955) made the largest attempt to build a systematic set of logical alternatives as a guide to action outside Scandinavian countries and the Netherlands, even before Tinbergen and Theil. He succeeded in pursuing this target only partially in his first works, as he studied not the abstract and general issues of economic policy but only how to manage international economic policy by using multiple instruments to pursue various targets: at the same time, in particular, balance-of-payments equilibrium, full employment and, more generally, economic welfare. However, in later investigations he enlarged his analysis of economic policy and mainly dealt with the basic design of economic policy. In his lecture at Manchester on 'The Controlled Economy' of 1970 (see Meade 1971), he depicted three kinds of interconnected programmes:

1. An indicative plan, designed to enable private and public decision-makers to make better forecasts of future market conditions, which would facilitate their decisions, in the absence of future markets. This would derive from the indication by citizens of their decisions as to the amount of goods and services they would demand or supply, conditional on a matrix of alternative current and future prices of all of them. This process would converge towards a situation where a specific matrix of prices equating demand and supply for all goods and services could be found. An econometric model would be an inferior, even if simpler, system to carry out the basics of this plan.

2. A long-run structural plan, whose aim is to enable the government to set its instruments, both in the present and at various future periods, at levels that should allow for the best use of the community's resources.

3. A short-run stabilisation plan to cope with the effects on inflation and unemployment of residual uncertainty

and unpredicted events in a way to avoid cumulative inflationary or deflationary situations.

Meade (1971) got very close to conceiving planning as an interactive action with the private sector, i.e. to a strategic conception on economic policy. His triple level of planning, through a structural and short-run control plan, on the one hand, and an indicative plan, on the other, is his solution to the issue.

The purpose of an indicative plan is to influence the expectations of private decision-makers. The other plans are designed to set the government's instruments at a level that will allow them to attain their social objectives. Preparing these plans can be done only if, by means of an indicative plan, the government has some forecast of the private sector's intentions (or an econometric model of the economy). Similarly, an indicative plan needs knowledge of the solutions of the other plans. Other British contributions were Heal (1969, 1971, 1973, 1987, 2005),[20] Hughes Hallett and Rees (1983) and Holly and Hughes Hallett (1989).

All the theoretical contributions to economic policy and the whole economic policy discipline in the United Kingdom had only a short-run impact on the whole British academic community. A partial explanation of this apparent exception of the United Kingdom to host a 'school' of economic policy could be that in the 1950s and the following decade the attention of at least part of British academia was directed towards some alternative target, i.e. developing a more radical critique of the prevailing marginalist credo, as done by the Neo-Ricardians.[21]

---

[20] This author also contributed to the other pillar of economic policy, in particular, dealing with the impossibility theorem, publishing papers of his own (Heal 1972, 1997) or as a co-author (Chichilnisky and Heal 1983, 1997).

[21] It must be said that the writings by Sraffa (1960) and a number of his followers contributed to the so-called capital debate, which added to the doubts about the efficiency of markets.

The discipline seemed to have a possibly larger impact on practical public intervention in the United Kingdom. Efforts were initially made to introduce optimal control in the economic administration of the country. In fact, the Treasury established a Committee on Policy Optimisation chaired by Professor R. J. Ball, which produced a report that was presented to Parliament (Ball 1978) favouring implementation of techniques of optimal control for use by the UK government.[22] The committee concluded favourably, but practical implementation came to a halt, as soon after the report, policy attitudes towards laissez-faire and government intervention in the United Kingdom changed, suggesting large dismantlement of positive policy action.

The explanation of the relevance of the discipline in a country depending on the extent of that country's degree of public intervention in the economy can find some application with reference to Australia. In fact, in Australia there were a number of additions to the literature on economic policy. Trevor Swan, well known for his contributions to the development of growth models, contributed to the 1945 'White Paper on Full Employment', setting the framework for Australian macroeconomic policy in the following three decades (see Coombs 1994: appendix). Above all, Swan can be considered to be one of the main contributors to the theory of economic policy. In fact, already in 1953 he had devised the essential concepts of controllability that were being developed by Frisch and others and applied them to summarise the content of the many hundreds of pages devoted by Meade

---

[22] Some eminent economists and statisticians – mainly British but also Austrian, such as R. Neck, and American – presented evidence to the committee or talked to its members. The committee discussed a number of aspects of the problem: first, the pretention of a superiority of markets, the possibility and opportunity to refer optimal policies to the Cabinet's or the Treasury's preferences, the relevance of forward commitment of ministers with respect to the use of either open- or closed-loop optimal control and the limits of programming procedures for capturing some of the issues relevant to the distribution of resources and benefits.

to the analysis of internal and external equilibrium. This was the so-called Meade(-Corden-Salter)-Swan diagram. Swan's tendency to delay publication of his results meant that the diagram did not appear in print until 1960 (Swan 1960; Butlin and Gregory 1989). Finally, work by Preston and Pagan has been path-breaking for some extensions of the theory of economic policy (Preston 1974) and its almost final systematisation (Preston and Pagan 1982).

However, the explanation of a scarce penetration of the new discipline in a country in terms of the extent of policy intervention in that country would not fit the case of France, where the government played an important role in a number of fields, and indicative plans were prepared for some decades after World War II. Perhaps other factors – in addition to those of a casual nature, such as the limited role of economists vis-à-vis politicians and bureaucrats or technocrats – were more relevant.

Somewhat relevant could be the general attitude towards science (e.g. positivism) in Anglo-Saxon countries (as this type of epistemology denies a scientific status to normative statements), whereas Frisch insisted on adopting a normative perspective in the planning procedure for assessing the size of the variables involved and their relations (e.g. Frisch 1961). However, the homogeneity of Scandinavian and Dutch societies and the relative weakness of groups in favour of specific interests and acceptance of the implications of a social consensus tended to facilitate a unifying approach to policymaking. The very notion of a unitary Scandinavian economic policy model has been debated (Pekkarinen 1988), but the degree of homogeneity was and still is very high – certainly within each country (see e.g. Bjerkholt 1998, 2005 for Norway) and to a large extent also for all of them with respect to other European countries. In particular, three features common to all Scandinavian countries are: implementation of incomes policy, relevance of the welfare state and other institutions typical of this particular version of capitalism (the so-called Nordic model). Insofar as the Netherlands are concerned, one must consider the existence of a similar degree of social homogeneity, notwithstanding that at the end of the war the government was an uneasy coalition of different political parties (Hughes Hallett 1989: 192).

In addition, an important role might have derived from the existence of bodies composed by economists intermediating between politicians and bureaucrats for devising a set of consistent policies. In Scandinavia and the Netherlands, technical institutions participating in academic economics, ancillary to the political bodies, were instituted. A Central Plan Bureau was established in the Netherlands in 1945. In Norway, an Economy Department and, later, also a Planning Department were created at the Ministry of Finance, which together with Statistics Norway (with a Research Department established in 1950) and the Institute of Economics of the University of Oslo constituted an 'iron triangle' for the buildup of economic planning (Eriksen, Hanisch and Sæther 2007). A very detailed account of the interaction between the theoretical innovations and the use of macroeconomic models for policymaking, especially under the influence of Frisch, can be found in Bjerkholt (1998). Similarly, a detailed account of the procedures implemented at the Dutch Central Planning Bureau, as well as the insights derived from Frisch's suggestions during his visit to the bureau, can be found in van Eijk and Sandee (1959).

A related and very important factor that could explain the birth of economic policy as a discipline in Scandinavian countries is the tendency of Scandinavian economists to tune into public debate on economic policy issues. In particular, in the two or three decades after the war in Scandinavia and the Netherlands, the international community of economists interacted with public and private decision-makers, interest groups, the press, other scientists and the general public through the intermediation of the economists of these countries, who were open minded and had no vested interest in implementing their ideas. The interaction operated in a way that can be thought of as being conducive to a policy model that was specifically national.[23] They still do so now after a further wave of globalisation, even if less than in previous decades.

In explaining the birth of economic policy as a discipline in Scandinavian countries, we can thus speak of a kind of national (economic) policy model, as done by Pekkarinen (1988) in dealing with an issue central to our analysis but of a more limited content, that of Keynesianism and the framework of policy ideas prevailing in Scandinavian countries. The model 'is created out of the broad structural, cultural, social and institutional context of each country' (Pekkarinen 1988: 4). These factors all converged in Scandinavian countries to produce an environment favourable to the birth of a discipline such as economic policy. If one factor can be privileged in this context as a synthesis of other influences, possibly the common cultural ascendant in Scandinavian countries of economic policy as an autonomous discipline can be traced back to Wicksell. His socialist orientation, his support for the welfare state, his critical analysis of Pareto's maximum principle (for which see Palsson Syll and Sandelin 2001) and his analyses of macroeconomic failures in terms of employment and inflation are all elements having an influence on many parts of the future discipline. Our way of proceeding to explain the emergence of economic policy as a discipline in some countries is necessary for a number of reasons. We refer only to a couple of them here.

First, there is a problem of hysteresis of theories due to the cultural and economic factors underlined by Galbraith (1987). In addition, still now there may be a certain lack of

---

[23] In some cases economists took the part of technical organisations and consultation bodies to policymakers. Sometimes they also transited to politics. On the Swedish experience, an important source is Carlson and Jonung (2006), but this also hints at other Scandinavian countries.

correspondence between rather recent developments in the economic science – which certainly now have an international span and to some extent were already so around World War II – and current policy debates and action. Acocella (2013) suggests a reason why the hysteresis might not have operated in the case of the innovations introduced since the end of the 1960s. In fact, already towards the end of 1970s and in the following years, both the international and the local communities of economists were ready to accept them because the new theories brought them back to the classical ones (Johnson 1971).

1.9   Economic Policy in Italy since the 1960s

In Italy, economic policy was hardly taught or investigated as a discipline, at least until the mid-1930s. Most Italian economists followed the autarchic and corporatist credo dictated by the Fascist regime, thus being largely isolated from theoretical developments abroad. Some of them were engaged in the administration of practical policies of the regime. Trade and colonial policy and law, as well as banking policy, were the main substitute of a systematic policy discipline. A minority of enduring pro-market economists, instead, were not inclined to accept Keynesian thought, and some of them migrated abroad.

Because of this prevailing conformist attitude, Italian economic academia had thus exhausted the main innovative tradition characterising it at least until the 'Great War' and had to import the seeds for new progress from abroad. In the early 1950s, practically only a few Italian scholars had introduced – or were about to introduce – Keynesian thought in Italy (Marrama 1948; Papi 1953; Franchini Stappo 1955; Di Fenizio various years). Even fewer Italian scholars had studied progress in welfare economics (Caffè 1953a, 1956a; Lombardini 1954; see also Caffè's translation of the papers on the 'new' welfare economics: Caffè 1956b, Caffè's translation of Zeuthen 1958). This is apparently strange, as the 'new' welfare economics was based on Pareto's foundations, and there were Italian economists, such as Luigi Amoroso, following Pareto's method, but only insofar as the use of mathematics for economic analysis was concerned. Pareto had a very extensive, if lagged, impact on the academic profession abroad, in particular, for what we are interested in in this book, not only for his welfare principle but also for laying down the tools of mathematical economics that contributed to the foundation of econometrics (Tinbergen 1949).

Similarly, very few Italian scholars had introduced the theory of economic policy in the form of either translations and preparation of updated textbooks (in addition to those already mentioned; see Marrama 1962) or reflections on foreign experiences in Western countries, particularly in the Netherlands, under the impulse of Jan Tinbergen (Caffè 1943b, 1946a, 1946b). But some Italian journals hosted either important original articles by foreign authors or their translations. This was the case for a number of contributions – by Frisch, Tinbergen, Theil and, outside the proper realm of economic policy, Shackle and even K. Godel – published in *L'industria*, a journal edited by F. Di Fenizio, and *Metroeconomica*, founded and edited by E. Fossati. The intellectual openness of the economists mentioned also was crucial in their propensity to encourage their pupils to complete their preparation abroad, even if mainly in the United Kingdom and the United States.

By the beginning of the 1960s, all the premises existed in Italy for devising a consistent and rather autonomous set of propositions to fill the discipline of economic policy with new content. The only problem was about the weights to assign to the different possible ingredients. There were two main lines along which the discipline was systematically introduced by two scholars: in a rather loose form, Ferdinando Di Fenizio and, mainly, Federico Caffè.

Di Fenizio gave preeminent relevance to the theory of economic policy. Caffè searched for all the possible key

ingredients for conceiving economic policy as an autonomous discipline. Indeed, as already said, he did so first by
studying policy design and planning experiences in Western
countries, including Italy, before 1958 and then by critically
reviewing progress in the development of welfare economics, translating them into Italian and editing a collection of
papers on the new welfare economics and the SWF, as well
as editing the Italian translation of Zeuthen (1958).[24]
Moreover, he finally published a textbook in two volumes
on economic policy (Caffè 1966a, 1970). This followed to
some extent the path of Zeuthen (1958), but with a more
balanced weight of the various ingredients of the discipline.

A path to some extent similar to Caffè's was followed by
a group of economists in Naples, led by Augusto Graziani,
who wrote a book containing, first, the foundations for public
economic intervention, then the theory of economic policy
and, finally, detailed policies aiming at specific short- or
long-run targets (D'Antonio, Graziani and Vinci 1972,
1979). Other books, such as Rey (1967) and the work done
in conjunction with the attempt to lay down a framework for
the indicative planning schemes prepared by the central
government, applied some of the principles of the discipline,
specifically those of the theory of economic policy (e.g. Fuà
and Sylos-Labini 1963).

For many years, these, together with a few others, were the
main economic policy textbooks circulating in Italy, widely
adopted in most universities. After 1990, other textbooks
were written along lines similar to those of Caffè and
D'Antonio, Graziani and Vinci but with greater attention to
social choice and positive economic policy (Balducci
Candela 1991; later Balducci, Candela and Scorcu 2001,
2002; Acocella 1994, 1999; Cagliozzi 1994). By including
a positive approach in addition to the normative one, these
books complemented the 'normative' theory of economic

---

[24] See more in Box 1.1 at the end of the chapter.

policy, thus completing the set of ingredients that ideally can be thought of as constituting the discipline of economic policy. Some of these books also introduced cases of economic policy to be analysed as a game and discussed in terms of how they involved issues of reputation and the use of rules. In addition to the books already cited, Persson and Tabellini (1990) dealt more specifically with issues of commitment and reputation, which were familiar after the Lucas (1976) critique and Barro and Gordon (1983). To our knowledge, the idea of policymaking as the interaction of governmental action with that of major private institutions was already in Caffè (1966a), but he only hinted at it and did not express it in detailed and formal terms.[25]

Some of the Italian books that had developed and complemented the 'Scandinavian-Dutch approach' to economic policy were translated into English and other foreign languages (e.g. Chinese, Polish and Croatian) and now enter the syllabus of some tertiary-level courses abroad (this was the case for e.g. Acocella 1994, 1999). Notwithstanding this, the approach has apparently failed to largely develop abroad in the period when it did not find any objection; by the end of the 1970s, it had practically been abandoned in the countries where its core originated (see more in Section 2.1).

1.10 Conclusions

Economic policy as a discipline had clearly emerged in the 1950s in some European countries – mainly Scandinavian countries, the Netherlands and Italy. Australia was the main country where it had developed outside Europe. Elsewhere, it had a limited impact. Very limited contributions, mainly in the form of textbooks, came from the United States.

---

[25] More details on developments of economic policy can be found in Acocella (2016c).

Economic policy was built as a discipline mainly by collecting various innovations introduced in different fields of economics, in addition to mathematics and statistics (insofar as the 'theory of economic policy' is concerned), political philosophy and political science (for welfare economics and social choice, i.e. the 'logic' of economic policy). But it also drew on the evolution of the economic and social systems.

The logic and theory of economic policy constituted the 'core' of the discipline. Various parts of this core were the object of both minor and vital critiques concerning the existence of government failures. Critiques moved to its core can partly explain why the discipline did not pass over to other countries and did not survive, even in Europe and Australia, after the 1970s or, in some cases, the 1980s. This is apparently strange. Section 2.2 offers other possible reasons that could jointly explain this setback.

Box 1.1 Caffè's Method and Anticipation of Economic Policy As a Discipline

Caffè's first writings were in applied economics. His first paper, entitled, 'Spontaneous and Forced Savings in War Financing' (Caffè 1942), dealt with grievous current issues. In the following years it was always his propensity to care for current important issues that absorbed his energies as an employee of the Bank of Italy and as an expert or member of various public bodies directed at the economic reconstruction of the country and the draft of its new constitution.

In some of his numerous papers published between 1943 and 1948 he explicitly referred to both microeconomic and macroeconomic market imperfections as a justification for government intervention. Caffè (1943a) suggested democratic planning as a vital instrument for dealing with the many problems of reconstruction and possibly also with the different goals that would arise in normal times by using the whole set of policy instruments. He also cited experiences abroad, particularly in the

Box 1.1 (cont.)

Netherlands under the impulse of Jan Tinbergen (Caffè 1943b, 1945, 1946a, 1946b, 1947, 1948a, 1948b). In these papers he linked planning to market failures not only for the contingencies of that time but also for more enduring reasons. In a series of reflections from 1947 to 1949, starting again from market failures, he also firmly criticised current policy attitudes. He also implicitly, but clearly, stated a programme of macroeconomic policy dealing with the main issues of the time, i.e. employment, inflation and the balance of payments, making use of public investment, monetary and credit action, the exchange rate and foreign aid. His awareness of the changing nature of policy issues, which need flexible actions, is to be stressed (Caffè 1949a, 1949b). In other papers he discussed the role of public investment (1954a, 1958), interest policies and investment (1954b) and other policy instruments.

Starting in 1953, he deepened his theoretical apparatus, being interested in one of the issues he had briefly touched on in his papers on planning, i.e. market failures and the microeconomic policy agenda. He wrote a number of papers on what he later would call the 'logic' of economic policy, thus dealing with microeconomic failures of the market. He followed the evolution of the debate on them through time, from the old to the new directions taken on this topic. He also translated the main contributions of the new welfare economics into Italian (Caffè 1953a, 1956a, 1956b).[26]

Caffè's interest in problems of practical relevance had found two firm theoretical foundations, the logic and the theory of economic policy, i.e. what in the text we call the core of economic policy.[27] However, his intellectual formation was completed only

---

[26] In the interwar period, few Italians were interested in welfare economics. One of them was Tagliacozzo (1933, a text that Caffè certainly knew about when he wrote his textbook on economic policy). On the contribution by Caffè to the foundation of economic policy as a discipline in Italy, see also Pomini (2015).

[27] As said earlier, the definition of the core is mine. However, in the first chapter of his main book and in the whole book, his need to define it is clear, through a systematic analysis of the microeconomic and macroeconomic foundations for government intervention, as well as of the set of logical alternative courses of action open to government, based on different possible relations between economic variables (see in particular

Box 1.1 (cont.)

when he found two important links. The first is what he drew from his mentor, Gustavo Del Vecchio, conceiving the path from analysis to policy as given by different stages of a unitary science, each having a theoretical setting. Thus, by mid-1950s, he possessed all the ingredients for conceiving economic policy as an autonomous discipline in the realm of the economic science, together with a deep knowledge of institutions and history. However, he failed to link the two parts of this core to each other. Knowledge of Zeuthen (1958) finally sparked his conception of economic policy, and he edited the Italian translation of this book. How Caffè discovered the book, published only in Danish, is unclear. Most probably, Caffè already knew Zeuthen both from his previous publications in English (including an incomplete paper that had been requested from him by the editor of the *Quarterly Journal of Economics* and was published posthumously (Zeuthen 1959) and the Italian translation of part of one of them. He certainly did not trace Zeuthen (1958) directly, as he did not speak Danish, or indirectly, e.g. through Schneider's obituary in *Weltwirtschaftliches* (Schneider 1959), as he did not read German either. In addition, no reference to Zeuthen's (1958) book is in Schneider's article in memoriam of Zeuthen published in *Econometrica*, and thus Caffè cannot have traced the book through it.

Caffè required Zeuthen (1958) as one of the compulsory references in his academic course on economic policy from 1961 to 1964. The book, while being very suggestive, proved to be rather

Caffè 1966a: 22–23). In doing this, the set of tools created at a more abstract level (Meade's 'tool-making') should be exploited (Caffè 1966a: 20) 'in order to develop a set of possible economic situations, sketched in a simplified way, i.e. by abstracting from the greater complexity of real situations' (Caffè 1966a: 23). This systematic analysis of government action should be followed by an applicative stage, which will determine the real relevance of the relations between the different variables in specific actual situations (Caffè 1966a: 24). Application to real situations, both domestic and international, was indeed done in Caffè (1970). In this second volume he also presented some formal aspects of a social-welfare function, following discussion of two new macroeconomic targets, growth and balance-of-payments equilibrium. A unified presentation of both the core and its applications to real situations can be found in Caffè (1978a).

Box 1.1 (cont.)

hard to digest for most students. This might have been one of the reasons why Caffè decided to write his own book and prepared the necessary bricks for it. He both drew from his previous research and undertook new research for filling the process forming the policy agenda through the contributions of classical and neoclassical economists (Caffè 1962, 1964a). The logic of economic policy, including both micro- and macroeconomic failures, was completely developed in a historical perspective in Caffè (1964b). Finally, in 1964–66, the first volume of his new book on economic policy was published, where he stated his version of the whole core of the discipline, with a weight attributed to its two parts more balanced than Zeuthen's (1958), where the logic of economic policy was predominant (Caffè 1964b, 1965, 1966a). Application of these principles to current policy, especially with reference to Italy, was made in the second volume (Caffè 1970).

Caffè's systematic statement of the foundations of public intervention, its design in theory and in practice – what goes under the name of 'normative' economic policy – apparently omits a detailed discussion of government failures, what later was often referred to as 'positive' economic policy. This is not so, as he does not think that government failures are irrelevant. In fact, many of his papers refer to such failures.[28] Probably, at

---

[28] He was aware of these failures and underlined them in a number of points. He certainly referred to the experience of Italy and the course of policy action implemented there from at least a couple of points of view: the 'strategy of alarmism' undertaken by the government immediately after the war to justify a certain political and policy stance (Caffè 1972) and the choice made in the same period – also as an effect of vested interests – of adopting a pro-market attitude without tackling structural problems, which impaired the lasting nature of growth in Italy (Caffè 1985). In addition, he dealt with failures of international institutions, which involved the action of technocrats, power groups and national powers. An example of all these 'distortions' is his numerous papers on informal and formal changes of the original statutes of the international organisations created at Bretton Woods (see e.g. Caffè, 1966b, 1978b). In addition, mention must be made of his reservations with respect to European Economic Community as an acceptable and workable form of integration and as an institution de facto allowing free capital movements. This was against the letter and the spirit of the Treaty of Rome and represents a specific example of distortions deriving from the

Box 1.1 (cont.)

the time he wanted to state the normative approach as a useful innovation to use as a yardstick. In any case, he thought that a large number of government failures are simply due to the scarcity of public information, participation and control.

Why didn't Caffè write a book on economic policy as a discipline himself, before Zeuthen, while possessing all the ingredients of its core and also having deep knowledge of the working of economic systems, in particular, of the institutional and historical features of the Italian one? There may be a number of reasons, among which a personal reluctance to make up something of the kind of a 'Harlequin costume' rather than a 'coveralls' (a quote borrowed from a philosopher, Guido Calogero; see Caffè 1977: 11) drawn from critical analysis of the various contributions to economic thought. This reluctance is apparently disproved by his wealth of quotations, which often hide his personal convictions. But this is only appearance. Again, a scientist can follow two roads when expressing his ideas: hiding the sources of his reflections or hiding his ideas and letting the sources of his reflections speak. The former was chosen by Adam Smith. Federico Caffè preferred the latter, as an effect of his personal inclination, respect for others and for pluralism, modesty[29] and reluctance to speak in the first person, associated with consciousness of the vastness of his ignorance, of 'the little light and the large circle of shadow' prevailing at all levels of learning (to repeat the expression he used in a letter to a former student and friend of his, drawn from a popular Italian novelist of the twentieth century, Virgilio Brocchi) (Amari and Rocchi 2007: 1011). Contrary to the apparent derivation of bits of his analysis from other authors, he followed a very clear line of reasoning of his own not only in each paper but also in his whole contribution to economic policy (see also Faucci 2002). Added to this is his preference, also for didactical purposes, for open and critical analysis of the history of economic thought rather

---

imbalance of power among the member countries, as well as from the excessive role of technocrats (see, e.g. Caffè, 1957, 1985).

[29] Ciocca (2014: 20) speaks of 'proud modesty', an expression that perfectly depicts one of Caffè's qualities. Acocella (2015) underlines his tendency to prefer subliminal messages.

Box 1.1 (cont.)

than formal and closed analysis, a derivation of his inclination to apparent eclecticism, as well as his theoretical background. His eclecticism – which was 'rigorous, selective, critical' (Ciocca 1995: 149) – might also derive from acceptance of Del Vecchio's (and, before him, Pantaleoni's and Einaudi's) 'whig' conception of economic science as being characterised by progress without breaks (Faucci 2002: 366–67).

Source: Redrawn, with a few changes, from Acocella 2014b.

2

Progressive Dismantling and Demise of the Classical Theory of Economic Policy

This chapter deals with the critiques against the first and second pillars of economic policy as a discipline. Section 2.1 tries to explain why the discipline did not pass to countries that were different from those where it was born as well as why it did not survive there. Section 2.2 sketches the pre-conditions for a discipline to exist and the different kinds of critiques aimed at economic policy as a discipline. The following sections investigate the critiques, both minor (Section 2.3) and vital, addressed to the two pillars of the discipline (Section 2.4 for the first pillar, Section 2.5 for the second). The consequences of these critiques for policy attitudes – in terms of the preference for constraints and rules rather than discretionary action – are dealt with in Section 2.6. Finally, Section 2.7 links this chapter to Chapter 3, where the manner in which the first pillar was re-established and the long process for re-establishing the second pillar are analysed.

2.1 Why Economic Policy Did Not Pass Over to Other Countries or Survive

Specific circumstances had favoured the emergence and flourishing of the discipline of economic policy in Scandinavia, the Netherlands, the United Kingdom, Italy and a few other countries. After all, these countries shared

some common features distinguishing them from other countries: the weight and left-wing orientation of the 'intelligen-
tsia' as well as of the political parties supporting the
governments or of some strong opposition parties and institutions (such as trade unions), together with the idea that
public happiness should be served by a 'visible hand'.
To these we should add another circumstance for Italy: an
idealistic epistemological attitude of the Italian scientific
community, the importance at the time of the Marxist and
Catholic credos – which are both pro-government – and the
relevance of civil society.

To illustrate why the idea of economic policy did not pass
over to other countries – and indeed did not survive in the
countries where it flourished for some time – multiple explanations can be offered. Reference could be made not only to
the absence of features similar to those listed in Chapter 1 but
also to the strength of the bureaucracy (including the status of
the central bank) in some countries. This may 'insulate policy
from various political pressures, although it may also limit the
influence of outside economic theorists over policy'
(Pekkarinen 1988: 5), which could explain why a theory of
economic policy did not develop in France or Germany.
A reason for the scarce attention to long-term planning (and
then to an ingredient of the core) in some countries might be
tied to the importance of the Nordhaus political business
cycle and the political aspects of policy, at least in some
countries, such as the United States, Canada, Japan and, possibly, Germany, in contrast to the Scandinavian and other
countries mentioned earlier. However, on the one hand, this
explanation would not fit all situations, such as e.g. that of
France; on the other hand, there appears to be no reasonable
explanation for rejecting the remedy suggested as optimal by
Nordhaus (1975: 189) in referring to a 'planning framework'.

The only possible explanation is that in most of the countries where economic policy did not develop, as well as in
those in which it was in progress, either the orientation of

people in favour of markets, political pressure or both also were really very powerful in intellectual circles, merging with the developments of economic theory, as we will discuss later. In fact, these developments at least partly questioned the preconditions for the existence of an economic discipline. I discuss them in the following sections.

2.2 Preconditions for the Existence of an Economic Discipline: The Core of Economic Policy under Attack

Any analytical discipline cannot be conceived if some minimal conditions are not satisfied, in particular, as far as the abstract preconditions for its existence are absent, insufficient or defective. As for economic policy as a discipline, these preconditions are two: (1) the existence of market failures requiring intervention by an institution based on a logic that is different from that of self-interest and (2) The validity of what I called its 'core', allowing for the possibility or necessity of supplementing (or substituting) market decisions (as an institution expressing people's preferences) with democratic, consistent and effective public action.

No theoretical or practical objections were raised against the existence of market failures, even if their term of comparison – the maximand that the market could not reach – was unclear or could not be derived from people's preferences. Indeed, Akerlof (1970) added to these failures by introducing asymmetric information.

It is true that Coase's propositions (Coase 1960) had tended to rehabilitate markets or at least part of their failures, but his arguments came up against fundamental theoretical difficulties noticed already in the 1970s, such as the existence of fundamental non-convexities, which makes it impossible for an equilibrium in the pollution permits to exist (see Acocella 1994: 104–6 English trans.). This notwithstanding, over time the idea of market primacy spread through the academic community, was enriched by other arguments, gained momentum and dominated the prevailing theories, transmitting also to the countries where the discipline of economic policy was born.

From this last point of view, Kærgård, Sandelin and Sæther (2008) cite the influence of K. H. Borch, who was recruited to the Norwegian School of Economics and Business Administration as a professor of insurance from 1963 and urged his students to pursue doctoral studies in North America, thus weakening the influence of the Oslo school in Norwegian economics and politics. This aggravated the asymmetric openness of the Scandinavian academic community (see Section 1.8).

Other factors leading to the decline of the Oslo school are given by Eriksen, Hanisch and Sæther (2007) and replicated in Sæther and Eriksen (2014a), on which, however, see the highly critical comments by Bjerkholt (2014), partially accepted by Sæther and Eriksen (2014b). Dixit, Honkapohja and Solow (1992) explain the disappearance of the tracts of the Swedish school due to the globalisation of economic analysis along lines dictated by the Chicago school. Asymmetric openness turned into the importation of a standardised commodity into a 'small' country.

Dealing specifically with Sweden but with implicit reference also to other countries, Jonung (2013) points out the attractions and constraints of the younger generation of Swedish economists that led them to publish in English, prefer occupations in North American universities and disregard policy issues and applications of theoretical thought. Jonung's analysis applies to Italy and to other countries as well. To be fair, Siven (1985: 592) explains the end of the Stockholm school as due in particular to its methodology ('disinterest for equilibrium analysis, a preference for casuistic analysis, and lack of instruments for analysing the questions posed by the School itself'). It is natural that the homogeneity of the Chicago school had been reached at the cost of taking national specificities out of the realm of analysis. It is not so natural that policy applications to solve specific issues in a given context follow analysis with scarce reference to history and institutions, which is also due to uncritical understanding of the respective contents of economic analysis and policy. 'Economic policy' is not even listed as a subject in the *Journal of Economic Literature* (*JEL*) classification system, and only 'macroeconomic policy' appears as a subcategory.

These developments were favoured – indeed strengthened – by the multiple objections to the possibility that democratic policy action could effectively amend market failures, as indicated by the discipline of economic policy born in Scandinavian countries. Most such objections dealt with some kind of government (or 'non-market') failures. We divide them into two types: those we can call 'minor failures', on the one hand, and 'vital failures', on the other, according to whether or not they can be incorporated into the 'core' of the discipline or are – at least unless they are the object of much closer scrutiny – destructive of it, respectively.

Minor critiques – most of them of a 'political economy' kind, when such critiques are not so extremely articulated as to involve the self-regulating ability of all human actions – can enrich the discipline and be easily incorporated into it. I deal with them in Section 2.3.

Vital critiques have left the logic of economic policy untouched insofar as the existence of market failures is concerned, thus setting, from this point of view, the stage for government intervention to cure such failures. Vital objections have been directed instead mainly at the existence of 'critical' government failures. They refer first to the impossibility of taking people's preferences as a reference for public action, stated by Arrow (1951). In addition, there are the 'radical' objections to the effectiveness of public action of the kind raised by Lucas (1976), based on the introduction of rational expectations (REs) into the analysis, together with other assumptions.

Differently from minor critiques, these critiques could not be incorporated into the discipline. They were really a barrier opposing its very existence, because, on the one hand, they limited the very possibility of fixing market failures in a democratic society starting directly from individuals' preferences. Definition of the society's goal had to be delegated to politicians through the political process. On the other hand, the effectiveness of discretionary economic policy was put in question, thus severely limiting the range of public action, which was confined to the definition of rules. Only when these critiques were overcome did the very possibility of founding economic policy as a discipline come to exist.

2.3   Minor Failures: The Identity of Policymakers

What we call 'minor failures' are the government failures that have been emphasised by the 'positive' approach to economic policy. This perspective stresses very important factors, such as the corruption of politicians and their capture by powerful interest groups.

The 'classical' theory of economic policy is accused of ignoring the identity of policymakers, their political and personal objectives and thus the numerous agency problems arising in public governance.[1] The egoistic or populist tendencies of politicians were first introduced by the school of public choice, starting from the idea of the political process as being determined by a collection of self-interested decisions (Buchanan and Tullock 1962). This applies not only to politicians but also to other agents. As far as politicians are concerned, their

---

[1] Here and below I use the term in its general meaning, as a substitute for government action. Some authors put the emphasis of government action on its *enablement skills*. These are required in order to link multiple stakeholders and organise horizontal forms of societal self-coordination for a common end in a situation of interdependence. This should be implemented through a larger role of markets and 'third parties' (in particular, various private institutions) rather than by command and control regulation (Salamon 2000; Peters 2002; Jordan, Wurzel and Zito 2005).

attempts to maximise the length of their tenure (Downs 1957) or to win re-election (Nordhaus 1975), their partisan inclinations (Hibbs 1977; Wittman 1977) and their representation of interest groups (Olson 1965) rather than all citizens imply reaching an employment target higher than the natural one, running budget deficits, accumulating public debt and so on. This is possible if there arise principal-agent problems as an effect of 'rational ignorance' (Downs 1957) or asymmetric information (also Dixit 1996).[2] To be sure, similar problems affect not only macroeconomic policies but also the provision of public goods and are particularly important if the principal is composed of a large group of individuals (Olson 1965). Niskanen (1971) underlines the personal interests of bureaucrats in enlarging their share of the budget they have to administer in order to be paid higher salaries. This leads them to over-provide public goods. In addition, the kind of electoral system, e.g. proportional representation, and electoral uncertainty can exacerbate the tendency to enlarge expenditures and deficits. Other important contributors to an analysis of the 'political economy' or 'political economics' approach were Alesina, Persson and Tabellini (Alesina 1987; Alesina and Tabellini 1990; Persson and Tabellini 2000).

However relevant, the factors underlined by the political economy approach are not vital failures of the classical discipline of economic policy. They need to be taken into account in practical policy together with a number of other institutional and historical features characterising the issue in question and should be part of the discipline when policy action is to be devised in practice. These objections can be dealt with partly in analytical terms similar to some of those referred to as 'market failures' (asymmetric information). Both markets and governments, as human institutions, are imperfect. Having recognised this, economic policy as a discipline

---

[2] This is the reason why control over bureaucrats can never be complete, even when political power is concentrated in the hands of a sovereign (Tullock 1965).

could be a way to devise how they can complement each other and be designed in a more rational way (I trace some of their consequences on policy actions later). On practical grounds, as a consequence of these theories, the need arises to devise rules to constrain governmental action (see Section 2.6).

Instead, logical and empirical objections were moved to the second precondition, as mentioned by Arrow (1951), and new ones were added as an effect of the innovations introduced in the two decades after the mid-1960s. Some objections of this kind contributed to developing parts of economic policy and generated new fields of inquiry. Some other objections, such as the Lucas critique, tied to REs, have been fatal to the survival of economic policy as an autonomous discipline until recently and have contributed to its decline while supporting the theoretical orientation of the Chicago school, referred to earlier. The absence of theoretical advances in crucial areas of the core of economic policy, such as the theory of economic policy, after its practical demise as an effect of the Lucas critique has been a determinant for the persistence of critical positions against the discipline.

2.4   Vital Failures and the First Pillar: The Impossibility of a Democratic Social Welfare

Vital failures are tied to two types of objections: the impossibility of taking people's preferences as a reference for public action, underlined by Arrow (1950, 1951), and the 'radical' objections to the effectiveness of public action of the kind raised by Lucas (1976). The former objection was drastic but relatively short-lived, and it was rather easily overcome in a number of ways. I will deal with it and the suggestions for coping with it in this section. The latter objection, instead, had a long and composite gestation, complemented all the previous objections aimed at the effectiveness of government action and led to widespread negative attitudes towards it. I deal with it in Section 2.4.1 and defer the difficult process of suggesting appropriate theoretical and institutional solutions to Chapters 3 and 4.

The impossibility of a democratic social welfare function prevented the identification of a term of comparison for market failures. Without such a term of comparison, in fact, market failures could not be easily defined and identified.

This section is organised as follows. The first subsection is devoted to the axiomatic demonstration of the impossibility of a democratic social welfare function, i.e. to the conclusions derived on the basis of preconceived sensible requirements for the construction of social ordering starting from multiple individual orderings. In Section 2.4.2, I discuss the procedural aspects of this construction, involving voting mechanisms.

2.4.1　The Axiomatic Impossibility

In order to overcome the partial nature of Pareto orderings, Arrow (1951) took an approach that was different from that adopted by the proponents of the compensation principle (see Chapter 1). He tried to construct a complete social ordering axiomatically by supplementing the Pareto principle with other widely accepted axioms having the nature of both ethical norms and procedures satisfying them.

For example, let us consider a set of alternatives *a, b* and *c* and suppose that all consumers prefer *a* to *b*, but some prefer *c* to *a* and others prefer *a* to *c*; similarly, some prefer *b* to *c* and some *c* to *b*. If we apply the Pareto principle, the unanimity of individual preferences for *a* over *b* allows us to construct a social ordering of *a* and *b*; in other words, society will prefer *a* to *b*. However, the Pareto principle does not allow us to order *c* with respect to *a* and *b*. Arrow attempts to construct a complete ordering by employing the Pareto principle with additional conditions that enable us to order Pareto-non-comparable states as well. These additional conditions can be expressed in axiomatic form. The normative content of the axioms used by Arrow is underscored in Mueller (1989: chap.

20). The axioms also have a procedural counterpart; i.e. there are voting procedures (majority voting, for example) that satisfy the axioms, as we will see in Section 2.4.2.

Take the weak version of the Pareto principle, which states that society must prefer social state a to social state b if all its members prefer a to b. In order to extend this ordering and make it complete and 'rational', it seems necessary (or reasonable) to supplement the Pareto principle with the following conditions:

1. **An Unrestricted Domain Condition.** The 'rule' for constructing a social ordering out of individual orderings must be defined for all possible sets of individual orderings. In other words, the rule for the social ordering of individual preferences holds whatever these preferences may be, as long as each system of individual preferences is not contradictory.

2. **An Independence of Irrelevant Alternatives Condition.** In choosing between a and b, we must only take into account individual preferences with regard to those alternatives, ignoring individual orderings of other possibilities. This hypothesis is introduced in order to economise on the information necessary for social ordering, but it also enables us to exclude insincere expressions of preferences made for strategic reasons.

Following Arrow, it can be demonstrated that with this set of hypotheses, the Pareto principle enables us to obtain a complete social ordering. However, this can only happen if the preferences of one individual are 'decisive'; that is, if the choice of one individual determines society's choice, regardless of the preferences of the other members of society (i.e. there is a dictatorship in determining social preferences).

The practical significance of this result is of considerable importance: the members of a community who wish to construct a complete social ordering satisfying the conditions of unrestricted domain and independence of irrelevant alternatives, as well as the weak Pareto principle, must necessarily accept the preferences of one individual regardless of those of the others. Under these conditions, rejection of dictatorial choices makes it impossible to define a complete ordering that overcomes the partial character of the Pareto principle while still applying the principle itself. This is the Arrow 'impossibility theorem'.[3]

The outcome of Arrow's attempt to construct a complete social ordering put an end – with little or nothing to show for its efforts – to the scientific programme initiated by Robbins' (1932) essay. The attempt to direct welfare economics towards the exclusive study of problems of efficiency, separated from those of equity – and, thus, of values – was a failure.

2.4.2 The Procedural Impossibility

I have reviewed the main problems that arise in the axiomatic attempt to devise a social ordering based on individual preferences. The axioms normally reflect value judgments, which may be more or less acceptable. This apart, the axiomatic approach is a purely logical exercise and apparently almost entirely ignores the procedures normally used in the real world to aggregate individual preferences, i.e. forms of voting.

This subsection shows that

1. Different procedural methods are based on different value judgments;
2. There is a correspondence between the criteria used in logical schemes for the construction of social orderings and voting procedures; and
3. It is difficult to construct a social ordering in a democratic society.

---

[3] I have presented the impossibility theorem in a way that emphasises the impossibility of non-dictatorial choices, given the other axioms. However, if we underline the need of non-dictatorial choices and take this as an axiom, the impossibility still holds, unless another axiom is dropped.

Voting theory therefore enables us to extend the analysis of previous sections and look at it from a different point of view. Every voting situation presupposes a set of rules of varying complexity, each of which is the product of choices that have significant effects on the results of the vote itself. One group of rules regards the choice of who can vote and the number of votes each participant will cast; this calls for the same sort of interpersonal comparisons as those used in the axiomatic construction of the social ordering and for the selection of a dictator.

A second group of rules concerns the voting procedures and involves establishing

1. The proposals to be put to a vote (in particular, deciding who can formulate the proposals);
2. The voting procedure proper; this can be either a binary rule (in which pairs of alternatives are voted on) or a plurality rule (in which more than two alternatives are voted on simultaneously); and
3. The order of voting, which is important in cases where not all the alternatives are voted on at once.

The influence of value judgments in determining the procedure for formulating proposals is clear, but we will shortly see that they are also involved in the other procedures.

A final group of rules concerns the procedure for determining the outcome of the vote; for example, we can choose between unanimous or majority voting. The degree to which individual preferences are respected in social choices differs in the two cases. In the two following subsections I will concentrate on the problems connected with this last group of rules.

To sum up, there are difficulties in constructing a social ordering in a democratic regime. They regard, in particular, (1) insincere voting for strategic purposes and (2) 'multi-peaked' individual preferences.

Political institutions nevertheless can be arranged in such a way as to reduce or even eliminate these difficulties by skirting the conditions under which they arise. For example, strategic voting can be reduced if participation in votes on specific alternatives is voluntary, which in practice limits the vote to people interested in those (and not other) alternatives. In addition, despite the existence of multi-peaked preferences (which is often a consequence of the fact that choices are multidimensional), we can still apply the median voter theorem if voting regards 'slates' of proposals, candidates or parties. What is more, while cyclical majorities can emerge from single votes, multiple votes on different questions might avoid them (see Ingberman and Inman 1988). I will not extend my analysis of actual political institutions here because I wish to keep this part of the discussion on a more abstract level. Such an analysis in any case lies within the domain of political science. The last forty years have seen the emergence of a new approach, the public choice school and political economics, which deal with the economic study of non-market decisions or, simply, the application of economics to political science, as indicated earlier.

My objective so far has been to show that

1.   All the procedures in the construction of a social ordering through voting constantly reflect value judgments about the best action to take; these judgments lead to the selection of one or another of the possible alternatives and therefore benefit one or another of the members of society.
2.   There is a correspondence between the value judgments underlying the voting rules and the conditions that make the aggregation of individual preferences possible.
3.   It is difficult to define a social ordering in a democratic regime. It was shown that using either unanimous or majority voting rules as an aggregation procedure for individual preferences.

    a.   Does not guarantee that a well-defined social preference will be expressed and

    b.   Can lead to different results depending on the circumstances (in particular, on voting procedures); social preferences therefore can be altered by voters and/or those in charge of the voting if special measures are not taken to avoid this.

2.5   Vital Failures and the Second Pillar: The Ineffectiveness of Policy Action

In this section, I deal with the second type of vital objections to the discipline, i.e. those concerning the effectiveness of economic policy.[4] These objections complement the critiques implicitly dealing with the effectiveness of policy action in favour of citizens that can be derived from the personal preferences of policymakers but, contrary to them, had a long and more composite origin and have been settled less easily.

These objections are essentially due to the introduction of expectations, initially adaptive expectations, with respect to monetary policy (see Section 2.5.1) and then, in a more forceful and general way (i.e. referred to all policy actions), due to the assumption of REs in a context similar to that of Lucas (1976) (see Section 2.5.2). These objections – while contributing to the general progress of economic thought in various ways[5] – negated the effectiveness of policy action even in the absence of agency issues and led to assertions about the low or negative value of fiscal multipliers and the need to avoid coordination of fiscal policy across countries (see Sections 2.5.3 and 2.5.4). In their weakest form, they constrained public policy into a Nessus shirt by prescribing

---

[4] This section largely draws on Acocella (2014a).

[5] As a matter of fact, I can repeat Lucas' words and say that 'dynamic economic theory ... has simply been reinvented in the last 40 years', which implied introduction of a 'new ability to incorporate dynamics and probabilistic elements into economic theory' (Lucas 1987: 2).

policy action only under a rather rigid set of rules to avoid time inconsistency and suboptimal outcomes. Stronger versions of this kind of criticism denied any active role to public policy when in conflict with the conduct of private agents (see Section 2.6).

These problems have long been unaddressed, thus contributing in a decisive way to the decline of economic policy as an autonomous discipline. To some extent, the very practical application of the discipline in its heyday could have distracted its founders and followers from further research and innovation, as was certainly the case for the Stockholm school and possibly also for the Oslo school.

2.5.1 The Role of Monetary Policy with Adaptive Expectations

In the second half of the 1960s, independent analyses by Edmund Phelps (1967) and Milton Friedman (1968) led to the conclusion that monetary policy aimed at higher employment and income is ineffective in the long run, when there is no trade-off between unemployment and inflation (the long-run Phillips curve is vertical). Thus, any monetary expansion that attempts to reduce the 'market' rate of unemployment below the 'natural' one is doomed to failure and can only cause inflation. Monetary policy should pursue a target of monetary stability rather than trying to influence real variables. This explains why the European Central Bank (ECB) has been assigned a monetary target (price stability) instead of a dual or multiple mandate, as in the case of the Federal Reserve. To be sure, price stability would not be the proper objective in this line of analysis because the Friedman (1969) rule must be obeyed, which should ensure (at least in a completely flexible price context) a zero nominal interest rate and a *deflation* rate equal to the real interest rate on safe assets. The decision taken by the ECB to choose an inflation target less than, but close to, 2 per cent – then a positive one –

is only apparently contrary to the Friedman rule, as in reality prices are not completely flexible and hedonic prices may be of some importance.

The issue of the independence of central banks seems, however, more remote from Friedman's thought. In his opinion attributing to the central bank an independent status is a second-best option, for both political and economic reasons. As far as the latter are concerned, rules are preferable to independence, as the main objectives of monetary policy are to avoid money itself being a factor in major disturbances in the system and to offer a stable background for the economy. It is true that Friedman's objections to independence refer to a situation where the central bank is given 'a good deal of separate power', whereas some central banks, like the ECB, are governed by a rule (i.e. a kind of 'flexible' inflation targeting). However, this rule must be obeyed in the medium run, which implies that cyclical manipulations of the interest rate (or the monetary base) are not only possible but also desirable. This is exactly the kind of monetary conduct Friedman wanted to avoid (Friedman 1962).

We therefore must refer to the theoretical foundations of the rules governing central banks and their targets other than those of Friedman, even if Friedman's (1962) argument contains the seeds of further thought justifying an independent and conservative central bank. This anticipation of further developments can be linked to one of the arguments Friedman makes use of, in particular, when, in the case of an independent central banker, he is a critic of the uncertain personality of those in charge of monetary control, who may or may not give any assurance of steady and firm conduct. This argument is a prelude to the assertion of the virtues of commitment and of a conservative central banker, which are linked either to the passage from backward- to forward-looking expectations or to political economy arguments – or to both.

2.5.2 *Rational Expectations, the Neutrality Proposition and the Need for a Conservative Central Bank*

Introduction of REs led, first, to a statement of the ineffectiveness of monetary policy that was even more forceful than that stated by Friedman (Sargent and Wallace 1975). Similarly, with rational forward-looking expectations, fiscal policy was considered to be ineffective as an instrument for managing income levels (Barro 1974), a result that will be considered into detail shortly. A proposition of policy neutrality or policy 'invariance' was thus stated concerning the most important macroeconomic policy instruments. From a more general point of view, Lucas (1976) showed that if the private sector has REs, it can fool *any* attempt by either the central bank or the government to pursue a given target for any real variable through the use of any instrument (generalised policy neutrality). The Phillips curve is then vertical also in the short run.

In the same vein, any promise by governments that is time inconsistent is deemed not to be credible by private agents having forward-looking expectations (Kydland and Prescott 1977). This result can be avoided by self-restraint of the policymaker, whose temptation to cheat is balanced by a fear that he or she might lose his or her reputation and no longer be able to act effectively in the case of repeated interactions with the private sector. However, in a world filled with uncertainty, signals are more difficult to interpret, and then the best practical solution to the problem of time inconsistency is that the policymaker credibly commits to some rule (Barro and Gordon 1983).

2.5.3 *Ineffectiveness of Fiscal Policy: Low Value of Multipliers*

In the vision of the policymakers of the 1980s and 1990s, which reflected to a large extent the economic theories that had been introduced since the end of the 1960s, problems do not come from markets, which should indeed be freed of any obstacle (or at least of regulations and obstacles deriving from the government action). They come from the discretionary action of public agents, as in each time period these tend to pursue targets that are unattainable in the presence of private agents having either backward- or forward-looking expectations. In attempting to obtain their objectives, governments are fooled by the private sector, and a suboptimal outcome results. Discretionary monetary and fiscal policies are ineffective with respect to real variables, and the first best desired by public agents can never be obtained. Complying with some kinds of rules can at least ensure a second-best outcome.

Setting rules to constrain monetary and fiscal policy (e.g. monetary rules, limits to budget deficits and public debts) has multiple theoretical roots. First of all, by referring to political economy contributions, one can have an analytical justification for the assumption underlying Barro and Gordon's (1983) model, according to which the government's desired unemployment rate is lower than the natural one. In this way, one goes to the roots of time inconsistency. In addition, this literature can explain the tendency towards accumulation of public deficit and debt. This offers a specific justification for constraints imposed on discretionary fiscal action and political economy contributions that predicate the need for rules in general and constitutional rules in particular.

The ineffectiveness of government action due to ultra-rationality (Barro 1974) or REs, the low values of multipliers, time inconsistency and other factors move in the same direction. Finally, within the realm of public action, the potentially negative influence of coordinated fiscal policy on the price level and the capacity of monetary counteraction by an independent and conservative central bank would justify the absence of fiscal coordination in currency unions and application of the principle of subsidiarity to this matter.

Of special interest are two issues raised in the literature that have inspired recent fiscal policy attitudes towards the crisis in some countries, e.g. in Europe: on the one hand, a widespread belief in the existence of a limit beyond which an increase in public debt would have negative consequences on growth (e.g. Reinhart and Rogoff 2010; Checherita-Westphal and Rother 2010; Kumar and Woo 2010; and, long before these contributions, Modigliani 1961; Diamond 1965; Saint-Paul 1992); on the other hand, the assertion of very low (in the limit, null) or even negative spending and tax multipliers (Giavazzi and Pagano 1990).

In the following sections, we deal only with two of the above-mentioned arguments in favour of policy ineffectiveness, i.e. the low value of multipliers and the negative effects of fiscal policy coordination. At this point, I must note that one reason for policy ineffectiveness really derived precisely from the space acquired by markets – specifically financial markets – over time. This was largely an effect of both globalisation and the stimulus given to these markets by relaxation of certain constraints that had been set at Bretton Woods under the influence of Keynes' pressure in order to leave some room for autonomous national policies (Carabelli and Cedrini 2014). This refers, in particular, to the relaxation of limitations on capital account operations and also to the possibility of drawing on the International Monetary Fund (IMF) for capital account deficits.

2.5.4 Inefficiency and Negative Spill-Overs from Coordinating Fiscal Policy in a Currency Union?

The neoclassical and New Keynesian approach that incorporates some sort of Barro-Ricardo (consumption-smoothing) effect – thus asserting a low value of multipliers – tends to suggest fiscal policy ineffectiveness for expansionary purposes and, in the case of a crisis, the need for fiscal contraction. The familiar investment saving–liquidity preference money supply (IS-LM) fixed-price textbook model teaches us that an increase in public spending leads to a greater than proportional increase in private consumption and output because of the Keynesian multiplier. Looking more closely at the text, the effect is not so simple. For instance, crowding out may reduce (or even offset) the effects of government expenditure, since the higher interest rates may discourage private investors.

Assuming fixed prices, as in the IS-LM model, all changes in aggregate demand are satisfied by a passive aggregate supply. However, this kind of analysis can be extended to explicit aggregate demand and supply functions to show the effects of policy changes on wages, prices and employment, as well as on real performance and financial conditions. Often the induced changes in wages and prices reduce, if not negate, the impact of expansionary fiscal policies. The effects of government action also can be offset by the central bank, when the monetary authorities do not accommodate the fiscal expansion.

As mentioned earlier, rational agents lead to a different result: increases in public spending financed by debt may lead to a reduction in consumption (a non-Keynesian effect) and possibly in output. The effect on consumers derives from their prediction that the increase in public debt should be repaid through higher taxes in the future.

In the real business cycle realm with price flexibility, the dynamics of fiscal policy and its effects are determined by aggregate supply. If prices are fully flexible and non-distortionary taxes are assumed, a change in public consumption does not affect capital or labour productivity but again influences the economy only by its wealth effect. Increases in public expenditure lower permanent income because rational agents expect future taxes. They therefore reduce private consumption, and real wages fall. Private investment then increases, offsetting part of the fall in consumption (Baxter and King 1993).[6]

The inclusion of price stickiness is not enough to avoid the effects described by Baxter and King (1993), which survive into the canonical New Keynesian dynamic stochastic general equilibrium (DSGE) model. Here the fall in consumption and the increase in labour supply add to labour demand. Then, if the monetary policy is not too active in responding to the production level, real wages can rise (instead of falling), but not by enough to arrest the fall in consumption and thus the non-Keynesian effects of fiscal policy (Goodfriend and King 1997; Linneman and Shabert 2003).

Even in these neoclassical and New Keynesian models, separable utility, deep habits consumption, rule-of-thumb consumers and spending reversals could restore positive and significant Keynesian-like effects of public spending increases on output (Hebous 2010). In the absence of such mechanisms, some kind of Barro-Ricardo effect not only would imply the ineffectiveness of Keynesian policies but also would suggest the need for fiscal consolidation, under the form either of a reduction in expenditures or of a rise in taxes. This suggestion would be strengthened considering also the negative long-term effect of debt on growth. A positive effect of government expenditure cuts both from a short- and a long-run perspective derived from some empirical research. As mentioned earlier, this was the conclusion of Giavazzi and Pagano (1990), who explained the positive effects on consumption of the cuts of the 1980s in Danish and Irish public expenditures as deriving from households' expectations of permanent cuts in the level of the government budget. Along similar lines followed Alesina and Perotti (1995, 1997) and Giavazzi and Pagano (1996).

[6] Nonetheless, if lump taxes are not available, the effects of public consumption on output and investment depend on the elasticity of labour supply and the tax path. In such a case, an increase in public spending may imply reductions in investment and output too.

This fin de siècle credo of low or negative values of multipliers was certainly not in favour of traditional Keynesian fiscal action and imbalances and can be thought of as influencing the draft of the European Monetary Union (EMU) institutional setup (Acocella 2014a). In addition, it has also inspired the idea of an expansionary fiscal consolidation (the doctrine of 'expansionary austerity') that has been at the basis of exit policies from the crisis – and the related idea of 'gain without pain'[7] from fiscal consolidation, or the so-called German view (Acocella 2015).

From this perspective, it is not strange that in Europe active fiscal policy had been put in plaster by the Stability and Growth Pact (SGP), and (more recently) the 'fiscal compact' has been agreed on. But these limitations on discretionary fiscal policy cannot be fully understood without considering open economies explicitly, in the context of other European institutions, which I do below.

Theoretical models of open economies are of specific interest to me. In this context, the impact of budget policies on the real exchange rate plays an important role in determining the size of the multiplier effect, as this could be increased by real exchange rate depreciation. Also, other effects must be taken into account in an open economy, such as the existence of incomplete international financial markets (Kollman 2010) and the possibility of a home bias in consumption (Ravn, Schmitt-Grohé and Uribe 2007), as both increase the expansionary impact of public expenditure. In an open economy context, positive spill-over effects operating via trade also have a special interest. Beetsma, Giuliodori and Klaassen (2006, 2008) and Beetsma and Giuliodori (2011) explore the international spill-overs from fiscal policy shocks in Europe. A fiscal expansion stimulates domestic activity, which leads to more foreign exports and, hence, higher foreign output. Erceg, Gust and Lopez Salido

---

[7] I use the expression of Perotti, who confuted the idea (Perotti 2013), as we will see later.

(2007) and Spilimbergo et al. (2009) argue in fact that fiscal coordination increases multiplier effects.

Some of these effects are scarcely relevant in the case of fixed exchange rates, as in the EMU. In fact, changes in the real exchange rate are possible only to the extent to which the price level can be lowered in the country with an expansionary fiscal policy, which contradicts what one should expect to happen in a monetary union. Also, the home bias is limited in the European Union as far as the effect of national protectionist policies is concerned, as both trade and non-trade barriers were drastically lifted. In fact, the income multiplier is reduced by the high value of the propensity to import from other EU countries. This high propensity, instead, while having a negative impact on expansionary fiscal action in one country only, would per se support a coordinated fiscal action.

This conclusion misses interactions between fiscal and monetary policies, which have an impact on the nature and value of fiscal multipliers and spill-overs. In a monetary union such as the EMU, assigning monetary authorities the primary target of price stability implies a negative spill-over of fiscal policy; in fact, any expansionary fiscal action by one country has an impact on the union's price level and thus calls for a deflationary intervention by the ECB. Beetsma and Bovenberg (1998), Beetsma and Uhlig (1999) and Beetsma, Debrun and Klaassen (2001), while using different modelling approaches, all find negative effects on income from fully coordinated fiscal expansion due to the deflationary reaction of the central bank.

According to Beetsma and Bovenberg (1998), in a monetary union such as the EMU, time inconsistency provides the rationale for a conservative central bank and against the coordination of national fiscal policies. In fact, in their analysis, the system suffers from both a spending bias and an inflation bias and thus faces a trade-off between them. By adjusting either monetary or fiscal institutions, not both, only a suboptimal outcome can result. Monetary unification enhances the strategic position of the monetary authority and introduces a disciplinary effect on governments. Fiscal coordination would eliminate this disciplinary effect and worsen the strategic position of the central bank. The need for introducing subsidiarity in fiscal policymaking is thus asserted.

The only problem left is whether the existence of a committed central bank alone and national fiscal authorities can avoid the negative effects on price stability of free-riding by the latter or whether other institutions are needed to complement the type of central bank that has been chosen. Beetsma and Uhlig (1999) claim that a pact like the Stability and Growth Pact (SGP) can reduce the negative spill-overs arising from political distortions that can be exacerbated in a monetary union. Beetsma and Uhlig (1999) give two possible justifications for constraining the action of national fiscal policy. One refers to a country, closed or open, that wants to draft a fiscal constitutional rule to tie the hands of its own government (based on the arguments developed in Section 2.3). The other lies in the existence, in a monetary union, of negative spill-overs deriving from a country's budgetary policy and accumulation of debt on the common inflation rate.

The same problem – i.e. sufficiency of a committed central bank for ensuring price stability – has been investigated from another point of view. The 'unpleasant monetarist arithmetic' of Sargent and Wallace (1981) held first the view of the insufficiency of a monetary policy rule for price stability due to REs. Given these kinds of expectations, bond financing of public expenditures and tight money could give rise to immediate inflation. Along similar lines, Woodford (1996) applied the fiscal theory of the price level to the case of the EMU. In the absence of fiscal self-discipline by governments, he found that the theory supported introduction of limits to public deficit and debt as a way to complement the monetary rule chosen by the common central bank – or even to set up a precondition for this bank to be charged with maintaining price stability.

A final justification for setting limits to national fiscal policy in the context of a common monetary system was suggested by Casella (1989): a country's fiscal deficit has negative spill-overs on the interest rates and bond prices of the area and should then be limited. In order to eliminate the tendency of governments to create inflation, the inflation bias, that may be present in the constituency and the government, many possible rules have been suggested.

The school of public choice suggested introduction, in particular, of constitutional rules to be decided by following a unanimity procedure. Quasi-rational individuals could agree to limit the temptation to draw short-run benefits and agree on such subjects as balanced-budget rules, limits to governmental growth and transfers (Brennan and Buchanan 1980; Buchanan, Brennan 1981). One thus could explain both the reason why some rules adopted by the EU – such as the SGP – were required to be constitutionally grounded (Inman 1996) and the recent provision of the EU fiscal compact according to which constitutional rules constraining discretionary fiscal policy should be passed.

2.5.5   Summary

Then, in the 1970s and 1980s, the rationales were laid for advocating rules setting constraints to discretionary fiscal policy. These were

1. Political economy considerations about the attempts of governments to force the unemployment rate below the natural one;
2. Time inconsistency; and
3. Ineffectiveness of fiscal action, with possibly negative multipliers and effects of accumulated public debt on growth.

The SGP and the fiscal compact in the European Union and the ceilings set to the size of federal debt in the United States[8]

---

[8] The US ceiling was first introduced in 1917 but had largely lost its role after 1974.

were the legal transposition of such statements, reflecting the idea that the true problem was of ensuring that no harm could derive from fiscal policy. In the United States, these limits were tempered by a non-conservative central bank.

In the EMU, other rules tended to prevent

1.   Negative spill-overs on the real interest rates abroad; and
2.   Negative spill-overs on the price level, aggravated by policy coordination and the ensuing monetary policy counter-reaction (Hughes Hallett and Acocella 2016b).

A specific consequence of the theoretical developments in the 1970s and 1980s was the introduction of independent central banks and authorities. Again, a wide array of institutions were implemented in the EMU as a consequence of this. I deal with this topic in Section 2.6.

2.6   The Need for Rules and Constraints: Independent (and Conservative) Central Banks and Authorities to Limit Discretionary Policy Action

Another solution for limiting the tendency of governments to create inflation could be tying money growth to some macroeconomic indicator. A further alternative is for the constituency or government to delegate monetary policy to independent institutions not plagued by time inconsistency and opportunistic behaviour, with incentive structures different from those of politicians, in order to acquire a credible commitment. Such an institution could be a conservative central banker, i.e. a banker assigning employment a lower weight than that of society or the government. Rogoff (1985a) shows that this will be able to attain a lower level of inflation without reducing employment. On this, see also de Haan and Sturm (1992), Cukierman (1994) and Akhtar (1995). Appointing a conservative central banker introduces a conflict with the government that can be avoided by setting rules that govern the independent monetary authority, i.e. by establishing a target conservative central bank (Svensson 1997). These steps represent the best way to obtain a commitment not to pursue inflationary, and ineffective, policies.[9] We are thus (almost) back to Friedman, with two (significant) details to be added: one that rules are a way to cope with a more general problem faced by governments, that of their credibility, and the other that once price stability is not in question, stabilisation policies are possible. However, this is exactly the description of the status of the ECB, which has to guarantee a certain inflation rate in the medium run as its preeminent target but can also pursue other objectives, provided that these do not prejudge the attainment of its predominant target.

Delegation to independent authorities is a case more general than that of conservative central banks, as other independent authorities could be devised (Majone 1994, 1996). One recent suggestion is that of 'fiscal councils' (for recent literature, see Hagemann 2010; Calmfors and Wren-Lewis, 2011; IMF 2013). These institutions are responsible for monitoring the economic health of the world's larger economies. The IMF and the European Commission recommend that politicians place themselves under the scrutiny of an independent fiscal council, which could ensure monitoring of the government budget in the light of its impact on growth, employment and long–run sustainability of public and private finances. These councils should increase credibility and commitment to a set of sustainable fiscal policies by providing politically neutral monitoring to the economy as a whole. This idea has been implemented

[9] However, there are alternative ways to reach a similar outcome. In fact, Neck and Dockner (1987, 1995), with reference to a dynamic game between the government and a conservative central bank, both having unemployment and inflation as their targets, show that subgame perfect Pareto-optimal non-cooperative equilibria can derive from repeated interaction of the players when memory strategies accounting for threat and retaliation are admitted.

in many European countries, such as Sweden (Swedish Fiscal Council), the United Kingdom (Office of Budget Responsibility) and, more recently, the European Union (European Fiscal Board).

In countries where the creation of independent authorities is difficult to implement or commitment to a rule is not credible, other solutions have been devised. In general, the favour for an 'external constraint' was very diffuse (Giavazzi and Pagano 1988; Sibert 1999) as a prescription for governments in high-inflation countries. Such constraints should tie their (inflationary) hands by committing them to a fixed exchange rate with lower-inflation countries. Thus, monetary policy would credibly be delegated to an external entity, and private agents would no longer expect their governments to inflate the economy and would act consistently. Therefore, they would adjust their conduct and rely on instruments other than higher mark-ups to pursue their revenue or profit targets (Carli 1996). In particular, the idea was common of the need to tie these countries' monetary policies (and possibly also other policy tools) to some kind of policy rule, such as dollarisation or a currency board or a system of fixed exchange rates such as that represented by the European Monetary System (EMS), first, and by a currency union of the EMU kind, later.

2.7 Waiting for a Revaluation of Policy Effectiveness

All these constraints on discretionary policy action derived from the roots already investigated in previous sections. A reevaluation of this action had to wait for a long, almost silent revolution concerning numerous aspects of policy action. In Chapter 3, I will recall the steps of this revolution that finally led to rehabilitation of policy effectiveness and the second pillar of economic policy, after having briefly dealt with the reasons that led to reestablishment of the validity of the first pillar.

3

Re-establishing the First Pillar
and a Silent Revolution for the
Effectiveness of Policy Action

The critique of the first pillar of economic policy as a discipline emerged rather early, really even before a complete statement of the discipline, and required some time to be overcome. As said earlier, a pragmatic solution was provisionally adopted, but one based on logical, political and philosophical premises was suggested only about two decades after the critique. Re-establishing the second pillar required a longer time span, which also began some decades after the initial critique, but it has been accomplished only rather recently. In this chapter we deal with the solution suggested for the critique of the first pillar in Section 3.1. All the following sections of the chapter are devoted to the long process that laid the premises for overcoming the critique of the second pillar. The re-establishment of the second pillar is the object of Chapter 4.

3.1 Possibilities of a Democratic Social-Welfare Ordering: The Need for a 'Theory of Justice'

As said earlier, the attempt to derive a social order from individual preferences based on a set of postulates resulted in Arrow's (1951) 'impossibility theorem'. This established a vital failure of the first pillar of economic policy. The practical 'shortcut' devised by Frisch of referring the SWF to policymakers seemed not to be acceptable in theoretical terms. In fact, this solution was based on the assumption that the policymakers (and thus their preferences) reflect citizens' values. The process of selecting politicians would be delegated to the political arena – hopefully in a way that ensures democracy. However, choice of democratic institutions and the form of voting that can ensure them then are also expressions of values. This choice is possibly the most preferred outcome for most citizens, but it remains a choice between values having a subjective nature. This cannot be introduced from the outside if the issue is to be the derivation of social values from individuals' preferences with no external interference, i.e. if values are not given explicit citizenship in the process of searching for a social order.

It was Leibenstein (1962: 316) who first stated that 'the choice rules suggested by contemporary welfare economics are really ethical rules' not only because some of the terms employed – for example, 'efficiency' and 'the optimal allocation of resources' – are value loaded but also because procedural rules for (possibly) reaching a social outcome (e.g. the voting rule or the choice principle) protect some individuals or better ensure democratic choices. We can then draw the conclusion that it is a theory of justice that must tell us which is the preferred principle of fairness, according to which the social-choice paradox must be solved.

Various attempts have been made to get around the 'impossibility' result along this route by eliminating one or another of the axioms that Arrow (1951) thought necessary for constructing a complete social ordering. Special attention has been directed to assumptions regarding the information on individual satisfactions (measurability and comparability). The Pareto principle is founded on the specific 'informational' postulates of ordinal measurability and non-comparability. It has been shown that the other axioms introduced by Arrow also rule out cardinal measurability and/or interpersonal comparability of utilities (see, among others,

Mueller 1989: chap. 20). Some have argued that these are the key hypotheses – originating from specific values – and that removing them would allow us to construct a complete social ordering.[1]

Abandoning simple ordinal measurability does not enable us to avoid the impossibility result, however (Sen 1970a). A complete, non-dictatorial social ordering can be obtained if, in addition to cardinal measurability, some degree of interpersonal comparability is admitted. In particular, if we allow full interpersonal comparability in addition to cardinal measurability of individual utilities, it is possible to construct a simple or generalised utilitarian SWF (see below). 'The additional information availability allows sufficient discrimination to escape impossibilities' (Sen 1999b: 357).

Given the necessity of using some sort of interpersonal comparison to define complete social rankings, we must specify the principle that will enable us to evaluate all possible alternative situations, especially in cases where opting for one or another state means improving one person's situation while worsening that of another. This implies a problem of distributive justice, which consists in defining criteria to judge the desirability of alternative ways of (1) assigning the participants in the productive process (more generally, the members of a society) the benefits of that activity and (2) apportioning the related costs.

Obviously, such criteria depend on each individual's view of the world. It is therefore no surprise that economists attempting to construct social orderings have often taken their inspiration from principles of social or political philosophy. This was so e.g. for Pigou (1920), who adopted certain principles of utilitarianism. In some cases, economists have

---

[1] However, a different route has been followed by Fleurbaey and others, who have instead relaxed the independence from irrelevant alternatives postulate (see e.g. Bossert and Weymark 2008; Fleurbaey and Maniquet, 2011), which can allow the incorporation of some principle of fairness.

studied these disciplines directly, as e.g. for Harsanyi (1976) and Sen (1970a). In a number of cases, principles of distributive justice have been developed by social philosophers, such as Nozick (1974) and Rawls (1971).

When the need for criteria to evaluate distribution became clear to economists, efforts to construct a social ordering found many points in common with contemporary social or political philosophy, which carries on the work begun by modern moral philosophy with partly new concepts and methodologies. In evaluating distribution (and any other aspect of social life), the big issue is whether to accept or not the view that (1) each individual is the best judge of his or her preferences and (2) the value of possible social states is determined by the individual's perception of these states (and the satisfaction obtained). According to this view, which constitutes the postulate of 'ethical individualism', this should be the only allowable basis for assessing social states, and anything not considered relevant by the individual must not be assessed by society as a whole. This principle ('welfarism', as Sen terms it; see e.g. Sen 1987), again, is the object of choice and can be debated.[2]

---

[2] There are two types of objections to it:

1. One can object to the idea that the social ranking must only take account of the satisfaction effectively enjoyed by individuals at a certain point in time, ignoring other aspects that might be worthy of consideration. These could be the existence and ability to exercise rights and liberties and the quantity of goods actually available to the different members of the community.

2. In reducing the situation of society to the satisfactions of individuals, the latter's preferences are often considered to be given. This is done without going into the factors that formed them, especially the influence of the environment and the attitudes and judgments of groups and so on (Schumpeter 1954: 889). In reality, individual preferences and the behaviour of individuals are not 'genuine' but endogenous. They do not emerge independently of the economic and social context but are instead affected by many factors, including other people's habits (Duesenberry 1949), fashion and social 'norms' (Leibenstein 1950; Etzioni 1985), which expose preferences to manipulation, especially by firms.

There are criteria of distributive justice that incorporate the postulate of ethical individualism and can be expressed in the form of a SWF, such as the utilitarian and those suggested by Bernoulli-Nash (see Nash 1950), Rawls (1971), Bergson (1938) and Samuelson (1947) (see Acocella 1994 more extensively). Other criteria do not accept ethical individualism but are still of much interest (e.g. Nozick's and Sen's theories of justice).

In particular, Sen has not only demonstrated that the principle of Pareto optimality can be in contrast with democracy (Sen 1970b), but he has also indicated remedies (Sen 1970a). By introducing the innovative concepts of 'functionings' and 'capabilities', Sen (1980, 1985) succeeded in merging consideration of material aspects and the results achieved by individuals (including distribution), on the one hand, and rights and liberties, on the other. He began by observing that both the quantity of a good (food, for example) and the utility generated by its use are inadequate indicators of the welfare of an individual or a community. The total quantity of food available to a community is inadequate as a guide because some people may not have access to it. Nor is utility of individuals any more successful as a criterion because it is a psychological indicator that is incapable of (fully) revealing certain effects. For example, the effects of malnutrition – intended as either a shortfall or excess of food – are not always perceived by the individual; one may take pleasure in a single crust of bread, but the lack of certain fundamental nutrients may scar one's body for life.

There are in fact non-psychological aspects of goods that are central to evaluating their advantages to people and

Advocates of ethical individualism hold that if the preferences of individuals are replaced by those of one person (e.g. a philosopher or social reformer) – perhaps not even a member of the community – paternalistic or authoritarian consequences can follow. Such a risk undoubtedly exists, but it can be practically eliminated by setting out which features of the social state – such as certain rights and liberties – must be preserved, by granting them constitutional status.

society. Goods have characteristics that people may use to perform certain functionings, and it is the achievement of these functionings (being well nourished, healthy and able to move; having self-respect; being respected; being able to take part in the life and progress of the community) that indicates the benefit enjoyed by people, allowing them to exercise positive liberty. Moreover, it is not only the effective performance of certain functionings that is important but also the very possibility (the 'capability') of performing them even if they are not actually performed. For example, it is important to have the right to move without legal or material obstacles, even if a person should decide not to move. Similarly, freedom of speech is a capability, in that it allows everyone to express their views: it does not 'require that a person should be continuously speaking but that he should be able to speak if he were to so choose'. Obviously, for basic 'capabilities' such as feeding oneself adequately, enjoying good health and acquiring an education, the element of choice may be unimportant, since people will normally take advantage of them when possible. In this case, the capability of performing certain functions corresponds to their effective performance, and the distinction between capabilities and functionings largely disappears; in other cases, however, the distinction remains important (Sen 1982: 29–31; see also Sen 1992: chap. III).

Other economists have moved in the same direction. Desai (1991) has found an application in the study of poverty and human development indicators constructed by the World Bank; in particular, purchasing power, education and health are the proxies of 'capabilities' that are used to construct indicators of human development. One specific aspect of these indicators, education, on which we will insist in Chapter 7 as an essential element for democracy, deserves more discussion. Achievements of educational functioning are of specific relevance, as they indicate that a wider range of educational choices and perspectives has been available to people. We should look at achievements in terms of education rather than the amount of money put into it or even years of schooling to really assess enhanced functionings and capabilities. This would involve evaluation of the content of schooling, whether it enhances literacy and the capability to process information (Unterhalter, Vaughan and Walker 2007).

Sen's conception of justice is also shared in particular by Martha Nussbaum, who holds that each person's capabilities should be considered as an end, not a means, for the life of people, and a minimum level of his or her capabilities that express his or her quality of life should be ensured by the state (e.g. Nussbaum 2011). Nussbaum (1999) lists ten 'central human functional capabilities' that must be respected by a just society: (1) life of a normal, natural duration, (2) bodily health and integrity, including adequate nourishment and shelter, (3) bodily integrity regarding, for example, freedom of movement and security against assault, (4) freedom to exercise one's senses, imagination, and thought as one pleases, which includes freedom of expression, (5) freedom to form emotional attachments to persons and things, which includes freedom of association, (6) the development and exercise of practical reason, the capacity to form one's own conception of the good and to try to plan one's own life, which includes the protection of freedom of conscience, (7) freedom of affiliation on equal terms with others, which involves provisions of non-discrimination, (8) concern for and possible relationships with animals, plants and the world of nature, (9) the freedom to play, to seek amusement and to enjoy recreational activities and (10) some control over one's own political environment, including the right to vote, and one's material environment, including the rights to seek meaningful work and to hold property. All these capabilities are essential to our functioning as flourishing human beings and should be ensured for all citizens of a just society. Anand, Hunter and Smith (2005) find strong evidence that the Nussbaum's list of capabilities influences well-being.

Starting from acceptance of many of the ideas indicated, other later investigations have also added to the 'possibilities' of constructing social-welfare orderings or social-ordering functions that had been indicated by Sen (see e.g. Arrow, Sen and Suzumura 1997, 2002, 2011). More specifically, they are now addressed by an ancillary discipline that has emerged in more recent decades from previous studies, i.e. 'implementation theory' (see e.g. Maskin and Sjostrom 2002; Fleurbaey and Maniquet 2011). This takes the incentive problem to the forefront of analysis and heavily relies on game theory, thus to some extent dealing also with some of the minor problems raised by asymmetric information. Designing a mechanism that provides incentives is equivalent to solving a problem of devising the proper institutions in a way to guarantee equilibrium outcomes consistent with some choice rule, or to 'implement' it. These advances make the first part of the core of economic policy, i.e. the logic of economic policy, well founded and well connected to the second part.

3.2 Rip van Winkle and the Rebuttal of the Theoretical Convictions of the 1970s and 1980s on the Ineffectiveness of Economic Policy

Only a few economists and observers warned in those decades about – or have pointed out later – the fragility or the limits of the critique of the ineffectiveness of discretionary economic policy and the idea of a superiority of markets and strict policy rules.[3] In the early 2000s Alan Blinder (2004: 26) claimed that 'a sharp revision of the naively optimistic views (about the capacity of economic policy to control the economy) held by some economists circa 1966

---

[3] One of these rare exceptions was Franco Modigliani (1977).

was called for. But ... the pendulum may have swung just a bit too far', producing similar naively optimistic views about the virtues of markets and central bank independence and conservativeness.

Blinder's words are even more acute nowadays, as economic theory has further questioned the system of beliefs that had emerged in the twenty years or so after 1966, even if it still retains some assumptions that led to the propositions featuring that credo. Three decades later, Rip van Winkle's faith in this still-dominant credo would be crowded out by the analytical developments that have intervened in recent years.[4]

Think of

1.   The limited practical relevance of the surprise effect;
2.   The irrelevance of many critiques of the 'classical' theory of economic policy (in particular, to Tinbergen's 'golden rule' about controlling the economy) based on rational expectations (REs);
3.   The theoretical and practical limits to time inconsistency and thus to related prescriptions of monetary policy rules that should replace discretionary action;
4.   The existence of a non-vertical long-run Phillips curve;
5.   The need for more active fiscal policy and regulation (especially of financial markets and institutions) once some unrealistic assumptions of current models are ruled out;
6.   A critique of the arguments in favour of political independence of central banks;
7.   The suboptimality of a conservative central bank in a monetary union with active trade unions; and

---

[4] Rip van Winkle is the character created by Washington Irvin and evoked by Gordon (1976), who made a terrible 'environmental' mistake waking up in the Republican America, after sleeping for twenty years, by declaring himself a devote subject of King George III.

8.   A critique of the Friedman rule and the need for an inflation target well above zero in the presence of public transfers.

The irrelevance of critiques to the classical theory of economic policy and the limits to time inconsistency will be dealt with in Chapter 4. Specific details on the other critiques are given in subsequent sections of this chapter.

3.3   The Surprise Effect

Most econometric research (Sims 1980; Canova and De Nicoló 2002; Giannoni and Woodford 2005; Bernanke, Boivin and Eliasz 2005; Christiano, Eichenbaum and Evans 2005) do not distinguish between anticipated and unanticipated components of monetary policy. However, generally speaking, they find that monetary policy shocks are effective over a period of some years. This would confirm the relevance of the surprise effect, in contrast with the opinion of Lucas (1996: 679) himself. However, it mainly raises the need, underlined by Mishkin (1982), to introduce the possibility that monetary action could be partly anticipated but still effective. Thus, the reason why what appears to be a relevant surprise effect lies in misspecification of the model. In fact, Mishkin found that a lag specification of anticipated policies leads to results that tend to negate their ineffectiveness, thus invalidating Lucas' proposition.

This finding has been confirmed by later contributions. Cochrane (1998) again underlined the need to distinguish between anticipated and unanticipated components of monetary policy in all types of models. Anticipations can derive from explicit central bank communication, especially through forward guidance on its future action (we will deal extensively with this in Chapter 5 and 6) or simply reflect the private sector's expectations. This kind of analysis cannot be done through a vector autoregression (VAR), and various authors estimate a New Keynesian model in order to compare the response of output to policy surprises and news. The estimated effects of monetary policy shocks are very different from those usually found in the literature. Now the contribution of news is less than 2 per cent of fluctuations, whereas the effect of anticipated monetary policy varies from 15 to 25 per cent of medium-run output fluctuations and is more persistent. Real effects of systematic monetary policy depend on the shares of frictionless competitors having REs and rules-of-thumb agents or agents facing other frictions. Hoover, Jorda (2001), using a VAR, confirmed and strengthened these findings of significant real effects deriving from anticipating systematic monetary action (see also Flaschel, Franke and Semmler 1997: chap. 8).

Most recently, by estimating a benchmark New Keynesian model, Milani and Treadwell (2012) find that the contribution of monetary policy news to output fluctuations is larger than that of surprise shocks. This stresses the relevance of the communication policy followed by the central bank in recent times, especially of forward guidance.

3.4   The Non-Vertical Long-Run Phillips Curve

Recent developments in macroeconomics contradict the widely held belief that permanently higher inflation cannot affect unemployment, which – according to Blanchard and Fischer (1989) – derives from a priori reasoning rather being consistent with empirical evidence. Orphanides and Solow (1990) suggest that the long-run effects of money growth can depend on a number of assumptions, such as those of non-separable utility functions and cash-in-advance or money in the production function. Holden (2003) shows that they can also arise at low inflation rates in the case where wages are set through negotiations. According to Hughes Hallett (2000), regional or sectoral curves can have different slopes. If there is a mismatch between supply and demand in different sectors (or, by extension, in different countries or regions in a fixed-exchange-rate regime or monetary union), their aggregation always generates a long-run trade-off between inflation and output, which makes it possible to change the natural rate of unemployment by changing the sectoral or regional compositions of demand.

In New Keynesian models, a long-run relationship between inflation and real activity is obtained based on price staggering (see, among others, Goodfriend and King 1997 and Woodford 2003), where the implied effects of inflation on unemployment are unambiguously adverse. This implies that the optimal long-run inflation rate should be zero, an issue that will be discussed further in Section 3.5. Various authors have demonstrated the non-linearity of the Phillips curve (e.g. Ascari 2000, 2003).

Graham and Snower (2008) show that the interaction of staggered nominal wage contracts with hyperbolic discounting inflation leads to a significant long-run effect of inflation on real variables via money growth. With their baseline calibration, which takes the length of the contract period to be 1 year, a permanent increase in inflation of 1 per cent is associated with an increase in output and employment of approximately 0.2 per cent for inflation rates of up to around 10 per cent. This is roughly of the same order of magnitude as the empirical estimates of the long-run Phillips curve in the classical studies that have found a significant trade-off from Phillips (1958) and Samuelson and Solow (1960) to Akerlof, Dickens and Perry (1996, 2000). These authors derive a trade-off between unemployment and inflation via a static model with downward wage rigidities. Fair (1999), instead, finds that there would have been a rather low price level and inflation costs with rather significant gains in output and decreases in unemployment if the Bundesbank had been more expansionary in the 1980s.

In a dynamic stochastic general equilibrium (DSGE) model with RE agents optimally setting their wages, Benigno and

Ricci (2011) investigate the macroeconomic implications of downward nominal wage rigidities in a low-inflation environment. They derive a closed-form solution for the long-run Phillips curve. This shows an inflation-output trade-off that is virtually vertical at high inflation rates but flattens at low inflation. The need for stabilisation policies derives from two circumstances: (1) the flat section of the curve implies progressively larger costs in terms of output of attempts at reducing inflation, and (2) macroeconomic volatility shifts the curve outward, generating output and employment costs. The results question the conventional view that argues against the presence of a long-run trade-off and in favour of price stability. They also reconcile models with real life, where no central bank adopts a policy of zero inflation and in the long run the inflation rate is positive. This can be explained as due to the zero nominal interest bound and, as in Benigno and Ricci's model, the presence of downward nominal rigidities.

Di Bartolomeo, Tirelli and Acocella (2014) share the view that modern monetary models may underestimate the benefits of inflation on wage mark-ups but highlight a disciplining channel based on the idea that inflation is a tax on money balances. To model this effect, they introduce money in the utility function, as in Christiano, Eichenbaum and Evans (2005). Di Bartolomeo, Tirelli and Acocella (2014) then identify a channel that supports the inflation tax effect on money balances, which disciplines wage mark-ups. In line with a recent analysis of institutional features of wage bargaining in twenty-two European Union countries, the United States and Japan (Du Caju et al. 2008: 25), Di Bartolomeo, Tirelli and Acocella emphasise that wage contract renegotiations take place while expiring contracts are still in place, enabling wage setters to internalise their consequences for household choices. In their model, this is captured by the assumption that within each period wages are predetermined to macroeconomic variables (see Corsetti and Pesenti 2001 for a similar assumption). This allows setting a framework where wage setters internalise the effect of their wage choice on their own real money holdings. In the paper, the authors show that such an effect is negative and becomes stronger with the expected inflation rate, inducing wage setters to limit their wage claims. This is therefore a new justification for the existence of a non-vertical Phillips curve. Model simulations show that a moderate inflation rate can generate substantial output gains relative to both the Friedman rule and the commitment to price stability, popularised in standard New Keynesian models.

From an empirical point of view, a growing literature has shown that New Keynesian models significantly improve their ability to replicate business cycle facts if monetary policy rules are assumed to target time-varying, non-zero long-run inflation rates (see Cogley and Sbordone 2008 and the references therein). Ireland (2007) estimates a New Keynesian model to draw inferences about the behaviour of the Federal Reserve's unobserved inflation target. His results indicate that the target soared from 1.25 per cent in 1959 to over 8 per cent in the middle to late 1970s before falling back to below 2.5 per cent in 2004. He provides evidence that is consistent with the view that shifts in the secular trend in inflation (i.e. the expected long-term inflation rate) could be attributed to a systematic tendency for Federal Reserve policy either to limit the contractionary consequences of adverse shocks (Blinder 1982b; Hetzel 1998; Mayer 1999) or to exploit favourable economic conditions to eventually bring inflation down (Bomfim and Rudebusch 2000; Orphanides and Wilcox 2002). More generally, monetary policy should consider the possibility of unobserved shifts in sustainable growth rates (Lansing 2002). Blanchard (2016a: 31) re-examines the behaviour of inflation and unemployment and

> reaches four conclusions: (1) Low unemployment still pushes inflation up; high unemployment pushes it down. Put another

way, the US Phillips curve is alive ... (2) Inflation expectations, however, have become steadily more anchored, leading to a relation between the unemployment rate and the *level of inflation* rather than the *change in inflation*. In this sense, the relation resembles more the Phillips curve of the 1960s than the accelerationist Phillips curve of the later period. (3) The slope of the Phillips curve, i.e. the effect of the unemployment rate on inflation, given expected inflation, has substantially declined. But the decline dates back to the 1980s rather than to the crisis. There is no evidence of a further decline during the crisis. (4) The standard error of the residual in the relation is large, especially in comparison to the low level of inflation.

Each of the last three conclusions presents challenges for the conduct of monetary policy. Wisdom gained from the experience of the 1960s and later will be needed.

3.5   The Optimal Inflation Rate

A consensus seemed to exist until a few years ago that monetary transactions costs are relatively small at zero inflation and that implementing low and stable inflation is the proper policy.[5] Optimal monetary policy analyses (Khan, King and Wolman 2003; Schmitt-Grohé and Uribe 2004) identify two key frictions driving the optimal level of long-run (or trend) inflation. The first is the adjustment cost of goods prices, which invariably drives the optimal inflation rate to zero. The second is monetary transaction costs that arise unless the central bank implements the Friedman rule, i.e. a zero nominal interest rate implying a negative inflation rate in steady state. On balance, i.e. considering these two frictions together, the optimal inflation rate should be negative, but close to zero.

In their survey of the literature, Schmitt-Grohé and Uribe (2011) argue that the optimality of zero inflation is robust to

---

[5] Some paragraphs and the driving argument of a part of this section are drawn from Di Bartolomeo, Tirelli and Acocella (2015).

other frictions, such as nominal wage adjustment costs, downward wage rigidity, hedonic prices, the existence of an untaxed informal sector and the zero bound on the nominal interest rate. This result is broadly confirmed by Coibion, Gorodnichenko and Wieland (2012), who find that the optimal inflation rate is low, typically less than 2 per cent, but is in sharp contrast both with empirical evidence and widespread central bank practice of adopting inflation targets between 2 and 4 per cent.

Some contributions (e.g. Rogoff 2010; Blanchard, Dell'Ariccia and Mauro 2010; Aizenman and Marion 2011; Ball 2014) in some ways evoked the well-known Phelps (1973) argument that to alleviate the burden of distortionary taxation, it might be optimal for governments to resort to monetary financing, driving a wedge between the private and social costs of money. This argument has been neglected for about four decades, possibly also because the New Keynesian models widely adopted since the 1990s offer what has been called the 'divine coincidence' between low inflation and zero output gap (Blanchard, Dell'Ariccia and Mauro 2010).

After a few voices had risen after 2010 in favour of a higher long-run inflation target, the importance of the Phelps effect was reconsidered only recently, in a DSGE model (Di Bartolomeo, Tirelli and Acocella 2015; Tirelli, Di Bartolomeo and Acocella 2015). This leads to results that challenge the optimality of near-zero inflation rates when the tax system is incomplete. A non-negligible – but moderate – inflation rate can indeed be optimal, and inflation (and tax rate) volatility should be exploited in order to get rid of the debt accumulated after 2008 as well as to stabilise debt/gross domestic product (GDP) ratio in the long run. This is obtained simply by allowing for a plausible parameterisation of public consumption and transfers. As a matter of fact, public consumption accounts for a limited component of overall public expenditures in some Organisation for

Table 3.1 *Public consumption, other public expenditures and total revenues,[a] selected OECD countries (1998–2008)*

	Public consumption	Other public expenditures	Total revenues
Sweden	26.67	29.03	57.21
Switzerland	11.4	23.48	34.40
United Kingdom	19.83	22.28	40.38
United States	15.26	20.51	33.47
Euro area	20.17	27.11	45.39

[a] Average ratios to GDP.
Source: OECD 2012.

Economic Co-operation and Development (OECD) countries, and transfers are relatively large (Table 3.1).

Contrary to Schmitt-Grohé and Uribe (2004), the optimal inflation rate monotonically increases from 2 to 12 per cent as the transfers-to-GDP ratio goes from 10 to 20 per cent, a result their model can obtain only with very large public-consumption-to-GDP ratios, in an order of magnitude ranging from 40 to 47 per cent.

The rationale of this result is related to the different effects of public consumption and transfers on tax and inflation revenues and thus to the different incentives to use taxes or inflation to finance them. An increase in public consumption reduces private consumption and money holdings while potentially raising the labour supply (depending on the effects of public expenditure on output). Reductions in private consumption and money holdings erode the inflation tax base. The rising labour supply increases the tax base, making an increase in the distortionary tax rate unnecessary. In other words, increases in public consumption make it more likely that taxes can finance it compared with inflation. By contrast, transfers have no impact on overall

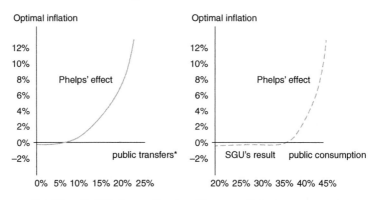

(*) Additional to 20% of expenditure in public consumption.

Figure 3.1 *Optimal inflation rates with and without fiscal transfers.*
(Source: Di Bartolomeo, Tirelli and Acocella 2015)

consumption and labour supply and thus do not favour ordinary tax financing of public expenditure vis-à-vis an inflation tax (see Figure 3.1).

In advocating a higher inflation rate, one should consider that it has both benefits and shortcomings. From the former point of view, while being useful as a way of paying down the value of outstanding public debt and reducing future taxes, it has other advantages. In fact, it also reduces the value of extant private debt, thus possibly stimulating investment and discriminating between types of assets in favour of mobilisation of capital. In addition, it can get rid of the 'zero-lower-bound' (ZLB) constraint by lowering real interest rates. Finally, contrary to other results (e.g. Albanesi 2007), it can reduce inequality if implemented in combination with lower income taxes (Menna and Tirelli 2017).

Some costs and risks of permanently raising target inflation rates exist. These can refer to the increase in long-term nominal interest rates that would follow as an effect of higher interest rates, but this is usually lower than the increase in the inflation target. Some authors also fear the ensuing loss in the credibility of central banks deriving from expectations of further increases in the target. However, this appears as well established, and a simultaneous increase in advanced countries' target inflation rate should do no damage.

As for dissent on the opportunity to raise the inflation rate, Mishkin (2011) argues that very deep recessions such as the one begun in 2007–8 are very rare, and then the risk of easily reaching a constraining ZLB is not very relevant. Then the benefits from a higher inflation target would not be very large.[6] Instead, a higher inflation rate would cause distortions in cash holdings and greater uncertainty about relative prices and possibly undesired redistribution of wealth. As a matter of fact, however, most empirical estimates find limited effects of this kind (Ball 2014). As to the effects on expectations, Mishkin fears that people's expectations on future inflation will keep on rising. Piketty (2013) holds that the initial positive effect can partly disappear over time because people's expectations can change. Bernanke (2010), Mishkin (2011) and Woodford (2009), in their papers cited by Ball (2014), are sceptical about targeting a higher inflation rate, say, at 4 per cent, since people would think that going to 4 per cent is only a first step to going to 6 per cent or more, and it would be very difficult to tie down expectations at 4 per cent. However, in Ball's opinion, the 'central bank should determine its optimal policy, explain this policy to the public, and carry it out. We have learned from recent experience that 4 per cent inflation is better than 2 per cent, because of the zero bound problem. Why can't policymakers explain this, raise inflation to 4 per cent, and keep it there?' (Ball 2014: 14), which seems to us a very reasonable argument. Along a similar line of reasoning, Blanchard, Dell'Ariccia and Mauro (2010: 11) provocatively ask 'is it more difficult

---

[6] In a similar way, Rogoff (2017: 63–4) holds that 'enabling effective negative [interest] rate policy is also much cleaner and more elegant than the second-best policy of raising inflation targets'.

to anchor expectations at 4 percent than at 2 percent?' This issue of expectations must be dealt with carefully. In fact, what matters is obtaining a stable pattern of higher inflation expectations. This can be very useful from another point of view, i.e. in lowering the expected real interest rate in a way that counteracts secular stagnation (see Section 5.7).

Another possible shortcoming of a higher inflation rate target can derive from the possibility that the inappropriate timing to implement this policy might generate or feed bubbles in the asset markets (Wolff 2014). This is really a relevant point, and we underline it later (see Chapter 5), but it should not be overemphasised. The true problem is that policymakers should be well aware of this possibility and introduce additional tools to counteract the risk, such as macro-prudential policies. Finally, there are the effects of distortions arising from a higher inflation. These are of two kinds at least. The first kind has to do with distortions on money holdings. Another argument in favour of a low inflation rate target is that a strong anti-inflationary policy mitigates the adverse effects of uncertainty on aggregate demand, as hiring decisions play a significant role in transmitting uncertainty (Guglielminetti 2016). Both distortions cannot be denied. The real issue is to compare them with those from higher taxation. In all probability, the costs of an inflation target of 4 per cent rather than 2 per cent are not significantly higher.[7]

3.6   Political Independence of Central Banks

The issue of political – or goal – independence of central banks, i.e. independence in setting their own goals,[8] was first

---

[7] Blanchard, Dell'Ariccia and Mauro (2010). In saying so, these authors do not account for the effects of uncertainty on hiring decisions, but their argument seems to be still valid even taking these into account.

[8] As distinct from instrument – or economic – independence, i.e. the possibility for the bank to freely choose the best instruments to pursue certain

discussed within the realm of positive economic policy. Bade and Parkin (1978) first inquired about the existence and degree of central bank independence in order to check whether it has an influence on the economy's performance. They measured political independence, making it depend on the existence of a body formally separated from the government to decide monetary policy and the presence of members of the central bank board that are government officials or have been appointed by it.

Bade and Parkin (1978) measured the impact of independence in twelve advanced countries, finding that most showed an association of higher independence of monetary policy with a smaller average government budget deficit. A number of later studies (ranging from Alesina (1988), to Grilli, Masciandaro and Tabellini (1991), Cukierman (1992) and Alesina and Summers (1993), to name only some of the first contributors) tried to refine the measurement of the degree of independence.

More recently, after studies by Fry et al. (2000) and Crowe and Meade (2008) and some previous investigations of their own, Dincer and Eichengreen (2014) measured trends in independence through time up to 2010 for more than 100 central banks, basing their measure on various indicators. These include political transparency as to policy objectives and their priorities, economic transparency referring to the information used for policy action (economic data, the model of the economy, etc.), procedural transparency and operational transparency concerning specifically indications of methods for correcting imbalances between targets and achievements. The authors found that independence is highest in the European Monetary Union (EMU) and some small countries and lower in the United Kingdom, the United States, Australia, India and other countries. They find a

goals. Definitions are from Grilli, Masciandaro and Tabellini (1991) and Debelle and Fischer (1994).

co-movement of transparency, which has risen through time in both advanced and less developed countries, and central bank independence. According to them, the former should tend to rise as a consequence of the need to ensure accountability of independent policy authorities in a democratic society. However, while the need for transparency is particularly evident in countries with strong political institutions, this is not rigorously true for independence.

In normative theory, as a first approximation, the status of independence and the issue of the identity of the central banker were not discussed until the 1980s. During that decade, the literature generally favoured separation of the authorities governing monetary and fiscal policy. Blinder (1982a) suggested a reason in favour of independent authorities, stating that dispersion of power can be a defence against its misuse. Then Rogoff (1985a) applied the concept of independence of central banks to the issue of time inconsistency and suggested appointment of an independent central banker to cope with it. The possibility of setting monetary policy without interference or restriction could at least partially solve the inflation bias problem, since an independent central bank could decide the monetary policy stance without any political calculation of its effects on voters.

In addition, Rogoff (1985a) faced the issue of the optimal degree of conservatism of a central bank from the point of view of a social-welfare function. We deal with this in the next subsection. He kept the two issues, conservativeness and independence, separate, even if claiming that both are necessary to pursue a higher welfare. In contrast to Rogoff, almost all following papers have not made this distinction and treat central bank independence and conservatism as a joint or indistinct variable. In empirical or theoretical analyses, the two are usually represented by a unique parameter expressing the relative weight attributed to inflation and stabilisation in the central bank's objective function.

Possibly also under the influence of Rogoff (1985a) and the subsequent literature, in the 1980s and 1990s the number of central banks that were given a statute of political independence increased. But this was not an effect of free political decisions. Cukierman (1994) suggested the possibility of political and economic factors influencing the degree of legal independence. According to Posen (1995), there were underlying forces pushing towards independence, taken as an indicator of a relatively lower preference for inflation. Hayo (1998) found empirical evidence in favour of the idea that central bank independence alone cannot explain macro-economic performance and found some proof for the idea that the culture of people in support of low inflation might have favoured it, even if the possibility of reverse causation cannot be excluded and data availability did not allow application of the test of 'Granger causality'. Political independence does not come at no cost, as it can involve a lower inflation rate and a higher unemployment rate, at least if monetary action is effective. Political independence was indeed supported by the financial sector, which has a low preference for inflation (Santoni 1986). This is a short way to saying with Posen that both political independence and inflation are the outcome of structural economic and social factors that result in the central bank statutes having no impact of their own – i.e., independently of these factors – on inflation. In fact, as we will see in Chapters 5 and 6, (vested) interests play an essential role in the formulation of policy action.

More recent papers have confirmed the previous dichotomy in the orientation of the theoretical literature, with a prevalence of sceptical views on the advantages of independence.[9] On the one hand, some maintain the idea of a positive effect of monetary policy independence on

---

[9] A rather recent review of the different reasons in favour of coordination can be found in Šehović (2013).

inflation and macroeconomic performance. Berger, de Haan and Eijffinger (2001) corroborate robustness of the negative correlation between the degree of central bank independence and inflation. Arnone et al. (2007) find an increasing trend in the political and economic autonomy of central banks in most of the two decades after the end of the 1980s, with the rise in the former lagging behind the latter's and a positive influence of this trend on reduction of inflation. Harashima (2007) develops a model explaining that an independent central bank is necessary simply because it guarantees that inflation does not accelerate, thus protecting against governments that are not weak, foolish or untruthful but simply corrupt (true economic Leviathans).

Others (e.g. Hayo and Hefeker 2002; Mishkin and Schmidt-Hebbel 2007) have confirmed the conclusions and empirical findings of Posen and Hayo. In particular, according to Hayo and Hefeker (2007), central bank independence does not encourage better monetary policy performance, as it is a condition neither necessary nor sufficient for monetary stability. Beyond all this, many central banks are only instrument independent, or it is very difficult to define whether instruments or political independence holds.[10] Hayo and Hefeker (2007), after distinguishing between independence and conservativeness, suggest that if there is an issue of time inconsistency, there are also other and less costly solutions to it, such as inflation targets, fixed exchange rates and inflation contracts. Central bank independence is not a necessary condition for price stability, even if it can be judged as an appropriate solution for some countries.

[10] The Bank of England does not have goal independence – in fact, targets are assigned to it by the UK government – whereas the bank has instrument independence. With reference to the most important central bank, Cargill and O'Driscoll (2012) say that by examining the history of the Federal Reserve, the hypothesis of its de jure independence from political authorities is more myth than reality. However, the Federal Reserve certainly has instrument independence. Similarly, de jure independence of other central banks does not correspond to their de facto behaviour.

On empirical grounds, some studies find a high positive correlation between independence and monetary stability, but others contradict this result. Moreover, correlation says nothing about causality. The correct way of dealing with the relationship between central bank independence and inflation would be to inquire at historical and political levels about the process leading to the decision about the importance of price stability as a major economic policy objective, if this has been the case for a country. If this is so, the analysis should be directed at understanding – through the same analytical tools already indicated – the process leading that country to choose central bank independence rather than the potential alternatives.

The relevant topics on which reflection must be entertained also concern issues that are different from the simple impact of independence on inflation. On the one hand, Demertzis, Hughes Hallett and Viegi (2004) find that the pursuit of different targets by an independent central bank and elected governments generates a conflict, and both will be unable to reach their respective objectives, the more so the larger is the difference between their preferences. These conflicts will drive fiscal policy to become more expansionary than is appropriate because of the need to offset/overcome the effects of more conservative monetary policies. This has consequences for efficiency and the long-run debt position, yet the endogenous voting extension of the model shows that the electorate will naturally vote for such outcomes.

Benigno and Woodford (2004) also underline this need for complementarity of monetary and fiscal policy. On the other hand, Woodford's (2000) recognises the tendency of monetary policy to overreact to cost-push shocks, a kind of stabilisation bias under discretion relative to commitment arising even when no inflation bias is present, as inflation is not higher than the average inflation under commitment. Albanesi, Chari and Christiano (2002) show that a stabilisation bias arises when monetary policy is the only policy tool to react to shocks. In these conditions, with discretionary monetary policy, expectation traps arise because the private sector tends to protect itself from inflation, which induces monetary authorities to react by supplying the expected level of inflation.

As seen in the preceding section, Di Bartolomeo, Tirelli and Acocella (2015) strengthen Benigno and Woodford's (2004) argument that the optimal fiscal and monetary stabilisation policies should be seen as complements by referring to a different, novel mechanism, acting when public transfers are introduced into the analysis. Thus, the monetary authority should consider the consequences of its actions for the government budget. In this regard, a substantial amount of inflation volatility is indeed desirable to deflate nominal debt and to limit the accumulation of real debt and stabilise debt/GDP ratios in the long run.

A final reason for coordinating fiscal and monetary action derives from the mixed nature of some innovative unconventional monetary policies. We deal with this in Chapter 5. Arestis (2015) suggests coordination of fiscal policy not only with monetary policy but also with financial stability policies in order to reduce unemployment and income inequality.

3.7   Conservative Central Banks and Alternative Ways of Governing Inflation

As mentioned earlier, Rogoff (1985a) first analysed the issue of a conservative – and not only independent – central bank as an instrument of maximising social welfare. According to him, the degree of the central bank conservativeness, in terms of the weight put on the inflation target in its loss function, should be higher than that of the government but less than infinity. In fact, as this weight of inflation increases, its marginal benefit, in terms of decreasing rates of inflation, decreases, whereas its cost, in terms of increasing unemployment, increases. At some point, if the marginal benefit and cost functions are well behaved, the two are equal, and that point marks the socially optimal degree of conservatism.

This solution has various drawbacks in terms of how it should be implemented: proper incentive schemes should be devised to induce the independent banker to implement this optimal degree of conservativeness. This can be done in terms of some form of optimal contract between the government and the central banker whereby incentives are set and a check of outcomes is required.

Guzzo and Velasco (1999) question Rogoff's conclusion by arguing that if wage setters are non-atomistic and inflation averse, conservativeness can lead to lower employment and output. Inflation can be lower either for low or very high degrees of conservativeness. The welfare of a representative worker tends to be maximal if a populist (i.e. a not conservative) central bank is in charge, ensuring low inflation and an optimal level of output and employment.[11]

By contrast, Rogoff's solution was supported to various degrees by empirical evidence in Grilli, Masciandaro and Tabellini (1991), Alesina and Summers (1993), Bleaney (1996) and Eijffinger, Hoeberichts and Schaling (1998). At least two problems arise when the issues of independence and conservatism are considered. The first refers to the distinction between the concepts; the other, to whether a conservative central bank is the only – or the best – instrument available for coping with excess inflation.

With reference to the former, Hefeker and Zimmer (2011) say that the literature about monetary policy delegation has usually taken the two concepts interchangeably. An important exception is Eijffinger and Hoeberichts (1998), who

---

[11] It is maximal in the case of a monopolistic union. In the case of many unions, the maximum is obtained for various degrees of conservatism depending on the value of some parameters (Guzzo and Velasco 2002).

introduced two different parameters for them and showed that there exists a trade-off between independence and conservatism and that a continuum of combinations of independence and conservativeness may be socially optimal, a result that holds also in a New Keynesian framework (Eijffinger and Hoeberichts 2008) but can be frustrated by uncertainty (e.g. Hughes Hallett and Weymark 2005). Crowe and Meade (2008) link introduction of independence and conservativeness of central banks to situations of market rigidities. However, rigidities cannot be considered as given. They are, instead, endogenous with respect to other institutional features (see Gros and Hefeker 2002 for a model). Posen (1998) had pointed out that a higher degree of central bank conservatism might cause nominal wage rigidities to increase, thus raising the costs of disinflation.

With reference to the second issue arising in connection with the optimal degree of conservatism, i.e. whether a conservative central bank is the only – or the best – instrument available to cope with excess inflation, one should first consider that depending on the labour market institutions, conservatism may be a second-best solution with respect to the first-best solution represented by a situation with no imperfection and rigidities.

Acocella, Di Bartolomeo and Hibbs (2008) show that conservative, tight policies have great capacity to offset the potentially negative employment costs of decentralised bargaining when nominal wages are pre-committed and unions internalise systematic responses of the monetary authority to their wage-setting behaviour. Moreover, conservative, anti-inflationary monetary policies always dominate liberal policies in the sense that inflation is always lower and unemployment is never higher under a tight policy versus a liberal policy. Yet, if monetary policy were compelled by law, social norms or some other reason to accommodate rising wages and prices, then macroeconomic performance would be enhanced by a flexible-wage labour market in which unions had the institutional capacity to adjust wages continuously to realisations of the money supply. In this respect, a flexible-wage labour market without binding contracts is more compatible with monetary policies that systematically accommodate nominal wage expansions.

Other institutions can act as substitutes for monetary policy conservativeness. In fact, Di Tella and MacCullock (2004) show the existence of a negative relationship between inflation and unemployment benefit programmes for a panel of twenty OECD countries over the period 1961–92. High unemployment provisions thus can make the monetary authority less concerned about unemployment. In addition, corporatism can, at least partly, substitute for monetary policy conservativeness.

In addition, by applying a New Keynesian sticky wage and price model, Debortoli et al. (2017: 2) have shown that a high weight on the output gap is beneficial for society 'as it serves as an overall proxy for other welfare relevant variables'. We can say that this kind of mandate for the central bank achieves a kind of 'reverse divine coincidence'.

3.8 The Changing Value of Multipliers and Fiscal Policy

Of special interest is a critical examination of two positions that have inspired recent fiscal policy attitudes against the crisis in Europe and the idea of limited effectiveness of fiscal policy. On the one hand, there is the assertion of very low (in the limit, null, if one accepts Barro's proposition – see Barro 1974 – or even negative) spending multipliers. On the other hand, there is a widespread belief in the existence of a limit beyond which an increase in public debt would have negative consequences for growth (Checcherita-Westphal and Rother 2010; Kumar and Woo 2010; Reinhart and Rogoff, 2010) as well as on the virtues of contractionary fiscal consolidation (Giavazzi and Pagano 1990, 1996).

As Galí, López-Salido and Vallés (2007) underline, the New Keynesian model does display non-Keynesian effects, unless liquidity-constrained agents are present, as their consumption will increase with real wages and other factors setting a constraint on their budgets. In reality, a significant fraction of consumers is liquidity constrained (see e.g. Di Bartolomeo, Rossi and Tancioni 2011), and this probably increases in recessions, which leads to time-varying fiscal multipliers. This, together with sticky prices, justifies the pursuit of countercyclical fiscal policies, with government spending set at a level above that warranted by the 'efficient provision of public goods' (Galì 2005: 587–88).

A number of factors can influence the effectiveness of fiscal policy. We are interested in knowing whether it increases in downturns relative to 'normal' circumstances and how the fiscal multipliers vary across different fiscal instruments or with other policy instruments in use at the same time and with market expectations of future events or with the size of likely shocks. The lesson is that these are all elements crucial to understanding the potential effects of fiscal policy, in particular, the sign and the size of the different fiscal multipliers, and their interaction with, and dependence on, the monetary policy stance.

Blanchard, Dell'Ariccia and Mauro (2010) draw a number of lessons from the crisis. First, the Great Moderation was useful as a way to stabilise expectations in an environment of supply shocks (e.g. for oil prices) but has possibly nourished one of the sources of the Great Recession, i.e. neglect of risks by the agents. Second, financial intermediation matters, but its role can be impaired by a number of circumstances, in particular (as we will see below) as far as the transmission of monetary impulses from the short run to the long run is concerned. In addition, regulation is not macroeconomically neutral, as shown by the crises derived from the great bubble bursts in 2001 and 2007–8. Finally, countercyclical fiscal policy matters for a number of reasons: (1) because monetary policy has well-known limits of effectiveness, especially when the ZLB is approached and (2) because it has longer lags in its effects (even if lower implementation lags), which is in contrast with the longer administrative lag required for introducing fiscal policy. The total lag is shorter for fiscal policy, which has thus returned to centre stage, also due to the prospective length of the crisis.

Other studies stress the efficacy of fiscal policy in severely depressed economies when central banks do not offset its effects (DeLong and Summers 2012). Moreover, fiscal multipliers are shown to be asymmetric and regime dependent (Auerbach and Gorodnichenko 2012; Mittnik and Semmler 2012). They are 'stronger in recessions than in expansions, in particular in presence of financial market stress, so that contractionary effects can become very severe when fiscal consolidations are pursued' (Semmler and Semmler 2013: 2), as an effect either of some economies being locked in a bad equilibrium (De Grauwe 2011) or of macroeconomic non-linearities (Semmler and Semmler 2013). This result is confirmed by the analysis of seven structural DSGE models used for policy action as well as academic DSGE models (see, in particular, Coenen et al. 2012). With specific reference to the existence of a ZLB constraint to interest rates, Denes and Eggertsson Gilbukh (2013) suggest that both cutting government spending and increasing sales taxes can increase the budget deficit at zero interest rates according to a standard New Keynesian model calibrated with Bayesian methods. When monetary policy is stuck at the ZLB, it cannot offset the expansionary effects of fiscal policy via the interest-rate or exchange-rate channel, and private investment can even be crowded in. Expectations of higher inflation deriving from fiscal expansion could lower the real interest rate and add further stimulus (see Christiano, Eichenbaum and Rebelo 2011, IMF 2015 and OECD 2015, all cited by Furman 2016). Similar suggestions are expressed by Woodford (2011), who also indicates higher multipliers in case of price or wage rigidity. Eggertsson and Krugman (2013) show that expansionary fiscal policy is an effective instrument for coping with situations of crisis and debt overhang. Thus, again, the effects of fiscal policy are highly dependent on the policy regime. The analysis shows, however, that a permanent fiscal stimulus implies lower values of the initial multipliers and a negative impact on income in the long run. For a more general review of the recent literature, see Gechert and Rannenberg (2014).

These findings must be assessed in conjunction with those of Bilbiie, Monacelli and Perotti (2014), according to which usually government expenditures at the ZLB do not necessarily enhance welfare, even when their output multiplier is large. However, in another paper, Bilbiie, Monacelli and Perotti (2012) show that tax cuts financed with government debt at the ZLB are Pareto improving when there are constrained borrowers, as the cuts are a form of implicit transfer from unconstrained savers to constrained borrowers.

Of specific relevance are some analyses that take account of open economies (in some cases the EMU) and spill-over effects. In order to quantify these effects, Coenen and Wieland (2002) constructed a small macro-econometric model of the United States, the Euro area and Japan and found that international spill-overs of domestic shocks turn out to be rather small when exchange rates are flexible and short-term interest rates are set according to policy rules that focus on stabilising domestic variables. With references to eleven EU countries in the period 1965–2002, Beetsma, Giuliodori and Klaassen (2006) combined a panel VAR model in government spending, net taxes and GDP with a panel trade model. They found that a domestic public spending increase (tax reduction) equal to 1 per cent of GDP implies 2.2 per cent (0.8 per cent) more foreign exports over the first two years, on average. If Germany initiates such budget change, the effect on the GDP of its trading partners is 0.23 per cent (0.06 per cent) over the first two years. These figures are likely to indicate lower bounds for the effects that will actually occur (Beetsma, Giuliodori and Klaassen 2006). Beetsma, Giuliodori and Klaassen (2008) found that a 1 per cent of GDP public spending impulse produces a 1.2 per cent output rise on impact and a 1.6 per cent peak response of output. In addition, rising imports and falling exports together produce an impact fall of the trade balance of 0.5 per cent of GDP and a peak fall of 0.8 per cent of GDP. The public budget moves into a deficit of 0.7 per cent of GDP on impact. Similar results are presented in Beetsma and Giuliodori's (2011) estimation for the period 1970–2004 of the effects of government purchases on income in open European economies, which are higher than 1 on average in the short to medium run. The public and trade balances deteriorate. Even if the value of the multiplier is greater than 1, it is lower in open economies because of leakages. This strengthens the rationale behind a concerted fiscal expansion among European countries and, by contrast, implies that decisions to introduce fiscal discipline – either independently decided by a country or imposed by some common rule – have cumulative negative effects that may impair reaching the target of a reduction in the debt/GDP ratio.

In summary, the size of multipliers varies according to a number of circumstances: the type of fiscal instrument used for consolidation, the cyclical situation of the economy, the expansionary or contractionary nature of other policies (notably of monetary policy), the degree of price and wage flexibility, the degree of openness of the economy and the policies enacted in related economies as well as their rates of growth.

Let us turn now to the second issue mentioned at the beginning of this section, i.e. the need for fiscal consolidations. This can arise from different considerations. The first consideration is that accumulation of debt aggravates the fiscal burden of future generations. In addition, it could have negative effects on various other relevant policy targets.

In particular, it could reduce growth. The assertion about the beneficial effects of fiscal austerity has passed through a long process of theoretical refinements, confutations and empirical evaluations. Recently, the negative effects of debt on growth have received theoretical support by Checherita-Westphal et al. (2014). However, doubt with respect to some tenets of this idea was first raised by Blanchard and Perotti (2002), who gave a substantially Keynesian answer to the issue of the effects on income of the tax increases and expenditure cuts needed for consolidation. In fact, they found that the former have a contractionary effect, whereas the latter have an expansionary one. The authors did not engage in a discussion about debt-consolidation strategies, but on the basis of their findings, one could hardly assert that a policy of expenditure reductions and (to a less extent) tax increases, while certainly contributing to the reduction of the numerator of the debt/GDP ratio, would give an impulse to the denominator. Instead, their findings might support debt consolidation not based on a budget contraction, at least as far as the effects on income are concerned. In addition, with specific reference to the effects on growth of one item of public expenditures, i.e. government investment, the 'New View' of fiscal policy has underlined that, especially when devoted to innovation, it should be sustained in order to expand productivity and aggregate supply and create future fiscal space (Gaspar, Obstfeld and Sahay 2016 and IMF 2016, as cited by Furman 2016).

As far as empirical tests are concerned, on the basis of a long time series of data referred to a wide range of countries, Reinhart and Rogoff (2010) draw the conclusion that the relationship between debt and growth is weak for debt/GDP values below 90 per cent but becomes significant and negative beyond that level. Herndon, Ash and Pollin (2013) have criticised these results due to the omission from the Reinhart and Rogoff's test of important developed nations – which experienced high growth even with a high debt burden – and low weights on countries for the duration of high debt and growth performance. When account is taken of this, the 90 per cent value is no longer a ceiling beyond which growth is reduced.

A rather complete and detailed – unfortunately, not updated to the wealth of more recent contributions – empirical analysis of the effects of fiscal consolidation is presented in IMF (2010), which takes account of numerous aspects of the effects of fiscal consolidation policies: in particular, their timing (i.e. whether they are short or long term), the monetary policy stance and the expansionary or contractionary nature of budget policies in other countries. Its conclusion is that, first, the idea that fiscal austerity triggers faster growth in the short term finds little support in the data. Typically, fiscal retrenchment has contractionary short-term effects on economic activity, with lower output and higher unemployment, but 'fiscal consolidation is likely to be beneficial over the long term' (IMF 2010: 113). In addition, a budget cut is less expansionary the lower the interest rate (as monetary policy has little room for partially accommodating the deflationary effects), the lower the likelihood of a currency depreciation and the less expansionary are the policies of other countries, which gives little scope for raising net export. Also critical towards the expansionary effects of fiscal consolidation is Perotti (2013), who shows that at least in the three episodes referred to by Giavazzi and Pagano (1990, 1996) in their papers on the expansionary virtues of fiscal consolidation, those of Ireland, Denmark and Sweden – the expansion derived from either external demand or by other factors. Similar results hold for consolidations implemented by Belgium, Finland and the United Kingdom. An important ingredient of the success of consolidation was incomes policy, even if it offered only temporary beneficial support.

Some authors point out that smoother fiscal consolidations are more successful than stiffer ones (Batini, Callegari and Melina 2012). In addition, consolidation is more successful if policies are well coordinated, the growth rate is positive, and tax yields or welfare spending is not too high a share of GDP. When the monetary policy stance is accommodative – and the longer so – multipliers rise. Coenen et al. (2012) and Gechert, Hughes Hallett and Rannenberg (2015) have estimated that if this lasts, the value of cumulative spending multipliers rises well above 1. Similar is the effect of the private sector's lasting expectations about an accommodative monetary policy. Finally, the degree of openness of the economy and the rate of growth of other economies are relevant due, as indicated earlier, to the fact that multipliers are lower for an open economy, the more so the higher is its degree of openness and the size of demand abroad. Moreover, consolidation is more likely to lead to success when it takes place in a small economy, out of pre-election years and where governments face coherent oppositions (Fatás et al. 2003).

Anyway, Blanchard and Leigh (2013a) find that stronger planned fiscal consolidations were associated with lower growth in developed economies. Thus, Blanchard and Leigh's advice (2013b) is to proceed very carefully in deciding when to proceed to choices of consolidation and how much consolidation to implement. An important variable is political, in that deferring consolidation can require consideration of political factors at work. Consolidation, in fact, may need to be continued for a long time, spanning the length of a government's mandate.

These findings have important consequences for our topic, as far as both institutional and short-run implications are concerned. We will briefly deal with them in the next section.

3.9   An Application of Values of Multipliers: Inconsistency of the EMU Institutions

In the EMU, monetary policy has tended to be contractionary until recently. The European Central Bank (ECB) has taken over the task that should have been entrusted to fiscal policy, i.e. that of a better coordinated countercyclical policy action (Tabellini 2016). Thus, it is the whole institutional design – and not only current policies – that imposes a deflationary bias.

The risk envisaged before the start of the EMU by Gregory and Weiserbs (1998: 48) about the 'potential deflationary bias that the Maastricht criteria are likely to impose throughout the EU' has materialised. It has also caused a tendency to secular stagnation, resembling the situation that emerged in the 1930s as a consequence of the deflationary policies enacted by European countries trying to stay on the gold standard (De Grauwe 2015).

In addition to the conservative nature of the ECB, the bias can be deduced from at least three aspects of the EMU institutions: the content of the Stability and Growth Pact (SGP), the fiscal compact and the asymmetric nature of the scoreboard of the 'macroeconomic imbalance procedure' (MIP) (Altavilla and Marani 2005; Acocella 2011; De Grauwe 2013; Stockhammer and Sotiropoulos 2014). Before the financial crisis, it was mainly the SGP that impressed a deflationary bias on the area. After this, the fiscal compact (formally, the Treaty on Stability, Coordination and Governance in the Economic and Monetary Union (TSCG)) and asymmetry of the limits to current account imbalances deriving from the MIP have stressed the bias.

As to the SGP, the bias derives first from the limitation imposed on the operation of automatic stabilisers in countries where they are stronger and may imply a fiscal deficit of more than 3 per cent. Moreover, the SGP does not limit public balance surpluses in a similar way. Finally, a debate has recently involved the method for calculating potential output and – as a consequence – the output gap of current output on which the structural balance depends. According to some authors (Tereanu, Tuladhar and Simone 2014; Darvas and Simon 2015) and countries (this was the position of eight financial ministers of EMU countries in 2016), the method currently in use by the EMU underestimates potential output and imposes a deflationary bias on countries having a high deficit and debt and the whole Euro area. These are requested to implement fiscal consolidation efforts in terms of the structural balance that a country under the 'excessive deficit procedure' (EDP) has to take.

A fiscal adjustment of at least 0.5 per cent of GDP per year is required according to the SGP and a higher one is asked from countries having a debt/GDP ratio over 60 per cent. The fiscal compact established in 2011 has accentuated the contractionary orientation of fiscal rules in the EMU in a situation of lasting deflation. It prescribes a structural budget deficit not larger than 0.5 per cent of GDP (whereas it is 1 per cent of GDP for countries having a debt/GDP ratio significantly lower than 60 per cent).

As to the limits to current account imbalances, it must be first noted that before the crisis, unchecked current account balances and the surpluses accumulated by the EMU 'core' countries moderated the deflationary environment in 'peripheral' countries due to inflow of capital into the latter, thus issuing wrong signals to investors (Acocella 2016a). In addition, the asymmetric nature of foreign imbalances indicated in the more recent MIP (6 per cent for surplus countries, 4 per cent in case of deficit)[12] translated into a very powerful deflationary bias due to debt deleveraging when the effects of both current account and public account became clear after the financial crisis, as is well known since

---

[12] This is no more than an issue of an improper way of introducing effective signals for a correct conduct of private and public agents (see Chapter 6).

Fisher (1933) and Keynes (1936) and revived by Minsky
(1993) and, more recently, by others, among whom Chiarella,
Flaschel and Semmler (2001) and Semmler and Haider (2015).

The mechanism is well illustrated by De Grauwe (2013).
A consumer or a firm that must reduce its debt will reduce
consumption and/or sell assets. Increased saving will reduce
demand, production and income. Sale of assets will lower
prices, creating new insolvencies and the need for deleveraging. Both actions will frustrate the private sector's attempt
to reduce its debt in a deflationary spiral unless the public
sector counteracts them by increasing its consumption and
taking over private debt.

The effects on GDP of the contractionary policies and debt
required in the EMU have recently been assessed in a number
of studies. Using a Keynesian model, Stockhammer and
Sotiropoulos (2014) estimate that had core countries
expanded their public budgets or raised their wages, a high
loss in the GDP in peripheral countries would have been
avoided. If, by contrast, in 2007 these countries were
required to fully eliminate their current account deficits by
deflationary measures, the cost would have been on the order
of 47 per cent of their GDP.

Rannenberg, Schoder and Strasky (2015) have applied the
analyses of multipliers developed by Coenen et al. (2012),
Gechert and Mentges (2013), Gechert (2015) and Gechert,
Hughes Hallett and Rannenberg (2015). Gechert, Hughes
Hallett and Rannenberg (2015) calculate the fiscal multipliers of tax increases: these lower GDP by around 1, whereas
expenditure cuts have a similar, but higher, effect on GDP, as
their multiplier has been estimated at about 2.5 on average,
in depression years. They find that the cumulative measures
of consolidation in the EMU in the three years up to 2013
have been roughly equal to a reduction of almost 4 per cent of
the EMU GDP. By applying the appropriate multipliers of
different expenditures and taxes, a cumulative negative
effect on GDP of almost 8 per cent in the same years has

been calculated. The budget balance effect would have been a meagre 0.2 reduction. The mountain has thus laboured and brought forth a mouse. More generally, if cumulative multipliers are applied to estimated changes in the individual fiscal instruments, the Euro area's fiscal consolidation effort reduced GDP by 4.3 per cent relative to the no-consolidation baseline in 2011 and by 7.7 per cent in 2013. Thus, austerity came at some cost. The biggest contributor to this GDP decline came from transfer cuts, not surprisingly, given their high multiplier and their high share in the overall consolidation effort.

According to Rannenberg, Schoder and Strasky's (2015) simulation, in the three years after 2010, Eurozone GDP had decreased by almost 6 percentage points with respect to the pre-crisis trend. This could be explained by one-third or one-half in terms of fiscal consolidation, and these fractions increase to almost two-thirds and more than 80 per cent.

An application of Gechert and Rannenberg's (2014) and Gechert, Hughes Hallett and Rannenberg's (2015) methodology to the policies that have been imposed on Greece to 'remedy' the crisis shows that austerity had a very heavy negative effect on the economy of this country, which has entered a profound depression because of it. First, the measures prescribed since 2010 implied a total reduction in public expenditures in Greece of about 30 billion euros – and an increase in revenues of about the same amount – in the five years following 2009. By combining the multipliers found by Gechert, Hughes Hallett and Rannenberg (2015) with the fiscal consolidation measures prescribed for Greece between 2010 and 2014, Gechert and Rannenberg (2014) explain 'almost the entire collapse of Greek GDP after 2009'. The reduction in GDP has been above 25 per cent with respect to the level in the absence of fiscal consolidation. As a consequence of this reduction, the debt/GDP ratio has increased by slightly less than 2 per cent compared with what it would have been in the case of no consolidation and more than in the case of consolidation based only on taxes.

Simply postponing this to a period when GDP had returned to its growth path should have ensured the desired consolidation. In fact, 'if the consolidation would have been postponed until after the recovery of the Greek economy and implemented gradually, almost 80 per cent of the cost in terms of lost output could have been avoided' (Gechert and Rannenberg 2015: 2). The reason stays simply in the variability of multipliers, which are very high in times of recession and lower in normal times, as a cut in expenditures would have depressed the economy less. For recessions of −4 per cent of GDP, Bilbie, Monacelli, and Perotti (2014) find that the optimal increase in government spending is about 0.5 to 1 per cent of *steady-state* GDP. For recessions implying a fall in GDP on the order of 28.8 per cent and a high annual deflation − such as for the Great Depression and not very different from the situation in Greece − the optimal increase in government spending at the ZLB is about 14.5 per cent (13.5 per cent if public expenditure is wasteful) of GDP.

3.10   What Have We Learned from the Crisis?

While originating a number of problems not only for its short- and long-run consequences but also for the ensuing limitations on the use of instruments, the crisis has taught us a number of other lessons on how to face problems. It may be that the number of new problems raised outpaces that of answers − as Blanchard, Dell'Ariccia and Mauro (2014: 1) say − and that we have entered a 'brave new world', but certainly policymakers and economists have devised new tools to face old and new issues. Not only have we discovered new instruments of monetary policy, but we have also learned that the timing of all the existing instruments and of new ones should be used in a consistent and coordinated way to pursue the government policy targets through time.

This is indeed a lesson deriving from the theory of economic policy, long ignored.

Consistency refers to the use of instruments in an economy in a way to simultaneously get the government's targets. As Yellen (2014: 31) notes, before the crisis, the usual way of reasoning (at the Federal Reserve) did not go much 'beyond "one instrument and two targets"', and only the financial crisis and its aftermath – in presenting central banks with great challenges – transformed 'how we look at this topic'.

The need for coordination of policy action also raises the issues of independent authorities governing in particular monetary, macro-prudential and structural policies, which should act by supporting and redirecting the economy. Finally, coordination involves agreements at an international level to reduce negative spill-overs deriving from a country's choice and to reinforce positive ones.[13]

One cannot say that reflections of the kind we have illustrated here have led to a new conventional wisdom or are prevailing in the theoretical and practical implementations. In this respect, two levels of the effects of the Great Recession must be distinguished: a theoretical one and a practical one. As to the former, there is always some degree of autonomy of theory from practice. As to the practical acceptance of the idea of the need for government intervention, the situation is different from country to country (or region). In Europe, the conventional wisdom emerged since the end of the 1960s is still largely implemented. This was not so in the United States until recently.[14] In emerging economies, policy intervention is certainly more common.

---

[13] On this, see also Gaspar, Obstfeld and Sahay (2016).

[14] The new American administration is practicing a kind of conservative attitude, which, however, starts from an idea different from that of the Washington Consensus. In fact, it is pursuing protectionist policies that imply clear divergence from the idea that free markets offer a superior solution.

4

Revaluation of the Classical Approach to Economic Policy
Re-establishing the Second Pillar*

4.1 Introduction

In Chapter 3 we saw that the 'impossibility objection' was addressed in a satisfactory way and has been largely overcome by a literature that is now developing in new and interesting branches of the discipline, such as the 'implementation theory', which involves the use of a strategic setting. Critiques moved to the other branch of the discipline on the basis of considerations of 'political economy' – involving the effectiveness of policy action – were not vital, and the discipline can survive and possibly be enriched by incorporating them in its main corpus.

However, when the vital Lucas critique referring to the effectiveness of policy action defied the other pillar of the core of the discipline (i.e. the theory of economic policy), there was no possibility of maintaining the discipline as it had been originally designed. This critique was not addressed for a long time, which contributes to explaining the decline of economic policy as an autonomous discipline. As said, to some extent, the very practical application of economic policy in its heyday could have distracted its followers from further research and innovation, as was certainly the case

---

* This chapter draws heavily on Acocella, Di Bartolomeo and Hughes Hallett (2013).

for the Stockholm school (Siven 1985) and possibly also for the Oslo school (Eriksen, Hanisch and Sæther 2007).

The theoretical advances of the last two decades described in Chapter 3 laid down some premises for a restatement of the second pillar of economic policy, asserting the effectiveness of economic policy and the possibility for policy action to lead the economic system towards goals set by governments. The final obstacle – really, the major one – was defying the Lucas critique. In fact, there would have been no or scarce use of new knowledge involving a higher value of multipliers or of the higher optimal inflation rate in the case that discretionary economic policy could not be used as an effect of the impending Lucas critique. Overtaking the obstacle of this critique involved a series of steps leading from the parametric setting of the classical theory of economic policy to a non-parametric one, i.e. to a strategic setting. Now policy action has been shown to be exempt from the critique if the policy action is designed in its proper strategic context, a setting analytically similar to that of the implementation theory. In addition, it can also produce new and interesting results insofar as existence, uniqueness or multiplicity of equilibria in the game are concerned (Acocella, Di Bartolomeo and Hughes Hallett 2013).[1] The possibility of accommodating in a strategic setting both pillars of the classical core of economic policy offered by the simultaneous development of the normative branch of the theory of economic policy and the implementation theory might open new horizons to economic policy as a consistent and autonomous normative discipline. In addition, the positive branch of the theory of economic policy also can be dealt with in the same setting.

One thus could hope that the discipline could gain momentum and challenge mainstream thought, which assigns a very

---

[1] It may be of interest to notice that these authors are economists trained in the tradition of the classical theory of economic policy who are working or have worked either in Italy at Sapienza University or in Britain and the Netherlands.

limited role to it. This would avoid confining policy discussions to a few considerations following very abstract – and sometimes unfounded – theoretical reasoning that often neglects any institutional and historical elements and lacks the theoretical background deriving from the logic and theory of economic policy. We are conscious, however, that this needs to overcome the power of some hysteresis in the development of economic thought that delays the dissemination of new ideas (Galbraith 1987), which is not an easy task, at least in the short run.

This chapter is organised as follows: Section 4.2 establishes the equivalence of a strategic game to the rational expectations assumption used by Lucas. The equivalence defines a strategic environment as the one that can deal with his critique. This is a proper context for investigating situations of possible conflict and the ways they can be resolved. The link between this environment and the content of the literature of the 1970s and 1980s and the implications of this new environment in terms of conflicts and their resolution are investigated in Section 4.3. Sections 4.4. and 4.5. constitute the core of this chapter: they state the conditions for controllability in a strategic setting for any number of players in a static and a dynamic setting. Section 4.6 summarises the contents of the chapter as well as theoretical progress in terms of restatement in a new setting of economic policy as a discipline. Moreover, it hints at open issues still to be dealt with further, in particular, with respect to coalitions, announcements and other possibilities of conflict resolution.

4.2 Equivalence of Rational Expectations to a Strategic Game

The root of the problem raised by the Lucas critique is that it shows the private-sector behaviour to be invariant to the policy vector itself if rational expectations (REs) are introduced. In other words, when the private sector has REs of future developments, the policymaker loses control of the economic system, as those expectations deny the existence of an equilibrium influenced by policy action, such as that postulated by the classical theory of economic policy.

As a consequence of assuming REs, for a long time mainstream economics has been trapped in Lucas critique. Ways have been suggested for alternative formulations of the agents' conduct in order to explain the economy's fluctuations. One has been pursued by De Grauwe (2012: vii), who shows that the view according to which 'everything becomes possible when we move into the territory of irrationality' is based on the false idea of what a rational agent is, since there are alternative ways to formulate it. He thus develops a behavioural model based on the limited cognitive ability of agents, by which he shows that fluctuations can be explained not by assuming external shocks to the economy but by accepting that they can be endogenously determined. We are only marginally interested in the issue of explaining busts and booms. Our focus is instead on the possibility for the policymaker to steer an economy that does not comply with his or her goals. We will show that this is possible by maintaining the RE assumption.

It is easy to understand that assuming REs amounts to an implicit change in the nature of the economic system confronting the policymaker. In a parametric setting such as that assumed by the classical theory of economic policy, there are certainly links between the decisions of the government and the private sector. Otherwise, the former could not have any influence on the latter. However, such links are defined, at least from the point of view of the public sector, in an unchanging context of the rules of the game. In fact, the policymaker perfectly knows the parameters of the latter's choice functions (e.g. the consumption function), and these do not change when it sets its instruments (interest rate, tax rates, etc.). The private sector has objectives that conflict with those of the policymaker but can only change its behaviour in a way known to the public sector and does not neutralise its action.

In a RE context, instead, the private sector reacts to actions or changes of regime decided by the policymaker by changing the rules dictating its choice and thus can neutralise the policies in advance due to its REs. This would change not just the outcomes but also the way the system itself behaves. The policymaker then faces a system that is no longer parametric, and this in itself leads, according to Lucas, to a loss of control of the economy, i.e. policy ineffectiveness. In formal terms, this would make the multipliers of policy instruments endogenously determined and conditional on the responses by the private sector.

This implication – though reasonable – might not survive an explicit way of dealing with the underlying conflict between the policymaker and the private sector in terms of a policy game.[2] Put differently, this critique holds for the Tinbergen-Theil theory of economic policy, but that is not to say that it is also true of a revised or new theory of economic policy based on strategic setting. It all depends on whether the private-sector reactions (or anticipations) can be accommodated in the policymaker's decisions or whether the private-sector reactions are strong enough to exactly offset what the policymaker is trying to do. In general, private agents can neither offset those actions completely nor would they try to do so, as we shall show.

Let us examine now in more detail how the Lucas critique should be expected to apply in a world of rational private agents and/or rational policymakers by discussing how it works in a strategic environment where each agent has his or her reaction function. It is clear that the reaction function of each player will depend on the policies or decisions made by others. Consequently, as soon as one player adjusts his or

[2] A 'policy game' is a game that explicitly models the behaviour of players, which are each conscious that their actions affect each other and can change them accordingly.

her policies or policy rule, the other players whose decisions depend on the decisions of the first player will adjust theirs – thus invalidating the premise of constant parameter values in the response by others that must have underlaid the first player's original calculations.[3] Hence, the critique is clearly true and needs to be taken into account. However, the obvious way to overcome it is to solve the implied policy game directly in extensive form.

In other words, using REs amounts to implicitly assuming some kind of reaction of the system to the policy enacted. This assumption, and the underlying conflict between the policymaker and the private sector that it reflects, can be made explicit. To this end, the issue facing the policymaker must be framed in a context (that of games) where the private sector's behaviour is explicitly modelled as having been derived from its preferences and objectives. Strategic inter-actions between the private sector and the policymaker then ensure that the REs of both are satisfied.

RE models are indeed semi-reduced forms of linear quad-ratic policy games that transform a two-player optimisation problem into a one-player optimisation problem constrained by some additional condition implying the REs of the rival on the optimising player's policies. Hence, they correspond to a Stackelberg game with the private sector as the leader, implying a discretionary equilibrium.[4] However, notice that RE games are often solved by using the Nash equilibrium. This occurs because the control variable of the forecaster is the same forecast on a target (not an instrument) variable.

[3] Unless the first player is a Stackelberg leader. However, even then, if the leader's decision causes the follower to adjust his or her policy rule (reaction function), as opposed to his or her choice of policy values, the leader will want to revise his or her decision if he or she is to continue to choose the best policies to pursue his or her objectives.

[4] The equivalence was first demonstrated by Brandsma and Hughes Hallett (1984). But because one could do the same in a (sequence of) linearised quadratic approximations, it obviously applies more generally in some form, provided that some conditions as to the existences of inverse matrices hold. See also Petit (1990: chaps. 8–10).

In addition, in these, the Nash and Stackelberg equilibria with the forecaster leadership coincide.[5]

More generally, in models with strategic behaviour by multiple players, these players (one of whom may be the private sector or a representative agent) have well-defined objectives in terms of the endogenous variables of the model. The objectives would be the normal goals of economic policy if the player is a policymaker (Acocella, Di Bartolomeo and Hughes Hallett 2013: 90–93).[6]

A dynamic game between two or more players (including at least part of the private sector) can always be transformed, although not always uniquely, into a conventional single-player RE model.[7] This is convenient; the implication is that a forward-looking RE term can represent not only the strategic behaviour of the private sector but also the implicit shifting responses of the private sector to any policy changes or interventions by policy authorities. This covers the case where the private sector's chief concern is to forecast the outcomes of the economy or government policy (i.e. set expectations) accurately. It also means that the Lucas critique can be overcome if we learn to control a RE model correctly without time-inconsistent policies. The remaining sections of this chapter in particular show how to do this – through explicit policy games. However, this also can be done indirectly – and, in some cases, imperfectly – through single-player RE models.

---

[5] However, it should be noticed that when REs express rational observations by the public, conceiving this as a player amounts to assuming collusive behaviour of the individual members of the public. This can be assumed properly only under certain conditions. In any case, the equivalence offers a useful perspective (Holly 1987).

[6] Alternatively, they might be able to achieve a particular wage or price level in the economy as a whole if the player is the private sector, or interest rates in the financial markets, or just to forecast as accurately as possible what the government's policies and outcomes are likely to be.

[7] On the need to generalise the correspondence of REs to strategic games, see Schelling (1958).

We can deduce that making use of a strategic model is to be preferred not only because the conflict and the strategic interaction are made explicit but also because the RE representation of strategic behaviour is typically not unique. In practice, this needs to be tied down by specifying a theoretical model of the underlying economy or by estimating the parameter coefficients directly.

In particular, the strategic behaviour at issue in the Lucas critique can come from any kind of policy game, i.e. a Nash or Stackelberg game. Alternatively, a conjectural variations game could be introduced, with a contraction mapping designed to create Pareto improvements over the simple Nash solution. In this game, if the iterations take time to complete, the conjectural variations formulation shows how the Lucas critique can also be represented as a sequence of reactions by the private sector followed by adjustments by the government or other players. According to these remarks, the Lucas critique is just a reflection of the steps in an extensive form game and can be overcome by computing the final solution of that game.

In fact, the only games that do not fit this analysis are cooperative games. Such games are solved by appointing a 'social planner' and therefore do not require strategic interactions at the policy level, as opposed to what may happen between the players at the negotiating stage beforehand. Hence, policies derived from such cooperative games are Lucas critique proof.

As a final note to the Lucas critique, one can say not only that this critique can be overcome in a strategic setting and hence the theory of economic policy can be rehabilitated but also that (1) REs provide additional policy 'instruments' in the form of policy announcements (see Chapters 5 and 6) and therefore make the classical policy intervention stronger rather than weaker and (2) the scope for time-inconsistent policymaking is substantially reduced, thus taking away one of the major objections to the theory (Hughes Hallett, Di Bartolomeo and Acocella 2012a, 2012b).

4.3   An Example of Conflicts Rather Than Passive Subordination and the Need for a Theory of Conflicts

In order to illustrate the existence of a conflict that can be represented in terms of both REs and strategic games, think of the Barro-Gordon model. At the time of Barro and Gordon (1983), the emphasis of the policy debate was still far from the search for conditions of existence of an instrument vector that could guarantee satisfaction of some fixed targets (Tinbergen's fixed-target approach) or of an optimal policy that could minimise a given loss function (Theil's flexible-target approach). In fact, the Lucas critique was usually deemed to negate the possibility that the policymaker could control the system at all. The discussion therefore concentrated instead on issues of effectiveness or neutrality of specific instruments when the private sector has some specific target(s) and instrument(s), thus continuing, in a new setting, the debate that had started in the preceding two decades.

Barro and Gordon in fact studied a situation of conflict where both players, the central bank and the private sector are active. This can be represented simply by introducing the assumption of REs by the private sector in a model where the government wants to minimise a loss function depending on employment and price deviations from some target values. Alternatively, the model can be stated as a Stackelberg game between the private sector (acting as the leader) and the public sector. It is also interesting to note that in this case, one player, the private sector, whose loss depends on deviations of employment from its target value, has one instrument (price expectations). It thus has one target and one instrument. By contrast, the government's loss depends on two targets, employment and price deviations from some target values (the one for employment is higher than that of the private sector), but the government has only one instrument by which it can control inflation only.

By solving either the game or the system with REs, one can show that the private sector fully crowds out monetary effects on real output. A superior solution, for the public sector, would be to commit to a certain rule. However, having induced favourable private-sector expectations, the policymaker would always be tempted to cheat and renege on his or her commitment, the classic time-inconsistency argument (Kydland and Prescott 1977), in an attempt to achieve yet better outcomes. Being aware of this possibility, in self-defence, the private sector would anticipate worse results; these can be avoided only if the policymaker's temptation to cheat is balanced by a fear that he or she might lose his or her reputation and no longer be able to act effectively if this game of interactions with the private sector is repeated.

Thus, with Barro and Gordon, we have a result of policy neutrality. The conflict is solved favourably to the private sector. However, their result is specific to the assumptions of their model, as we see below. They certainly do not have a general theory of policy neutrality, even if much of the literature has acritically accepted it as such. A part of later studies has tried to elaborate such a theory in different ways, without making any reference to Tinbergen's contribution.[8]

What we need, however, is a theory of conflicts within which this result can be generalised. Such a theory should first show when and to what extent a conflict arises and what the terms of the conflict are. In this respect, a conflict arises every time the players' targets differ, at least in terms of target values. No conflict can arise where two agents aim to obtain the same desired target values for all their targets, as there is a convergence of interests between the players. Enlarging the focus of our analysis to multiple-player (non-cooperative) games, only some target values of the shared targets might coincide for some players, whereas each of them also pursues other targets, different from those of other players. The

---

[8] For this, see Acocella and Di Bartolomeo (2004) and references therein.

possibility of a partial convergence of interests arises in this case. In fact, 'implicit' coalitions can derive from situations where some players share the same target values of some common target variables. We would thus move from a situation of conflict among all players to a situation where conflict is absent among some players, but there is a residual opposition or rivalry among certain groups of them. Conflicts can refer to the relationship between a public and a private sector or among different public bodies, national (e.g. fiscal and monetary authorities) or international (think of decisions of different governments on monetary or trade issues).

In addition, a theory of conflicts should state when and how these can be solved, defining the features of the equilibrium solution (e.g. if there is or is not policy neutrality), if any, and how they depend on some critical assumptions of the game, in particular, as to numbers of targets and instruments of each player as well as his or her propensity to negotiations and agreements with other players. More generally, it should show how other possible outcomes of the game, such as no equilibrium or multiple equilibria, might depend on those assumptions – or others.

4.4   Conditions for Controllability in a Static Strategic Setting with Two or Multiple Players

The theoretical tools devised by the classical theory of economic policy are relevant for finding the outcome of a conflict. In fact, when a player has a number of instruments at least equal to that of his or her targets, his or her actions will determine the outcome of the game and reach the desired target values, notwithstanding actions by opponent(s). This can also control the system, unless another player with target values different from those of the first player has a number of instruments at least equal to that of his or her targets. In this case, no equilibrium would arise. If the target values do not differ, in principle, there are multiple solutions in the target space, but – because of this – the equilibrium in the space of instruments cannot be defined.

In the case of more than two players, as mentioned earlier, implicit coalitions can arise. The properties of equilibrium will be similar to those indicated for two players, but now the concepts of conflict, controllability and existence or multiplicity are referred to coalitions and no longer to single players. In addition, the concept of implicit coalitions can be generalised. In fact, an implicit coordination can also emerge if some players only partially share the same target values and the concept of controllability can be substituted by the more powerful one of 'decisiveness'. The latter implies a degree of control of some variables by a group of players, but not necessarily the achievement of any desired targets. Let us deal with these issues in a more analytical form in the following subsections.

4.4.1   Neutrality and Existence of an Equilibrium in a Two-Player Static Game

We consider two players: the public sector ('government'), indexed by 1, and the private sector ('agent'), indexed by 2. The government has $q(1)$ targets. The number of the agent's targets is $q(2)$. Since the players may share some target variables, we also have $q(1) + q(2) \geq K$. Each player minimises a quadratic loss functions depending on the deviations of each target from its target value.

The loss functions can be expressed as

$$(4.1) \quad L_i = \frac{1}{2}\left(y_i - \bar{y}_i\right)' Q_i\left(y_i - \bar{y}_i\right) \quad i = \{1, 2\}$$

where $y_i \in R^{q(i)}$ is a vector of target variables, $\bar{y}_i \in R^{q(i)}$ is a vector of target values, and Q is an appropriate positive-definite diagonal matrix. Note that Q is a square matrix of full rank by assumption. Player i's first best (or the *optimum optimorum*) corresponds to his or her target values.

In this setup, all the vectors of target variable are sub-vectors of $y \in \mathbb{R}^K$. The K target variables are linked together by the following linear equation system:

$$(4.2) \quad y = Au + f$$

where $u \in \mathbb{R}^M$ is the vector of the controls set by the two players, and vector $f \in \mathbb{R}^K$ is a vector of given constants that are outside the players' control.[9] Each row of (4.2) corresponds to a linear relationship between one target and the full instrument vector u. To keep things simple, we will assume that the basis of A is the identity matrix.[10] All the players' control vectors, i.e., $u_i \in \mathbb{R}^{m(i)}$, are sub-vectors of $u \in \mathbb{R}^M$. We also assume that $m(1) + m(2) = M$ because a policy control, by definition, cannot be set by more than one player at a time. For the sake of simplicity, we also assume that each player cannot control more instruments than the number of targets under that player's supervision: i.e. $m(i) \leq q(i)$.

We consider three kinds of interactions (solution concepts), which are based on different information sets. In the non-cooperative 'Nash equilibrium', both decision makers play simultaneously, and each of them has to form expectations of the opponent's policy choices. In the case of a 'commitment equilibrium', the government is a Stackelberg game leader who forms expectations of the opponent's behaviour. The government can commit itself to a policy rule, optimal or otherwise, and hence to a policy that is not contingent on that formulated by the other player. The follower (agent) can then choose, given whatever the government has chosen. The decisions are sequential across players. Finally, in a

---

[9] It can also contain zero mean shocks. In this case, our results hold in expected terms by the certainty equivalence principle.

[10] It means that system (4.2) cannot be reduced to many independent sub-systems. However, our results stand even without this assumption by using the concept of decisiveness, for which see Section 4.4.5. For a more detailed discussion, see Acocella and Di Bartolomeo (2005, 2006) and Acocella, Di Bartolomeo and Hughes Hallett (2013).

'discretionary equilibrium', the government is a Stackelberg follower and cannot pre-commit to a particular policy, although the agent forms expectations for the government's policy.

By rearranging the matrix equation representing the economic system, we can reduce a decision problem in a two-player strategic context to two separate optimisation problems, one for each player. Player i's problem consists in minimising his or her loss function subject to the constraint of a system derived from the model of the entire economy, indicating the value of that player's targets as a function of his or her instruments.

The relevant subsystem for player i is

$$(4.3) \quad y_i = C_i u_i + E_i u_j + f_i \quad j \neq i$$

where $C_i \in R^{q(i) \times m(i)}$, $E_i \in R^{q(i) \times m(j)}$ and $f_i \in R^{q(i)}$ are appropriate matrices and vectors. Each problem can be studied and solved individually with the tools used in the traditional approach to economic policy. In our decoupled representation of the policy game, a straightforward condition for neutrality can be stated as follows.

Theorem 4.1   (*policy neutrality*). If equilibrium exists, the government's (agent's) policy is neutral with respect to the targets shared with the agent (government) if the subsystem relevant for his or her targets is controllable by the agent (government). It is worth noticing here that controllability by one player (e.g. the agent) implies that that player will always achieve his or her target values because his or her decisions correspond to his *optimum optimorum*.

Although intuitive, the above-mentioned condition may appear to contain a contradiction, since controllability by the agent does not exclude the possibility that the government can also Tinbergen-Theil control their own subsystem. However, this contradiction is in fact only apparent. Indeed, were it more than just apparent, a policy equilibrium would not exist. The issue of equilibrium existence is therefore crucially related to that of controllability and neutrality.

Formally, the following theorem can be stated and proved:

Theorem 4.2   (*existence of an equilibrium and the government's policy neutrality*). (i) The equilibrium of the game in target space exists if the intersection of the players' controllable sets is empty or if the players share the same target values for the variables contained therein. (ii) The government's policy is neutral for all the government's target variables contained in the agent's controllable target set. (iii) Symmetrically, the agent's decisions are neutral for all the agent's target variables in the government's controllable target set. These results apply not only to Nash but also to Stackelberg equilibria.

In the case where there are costs for the use of an instrument (or more instruments), these must be included in the players' loss functions by adding for each costly instrument an auxiliary target variable and an equality constraint between it and the instrument in question, in a way that indicates the need for minimising the costs of deviations from the target value of the instrument itself. This will affect the results of the game and the existence of a policy equilibrium as the number of targets is now higher. Controllability by a player then would require the availability of a correspondingly higher number of his or her instruments. Other generalisations are possible for linear quadratic loss functions.

One advantage of this approach is that conditions for model building and solving, i.e. policy effectiveness or neutrality and equilibrium existence, can be detected without solving the model but simply by looking at the number of targets and independent instruments of each player or – more precisely – by checking the order of matrix C_i. In particular, player i controls his or her sub-system if $m(i) \geq q(i)$; however, if this condition is satisfied for both players, no equilibrium exists.

4.4.2 Equilibria in an n-*Player Static Game from the Point of View of Each Player*

From this point of view, Theorems 4.1 and 4.2 can easily be extended to problems with any number of players, as indicated by the following theorem.

Theorem 4.3   (*equilibrium existence and neutrality generalised*). (i) The equilibrium of a policy game between any n players exists (in target space) if the intersection of their controllable target sets is empty or if the variables contained in the set are associated with the same quantitative target value for all the players that control them. (ii) Player i's policy is neutral for all his or her targets contained in the union of the other players' controllable target sets.

Analysis so far has been performed with reference to the outcomes relevant for each player (i.e. in outcome space only), and issues of multiplicity of equilibria either in this space or in instrument space were not investigated from the point of view of the whole system. By contrast, now we focus on the entire system to derive general conditions for equilibrium existence and multiplicity, in terms of the controllability of the whole system.

4.4.3 Policy Neutrality and Equilibrium Existence with Respect to the System As a Whole

Let us refer to games where players aim to maximise preferences defined on the same target variables (but with potentially different target values) as 'fully shared preferences games'. If all players share the same bliss point, we have a 'common-interest game'.

The possibility of interactions between policymakers has raised problems of coordination and comparisons between the outcomes of decentralised and centralised solutions.[11] Only occasionally have these issues been dealt with in terms of controllability of the system and the existence of an equilibrium. However, the essence of this problem is already well known in the economic literature, at least since Mundell (1968) raised the 'nth country problem'. In a world of n countries, there are $n - 1$ independent external balances, trade balances or exchange rates as possible targets but n possible independent policy instruments, such as interest rates, which could, in theory, be set by the n policymakers. As a result, if each policymaker made independent use of his or her instrument, a conflict would arise among the n countries, and no equilibrium would exist because of the adding-up constraint that must hold between the n external balances or n exchange rates.[12]

The conditions for existence derived in the above-cited theorems by first decoupling the policy game in a set of single-player problems and then applying the Tinbergen and Theil tools to each of them refer to the point of view of single players. By contrast, now we focus on the entire system to derive general conditions for equilibrium existence and multiplicity in terms of the controllability of the whole system.

Specifically, a decentralised equilibrium is characterised by multiple equilibria in the instrument space whenever the total number of independent instruments, summing across players, is greater than the total number of their (independent) targets when taken together. Surprisingly perhaps, the availability of instruments more numerous than the targets,

---

[11] Starting from the pioneering studies of Mundell (1962) or Cooper (1969), through the policy coordination work of Hughes Hallett (1986), to more recent works such as Corsetti and Pesenti (2001), Benigno (2002), Pappa (2004) and Plasmans et al. (2006).

[12] Robert Mundell was well aware that the existence of a redundancy issue depends on the set of assumptions about targets and instruments as well as on the working of the economic system (see Mundell 1962, 1968). This was even more evident in von Neumann Whitman (1969).

which is a virtue of a centralised or 'social planner' solution as it confers some degrees of freedom, is problematic in a decentralised environment because coordination on an equilibrium is difficult.

The equilibrium existence is shown to be unlikely in games with conflicts about the target values. Instead, in common-interest games, at least one equilibrium exists that is also Pareto optimal. However, the excess of instruments may cause a problem of coordination on how to set instruments to achieve it. It can be shown that the players can be given an incentive to choose exactly the values of the instruments leading to that Pareto-optimal equilibrium.

Let us assume that the total number of independent instruments available to the players is not smaller than the number of independent targets $\sum_{i \in N} m(i) \geq K$; i.e. we have a Tinbergen system. Then the following theorem can be stated (Acocella, Di Bartolomeo and Hughes Hallett 2013).

Theorem 4.4 (*instruments, targets and multiple equilibria*). If the total number of instruments exceeds the total number of independent targets, Nash equilibria are multiple in the instrument space, if they exist.

This does not necessarily imply that there are multiple equilibria in the target space. In a common-interest game with a Tinbergen system, at least one Nash equilibrium exists in the space of outcomes. But counterintuitively, this is not sufficient to guarantee that this equilibrium is unique. Although the outcome of the equilibrium where all target values are reached is 'privileged' by being the unanimous best choice for all players, there might be cases in which other vectors of targets satisfy the system as well. A possible example arises when the quasi-reaction functions of all players are coincident: at each of these infinite points, no player has any incentive to deviate as each of all the multiple equilibria in the outcome space is supported by multiple equilibria in the instrument space, given the assumption of a total number of instruments larger than the number of targets.

As a way of partial conclusion, we can say that in n-person games in general, if at least one player satisfies controllability, Nash equilibria (if they exist) are multiple in the instrument space and unique in the outcome space. By contrast, in a common-interest game, if at least one player satisfies controllability, there exist multiple equilibria in the instrument space and a unique one in the outcome space.

At a practical level, if there are too many instruments available in the game, it might become impossible for each player to make conjectures about the policies of the opponents.[13] The inability to forecast the strategy selected by the other players may then lead to a series of randomised policy interventions, which would destroy the policymakers' ability to coordinate on a Nash equilibrium, and even in the case of common-interest games, a unique equilibrium in the instrument space will not exist and instrument values remain somehow 'indeterminate'. By contrast, the over-determination of an economic system has no consequences for the centralised solution. In fact, a social planner can always select one of the infinite solutions arising when the economic system is over-determined. They are obtained simply by fixing the values of the instruments in excess of the targets.

A way to solve the problem of multiple equilibria in decentralised solutions is to introduce instrument costs. This would add to the number of targets and make the number of instruments always less than that of the targets. The introduction of extra costs for the players in excess of the number of instruments really acts as an equilibrium-selection device by selecting one of the multiple equilibria existing in the instrument space. If the equilibrium is unique in the outcome

---

[13] Here we implicitly interpret the Nash equilibrium as the result of each player making REs about the policy of its opponents.

space, instrument costs clearly coordinate players towards the desired target. Moreover, if there are multiple equilibria in that space, introducing costs can coordinate players on the Pareto-efficient one. Usually, they should be introduced only when operating instruments really imply costs. However, from a practical point of view – and not only at an analytical level – the imposition of a cost is fictitious in common-interest games. In fact, in this case, any arbitrary deviation of cost imposed implies that the players will not actually bear that cost, since they would prefer to do nothing. In that way, they would obtain their first best solution.

4.4.4   Conflicts and Coordination among Groups: Implicit Coalitions

A situation of no conflict can arise when there is a convergence of interests between different players. In this case, 'implicit' coalitions can arise among the players that share the same target values of the common target variables. This results in a move from a situation of conflict among all players, such as that assumed in the preceding subsections, to a situation where there is absence of a conflict among some players but a residual opposition or rivalry among certain groups of them. In a nutshell, similarly to the preceding cases, the existence of a conflict implies an opposition among the (implicit) coalitions that will lead to the nonexistence of an equilibrium if more than one coalition controls conflicting targets. By contrast, if only one coalition controls (in the same sense) the economic system, we end up with policy invariance. In addition, the concept of implicit coalitions can be generalised to the case where some players only partially share the same target values, and the tool of decisiveness can be introduced to solve the game.

In the two-player case, implicit coordination may emerge as the result of a decentralised setting without conflict between the two players. In a multiple-agent context, more general situations can be considered, e.g. implicit coordination among a subset of players or among a subset of target variables. This subsection explores the former; for the latter, the reader can refer to Acocella, Di Bartolomeo and Piacquadio (2009).

Let us consider an economy where n agents interact strategically. We assume – without loss of generality – that each agent aims at minimising a quadratic criterion defined in terms of deviations from a desired target value vector $\bar{y}_i$,[14]:

$$(4.4) \quad L_i = \left(y - \bar{y}_i\right)' Q_i \left(y - \bar{y}_i\right)$$

and is endowed with only one instrument; implying there are n instruments in total. Targets and instruments are both linearly independent. Agent i's first best solution is obtained for $y = \bar{y}_i$ and, as a consequence, $L_i = 0$.

The economy is described by the following linear system:

$$(4.5) \quad Ay = Bu + c = \sum_{i=1}^{n} B_i u_i + c$$

where y is a vector of K target variables, $u' = (u_1, ..., u_n)$ is the vector of the n instruments, and A, B and B_i are appropriate matrices of parameters $(A^{-1}B_i$ is the vector of policy multipliers for $u_i)$. We assume that the total number of instruments is not greater than the total number of target variables (i.e. $n \leq K$).

An (implicit) coalition is the set of agents for whom a certain target set Y contains their first best. We say that two coalitions have a conflict of interests if there exists at least one desired target value different for the same variable that is of interest to both of them. A coalition is said to possess coalition controllability if the strategies of coalition members always imply that they reach their first best outcomes for any given strategy of the other players.

---

[14] Q_i is not required to be of full rank as one agent may not be interested in one or more of the target variables.

Coalition controllability implies that a combination of instruments of the coalition members (coalition policy) exists such that for any given set of values for the instruments chosen by non-coalition members, the coalition members always achieve their first best outcomes. Conditions ensuring coalition controllability have been stated.

The concept of coalition also can be generalised to situations where not all target values – but only some of them – are shared. In this situation, differences in some target values can be settled within this group of players, where a Nash equilibrium can be reached. Even with partially differing target values, consideration of this case is important because the group can neutralise other external groups' policies. It is then relevant for policy effectiveness and institutional discussions.

These results are essential to fully understand policy games and, thus, for model building, as they state the conditions for the consistency of the optimal strategies of all the players (and thus the existence of an equilibrium to the game) as well as the effectiveness of policy instruments. In addition, they are relevant for institution building, as they can help us to show the conditions under which a decentralised equilibrium may hold or fail to exist or to be Pareto efficient.

4.4.5   Announcement Games

We have seen that cases of multiple equilibria can emerge in policy games and have derived the formal conditions under which this occurs. In such a case, the Nash equilibrium concept is too broad to tell us how policymakers interact and what the outcome of the game will be. Consequently, the issue of how to select one equilibrium arises. Non-binding announcements ('cheap talk') can be used as a device for coordinating the policymakers onto a solution. Along the way, we consider the 'credibility' of those announcements and their consistency across players and reaction functions.

The problem of multiple Nash equilibria has often been discussed in the literature. For instance, David Kreps considers multiple equilibria, and how to choose between them, to be one of the paramount problems in game theory. Many sorts of games have, in fact, multiple equilibria, 'and the theory is often of no help in sorting out whether any one is the solution and, if one is, which one is' (Kreps 1990: 97).

In some games with multiple equilibria, players know what to do. This knowledge comes from directly relevant past experience and from a sense of how individuals act generally. However, formal mathematical game theory still has much to say about where these expectations come from, how and why they persist or when and why we might expect them to arise (Kreps 1990). The problem of equilibrium selection in particular is closely related to various kinds of coordination failures (see e.g. Cooper and John 1988).

The natural solution to coordination failures is based on the idea of focal points (Schelling 1960), which is, however, not always appealing – in particular, when there is a conflict of interest among the agents. More interesting are the solutions that prevent the emergence of coordination problems by considering small two-stage variations of the standard coordination game that are based on pre-play communication or the introduction of outside options. Adding the option for one player to make an announcement does not alter the set of possible Nash equilibria.

We consider a general linear-quadratic (LQ) coordination game and introduce a pre-play stage that takes account of both cheap talk and outside options. In particular, we assume that an agent can make an announcement in the first stage of the game that other agents can take into account or not as they wish. If they do not coordinate on the announcement equilibrium, they expect the payoff given by the outside option. Therefore, the sender has to take account of this possibility in determining his or her self-committing announcements.[15]

Finally, we investigate the traditional time-inconsistency issue by clarifying the relationship between credible and non-credible promises. Costless announcements and the traditional commitment solution are briefly compared as alternative techniques for creating credible policy commitments. For a more exhaustive comparison, see Acocella et al. (2014). The LQ structure of the game allows us to derive closed-form solutions and to describe the entire taxonomy of it, including necessary and sufficient conditions to observe and solve coordination failures.

We consider a static LQ game between two players with complete information.[16] Each player k sets an instrument u_k to minimise the following loss functions:

$$(4.6) \quad L_k(z) = \frac{1}{2}\left[\left(x - \overline{x}_k\right)^2 + \beta_k\left(y - \overline{y}_k\right)^2\right] \quad k = \{1,2\}$$

defined over the weighted deviations of two target variables from their desired values. The relationships between targets and instruments are summarised by a system of linear equations that describes the economy: $z = Au + c$, where u are linearly independent instruments.

The Nash equilibrium is a vector $u^* = \left(u_1^*, u_2^*\right)$ if $u_1^* \subset \mathrm{argmin} L_i\left(u_k^*, u_{-k}^*\right)$, for $k = 1, 2$. Necessary and sufficient conditions to obtain multiple Nash equilibria in this linear setting imply that the first best outcomes for the two players lie along the same quasi-reaction function.

Among this set of Nash equilibria, we can identify the efficient subset: that is to say, equilibria not Pareto

---

[15] The possibility of announcement wars can also be considered, which we do not investigate here for simplicity.

[16] This case can find a practical application when the number of players is limited not only for public players such as monetary and fiscal authorities of the same country or policymakers of a few countries but also for private players as oligopolistic firms.

dominated by any other Nash equilibrium. This is given by all the (linear) convex combinations of the first best outcomes of the players. By contrast, Nash equilibria outside the subset of these equilibria represent coordination failures in the sense of Cooper and John (1988). Of course, if the target values of all players coincide, then all Nash equilibria that lead to different outcomes are Pareto inefficient (when the β are finite and different from zero, and players are interested in both targets).

All these cases of multiple equilibria, however, need some kind of 'story' of how a particular equilibrium may finally be selected. This can be provided by showing that sequences of announcements can lead players to coordinate their actions around one set of outcomes.

Here we consider only one-sided announcements for simplicity. For a more developed analysis, see Acocella et al. (2014). We allow players to make an announcement in the underlying game described earlier. At the beginning of the period, a player makes a public announcement about his or her policy. Thereafter, without any binding commitment, the two players simultaneously set their instruments. Since the announcement is not binding, the players can take it into account or not as they prefer. If they do not take account of that announcement, the outside option, which is naturally defined as the expected outcome of the underlying Nash game, is obtained.

Following Farrell (1988), we assume that credible non-binding announcements exist.[17] If a credible announcement is made, it will not be ignored by the receiver and will be used to coordinate the agents' actions. This means that agents will act according to that announcement. Credibility of nonbinding announcements is based on 'self-committing'

[17] It is worth noticing that as the announcement is cheap talk, it will not restrict the set of the Nash equilibria of the underlying game ('babbling equilibrium'). As in Farrell (1988), in fact, we are restricting the outcomes by changing the concept of equilibrium of the game.

messages and on an additional constraint, induced by the introduction of the outside option, which ensures that the coordination phase is implemented.

We assume that agents can communicate by a common language. Since an announcement can be seen as a nonbinding commitment about the agent's own supporting strategy, we assume that the agent receiving the announcement interprets it correctly. He also correctly links the announced outcome to the supporting strategies.

If an agent decides to ignore the announcement, the outcome of the underlying game is driven by an exogenously given probability distribution defining both the sender's and the receiver's outside option. Without entering into a discussion about its possible derivation, we just point out that this outcome distribution could have had its origin in a mixed-strategy equilibrium as well as in the players' beliefs, which may ultimately be derived from institutional or historical experiences. However, a detailed analysis of the form of the probability distribution is beyond the scope of this chapter.

We define the set of credible announcements as the set of announcements for which a series of axioms on self-commitment and acceptability holds. Clearly, given our assumptions, if an announcement equilibrium exists at all, it will completely describe the outcome and actions of the two agents in the game. Then the outcome of the game is the one first announced by one of the players, which corresponds to his or her most favourable outcome from among all the credible announcements. If there is at least one outcome on the quasi-reaction functions that Pareto dominates the random solution, then the one-sided announcement game has a unique announcement equilibrium.

As the announcement equilibrium is always unique and always a Nash equilibrium, it acts as an equilibrium-selection device. The idea is simply that the player making the announcement can use his or her 'announcement power' to eliminate the random outcomes to obtain his or her most favoured of the credible outcomes. However, if there is no outcome on the quasi-reaction functions that Pareto dominates the random solution, no credible announcement can be made, and the random solution is to be expected. The announcement therefore succeeds in solving the equilibrium-selection dilemma because it is a way to signal a common strategy that will lead to an outcome that is better than the random outcomes for both players.[18]

A one-sided announcement is a 'weak' promise in comparison to commitment. It is less favourable for the agent that makes the promise but crucially does not need any external credibility support in order to be implemented. Announcements therefore allow the players to convert a desirable outcome into a focal point upon which to coordinate, and thereby reduce (but not in general eliminate), inefficiencies even if the players are in conflict. In this way, they solve two very annoying problems of games with multiple equilibria: (1) how to arrange convergence to a Nash equilibrium and (2) how to solve coordination problems.

The introduction of an outside option strongly affects the results: this is a common-knowledge expectation about the payoff of the game when communication is not possible or unsuccessful. Specifically, the existence of an outside option restricts the set of credible announcements and forces the sender to announce a second-best outcome. Multiple announcements strengthen this result further because the sender has to take account of the possibility that the receiver can dismiss the proposal and announce a new one.

Finally, notice that announcements as an equilibrium-selection device are more likely to be observed when there is a large degree of uncertainty, little disagreement between agents about the targets and higher expected losses if players do not coordinate their actions. By allowing for cheap-talk

[18] When the outside option defines a (non-dominated) outcome with probability 1, the model recovers the prediction of Schelling's (1960) focal point idea.

announcements by both agents, additional insights into the outcomes can be derived without affecting the properties of the game. Indeed, in contrast to the case of commitment – where having two committing agents would bring no equilibrium (e.g. when there are two Stackelberg leaders) – using sequential announcements from both sides will always lead to a unique equilibrium. In the limiting case of a frictionless bargaining process (no transaction costs), this corresponds to implementing the Nash bargaining solution with appropriate weights representing bargaining powers.

4.5   Notions and Conditions of Controllability in a Dynamic Strategic Setting

In this section we will limit ourselves to very simple notions, leaving complexities to interested readers, who can refer to Acocella, Di Bartolomeo and Hughes Hallett (2013). We simply describe (1) the dynamic setting, (2) the information structures, (3) the solutions corresponding to the different structures and (4) how to calculate the minimum time needed for dynamic controllability. Point 1 will be dealt with in the next subsection, whereas the other points will be investigated in the following subsections.

4.5.1   A Simple Dynamic Setting

The simplest dynamic representation of an economy, in the form of a model, is as a linear difference equation system[19]:

---

[19] We use difference, rather than differential, equations to represent the economy's dynamics. Given the discrete nature of economic data, this is the conventional approach in economics. Petit (1990) provides an analysis in continuous time. We should also note that the model that we have presented does not include forward-looking components, which will be necessary for closed-loop information structures (see Section 4.5.2). For such an information structure, a more complex model is needed (see Section 4.5.6).

(4.7) $\hat{A}_0 y_t = \hat{A}_1 y_{t-1} + \hat{B}_0 u_t + \hat{C}_0 w_t$, $t = 1, \ldots, T$ (structural form)

where y_t is the vector of endogenous variables and potential policy targets in the system, u_t is the vector of policy instruments available, and w_t are random shocks and other exogenous influences or variables, which also affect this economy's outcomes. The matrices $\hat{A}_0, \hat{A}_1 \in R^{q \times q}$, $\hat{B}_0 \in R^{q \times m}$ and $\hat{C}_0 \in R^{q \times q}$ represent parameters and may also be the identity matrix. These matrices are all nonzero, meaning that they all contain at least one, some or many nonzero elements.

It is also easy to transform system (4.7) to its 'reduced form', equivalent to static reduced-form models:

(4.8) $y_t = A_1 y_{t-1} + B_0 u_t + C_0 w_t$ (reduced form)

where $A_1 = \hat{A}_0^{-1} \hat{A}_1$, $B_0 = \hat{A}_0^{-1} \hat{B}_0$ and $C_0 = \hat{A}_0^{-1} \hat{C}_0$. This reduced-form model takes account of all the contemporaneous simultaneity in the model and always exists as long as there are no redundant equations (equations linearly dependent on other equations). If that is the case, $\hat{A}_0$ is of full rank, and $r[\hat{A}_0] = q$ and $\hat{A}_0^{-1}$ will exist.

4.5.2 Notions of Controllability

If there are dynamic relationships describing how the economy evolves, there are likely to be dynamic objectives that policymakers would like to reach. There are four possible types:

1. **Static Objectives.** Hitting desired target values at each time from any initial condition.
2. **Multi-period Static Objectives.** Hitting and holding desired target values across a certain time interval, if necessary by changing instrument settings.
3. **Target-Point Objectives.** These are fixed targets to be reached at some specific point in time in the future.

4.   **Target-Path Objectives.** Hitting certain target values at a certain point in time and then holding a sequence of arbitrary point objectives for a certain interval thereafter.

Formally, the preceding problems can be illustrated in terms of four parameters. Assuming that the policymaker aims to reach his or her desired targets from t_0 (current period) or from t_0 on, the policymaker should act at least from the current period and anticipate his or her future policy changes. The relevant parameters can then be defined as follows:

1.   The degree of anticipation or policy lead $P \in \{0, 1, ...\}$;
2.   The target interval $T \in \{0, 1, ...\}$;
3.   The number of targets per period q; and
4.   The instruments per period m.[20]

This leaves us with a four-parameter theory of dynamic policy: P, T, q and m. A timeline for policy problems in a dynamic setting can then be depicted as in Figure 4.1. The line describes the policy interval (between $t_0 - S$ and $t_0 + T$) where the policymaker is active.

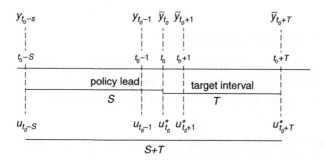

Figure 4.1 *A timeline for dynamic policy problems.*
(Source: Acocella, Di Bartolomeo and Hughes Hallett 2013)

---

[20] Normally, we assume that we have the same number of targets and instruments in each period (i.e. q and m are the same in each period). Relaxing this assumption causes additional issues to arise.

In the case of static objectives, the policymaker aims to achieve his or her target vector in the current period by setting his or her instruments in the current period. This corresponds to Tinbergen's static fixed-objective problem since the policymaker aims to achieve his or her target vector under linear constraints augmented by the given initial conditions. Multi-period static objectives imply a natural extension of the Tinbergen idea of fixed targets to a dynamic context as, in this case, the policymaker aims at achieving a configuration of desired targets $\bar{y}$ during a time interval between t_0 and $t_0 + T$. When there are target-point objectives, the policymaker wants to reach his or her targets at a certain time (i.e. in P periods), anticipating his or her action by P periods. In this case, one can also define the policy problem of endogenising P by interpreting it as the smallest time interval needed to achieve the target vector. Finally, target-path objectives imply that the policymaker aims to reach, after P periods, a certain dynamic path for the economy that is then held for T successive periods thereafter.[21] This representation of the policy problem should be generalised to models with multiple lags before specific policy measures can be calculated.

4.5.3 Information Structures

Three information structures are relevant. These are open loop, feedback and closed loop. We can informally define them as follows:

> **Open-Loop Policy Rule.** An open loop policy rule is one that can be calculated, optimally or not, at the first planning period and is then implemented irrespective of how the economy actually develops thereafter
>
> **Feedback Policy Rule.** A feedback policy rule reacts to the latest information on past realisations of variables in the

---

[21] We can also think of endogenising the policy lead P in this case too.

model but not to changes in expectations or probabilistic information on future variables or improved coefficients in the model (an improved understanding of the economy's behaviour) going forward.

Closed-Loop Policy Rule. A closed loop policy rule takes account of all the latest information available at each t, including probabilistic information on disturbances, any revised expectations for future variables and any revisions made to the model or our understanding of the policymakers' preferences and priorities. All of this in the same feedback-rule form.

Correspondingly to these rules, we could define open-loop, feedback and closed-loop strategies. Specifically, the open-loop strategy is a sequence of decisions for each time period, each of which depends on the initial state. The open-loop Nash equilibrium is derived from the presumption that at the beginning of the game each player can make binding commitments about the actions he or she will undertake over the entire planning period. That is, each player designs his or her optimal policy based on his or her own loss function at the beginning of the period and sticks to that policy sequence throughout the entire period. Hence, open-loop strategies are not usually time consistent. Feedback strategies provide instead a strongly time consistent (i.e. sub-game perfect) equilibrium. Sub-game perfectness requires that for every possible sub-game, feedback strategies u^* will remain the equilibrium and optimal value for that sub-game. In practice, a feedback strategy means that a contingent rule (dependent on the system's state vector at time t) is provided for each player and that the rules themselves can be obtained from the backward recursions of dynamic programming (Holly and Hughes Hallett 1989). That, in turn, requires the constrained optimisation problem faced by each player at each t to be recursively additively separable with respect to each $t, \ldots, T$. The recursive nature of the problem is upset if there are anticipation effects from REs or actions expected from other players in the future, when a closed-loop strategy is in order reacting to changes in expectations of future events as they appear, in addition to past outcomes.

4.5.4   Open-Loop Nash Solutions

The open-loop Nash context allows us to express each agent's optimisation problem as a static one, as he or she can set his or her optimal rule u_t^{i*} at the beginning of the game, taking as given the rules used by the other agents u_t^{j*} for $j \in n/i$.

If, for simplicity, the dimensions of the target and the instrument vectors and the vector of the desired targets are time invariant, $T = 2$ and we ignore stochastic disturbance and expectations (in a way certainty equivalence can always be advocated), each agent must minimise, given the initial condition y_0

$$(4.9) \quad L_i = \left(y_1^i - \bar{y}^i\right)' Q_i \left(y_1^i - \bar{y}^i\right) + \left(y_2^i - \bar{y}^i\right)' Q_i \left(y_2^i - \bar{y}^i\right) \quad \text{for all } i \in n$$

under the constraint

$$y_1^i = A_i y_0^i + \sum_{j \in N} B_{ij} u_1^j$$

in the first period and

$$y_2^i = A_i A_i y_0^i + A_i \sum_{j \in N} B_{ij} u_1^j + \sum_{j \in N} B_{ij} u_{2,0}^j$$

in the second period. Static controllability clearly requires $2q(i) = 2m(i)$, as in the static case, but the problem remains dynamic because the number of instruments (or targets) can vary over time, which changes multipliers from one period to another, or because the effects of instrument are distributed over time.

Let us see this with reference to cases where there are excess or fewer instruments with respect to targets in each period. Imagine, for example, that the policymaker has two targets over a two-period model (four targets); in the first period he or she has three instruments, and in the second one he or she can statically control the system only in period 1, but multi-period controllability is assured, as any four-target vector can be achieved in the two periods. This is because the effects of instruments are no longer purely static, and thus, both static and dynamic multipliers must be taken into account.

Ensuring that the number of instruments is at least equal to that of targets in each period is stronger than the conditions required for ensuring multi-period static controllability. This could be obtained also when the golden rule is satisfied neither in each period nor in aggregate, just as an effect of the dynamic nature of the instruments. However, if static controllability is satisfied, multi-period static controllability is also ensured.

We now refer to Figure 4.1 and derive the minimum time needed to reach targets by using the concept of dynamic controllability. In a classical, non-parametric context, dynamic controllability is obtained for any t equal to or larger than S and can be derived by solving the following optimisation problem:

$$(4.10) \quad \min_S L_S = \left(y_S^i - \bar{y}^i\right)' Q_i \left(y_S^i - \bar{y}^i\right) \text{ s.t.}$$

$$(4.11) \quad y_t^i = A_i y_{t-1}^i + \sum_{j \in n} B_{ij} u_t^j + v_t \text{ given } y_0.$$

A trivial case arises if $m = q$, as then $S = 1$ solves this problem. Thus, the policymaker always satisfies dynamic controllability. By contrast, if $m < q$, the policymaker should exploit the dynamic multipliers to obtain the desired targets, and this requires $S > 1$. The shortest time needed to reach his or her desired targets depends on how many targets and instruments the policymaker has. For instance, if only one instrument is available, he or she can expect to reach one target value in period one, two after two periods and so on; i.e. dynamic controllability requires at least $S = q$ periods. In general, if the policymaker has m instruments, dynamic controllability requires at least $S = q/m$ periods. For a formal proof of this, see Preston and Pagan (1982).

By applying the preceding result to a multi-player context, it emerges that if two (or more) players aim to solve a problem of the kind (4.10), where $q(1)/m(1) = S$ and $q(2)/m(2) = S$, both would be able to achieve their targets, and no equilibrium would exist. By contrast, if $q(i)/m(i) \leq S$ for all i, the existence of an equilibrium for problem (4.10) with multiple players is ensured. In other cases, the conditions for equilibrium existence will be more complex. But we do not analyse them here.

The second case of interest is where player i aims to reach certain target values in the shortest possible time. Assuming dynamic controllability, what can be achieved now depends on how many target values player i attempts to reach. Again, if a player has only one instrument available, he or she can expect to reach one target value in period one, two after two periods and all targets after a number of periods equal to the integer value of $q(i)/m(i)$ targets if $q(i) > m(i)$. In the absence of static controllability, this is as far as he or she can go in minimising the time taken to reach various targets.

If dynamic controllability applies in period S, player i can achieve his or her target values $\bar{y}_i$ exactly, in expectation, in period S at least. This means, applying certainty equivalence, that player i can achieve a value of $E(L_S) = 0$ in his or her loss function and maximum expected utility in period $t = S$. But the same result does not hold if there are instrument costs, since both static and dynamic controllability no longer apply. Nor does this result say anything about the costs along the way. In general, we should expect $E(L_t) \neq 0$, for all $t = 1, \ldots, S-1$ and $m(i)S \leq Tq(i)$. Analysing the utility costs in either of those two cases requires a full specification of the preferences in the loss functions $E(L_t)$ for each t.

There is one exception to the assertion that when the system is only dynamically controllable the policymaker must wait to achieve his or her target values. Section 4.5.6 shows that in an economy with forward-looking REs of future outcomes, dynamic controllability may be available from period one if announcements of future policy actions are used alongside the actual (current and past) policy interventions. If this is the case, and in the absence of instrument costs, then the costs along the way will fall away: $E(L_t) = 0$, for all $t = 1, \ldots, T$.

4.5.5   Feedback Nash Equilibrium

In a dynamic setting, controllability (or the golden rule of economic policy), policy ineffectiveness and the existence of a feedback Nash equilibrium are related to one another through the following two theorems.

Theorem 4.5   (*ineffectiveness in feedback Nash equilibrium*). In a LQ-difference game where an equilibrium exists, if one player satisfies the golden rule, then all other players' policies are ineffective for all the target variables shared with that player.

Theorem 4.6   (*nonexistence in feedback Nash equilibrium*). The feedback Nash equilibrium of the policy game described earlier does not exist if two or more players satisfy the golden rule and aim to achieve different target values for at least one shared target variable.

   Proofs: See Acocella, Di Bartolomeo and Hughes Hallett (2013).

Theorem 4.6 highlights the importance of these results for economic policy. This theorem says that if two independent policy authorities – say, fiscal policymakers and the central bank – decide to pursue different inflation targets, then the Nash equilibrium does not exist if both control the economy. When this is the case, the economy will not be able to reach a stable equilibrium position even when both policymakers try to optimise their policies. Moreover, the conditions for this are not particularly stringent. In fact, target independence may actually be unhelpful – not because fiscal and monetary policies cannot be coordinated properly but because the underlying equilibrium cannot be reached if both policymakers try to optimise their policy choices simultaneously and independently.

4.5.6   Dynamic Controllability with Closed-Loop Information

Policymakers routinely use announcements[22] as policy instruments to influence future expectations and, through them, future results. Announcement and signalling effects in fact imply that the announcement of a change in policy will typically affect agents' behaviour, even before the change is actually made. Rational policymakers should therefore internalise announcement effects and use the signals strategically. The economic policy literature, however, does not have a formal model of whether, and under what conditions, policy announcements can be used to systematically affect economic performance.

Time inconsistency and REs are said to imply that such commitments cannot be considered credible and would inevitably lead to Pareto-inferior outcomes. We discuss the credibility problem by considering REs within the traditional Tinbergen framework and show that under certain

---

[22] Here the role of announcements is different from that indicated earlier. In fact, now they tend to complement traditional instruments for the policymaker to reach his or her targets in a shorter time, whereas in Section 4.4.6 they served the purpose of helping a number of policymakers converge on one equilibrium out of the many that are possible.

circumstances REs will not only present the policymakers with no problem of how to set their policies consistently but may actually add to the scope of their policy instruments, in effect, giving them additional sources of effective policy power.

Let us consider an economy represented by a generic linear RE model in reduced form:

$$(4.12) \quad y_t = Ay_{t-1} + Bu_t + Cy_{t+1|t} + v_t \quad \text{for } t = 1, \ldots, T$$

where $y \in \mathbb{R}^S$ and $u \in \mathbb{R}^M$. This can be controlled by a policy-maker if a sequence of instrument values $u_1, \ldots, u_t$ can be found that will reach any arbitrary values $\bar{y}_t$ for the target variables in period t (at least in expectation) given an arbitrary starting point y_0. In this case, we are not concerned with the period-by-period controllability of the target variables between periods 1 and $t - 1$. Starting from period 1, dynamic controllability therefore requires a sequence of intended instrument values $u_{1|1}, \ldots, u_{T|1}$, say, that guarantee that $\bar{y}_{t|1}$ is reached in period $t < T$. This is possible only if the condition stated in the following theorem is satisfied.

Theorem 4.7   (*sufficient condition for dynamic controll-ability with REs*). The economy represented by (4.12) is dynamically controllable over the subinterval $(1, t)$, when $T \geq S$ and where $t < T$, if the sequence of policy multipliers and anticipatory effects is of full rank, i.e. if $r[R_{t,1} \ldots, R_{t,S}] = S$, given an arbitrary initial state y_0 and a specified terminal condition $y_{T+1|1}$.[23]

This means that if $S > t$, which is entirely possible for small values of t, dynamic controllability will be available through the *reactions* of $y_{t|1}$ to the implemented policy choices

---

[23] This theorem provides a sufficient condition for dynamic controllability. The corresponding necessary condition involves a smaller subset of R_{tj} having full rank depending on how many policy instruments are available.

$u_{1|1}, \ldots, u_{t|1}$ as well as through the *anticipatory effects* of announced or anticipated policy interventions that still lie in the future $u_{t+1|1}, \ldots, u_{T|1}$. In other words, a policymaker can use policy announcements, in addition to actual interventions, to guide the course of the economy. This can be done from the first period onwards, provided that $T \geq S$ and Theorem 4.7 both hold, even if there are insufficient traditional instruments $M < S$; i.e. the policymaker does not possess additional instruments such as announcements. In a conventional model with no REs, this would not be possible. In effect, the policymaker now has a greater number of policy 'instruments' at his or her disposal than he or she would in an economy without anticipations.[24]

One can object that while the $u_{1|1}, \ldots, u_{t|1}$ values will be implemented decisions, the remaining $u_{t+1|1}, \ldots, u_{T|1}$ values are only announcements that may never actually be carried out. However, because they lie in the future from the perspective of $y_{t|1}$, any subsequent time inconsistency plays no role in the controllability of $y_{t|1}$ as long as they are genuinely held expectations at that point and the policymaker will be able to reach his or her desired values for y_t in expectation.

4.5.7   Stabilisability under REs

The reasoning underlying Theorem 4.7 can be applied to show that any economy can also be stabilised to an arbitrary degree under rational, forward-looking expectations if it is dynamically controllable in the sense of this theorem. An arbitrary degree of stabilisation means that policy rules can be found to make the economy follow an arbitrarily stable path based on an arbitrary set of eigenvalues such that it returns to the original path following a shock. Theorem 4.8 gives the RE analogue of the standard stabilisability theorem for backward-looking or physical systems.

---

[24] Forward guidance is an announcement of this type (see Chapters 5 and 6).

Theorem 4.8   (*stabilisability and REs*). For any economy represented by (4.12), with arbitrary matrices A, B and C, we can find a series of forward-looking policy rules $u_{t|1} = \sum_{j=1}^{T} K_{tj}y_{j-1|1} + k_{t|1}$, say, such that the controlled economy is stabilisable up to an arbitrary set of eigenvalues if the economy is controllable in the sense of Theorem 4.7.

Note that (1) the control rule for use in period $t < T$ indicated in the theorem employs actions and anticipates actions up to the end of the policy period T and (2) policies implying stabilisability are not unique. The policymaker can use policies before t more intensively or, by contrast, do this with policy announcements about the future.

4.6   Summary and Open Issues

After the vital critiques moved to its two pillars, economic policy as an autonomous discipline has been rehabilitated by setting it in a new, strategic context. The possibility of constructing a democratic social ordering had been restated starting in 1970, with the important innovation that ways to do this were tied to values and conceptions of justice. More recently, the implementation theory developed in a strategic setting has enlarged the set of possible social-welfare orderings or social ordering functions.

The effectiveness of policy action required a longer process of reflection on the theoretical and empirical foundations of the various critiques moved to it. However, it was not complete until the possibility of effective policy action in an environment of REs was demonstrated. This has finally been done rather recently, after reflecting on the intrinsic nature of strategic reasoning and making appeal to the equivalence of REs with games. The strategic theory of economic policy also has added theoretical results of relevance for practical policy application. In particular, conditions for not only controllability of the economy but also existence or multiplicity of equilibria have been stated similar to those set by the classical theory of economic policy in a static and dynamic context. In addition, some roles of announcements as a policy tool have been clarified. In fact, these can let policymakers and other players converge on an equilibrium when there are many as an outcome of a game. In a dynamic setting, announcements about future action can also make this effective and eliminate time inconsistency if they allow conditions for controllability to be satisfied.

The theory of economic policy in a strategic setting has been of great help in the theoretical debate on policy effectiveness, leading to a critique of the leading conviction of policy neutrality. We have criticised the literature that is sceptical of government intervention by repeating the same analytical setting as that assumed by this theory. Our models can be useful for serving as a compass for real policy action. However, some relevant assumptions underlying both this theory and the strategic theory of economic policy (i.e. symmetric information about the model of the economy) should be relaxed. In fact, in practice, this is not the case, since the model of the economy differs as between the private and public sectors. Here the government has an important role in convincing the private sector of their superior knowledge. However, until and to the extent that this is not so, the effectiveness of public action, including announcements as to future policy, ought to be assessed in a more realistic framework.

The importance of the new theory as far as not only current policies but also institutions should be underlined. In fact, it has important implications for the theory of institutions owing to the fact that it can suggest whether a unique equilibrium, multiple equilibria or no equilibrium at all can be reached, which impinges on choice of a democratic institutional setting within a country and also has implications for international institutions.

Some issues are still to be settled in terms of the strategic theory of economic policy. First, the issue of coalitions and residual conflicts among players needs to be further investigated. In addition, the concept of decisiveness, as a way to generalise the concept of controllability, should be studied further, especially in its dynamic aspects for its possible impact on stabilisability. Finally, the whole theory, while being useful for crucial theoretical implications of policy action and debates on it, should be specified in a way to further serve this action in practical cases. The next two chapters will do this.

Part II

Economic Policy in the Present Tense

5

The Challenges of the Financial Crisis, Rising Inequality, Secular Stagnation and Globalisation

Economic Policy As a Lame Duck?

In this and the following chapter we introduce elements of realism in our conception of the economic discipline. In doing so, we want both to underline the important feedbacks for the theory that can be derived from a closer approximation to reality and to show the possibility of fruitfully applying our discipline – which has ensured taming of the Great Recession in most countries.

In this chapter we first look at the main issues that have risen to pre-eminence in the last decades, i.e. crisis, rising personal inequalities, a tendency to stagnation and globalisation (Section 5.1). We then deal with the pivotal role of the crisis, for the limits it has imposed on the use of fiscal and monetary policy (Section 5.2) and the need to devise new effective instruments. This, on the one hand, has imposed more stress on monetary policy, as new monetary policy tools and macro-prudential instruments have been introduced or projected (Section 5.3); on the other hand, it has provided an incentive to search for new rules of fiscal policy (Section 5.4) and coordination of macroeconomic tools (Section 5.5). The remaining three sections of this chapter deal with the policy deriving from rising inequality, stagnation and globalisation. The need to issue proper signals to avoid crises or reduce their size will be one of the objects of Chapter 6.

5.1   The 'Bad News': New Economic and Social Issues – The Great Recession

Economic policy has to face hard problems currently. As Blanchard, Dell'Ariccia and Mauro (2010: 10) say, defining a new macroeconomic policy framework is a very difficult task, more than before, but not a desperate one. 'The bad news is that the crisis has made clear that macroeconomic policy must have many targets; the good news is that it has also reminded us that we have in fact many instruments, from "exotic" monetary policy to fiscal instruments, to regulatory instruments. It will take some time, and substantial research, to decide which instruments to allocate to which targets, between monetary, fiscal, and financial policies.'

The bad news aspect is due to the fact that many issues have arisen with evidence at the same time. The Great Recession, rising inequality, secular stagnation and globalisation are the (partly) new issues that have arisen in recent decades. To be true, they had already manifested in the past, but they seemed to be dormant or to have been tamed. This was the case of the crisis, whose main occurrence dates back to the Great Depression of the 1930s, and the ensuing stagnation.[1] Globalisation and rising inequalities within both developed and less developed countries (LDCs) – even if inequality between them decreased – after World War II seemed to have been under control for a while (say, until the 1970s) but re-emerged in the following decades. Even if these tendencies are strictly intertwined, we will try to deal with each one at a time, starting from the crisis.

---

[1] The Great Recession emerged only a few years after Lucas' prediction in his Presidential Address to the American Economic Association – according to which the central problem of macroeconomics, i.e. depression prevention, 'has been solved, for all practical purposes, and has in fact been solved for many decades' (Lucas 2003: 1). The many roots of the crisis are illustrated by Fitoussi et al. (2010).

The recent crisis has been very heavy. The trends in income and employment growth in some important (both Organisation for Economic Co-operation and Development (OECD) and non-OECD) countries are shown in Table 5.1 for the former variable and in Table 5.2 for the latter. The time impact of the crisis has been different across countries. In fact, the United States has been hit very hard, followed by European countries and then Brazil, Russia, India, China and South Africa (BRICS). This difference in timing – similar to the propagation of a wave – has different roots ranging from the nature of the policies implemented in the various countries to the different structural positions of each.

Since its beginning millions of jobs have been lost. The crisis has hit some countries – especially European ones – more than others, driving up the unemployment rate in some countries to peak levels. In the Euro area it rose by around 5 p. p. to around 12 per cent in the 5 years to 2013 (see fig. 5.1), but in some European countries such as Spain it almost tripled, to 23 per cent. As a whole, the impact on OECD countries was not so heavy, reaching the peak in 2009–10 (8.4 per cent) and then slowing down to 5.5 per cent in 2017–18. In the United States the impact has been high until 2010–11, being relatively mild in recent years. Finally, in Japan the peak has been reached by mid-2009, but the country has remained relatively untouched by the crisis. However, it must be realised that in some cases, the unemployment rate underestimates the negative impact of the crisis, even in terms of unemployment. In fact, the number of youth 'Not (engaged) in Education, Employment or Training' (NEET) has increased as an effect of the crisis, almost all major developed countries, except Germany, Japan, Sweden and the UK, from 2007 to 2014, the year which signed the end of the crisis (see fig. 5.2).

The recession has been largely an effect of the pro-market policies enacted in these countries, which have favoured

Table 5.1 *Recent and projected growth rates for real GDP, 2007–17*

	2007	2008	2009	2010	2011	2012	2013	2014	2015	2016	2017
OECD countries											
OECD	2.7	0.2	-3.5	3.0	1.9	1.3	1.2	1.9	2.1	1.8	2.1
Euro area[a]	3.0	0.4	-4.5	2.0	1.5	-0.9	-0.3	1.0	1.6	1.6	1.7
France	2.4	0.2	-2.9	2.0	2.1	0.2	0.6	0.6	1.2	1.4	1.5
Germany	3.4	0.8	-5.6	3.9	3.7	0.6	0.4	1.6	1.4	1.6	1.7
Japan	2.2	-1.0	-5.5	4.7	-0.5	1.7	1.4	0.0	0.6	0.7	0.4
Korea	5.5	2.8	0.7	6.5	3.7	2.3	2.9	3.3	2.6	2.7	3.0
United Kingdom	2.6	-0.5	-4.2	1.5	2.0	1.2	2.2	2.9	2.3	1.7	2.0
United States	1.8	-0.3	-2.8	2.5	1.6	2.2	1.5	2.4	2.4	1.8	2.2
Non-OECD countries											
Brazil	6.1	5.1	-0.1	7.5	3.9	1.9	3.0	0.1	-3.9	-4.3	-1.7
China	14.2	9.6	9.2	10.6	9.5	7.7	7.7	7.3	6.9	6.5	6.2
India	9.8	3.9	8.5	10.3	6.6	5.6	6.6	7.2	7.4	7.4	7.5
Russia	8.5	5.2	-7.8	4.5	4.3	3.5	1.3	0.7	-3.7	-1.7	0.5

Note: Values for 2016 and 2017 are OECD projections.
[a] Aggregate of fifteen OECD countries of the Euro area.
Source: OECD 2016.

Table 5.2 *Recent and projected growth rates for employment, 2007–17*

	2007	2008	2009	2010	2011	2012	2013	2014	2015	2016	2017
OECD countries											
OECD	1.5	0.6	−1.8	0.3	1.0	1.0	0.7	1.3	1.4	1.5	1.1
Euro area[a]	2.0	0.9	−1.9	−0.5	0.2	−0.6	−0.6	−0.6	1.0	1.3	1.0
France	1.7	1.3	−1.0	0.2	0.1	0.2	−0.2	0.1	0.0	0.4	0.5
Germany	2.1	1.0	−0.3	0.8	2.5	1.0	1.0	0.9	0.7	1.6	0.8
Japan	0.6	−0.3	−1.5	−0.3	−0.1	−0.3	0.7	0.6	0.4	0.5	−0.2
Korea	1.2	0.6	−0.3	1.4	1.7	1.8	1.6	2.1	1.3	1.2	1.2
United Kingdom	0.8	0.9	−1.6	0.2	0.5	1.1	1.2	2.3	1.5	1.2	0.6
United States	1.1	−0.5	−3.8	−0.6	0.6	1.8	1.0	1.6	1.7	2.1	1.5
Non-OECD countries											
Brazil	1.6	3.2	0.5	0.7	0.7	1.7	1.4	1.5	0.0	−1.6	0.7
China	NA	NA	NA	NA	NA	NA	NA	NA	NA	NA	NA
India	NA	NA	NA	NA	NA	NA	NA	NA	NA	NA	NA
Russia	2.5	0.6	−2.3	0.7	1.5	1.0	−0.2	0.2	1.1	0.0	−0.2

Note: Values for 2016 and 2017 are OECD projections (NA = not available).
[a] Aggregate of fifteen OECD countries of the Euro area.
Source: OECD 2016.

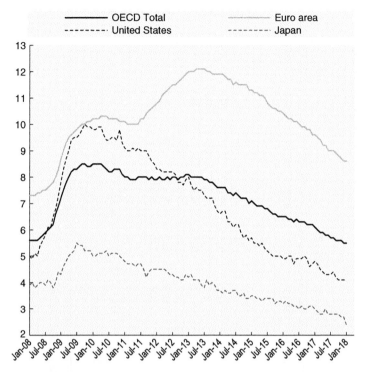

Figure 5.1 *Evolution of the unemployment rate in OECD countries, 2008–2018.*
(Source: OECD 2018)

unregulated growth of the financial sector, as well as other wrong policies, such as preference being given to abating inflation rather than unemployment and the instruments implemented for this (e.g. fiscal consolidation).[2] Unregulated globalisation has made it easier to transmit recessionary impulses from one country to another.

The most important pro-market policy behind the crisis was financial market liberalisation, which increased market

---

[2] 'The short-run costs in terms of lower output and welfare and higher unemployment have been underplayed, and the desirability for countries with ample fiscal space of simply living with high debt and allowing debt ratios to decline organically through growth' has been underappreciated (Ostry, Loungani and Furceri, 2016: 40).

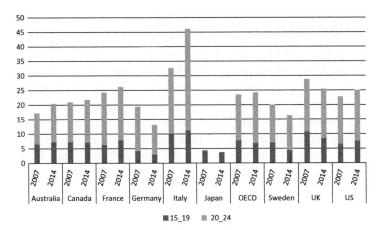

Figure 5.2 *NEETs in major OECD countries, 2007–2014.*
(Source: OECD 2016)

concentration, fed the housing and financial asset bubble[3]
and caused misallocation of resources.[4] As an effect of this
approach, the Fed was largely passive while financial inter-
mediaries and ordinary people took on increasing risk and
allowed the crisis to intensify for more than a year after it had
begun. As the Fed finally tried, but failed, to avoid allowing
the bubble to enlarge, the question arises whether this could
have been avoided by other, more effective and timely policy
instruments such as financial regulation. On the other side of
the Atlantic, the European Central Bank (ECB) action also
raised critiques. After a non-enthusiastic performance since
adoption of the euro, it was not able to prevent the contagion
of private debt into sovereign debt. To be fair, the failures in
the Euro area were related more to its general architecture than
to specific ECB policies. In addition, in the Euro area, other
policies and the general institutional design that were clearly

---

[3] According to Sardoni (2015), a satisfactory explanation of the current
crisis requires abandoning the assumption of free competitive economies
common to many theories, also those critical of capitalism, which offer a
different explanation of the crisis.
[4] An empirical analysis of these effects with reference to the housing bubble
in Spain is in Basco, Lopez-Rodriguez and Moral-Benito (2017).

in favour of free markets nourished the crisis and were unable to stop it for a long time (Acocella 2016b). The interaction of interest rates being stuck at the zero lower bound (ZLB), deflation and private indebtedness ('debt deflation') implies that a reduction of inflation, which usually has the effect of stimulating output, is contractionary (Neri and Notarpietro 2014). The general lesson from the crisis is that we are far from having achieved an optimal institutional design. Alternative explanations of the crisis in terms of other factors have been suggested, but institutions have certainly played an important role in feeding the crisis in the Euro area, as a comparison with the United States easily shows.

The next three sections of this chapter show the need for giving an image to the 'good news' and devising new policies (Section 5.2), in particular, new monetary and fiscal policy tools (respectively, Sections 5.3 and 5.4).

5.2   The Crisis As a Pivot: The Limits to Fiscal and Monetary Policy and the Need to Devise New Policy Tools

The recent financial crisis not only has led to a recession deeper and more severe than any since the Great Depression of the 1930s but also has shown the limits deriving from the previous policy. In addition, its length and size have put stress on both fiscal and conventional monetary tools, risking in any case to leave monetary policy as practically the 'only game in town', to echo the title of Bini Smaghi (2014).

New limits have also arisen. First, they refer to the use of some tools. In fact, soaring public debt has constrained expansionary fiscal policy, whereas zero interest rates have limited conventional expansionary monetary policy. The crisis has overburdened public finances in most countries. The limits to increases in public debt derive from the implied excessive burden thrown on future generations; the risks deriving for the stability of the system, possibly emphasised by the operation of financial markets; and the constraint deriving from high levels of public debt on the potential for fiscal policy to deal with the next negative shocks and secular stagnation. The attitude of governments has changed, and they have set or confirmed limits to public debt or both to it and the public deficit. The United States has confirmed existing constraints to rising debt in absolute terms by only slightly adjusting the ceiling. In the European Monetary Union (EMU), the 'fiscal compact' has set more stringent limits to both deficit and debt as a ratio to gross domestic product (GDP; see Section 3.8).[5] The length of the crisis and the unavailability of fiscal policy have put stress on conventional monetary policy as the ZLB has been reached.

Thus, insurgence of constraints practically implies dropping (at least) one policy tool (fiscal policy) or confining its use within strict boundaries, which is tantamount to the impossibility of respecting the golden rule of economic policy for reaching fixed policy targets and the need to resort to a second-best prospect. The implications for managing public policy thus have been negative, as the set of tools available for a lasting exit from the crisis has been impoverished, thus overburdening monetary action, which, on the other hand, remained stuck at the ZLB.

Hence, the need to (re-)invent a series of unconventional policy measures has arisen, with emphasis being put on monetary action in the long-term section of financial assets, as well as announcements on the future path of policy and possibly recourse to 'helicopter money' (see Section 5.3). Due to the mixed nature of some unconventional policies, response to the crisis has also blurred the distinction between monetary and fiscal policy to the point that the distinction between them may appear to have vanished. Microeconomic prudential rules have been adapted to face systemic risks, giving rise to macro-prudential policies. These new policies

---

[5] By contrast, in 2013, Australia repealed the debt ceiling instituted in 2007.

as well as the double nature of some monetary policies make the case for coordinating all macroeconomic policies, balancing their extent and timing, also in order to ensure proper functioning of democratic institutions. In addition, the need arises to reflect on the adequacy of the low inflation targets inherited from previous decades, which are set at too low a level for the monetary policy to relieve the economy at a sustained pace and reduce soaring public debt.

The issues we will inquire about in dealing with these instruments are as follows. Under what circumstances and through which channel can these new policies be expected to work? What lessons should be learned for the conduct of monetary and fiscal policies, and what roles should be ascribed to the central bank and to government in the future?

5.3   The 'Good News': New Monetary Policies and Macro-Prudential Instruments for Dealing with Crises

In order to enlarge the number of existing policy instruments, monetary policy has searched for unconventional tools (what Blanchard, Dell'Ariccia and Mauro (2010: 10) call 'exotic' instruments) to add to the usual interventions in the short-term market, with the intention of lowering long-term interest rates, which influence investment and thus recovery and growth. This is particularly difficult to do in conditions of ZLB, which prevents the current short-term interest rate and the expected future short-term rates – on which long-term interest depends – from reaching the level that would be required by the market for profitable investment.

The ECB and the central banks of other non-EMU countries (e.g. Denmark, Sweden, Switzerland and Japan) have introduced the practice of negative interest rates since 2014 in order to encourage banks to increase lending. The action, however, has been almost ineffective, and the enduring deflation has really hindered the effort to expand the economy. Instead, two (partially) new instruments, quantitative easing and forward guidance, have been implemented, and another one has been proposed again ('helicopter money'), that deserve more attention for their effectiveness.

5.3.1   Quantitative Easing

'Quantitative easing' is only a partially new monetary policy tool, since a form of it, Operation Twist, had already been used in the 1960s. It tends to lower long-term interest rates in order to increase private investment. The first such measures (usually referred to as Quantitative Easing 1 (QE1)) – addressed to large-scale asset purchases (LSAP) of government-sponsored-enterprise (GSE) debt, agency debt, mortgage-backed securities (MBS) and Treasury securities – began towards the end of 2008 in the United States. The second type of these measures (QE2) started in the second half of 2010 and concentrated on purchases of US Treasury securities. In fact, in September 2011, the Federal Reserve rediscovered Operation Twist, a commitment to extend the maturity of securities held on its balance sheet. In September 2012, a third round of QE was inaugurated, focusing on the purchase of MBS. In the European Union, QE had been implemented first at the beginning of 2015. In addition, other countries have tried it. QE operates directly on long-term interest rates, as public or private bonds are bought against money by the central bank, thus raising their current values and lowering interest rates, which could remedy the fall in the money multiplier and stimulate bank credit supply.[6]

These unconventional operations have been very effective in raising bond values and lowering sovereign yields (Cecioni, Ferrero and Secchi 2011; IMF 2013; Santor and Suchanek 2013) not only in the United States but also in other countries, as an effect of portfolio reallocation and repricing of the risk

---

[6] On QE, see Den Haan (2016).

in global financial markets (Fratzscher, Lo Duca and Straub 2013). They have also helped to lower bank funding volatility and to increase the loan supply (Carpenter et al. 2013). Weale and Wieladek (2014) find that announcements of these operations are associated with increases in output and inflation in the United States and the United Kingdom.

However, relying too much on them for too long can cause a liquidity glut, speculative activities – as the banks can find these operations profitable only for the capital account appreciation of their portfolio – distributional effects and capital movements both in the country where they are implemented and abroad. Moreover, the assets bought by central banks as part of their QE are certainly riskier than short-term government bonds, which could raise problems for the soundness of central banks' balance sheets.

As for distributional effects, QE can affect some persons and institutions positively and some others – at home or abroad – negatively (Bossone 2016; Den Haan 2016).[7] By pushing up asset prices, it benefits richer people and, in particular, those households holding a larger share of financial assets. In addition, this kind of unconventional monetary policy, on the one hand, can become less effective in a liquidity trap due to a diminishing money multiplier (van den End 2014); on the other hand, effectiveness is lower when they are terminated early (Burlon et al. 2016a).

Some – especially Germans, e.g. the Deutsche Bundesbank (2012), the German Constitutional Court (Bundesverfassungsgerich 2014), Sinn (2013) and Weber (2010), cited by De Grauwe and Ji (2015) – have criticised QE for having negative fiscal implications, as sounder countries can be asked to pay the bill in the case of default of some sovereign states. According to Benigno, Nisticò (2015), QE can cause some losses to the central bank if it relieves risky assets from the economy. These measures

---

[7] For this, see also the international spill-overs that we mention below.

would entail some kind of fiscal implication, unless the central bank implements a more inflationary policy to reduce its losses. These losses would increase if the assets bought by the central bank are issued by unsafe borrowers, such as Greece (for this, see Frankel 2014[8]). De Grauwe and Ji (2013, 2015) have shown, however, that QE for the Euro area can be designed in such a way as not to have such implications, at least for all countries in the area, e.g. by establishing that the sales of sovereign bonds are in proportion to the equity shares used for the purchase. In any case, as Armstrong et al. (2015) show, the risk deriving from the QE operations begun in 2015 are to be shared to a limited extent between EU institutions, the Euro system according to shareholdings and, mostly, the national central bank of the issuer. This would limit their burden for stronger countries.

International spill-overs (and thus, again, distributional effects) can derive from QE and other expansionary monetary policy tools. First, they act through the current account, as they imply positive direct and indirect spill-overs of such operations on the GDP of other economies, in particular, of LDCs. It has been estimated that a 1 per cent increase in the US GDP – as derived from expansionary monetary policies – can lead to a 0.2 per cent increase in China's GDP. With reference to QE, a 1 per cent decrease in the policy interest rate in advanced economies can imply a 0.1 to 0.2 per cent increase in the GDP of emerging economies (Blanchard 2016a). Together with these positive spill-overs, there are negative ones, linked to capital movements and exchange-rate changes. Emerging economies have complained about the ensuing macroeconomic and financial instability (Chen et al. 2016).[9] Before 2007, US current account deficits vis-à-vis the rest of the world were a cause underlying the global financial crisis. The crisis, together with the

---

[8] Frankel advises the ECB to buy US bonds, which would have the advantage of lowering the value of the euro, with beneficial effects on exports.
[9] An echo of the instability caused by the cessation of unconventional operations can be found in Cova, Pagano and Pisani (2016).

unconventional policies implemented in this country, put a relative halt to capital inflows. These inflows, however, suddenly appeared again when in 2013 the Fed announced a progressive upholding of the expansionary measures, causing an increase in long-term interest rates in the United States (the so-called taper tantrum), a rise in capital inflows also from the emerging markets and capital losses in these countries. Cooperation could mitigate the undesired effects of negative spill-overs not by bottling them up within their country of origin but by sharing them, in exchange for reciprocity (Engel 2015). However, some authors are sceptical about the possibility of implementing coordination of policies to pursue an international equilibrium that is more efficient than the decentralised one (Blanchard 2016b). Restrictions on capital flows could be implemented by each country to reduce spill-overs, but they are difficult to be introduced by a single country, since it would fear the negative consequences of discrimination from possibly beneficial foreign investment and outflows of foreign capital after the innovation.

The need and the form for international cooperation are highly dependent on circumstances. However, there is at least a case for contacts, exchange of information and dialogue between them

> under normal circumstances that make coordinated action possible in exceptional circumstances ... Global institutions and fora play an essential role for three reasons ... First, they achieve a better understanding and a common assessment of the global spillovers from domestic policy actions and the potential policy trade-offs. Second, even if the scope for coordination is limited in good times, they make coordination possible in bad times. And third, they prompt work at (international) regulatory bodies ... In so doing, they foster risk-sharing through decentralised markets, avoiding the need to coordinate in the first place. (Cœuré 2016: 10)

As a way of concluding on the benefits and dangers of QE, we can say that it is certainly effective and has indeed contributed to the expansion of the United States and the British economy, as well as avoiding a disruptive crisis in the Euro area. However, it should not be relied on too much and for too long, and a smooth exit from it is also necessary for its possibly overall negative international spill-overs.

5.3.2 Forward Guidance

'Forward guidance' may be defined as announcements made about the future stance of policy with the intention of influencing or managing expectations of future policy interventions and hence the expected path of future interest rates and outcomes for the economy.[10] It may be unconditional or indefinite (e.g. 'interest rates will remain low for a considerable – or for an indefinite – period of time') or time dependent ('for two years') or conditional ('interest rates will remain low until unemployment falls below 6.5 per cent'). It can be applied to achieve *controllability* and *stabilisability* of the economic system.

A form of forward guidance was first implemented by the Federal Reserve in August 2003 and again in December 2008 and by the ECB in July 2013. A time-dependent form of forward guidance was introduced by the Bank of Canada and the Swedish Riksbank in April 2009 and by the Federal Reserve in August 2011. The Federal Reserve shifted to conditional forward guidance in December 2012, and this was also adopted by the Bank of England in August 2013. The Fed indicated an unemployment rate of 6.5 per cent and an inflation rate of 2.0 per cent as its targets. No policymaker has hitherto announced marginal rates of substitution between targets or even a 'history-dependent' rule of the kind advocated by Eggertsson and Woodford (2003). However, in some cases, such as in the Euro zone, these can somewhat be inferred by rules stating priorities

---

[10] We do not consider forward guidance in the form of announcements made about the policymaker's projections on the future path of the economy here, although that is always possible and is indeed implied by the projections of the policy instruments – given access to a model of the economy and a matching information set.

of a target or some targets over others. Conditional forward guidance can be thought of largely as a kind of commitment more than an announcement. Forward guidance under the form of the announcement of the central bank's preference function has been termed 'Odyssean' just because it implies some kind of commitment, opposite to the case of 'Delphic' forward guidance, implying some kind of generic and loose engagement (Acocella and Hughes Hallett 2016[11]).

Forward guidance is therefore designed to make the private sector's expectations consistent with the policy intentions of the central bank or government with respect to interest rates, growth and investment – especially at the ZLB (Cœuré 2013). There is some evidence that it has reduced the volatility of expectations (Cœuré 2013; Filardo and Hofmann 2014). On this view, the governor of the Bank of Canada has argued that forward guidance is best used for stabilisation, especially at the ZLB.[12] Various papers provide greater detail on how this policy instrument works.[13]

Forward guidance is not a duplicate of QE but can or should complement it. Suppose that only the latter were implemented. QE should directly act on long-term interest rates, bypassing expectations on them. However, if no assurance were given on future interest rates, the risk might arise of unexpected rises in the interest rate. This would act contrary to the supposed effects of QE. Then forward guidance is useful in that it can or should directly influence the

---

[11] These authors give the meaning indicated in the text to these terms, which had been used with a slightly different meanings before.

[12] Stephen Poloz, Interview in the *Financial Times*, 15 October 2014.

[13] More recently, see Acocella and Hughes Hallett (2016) and Hughes Hallett and Acocella (2016, 2017), who use a macroeconomic model with rational expectations. However, Del Negro, Giannoni and Patterson (2015) point out that the effects of forward guidance can be overvalued when they are drawn from a micro-founded DSGE model. When an overlapping generation model is used, the effects are lower. McKay, Nakamura and Steinsson (2016) show that forward guidance has less power to stimulate the economy when agents do not have complete markets to ensure income risk. If this is the case, a precautionary savings effect tempers their responses to forward guidance as to future interest rates.

expectations of future short-term interest rates by giving assurance on them. Obviously, forward guidance may fail if the expectations are not in line with QE. We will deal with forward guidance longer in Chapter 6.

5.3.3 Helicopter Money

The last type of unconventional monetary policies is 'helicopter money', initially suggested by Friedman (1969) and others (e.g. Haberler 1952) before him.[14] Not very different from helicopter money is the Keynesian idea of digging holes in the ground to bury banknotes and later digging the notes up again (Keynes 1936: 129). Both consist in distribution of money to citizens or to specific categories of agents, under various forms, by base money, grants or tax rebates, possibly financed by money issuance. It could be particularly effective in the case of interest rates stuck at the ZLB. Due to the form that it can take (especially in the case of tax grants), it can also be considered under the heading of fiscal policy and, just because of its mixed, monetary-fiscal, nature, can be more effective than other unconventional operations. In fact, differently from QE, which implies a true asset swap, it injects purchasing power with no counterpart from the agents. More recently, a number of economists have written in favour of helicopter money (Buiter 2004; Reichlin, Turner and Woodford 2013; Bernanke 2016; Draghi 2016; Bossone 2016) as an effective way out of a crisis.[15] Others – e.g. the head of the Reserve Bank of India, Raghuram Rajan (see Rajan 2013) – have indicated their fears

[14] Friedman warned that the money drop should be a one-time event, never to be repeated, in order not to increase market uncertainty, which might translate into a change of the demand for real cash balances. In addition, the money should not be saved, and most importantly, the economy should not be in a state of full employment.

[15] Analogies with helicopter money are shown by 'fiscal currency'. This is an instrument of payment (see Galbraith 2016b) issued and freely distributed by the government that will be accepted for future tax payments and other payments to the state allowing for some discount. Also this currency can circulate among people as a common currency.

of an inflationary pressure – which, frankly, at least in Europe and Japan, is currently not a problem – deriving from this type of unconventional monetary policy.

5.3.4   Instruments for Financial Stability

The recent financial crisis has highlighted the strengthening of financial regulation and supervision, which has gone beyond a purely microeconomic approach. The literature on this topic has soared, involving the foundations of macro-prudential tools – their nature, implementation and effectiveness – together with the need for relations with monetary policy and international coordination.

In this section we deal with the following specific issues that have been the object of study:

1. Identifying asset price bubbles and the unintended consequences of unconventional policies due to the possibility of financial instability;
2. Defining macro-prudential policies beyond micro action to counter instability;
3. Implementing macro-prudential policies;
4. Determining the consequences and effectiveness of these policies; and
5. Coordinating macro-prudential policies at an international level to meet cross-border spill-over effects.

We defer consideration of issues of coordination of all macroeconomic policies to Section 5.5.

5.3.4.1   Identifying Asset Pricing Bubbles and Unintended Consequences of Unconventional Policies

Galati and Moessner (2013) attempted to explain some of the roots of the financial crisis. Overconfidence in the self-adjusting ability of financial markets – helped by improper policies of financial deregulation – led to an underestimation of the consequences of a growing financial sector, increasing indebtedness and financial innovation and reduced risk premia. Soaring asset prices, bubble formation and financial imbalances were some of the consequences.

Some of the underlying theoretical reasons can be traced back to the implausible assumption of complete market participation underlying traditional asset-pricing theories. Limited participation implies a complete change in the properties of models, as even small shocks cause relevant price volatility and multiplicity of equilibria (Allen and Gale 1994). Interbank loans can transmit and amplify shocks and cross-border spill-overs and transmit them from one country to another (Allen and Gale 2000; Nocciola and Zóchowski 2016). The size and extent of unconventional policies to tame the crisis, which have sharply increased liquidity, put emphasis on the risk of new financial booms and asset bubbles and thus on the need to devise proper regulation.

When monetary policy was practically the only possible action for dealing with asset bubbles, the issue had been raised whether it should counteract them. A conclusion derived by Filardo (2001) was that consistently with the prescription of control theory, monetary policy should include asset-price bubbles in its reaction function, if asset prices contain reliable information about the state of the economy, in particular, inflation and output. Now it has been realised that monetary policy can be relieved of some burden if complemented by a suitable regulatory policy. Then the two can be geared together to deal with asset bubbles (see Section 5.5).

5.3.4.2 Defining Macro-Prudential Policies: Beyond Micro Action

Micro-prudential regulation – e.g. quality/quantity of capital, leverage ratio, liquidity requirements – aims at forcing banks to internalise possible losses on their assets to protect deposit insurance funds and reduce moral hazard. This kind of regulation – even if of general application to all banks – does not consider the links between the various financial institutions as well as the pro-cyclicality of the operation of the financial system, which can lead to financial imbalances and systemic risk that cannot be counteracted by simple micro-prudential regulation. In fact, this improves the resilience of individual financial institutions but disregards the issues of the financial system as a whole and can even have pro-cyclical negative effects. Systemic risk can arise from different types of externalities, such as the strategic interaction of financial institutions, which can lead to complementarities during expansions; a generalised sell-off ('fire sales') of financial assets initially due to asset sales of one bank facing difficulties; self-fulfilling equilibria generated by exogenous shocks; amplification mechanisms of negative shocks (e.g. contagion as an effect of linkages); endogenous financial instability; and the propagation of shocks through various kinds of financial links. Macro-prudential regulation has exactly the objective of coping with these externalities and thus increasing the resilience to systemic risk. It consists in many cases of the same tools as micro-prudential regulation, e.g. ceilings on credit, on credit growth or on the loan-to-value ratio, or foreign currency lending, or the debt-to-income ratio, or minimum values of liquidity-related values. These measures can be applied to specific sectors – e.g. a mortgage cap – or to the whole economic system. The former can be particularly efficient because they target the origin of the imbalance. Thus, their potential positive effects are enhanced, while the negative effects on output are lessened. Macro-prudential policies can also be discretionary or rule based – i.e. automatic stabilisers – such as countercyclical capital requirements (higher in times of prosperity, lower during contractions) and cyclically dependent liquidity requirements. In any case, also discretionary macro-prudential policies can and need to be adjusted at different phases of the cycle exactly in order to smooth out cyclicality. The various macro-prudential policies can be combined to better correct systemic risk, but capital requirements are likely to play a crucial role (De Nicoló, Favara and Ratnovski 2012).

5.3.4.3   Implementing Macro-Prudential Policies

Basel III (i.e. the Third Basel Accord) is a global voluntary regulatory agreement on bank capital requirements, agreed to in 2010–11, to be implemented by steps and finally by 31 March 2019. It arose as a reply to the deficiencies in financial regulation revealed by the financial crisis that began in 2007–8. It increases bank liquidity and decreases bank leverage by strengthening capital requirements. In particular, it deals with systemic risk in stating the potential for national financial regulators to introduce 'discretionary counter-cyclical buffers'. This can be done by requiring up to 2.5 per cent of capital during periods of high credit growth. Doubts, however, have been raised about the size of the requirements being enough to address systemic risks (Schoenmaker and Wierts 2015). Other doubts can also arise with reference to the discretionary nature of the change in requirements. We deal with them below.

Any indication about the practical effectiveness of this agreement – even in the process of its implementation – is obviously premature. As to previous tools of macro-prudential policies, Lim et al. (2011) provide a first exploration of available data from forty-nine countries. Many instruments have been shown to be effective in reducing pro-cyclicality, even if their effectiveness is different based on the type of shock faced by the financial sector. Cerutti, Claessens and Laeven (2017) use an even richer data set, exploiting data for 119 countries in the period 2000–13, and find that these policies tend to lower credit supply, the more so in emerging countries. Borrower-based measures – such as loan-to-value and debt-to-income ratios – are effective for most countries, and foreign currency–related measures are effective mainly for emerging markets. Başkaya, Kenç et al. (2016) first draw a distinction between price- and quantity-based tools, the former immediately leading to a change in the price/cost of the various alternatives and the latter putting a limit directly on the amount of the targeted item, either asset or credit. Quantity-based measures reduce total credit growth for all levels of financial development, whereas price-based tools are relatively more effective in the case of financially developed systems.[16]

In addition to the choice of tools, an issue arises about the governance of supervision. Since supervisors have to look at various microeconomic and macroeconomic indicators in order to implement the most appropriate tools, the mandate to be conferred on them is necessarily of the kind of an incomplete contract. Then an issue of principal agent arises, which has consequences on the effectiveness of macro-prudential policies (Masciandaro and Quintyn 2016).

5.3.4.4   Determining the Consequences and Effectiveness of These Policies

When macro-prudential policies of the kind required by the Basel III agreement are implemented, the risk arises as to their effectiveness being impaired as a consequence of Goodhart's law. Rational agents can, in fact, react to the rules and make them ineffective or even dangerous. Moreover, they could anticipate that regulators will tend to be lenient in their countercyclical policies, as an effect of pressures from the financial industry and politicians, thus creating ex ante moral hazard (Horvàt and Wagner 2016). Finally, some macro-prudential policies may be not only ineffective but also counterproductive, as they can increase systemic risk.

Countercyclical capital requirements can add to the problem of excessive correlation of risks, since these can be endogenous. In fact, such requirements 'protect banks against common shocks, but not against bank-specific ones', thus lowering costs from aggregate risk and increasing their incentives to invest in common projects. This can increase systemic risk rather than decrease it. A solution could be that capital

---

[16] The same result is obtained by Nocciola and Żochowski (2016).

requirements are raised for systemic banks (Horvàt and Wagner 2013: 5). This could have the effect of reducing the internationalisation of banking, which is really due also to other factors (Forbes, Reinhardt and Wieladek 2016).

However, in general, macro-prudential policies can reduce the negative effects of capital flows volatility (see e.g. Başkaya, di Giovanni et al. 2016).

5.3.4.5   Coordinating Macro-Prudential Policies at an International Level to Meet Cross-Border Spill-Over Effects

Cross-border financial operations raise international spill-overs, whose sign and magnitude depend – *inter alia* – on the ownership structure of financial institutions and their linkages. Cross-border financial linkages are the channel through which not only shocks and bubbles but also policies (in particular, macro-prudential policies) in one country can transmit to other countries, as shown by the experience of the financial crisis that began in 2007 and of the ensuing policies. This raises a number of issues about how to coordinate national macro-prudential policies in a way to avoid excessive negative spill-overs and reduce their impact. In particular, the existence of a common prudential standard and supervisory body can be useful (Cecchetti and Tucker 2015).[17] In any case, bilateral agreements for stronger reciprocity arrangements between countries and – at least – some notification of the looming bubbles and policy actions are necessary for mitigating leakages. An (un-)intended consequence of monetary and regulatory policies can be banking de-globalisation (Forbes, Reinhardt and Wieladek 2016).

5.4   Searching for New Rules of Fiscal Policy

Since 1995 at least, there has been a continuous decline in real interest rates, which are unlikely to return to pre-crisis levels

---

[17] Applications to a currency union will be discussed in Section 5.5.

(see e.g. Gottfries and Teulings 2015 for the United States and Europe and Fujita and Fujiwara 2016 for Japan).[18] The causes of this decline range from increased global savings and a reduction in global demand for investment to changes in potential output and productivity growth. Regardless of the cause, the decline raises difficulties for conventional monetary policy. The need for either unconventional measures and/or fiscal policy then arises.

On the side of the latter, the impending issues deriving from high public debt have raised the need for revising the rules limiting fiscal policy and devising more proper ones. We are used to speaking of fiscal policy in terms of public balances and debt. However, neither of these variables is a policy instrument. Both are endogenous, as their values depend on the effects on GDP of the true fiscal tools (e.g. tax rates). In addition, both are usually assessed not in absolute terms but rather in relation to the GDP itself or to other indicators such as – for the value of debt – the value of total financial assets.

Projections of these ratios are to be considered from both short- and long-term perspectives. The short-term perspective is certainly useful and is the one that often determines fiscal action, but it can be misunderstanding if its future positive or negative consequences on GDP growth are neglected. Thus, the short- and long-term perspectives must be balanced against each other by considering the consequences of each policy for both. First, fiscal stimulus has a positive short-run impact and from this point of view can improve growth if its short-run effects are high enough to have a positive impact on fiscal sustainability. This is especially true when fiscal policy is accompanied by monetary policy constrained at the ZLB, as output can rise more than debt, which is not overburdened by positive interest rates. Financial markets have an ambiguous role in this respect, which is, however, important, considering

---

[18] Many concepts in this section are drawn from Acocella, Di Bartolomeo and Hughes Hallett (2016: chaps. 8 and 9).

the increased space assigned to – or taken by – them in recent decades. In fact, on the one hand, their tendency to reap short-term benefits can raise doubts about the consistency of this conduct with long-term projections and sentiments. On the other hand, even if their telescopic ability can be questioned, they could set the market sentiments in proper perspective, considering also the positive outlook that should derive from a future growth that is higher for output than for debt. Moreover, this very short-term conduct can negatively influence long-term outcomes.

Obviously, a rise in the budget deficit could not be accepted if it depended not on the choices of a benevolent policymaker but rather on politicians' profligacy. Ensuring this principle motivates suggestions about rules and institutions (including the introduction of fiscal councils) in order to constrain their action. In addition, the issue of how to complement fiscal policy with other policy tools arises from the perspective of containing public debt and other policy objectives (see Section 5.5).

The following subsections deal with the proper yardstick to assess public deficits from a long-term perspective (Section 5.4.1) and to discuss golden rules for the budget and debt target rules as an alternative to more common rules in terms of deficit (Section 5.4.2). Section 5.4.3 investigates the proposal to institute fiscal councils to monitor public finances.

5.4.1   Rules for Public Budgets

Economic research has developed an analysis of public finances that, together with that of macroeconomic disequilibria, describes how a benevolent policymaker might use fiscal policy to respond to economic shocks that affect government debt levels, both directly and indirectly.[19] The balance between the short- and long-run implications of budget

---

[19]   See e.g. Schmitt-Grohé and Uribe (2004), Benigno and Woodford (2004), Leith and Wren-Lewis (2011), Di Bartolomeo, Tirelli and Acocella (2014) and Tirelli, Di Bartolomeo and Acocella (2015).

policy is rather delicate. In particular, after a negative external shock and a deliberate expansionary budget policy, returning debt to its previous level should be undertaken only slowly and carefully, as we have seen in Section 3.8.

As mentioned earlier, we want to describe the policies that would be undertaken by a benevolent policymaker who is able to make credible promises on future behaviour. In the real world, fiscal policy is typically implemented by governments facing the constraints and the incentives of the political process. For a number of reasons, this may result in a 'deficit bias', which accounts at least in part for the rising government debt levels in many economies. Recognising the costs of such bias, it may be advisable to tie the discretionary hands of politicians by adopting some type of fiscal rule, which typically requires debt or deficits to be stabilised over relatively short time horizons.

A number of different fiscal rules could be applied. For example:

1. **Balanced Budget Rules** (which include the European Union's Stability and Growth Pact (SGP) and fiscal compact and can be applied to nominal or structural deficits). Recalling the endogeneity of deficits and debt, the government has only imperfect control over them. One consequence of this is that strict deficit rules are often violated, even in the absence of irresponsible or undisciplined policymakers, especially if correction is required in each year. Monitoring structural deficits (deficits averaged across the cycle), instead, has its own problems, given the difficulty of measuring potential output accurately, which requires measuring the cyclical budget deviations. Rules of this type can be manipulated or be the object of quarrels and lack credibility.

    A variant of this rule is the 'golden rule of deficit financing'. This prescribes that current revenues must match current spending over the cycle. Borrowing is permitted only to fund public investment.[20] As a consequence, growth can be enhanced, and both stability of public finances and a fair distribution of the fiscal burden will be ensured if certain conditions are met. Public investment should generate a rate of return at least equal – or in any case similar – to the private rate. This condition is satisfied depending, on the one hand, on monetary policy reaction and the crowding-out effect and, on the other hand, on the human capital and the externalities created by public investment. The golden rule was implemented in the United Kingdom in 1997 and has been abandoned recently (2009).

2. **Expenditure Rules**, i.e. limits on current spending in aggregate, limits to its growth, or limits in terms of a percentage of GDP or productivity. These may constrain the size of government and its fiscal agenda but will not necessarily achieve sustainable public finances unless a parallel rule places a floor under revenues and a ceiling on debt at the same time. This risks imposing costly austerity and deflationary policies at the same time.

3. **Revenue Rules.** These are even less easy to use. The difficulty is that revenues are both endogenous and more sensitive than spending to the state of the economy. Hence, revenues can easily collapse in a downturn when they are needed most: for example, when the budget comes under pressure in a recession, or when tax rises cause output to shrink yet further, or when austerity policies are imposed.

4. **Debt Rules and Debt Targets.** These imply a primary deficit control rule that needs to be agreed on in order to maintain fiscal sustainability over the medium to long term; we will deal with them in greater detail in the next subsection.

---

[20] There are, however, some possible shortcomings of this rule to consider when implementing it, such as the possibility of excessive emphasis on investment in physical rather than human capital and substitution of public consumption with low productive investment.

5.4.2   Debt Target Rules

Taking the steady-state level of debt out of a rule designed to maximise the rate of economic growth, subject to the golden rule of deficit financing, supplies an optimal *debt target*. This depends in particular on the marginal product of public capital and the discount rate. The lower the latter is, the higher is the optimal value of debt (Furman 2016). Given the tendency towards a reduction in interest rates, the optimal debt value should rise with respect to the computations of past years.

As discussed earlier, primary deficit and debt target rules could be designed in relation to the objective of maximising the rate of economic growth. This would preserve the principle of gradual adjustments. Sustainability is then secured by a primary surplus or deficit set above the growth-adjusted level of interest payments. The degree to which that primary surplus/ deficit exceeds this threshold determines the speed of return to the debt target and hence the debt ceiling that can be tolerated before collapse. There are both benefits and costs for this approach. On the side of the former, there is first the argument that debt, unlike deficit, represents a stock, not a flow. Even if both variables are endogenous with respect to the cycle, the stock nature of debt introduces persistence in the target variable, especially in countries with high levels of public debt. Debt targets therefore can be used to pre-commit or anchor fiscal policies to a path with sustainable public finances without impairing short-run fiscal action as an effect of the flexibility ensured by the existence of a debt ceiling. Second, debt targets focus on the ultimate risk: unsustainable public finances. They should be calculated in a way to maximise the rate of economic growth, taking into account a number of variables, among which are the different productivity of public and private capital, population parameters and age-related spending.[21]

---

[21] Checcherita-Westphal, Hughes Hallett and Rother (2014) show how to calculate a growth-maximising level of debt.

Moreover, debt rules can have the advantage of letting automatic stabilisers operate, thus also reducing the administrative lags that impair a prompt response of discretionary fiscal
policy to situations of crisis where automatic stabilisers are
weak. This is the case for the United States, where this weakness places 'much of the burden for fiscal stimulus on a political system that can be sclerotic on fiscal policy at best', even
if the fiscal system has become more progressive and universal
health insurance has been established (Furman 2016: 13). In
Europe, the action of automatic stabilisers is impaired by the
limits introduced by the SGP and the fiscal compact, especially for some countries, such as Denmark and Sweden.

In addition to a debt target, which is the reference value for
debt sustainability in the long run, a level of debt allowing for
flexibility of public finances for short-term management
should be set at a value that is a little higher than the debt
target, ensuring an absence of fatigue or poorly sustainable
policies, i.e. a *debt ceiling*. The space between debt target and
debt ceiling then allows policymakers to absorb shocks to
fiscal balances, i.e. to trade off good years against bad, confer-
ring flexibility to action for its management. Also, because the
target is a stock not a flow, this produces a *structural* balance
rule without having to calculate accurate cyclically adjusted
deficit figures. The space between the debt target and the highest permitted value will then allow debt ratios to rise in the bad
years (also leaving space for costly structural reforms that
could violate the rules of fiscal balances or solvency) but promote an automatic return in good years. This gives us the
flexibility to contain shocks without sacrificing the discipline
of monetary policy or stable public finances. Ruling out money
growth, the rule to obey to stabilise the debt ratio should be

$$(5.1) \quad p_d = (g - r)d$$

where the symbols mean, respectively, primary public deficit, growth rate, real interest rate and current level of the
debt/GDP ratio.

A balanced budget rule is neither necessary nor sufficient to this end. The primary budget can be positive or negative and can be geared according to the difference between the growth rate, the real interest rate and the initial value of the debt/GDP ratio. Otherwise, the debt burden will rise. Notice that neither the European Union's fiscal compact nor the United Kingdom's new Debt Commission Rule satisfy (5.1). These rules have created too much austerity, and the debt/GDP ratio has increased as an effect of their implementation (see Section 3.8).

On the side of the costs of this rule, it should be said that the level of sustainable debt (like that of potential growth, on which structural deficits depend) is also to some extent debatable, as it can be calculated only if the marginal product of public capital deriving from public investment can be identified with some reasonable approximation.

One implication of these observations is that it is easier to reduce a debt burden, or prevent its further increases, if r is reduced or if g is increased – the more so the larger is the existing debt burden d. In the Euro area at least, reducing r is problematic because monetary policy does not lie within the control of governments but pertains to an independent entity. However, debt restructuring, or announcements of aggressive moves to reduce budget deficits, will, if credible, lead financial markets to suppose that future financing requirements will fall and that the risk premia currently imposed need not be imposed on future borrowing. This would be a slow process because r refers to the *average* interest paid on existing debt, whereas reduced risk premia or interest rates would apply only to new or refinanced debt.

The alternative, raising g, seems more attractive. The growth rate is not a policy instrument. However, the government can influence g through public investment and structural reforms. The usual approach is to take steps to reduce the size of the public sector via wage and employment reductions; reduce the non–wage costs imposed on employers (shifting them onto employees; or using reforms to pensions or other benefit schemes to lighten the contributions levied on employers). Alternatively, we can reform the tax system to shift the burden from income, profits and employment taxes to consumption taxes or user costs; and introduce measures to encourage the private sector to limit wage settlements or increase productivity and R&D. The reductions in unit labour costs will lower domestic prices relative to competing economies (a *real* devaluation). Finally, public investment should be raised, in particular by creating infrastructures useful to give incentives to private investment, notably for energy, education and research. Private investment, instead of being crowded out by public expenditures, could indeed be crowded in not only for the positive effects of these policies on growth but also because of interest rates being stuck to the ZLB or, in any case, monetary policy being expansionary (Furman 2016).[22]

At this point, an analysis of alternative fiscal settings cannot omit mention of federal structures, where there is a federal fiscal authority insuring states against asymmetric regional shocks. This is done if a proportional (or, better, a progressive) income tax accruing to this authority, accompanied by cyclical (or, better, countercyclical) expenditures and transfers, can compensate the states (or regions) hit by a negative shock. The disadvantage of the states, in a nonfederal government, of having to accumulate debt incurred in a sovereign debt crisis thus would be avoided. Federalism would ensure that a currency area, possibly not satisfying the requirements of an optimal one, will survive asymmetric shocks.[23]

With reference to the United States, Sachs and Sala-i-Martin (1992) found that a one-dollar reduction in a region's per-capita

---

[22] Perotti (2014) is, however, a bit cautious about these positive effects for at least two reasons: on the one hand, he mentions the negative experience of some countries and, on the other, he notes the negative effects of this policy for savers.

[23] Sachs and Sala-i-Martin (1992) were good prophets in forecasting in 1992 that without the insurance mechanism provided by federalism, the entire process of monetary unification could be endangered.

personal income can trigger a reduction in federal taxes of about 34 cents, together with an increase in federal transfers of about 6 cents, i.e. a net federal contribution to disposable per-capita income of states between 33 and 50 per cent.

More recent studies have assessed the differential impact of a federal union on regions as a consequence of the asymmetric shock that hit Europe. Among them, Darvas (2010) underlines that federalism would have boosted confidence of the private sector and the political coherence of the Euro area and given scope for greater redistribution, risk sharing and a federal countercyclical fiscal policy to counteract the negative effect of consolidation in indebted countries (states). However, a note of caution on the absolute superiority of a federal design comes from Darvas himself, drawing on Aizenman and Pasricha (2010), as moral hazard about countercyclical fiscal policy also has been a major consideration in the United States. In fact, moral hazard can derive from common-pool and competitive borrowing considerations by states expecting a federal government bailout when needed; at the federal level, doubts can arise as to debt sustainability in the absence of plans for consolidation.

Henning and Kessler (2012) emphasise that any brake established on state budgets, as the Euro zone has done with the fiscal compact, being pro-cyclical, is not sustainable without a countervailing stabilisation action at the European Union's level, which needs a sufficiently high level of the central budget. In other words, any rigidity brought at the lower level that also limits the operation of automatic stabilisers should be compensated by flexibility at the higher level. From this point of view, the case of the United States is of particular relevance.

5.4.3 The Issue of Fiscal Policy Councils

Institutions responsible for monitoring the economic health of the world's larger economies (IMF, European

Commission) have recommended that politicians place themselves under the scrutiny of an independent fiscal council. Such monitoring can remind policymakers of the need to take account of the long-run sustainability of public and private finances. A fiscal council would highlight this whenever the policies being pursued look likely to endanger that sustainability. The key point is that this monitoring has to be forward looking. The purpose of this type of fiscal council would be to increase credibility and commitment to a set of sustainable fiscal policies and to make politically neutral monitoring available to the economy as a whole.

The Swedish Fiscal Policy Council has a mandate to comment on and recommend improvements to existing policies, especially when there is a risk of unsustainable levels of public debt or extreme tax liabilities or when there is a chance to reach those targets more cheaply. Where necessary, it can ask for explanations of and justifications for certain types of communications and recommend improvements to them. In practice, it has availed itself of the chance to do so (Calmfors 2012). The Swedish Fiscal Policy Council is also asked to examine the prospects for growth, employment, income distribution and structural reform programmes.

The United Kingdom's Office of Budget Responsibility is asked to provide independent forecasts of future fiscal revenues and budget positions, including the implications for growth and employment that may affect the fiscal position. It may use its own data and assumptions but only in the Treasury/Her Majesty's Revenue and Customs (HMRC) models. It may not examine or comment on the other targets of economic policy or the merits of alternative policies. The accent here is on forecasting rather than policy efficiency. Neither this agency nor the Swedish council is allowed to be involved in policy advocacy.

Reduced tasks are assigned to the European Fiscal Board, established in October 2016, whose terms of reference are to evaluate the implementation of EU fiscal rules, to advise the

European Commission on the fiscal stance appropriate for the Euro area as a whole, to cooperate with Member States' national fiscal councils and, upon request, to provide ad hoc advice on fiscal matters to the EC.

An important caveat must be added. First, adding this institution to the fiscal budget office, while supplying independent advice, also introduces another debatable source of information, as an assessment of debt sustainability now would come from two sources. It is true that one can be biased. However, no such assessment can be objective. In the end, sustainability assessments and policies are policymakers' responsibility. With respect to this, the argument can be raised as to the possibly short time horizon of governments' duration with respect to the time span needed to ascertain debt sustainability. The solution to this is twofold. On the one hand, institutional arrangements that warrant a sufficient length of duration of governments should be devised. On the other, citizens should be in a position to assess politicians' conduct and performance, which again is a task of optimal institutions, an issue we will return to in subsequent chapters.

Some independent researchers have suggested institution of fiscal councils as a way for ensuring 'fine tuning'. They would suggest short-term adjustments to the budget, whereas democratically elected authorities would be responsible for the 'coarse tuning' of fiscal policy (Wren-Lewis 2003; Arestis 2009).[24]

5.5   Coordinating Macroeconomic Policies: Down in the Trenches or Clearing Clouds for the Future?

In devising different policies, in particular, those of a macroeconomic type, the interactions between their effects must be recognised, even apart from the notation that some policies,

---

[24] More generally, on the issue of fiscal councils, see Von Hagen (2013) and Wruuck and Wiemer (2016), in addition to the references already given.

such as helicopter money creation, have a double nature, both of a monetary and a fiscal policy type, and that QE also can have fiscal effects, in particular, due to the fact that at the ZLB there is no clear distinction between the two policies (King 2014). In addition, there can be either substitutability or complementarity between the effects of the various policies that only a general model of the economy can account for. Policies are substitutes if each has a similar type of effect on some objective. This is the case e.g. of monetary, macroprudential and fiscal policies directed at raising employment and income. Policies are instead complementary if they operate better together. In this case, possibly each of them can be preferentially directed at one objective, which implies a kind of assignment of each instrument to some preferential target. A recent example of this kind of 'appropriate' assignment of instruments to targets has been derived by Menna (2016); in a dynamic stochastic general equilibrium (DSGE) model with non-Ricardian consumers, monetary policy can stabilise inflation, while fiscal policy can cope with the effects of productivity shocks on income distribution. In any case, the use of each instrument must be calibrated, as certainly all of them have an influence on all the targets.

In the rest of this section we deal with two specific interactions between policies, on the one hand, between monetary and fiscal policy and, on the other, between monetary and macro-prudential policy. The need to fight time inconsistency and inflation led some authors (not only, as mentioned earlier, Sargent and Wallace 1981 and Rogoff 1985a but also Walsh 1995) to require separation between monetary and fiscal policy and, in addition, monetary leadership and commitment. A consensus also gradually emerged on a similar position. This has lasted for three decades. Starting from the Great Recession, a rather unexpected event, it has somewhat lost its appeal, depending on the need to counteract the crisis, and a new orientation seems to have emerged afterwards.

However, the policy and the prescriptions that can be derived from it have been or are still almost generally accepted.

With the emergence of the crisis, the primary objective of economic policy changed from one of non-inflationary expansion to higher employment and income growth. This was pursued for a time by both expansionary monetary and fiscal policies, the latter being also to some extent coordinated at an international level, especially at the onset of the crisis. The crisis also required bailout interventions, in the immediate term, and the design of macro-prudential policies afterwards. The resilience of the crisis to policy measures (in most cases monetary action, after 2009), sometimes badly designed for a while, as in the Euro-area, has produced a rise in private and public debt not only in absolute terms but also with respect to GDP (Alcidi and Thirion 2016). This again required some kind of strict coordination between macroeconomic policies and, especially in the European Union, discarding the very strict target of non-inflationary monetary policy complemented by tight fiscal policy. Coordination, however, has not materialised, even if monetary policy is now stuck to the ZLB.

The 'old view' of the 1980s and the 1990s about the role of monetary and fiscal policies has changed from a number of perspectives. Innovative results also have emerged for coordination of the various policies. From the point of view of the results of the leaderships of different instruments, Hughes Hallett (2008) had challenged the old view by pointing out that – in a world of independent authorities in charge of different instruments – fiscal leadership leads to better outcomes not only for output but also for inflation and fiscal balances.[25]

---

[25] Acocella, Di Bartolomeo and Tirelli (2007) had already found that fiscal leadership has beneficial effects, confirming previous results obtained by Dixit and Lambertini (2001), Leitemo (2004) and Onorante (2006). However, this is true only with a conservative central banker. Central bank preferences also affect the desirability of fiscal coordination in a monetary union. In fact, contrary to Beetsma and Bovenberg (1998), they found that fiscal coordination improves outcomes in the case of a

In addition, almost as a preparation for the change induced by the crisis, it was shown that a changing degree of monetary conservatism and independence based on the contingencies can be desirable and produce sensible gains, in particular, if the economy is hit by a big shock such as a natural disaster or a banking crisis (Niemann and von Hagen 2008). As to the risk of time inconsistency, this can be avoided by well-designed and well-coordinated economic policies if governments have a long enough time horizon and sufficient instruments to control the economic system. Time inconsistency and the need for a commitment technology thus may appear only in certain cases (Acocella, Di Bartolomeo and Hughes Hallett 2013).

The new orientation is not generally agreed upon. A recent paper, in fact, shows that in a situation with multiple equilibria, by letting players move with a certain fixed frequency – which allows policies to be committed or, alternatively, rigid for different periods of time – monetary commitment can ensure a Pareto-efficient outcome (Hughes Hallett, Libich and Stehlík 2014). Contrary to this result, other analyses show that a fiscal leadership strategy can lead to a Pareto improvement from the perspective of both economic authorities (Cabral and Díaz 2015).

Apart from the issue of leadership, the extent to which monetary policy can relieve fiscal pain is worth discussing. Usefulness of a rise in the optimal inflation rate (Section 3.5) has already been underlined as a way to reduce not only present but also future public obligations. Moreover, monetary policy can be useful because unconventional monetary policies can rule out self-fulfilling sovereign default (Corsetti and Dedola 2016).

Cooperation also has an international dimension. This topic has come again to the forefront recently, as conventional

conservative central banker, whereas it leads to worse outcomes with a populist one.

monetary policy seems to be trapped at the ZLB and fiscal policy is impaired by rising debt. In this situation, the initial shock in a country can be exacerbated by the appreciation of the terms of trade of that country, and the shock propagates internationally. It cannot be countered unless common policies of low interest rates are carried out and complemented by fiscal policy (Cook and Devereux 2013).

The need then arises for a coordinated action both internally – by making joint use of monetary and fiscal policies[26] – and internationally. While the former seems to be feasible prima facie (except in the European Union), the latter appears less implementable. And this can even impair the feasibility of the former. In fact, at least during crises, the feasibility of coordinating monetary and fiscal policies at home depends on the prospect of the fiscal multiplier being high enough to lead to fewer deficits and debts. However, in an open economy, the multiplier is certainly lower, unless other countries also implement the same kind of expansionary policy.

Coordinating monetary and macro-prudential policies brings about a problem similar to coordination of monetary and fiscal policies, as both policies affect real economic variables. They are not mere substitutes and in some cases can be complements.

Economic outcomes are superior if monetary and macro-prudential policies are closely coordinated, especially when economic fluctuations are driven by financial or housing market shocks, as both macro-prudential and monetary policies have an influence on financial imbalances and inflation and output (Angelini, Neri and Panetta 2011; Guibourg et al. 2015). Galati and Moessner (2013), however, note that even if superiority of coordination should be recognised, practical problems, such as the lower frequency of macro-prudential decisions, imply that authorities governing these should

[26] Coordination would be particularly useful in a situation of crisis where there is a high level of outstanding debt. As mentioned earlier, debt can even be reduced when multipliers are high.

be the Stackelberg leader, similarly to what happens when dealing with monetary and fiscal policy coordination. A problem arises if macro-prudential regulation targets not only financial imbalances but also real stability. In this case, gains from coordination with monetary policy can be high. However, if the instruments are kept separated, each policy can be assigned to the target for which it is more effective: monetary policy targeting inflation and the output gap and macro-prudential regulation addressing financial stability (Svensson 2012). As to institutional arrangements, most authors agree that both policies can be implemented by central banks, which have superior monitoring abilities.

The source of financial imbalance is particularly relevant for small open countries such as emerging-market economies. If these economies have a large amount of foreign borrowing, this can typically cause financial imbalances that could explode after a financial shock. Coping with them by monetary policy – rather than using macro-prudential tools – is likely to aggravate financial instability (Ozkan and Unsal 2014).

In a monetary union, macro-prudential policies could be useful at the union level, unless the probability is low that financial imbalances arise at that level. This can be the case when integration of national banking sectors is incomplete, and there are heterogeneous financial cycles across countries. In these conditions, financial imbalances tend to arise mainly locally. This makes national macro-prudential policies necessary as a way to avoid financial imbalances and systemic crises at that level, without forcing the union-wide monetary policy to implement contractionary action or implying a union-level macro-prudential action (Kok, Darracq Pariès and Rancoita 2015). Otherwise, i.e., if financial cycles are common to the union area, application of the Tinbergen principle states that in order to ensure two targets – price and financial stability – monetary policy should be complemented by macro-prudential policy at the same level, and their coordination is equally desirable, given synergies or trade-offs between the targets (Boeckx et al. 2015). Macro-prudential policy at a union-wide level is particularly necessary in a situation where a prolonged expansionary monetary policy could feed common financial imbalances. Macro-prudential policies at the country level in a monetary union can help monetary policy and reduce changes in the nominal interest, partially substituting for the lack of national monetary policies (Brzoza-Brzezina, Kolasa and Makarski 2013; Quint and Rabanal 2014). In addition, macro-prudential policies can deal with local risks, avoiding the formation of asset bubbles, without the need to alter the expansionary stance of monetary policy (Visco 2015; Burlon et al. 2016b).

5.6   Fighting Inequalities

In this section we deal, in turn, with the following issues: the reasons for being interested in inequality and its effects on policy targets, measurement of inequality, causes of inequality and policies against inequality. To each of them we will devote one of the following subsections.

5.6.1   The Reasons for Being Interested in Inequality and Its Effects on Policy Targets

We are interested in income and wealth distribution for a number of reasons. First, we are interested because they are indicators of equity and fairness, which are important requisites for social cohesion (on this, see Wilkinson and Pickett 2009). Inequality is also important for health, education, political and economic stability (especially to avoid low aggregate demand and crises due to the lower propensity to consume of richer households). Moreover, inequality matters for its intergenerational effects, as a poor person tomorrow is likely to be the son of a poor person today (Raitano and Vona 2015; Franzini and

Raitano 2016). In addition, it has a negative impact on growth (Cingano 2014). Finally, it tends to reproduce itself over time, as it generates a conservative shift in sentiment among both the rich and the poor (Kelly and Enns 2010). The effects of poverty and inequality on long-term growth have been the object of inquiry of a number of modern theoretical and empirical studies that reach different conclusions.

Let us first deal with theoretical analyses. Voitchovsky (2009) indicates both the positive and the negative effects of inequality on growth. The former are linked to the top part of the income distribution, as this can boost savings available for investment unless they nourish corruption and rent seeking.[27] The latter are linked to the share of the bottom part of the distribution, as the poor cannot save or are trapped in a loop where high fertility rates, low education and low health perpetuate their state. It is true that the economic motive behind human action pushes towards the prospect of a higher income. Accordingly, some authors hold that inequality can have a positive influence on growth because it provides incentives for innovation and entrepreneurship (Lazear and Rosen 1981). However, just because of this, inequality can discourage effort by the poor (ILO 2015: 19, 20). In poor countries, inequality can allow at least some individuals to acquire a good education and accumulate the minimum needed to start businesses (Barro 2000).

But inequality may be harmful for growth because it: i) deprives the poor of the ability to stay healthy and accumulate human capital (Perotti 1996; Galor and Moav 2004; Aghion, Caroli and Garcia-Peñalosa 1999); ii) generates political and economic instability that reduces investment (Alesina and Perotti 1996); and iii) impedes the social consensus required to adjust to shocks and sustain growth (Rodrik 1999). The relationship between inequality and growth may be nonlinear, as in

---

[27] This is due to the higher propensity to saving of the rich (Kaldor 1957).

the theoretical model of Benhabib (2003), in which increases in inequality from low levels provides growth-enhancing incentives, while increases past some point encourage rent-seeking and lower growth (Ostry, Berg and Tsangarides, 2014: 8). Finally, Ravallion (2016) traces the various reasons underlying a negative impact of inequality on growth. Then different possible effects are at play. In order to assess whether positive or negative effects prevail, empirical analyses can be useful. We refer to only some of them. By exploiting a new data set offering information on inequality, redistribution and growth, Ostry, Berg and Tsangarides (2014) find a positive effect of equality on growth on average across countries and over time. The negative impact on growth of different features of inequality is found by Cingano (2014), who exploits a harmonised data set covering the OECD countries over the past thirty years. Redistributions typically enhanced growth. Higher growth causes a narrowing of inequality, which also supports faster and more durable growth. In any case, there seems to be no evidence that redistributive policies are harmful to growth unless they are of an extreme kind. Granger causality shows the existence of a double-direction effect between growth and inequality: inequality has a negative impact on growth, whereas growth positively influences inequality, but this latter effect is much lower than the former. In rich countries, lagged inequality is positively correlated with growth, whereas in poor countries, both correlations are negative and significant (Pagano 2004). Banerjee and Duflo (2003) use non-parametric methods and find an inverted U-curve between inequality and growth. This is consistent with Benhabib (2003) and could explain the inconclusiveness of other studies.

However, these empirical analyses can only indicate some possible regularities across countries and cannot be considered as diriment. In fact, history, the whole set of institutions and the economic and social conditions of each country can be decisive in indicating the possible effects of inequality on growth and other outcomes. Institutional differences can influence growth, as investment in physical and human capital depends on the security of property rights and the efficiency of policies (North 1981). The direction of causality from institutions to growth has been controlled in an attempt to find an exogenous variation of the former among countries colonised by Europeans. Institutions can emerge and persist that are inefficient, i.e., do not enhance growth, because of politically powerful elites, who dictate policies for rent extraction from the rest of the society (Acemoglu, Johnson and Robinson 2001).

5.6.2   Measurement of Inequality

Inequality has a multidimensional nature (Aaberge and Brandolini 2014). It can refer to a number of 'spaces', such as consumption, income, wealth, utility and capability. The most common spaces are income and wealth. Utility and capability are less common and more difficult to assess. For each space there can be different dimensions. As to income, dimensions of equality can be factor, personal or geographic distribution. Similar dimensions can be the object of analysis of other indicators. Wealth inequality can refer to total wealth, net of debt; specific wealth items such as houses and land; or financial wealth. For each space and dimension, different indices can be calculated. For example, personal distribution of income can be assessed using synthetic indicators such as the Gini or Theil index or more detailed indices, referring to deciles, quartiles or others.

Measurement of inequality is preliminary to any analysis and policy indication. Inequality of personal income and wealth seems to change from one period to the next. In addition, even if some common traits are discernible for the various countries, the size and trends of inequality are often divergent. Finally, the indices used for measuring such traits also can differ. But differences, rather than being detrimental, can be of help in detecting some sources of inequality.

Let us consider income inequality first and then wealth inequality. Income distribution can be assessed not only at a country level but also at a global level. We have different measures of equality in each case. The first such measure calculates inequality between nations across mean incomes without population weighting. The second weighs the mean income of each country by its population. The third, global inequality, is similar to the measure of personal income inequality within a country, as it refers to the income of each person (or family) in the world. The three indexes show a different trend through time (see Figure 5.3), as the first index has increased from 1950 to 2000 and then has decreased. The second index is continually decreasing, especially after 1990, mainly because of the rapid growth of two populous countries, China and India. Global inequality weighted by population continually decreases as an effect of the higher dynamics of population in developing countries. The third index, i.e. global inequality, as measured by the global Gini coefficient, is available only for the two decades after 1988 and oscillates from one year to the next. This is much higher than inequality within specific countries, being almost twice as high as in the United States, which, in turn, is higher than in Sweden (Milanovic 2013). Below we will deal only with the measurement of income inequality for specific countries and for the world as a whole.

As to income inequality within specific countries, the findings of various studies, referring to different periods, countries and indicators, differ. From the end of the Civil War to the start of World War II, the United States shows a profile of rising personal income inequality in terms of the Gini coefficient, mainly as an effect of rising monopolisation. The picture is rather different for European countries (Atkinson 2013: figs. 1–3). A general feature of all these countries is that 'it was the wars of the twentieth century that, to some extent, wiped the past and transformed the structure of inequality' (Piketty 2013: 118, English edn).

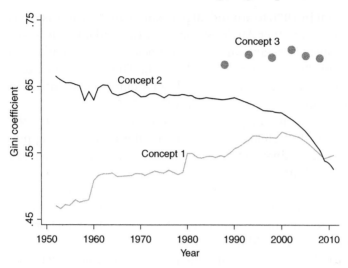

Figure 5.3 *International and global inequality, 1952–2011.*
(Source: Milanovic 2013)

More recently, the trend in income inequality has changed.
With reference to the last three decades, inequality – again
in terms of the Gini index – has risen more in transition countries (mainly the Baltic countries), the United States, the United
Kingdom and other English-speaking countries, followed by
some Nordic countries. It has increased less in other countries,
such as Italy, and has remained largely unchanged in Austria,
Denmark, France and Germany, in particular, after the eruption
of the Great Recession (Salverda et al. 2014). Some reversal of
inequality has taken place more recently in some South
American countries, partly as an effect of lower interest rates
and higher commodity prices, and in some cases due to a retreat
in many places from the free-market policies enacted in the
1980s and 1990s (Galbraith 2016).

Using a measure of personal inequality different from the
Gini index, this picture is confirmed, and some aspects of
the changes are enlightened. In the United States, the share of
the top 1 per cent has almost more than doubled from 8 to 9

per cent in 1976 to around 20 per cent in 2011, whereas it has risen less in other Anglo-Saxon countries and much less – or has stayed constant – in major European countries and Japan (Piketty 2013; Alvaredo et al. 2013). The same index also indicates a sharp rising inequality for emerging countries in the last three decades (see Figures 5.4 to 5.6).

As to world inequality, data are only available for the decades after 1998. However, they offer an interesting picture of the gainers and losers. If all the income recipients in the world are ordered from the poorest to the richest as in Figure 5.7, the gainers were mostly low- to medium-income earners from developing countries[28]; in addition, low- to medium-income earners in developed countries lost or had very low gains (Milanovic 2016).[29]

Strictly tied to personal inequality of income is personal inequality of wealth, which is even higher than income inequality. Today, in the second decade of the twenty-first century, inequalities of wealth that had supposedly lowered or disappeared are close to regaining or even surpassing their historical highs (Piketty 2013: 471, English edn). In what follows we will try to throw light on the causes of the rising inequality, both of income and of wealth.

5.6.3   Causes of Inequality

As to the causes of these trends, if we refer only to post–World War II experience, a reduction in the Gini coefficient had been fostered until around 1980 by Keynesian policies, active direct redistribution through the public budget and policy interventions in labour and capital markets. After 1980, the rise in inequality was given an important push by pro-market policies favouring liberalisation of goods, labour and capital markets and tax policy.

---

[28] Not the poorest, who were 'locked out of growth'.
[29] These were mostly workers displaced by trade, foreign investment and, to some extent, immigration.

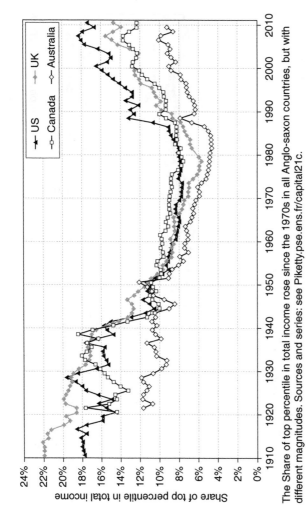

The Share of top percentile in total income rose since the 1970s in all Anglo-saxon countries, but with different magnitudes. Sources and series: see Piketty.pse.ens.fr/capital21c.

Figure 5.4 *Top 1 per cent income shares in Anglo-Saxon countries, 1910–2010.* (Source: Alvaredo et al 2013)

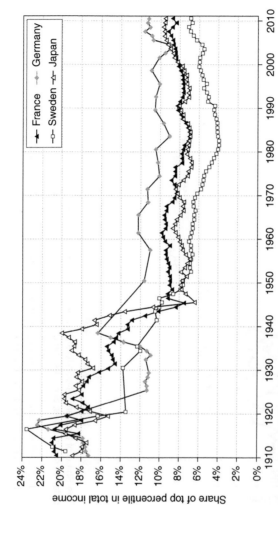

As compared to Anglo-saxon countries, the share of top percentile barely increased since the 1970s in Continental Europe and Japan. Sources and series: see piketty.pse.ens.fr/capital21c.

Figure 5.5 *Top 1 per cent income shares in Continental Europe and Japan, 1910–2010.* (Source: Alvaredo et al 2013)

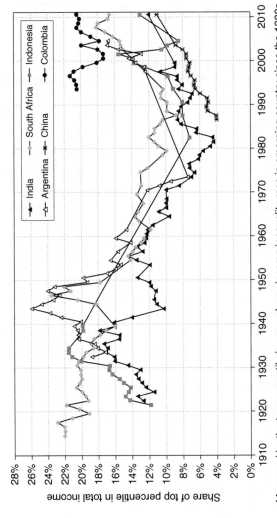

Measured by the top percentile income share, income inequality rose in emerging country since the 1980s rank below US level in 2000–10. Sources and series: see piketty.pse.ens.fr/capital21c.

Figure 5.6 *Top 1 per cent income shares in emerging countries, 1910–2010.* (Source: Alvaredo et al 2013)

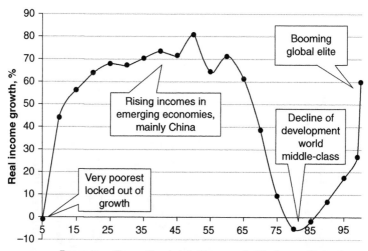

Figure 5.7 *Real income growth by percentile of global income distribution, 1988–2008.*
(Source: Milanovic 2013)

In fact, in advanced countries, the liberalisation of markets favoured a drop in earned income, which can be seen from both unadjusted and adjusted labour's share of national income. The former has fallen by around 10 per cent in the three decades to 2010 (Tridico 2017). The latter, ranging in 1991 from 59 to 66 per cent based on country, has fallen by around 4 per cent (Franzini Pianta 2016) (see Figures 5.8 and 5.9).

The role of tax policy is relevant. Its change is the first cause of the rise in the top 1 per cent share of income, as top income tax rates have been lowered (see Table 5.3).[30] Also relevant have been the changing bargaining power of different income earners, individualisation of pay and capital income deriving from accumulation of wealth, favoured also by lower inheritance tax rates (Alvaredo et al. 2013). Moreover, the

---

[30] See Steinmo (1993) and Pedone (2015), who mainly refer to the actual economic, social and political developments determining changes in tax policy in more than a century.

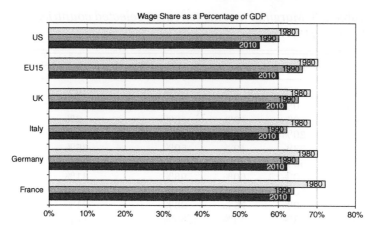

Figure 5.8 *Wage shares as a per cent of GDP, various countries, 1980, 1990, 2010.*
(Source: Tridico 2017)

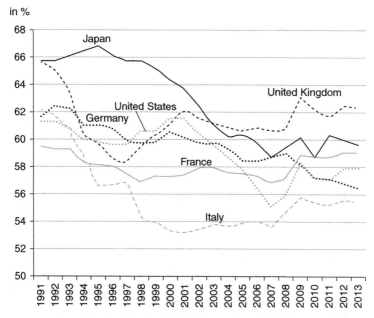

Figure 5.9 *Adjusted share of labour income in GDP in selected G20 countries, 1991–2013.*
(Source: Franzini Pianta 2016)

Table 5.3 *Marginal income tax rates, selected countries (1900–2013)*

	France	Germany	United Kingdom	United States
1900	0%	3%	0%	0%
1909	0%	3%	8%	0%
1913	0%	3%	8%	7%
1918	20%	20%	53%	77%
1928	33%	40%	50%	25%
1939	53%	60%	83%	79%
1941	60%	60%	98%	81%
1944	70%	60%	98%	94%
1951	60%	75%	98%	91%
1964	53%	53%	89%	77%
1980	66%	56%	75%	70%
1988	57%	56%	40%	28%
2000	61%	51%	40%	40%
2005	56%	42%	40%	35%
2013	53%	45%	45%	40%

Source: Pedone 2015.

combination of inflation and tax policies implemented has an influence on distribution, as discussed in Chapter 3.

But some of the underlying factors are unclear. Structural imbalances internal to countries – but also tied to financialisation, international relations and the global distribution of capital – are likely to be relevant. Inverse relationships between income inequality, on the one hand, and financialisation, weakened labour market institutions (for a decline of union density and a reduction in employment protection) and reduced public social spending, on the other, are found by Tridico (2015). It is not strange that income inequality rose less in countries that adopted different policy attitudes, such as some Scandinavian countries. By contrast, the surge in inequality did not derive from technology, or better to say, its role is disputed. The role of education can also be disputed, as in addition to it inequality can be created or

amplified by factors deriving from its intergenerational transmission due to networks, soft skills and other factors influencing inequality of opportunities, which are behind the
so-called Great Gatsby curve (Corak 2013).

Only partly, and indirectly, was it due to globalisation of
goods movements. However, to some extent, immigration
and, mainly, financialisation, the liberalisation of goods
and capital movements and the capital imbalances that
have been created in many countries and areas – such as
Europe – have nourished a rise in capital shares, capital
gains, bubbles, financial crises and inequalities (Tridico
2012; Duménil and Lévy 2014; Bogliacino and Maestri
2014, 2016; Stiglitz 2015b).[31] An idea of the rising bubbles
in the 2000s can be drawn from Figure 5.10.

In addition, globalisation has been given an incentive
precisely by pro-market policies and has led to some scaling
back of the welfare state and other policies in favour of equity.[32]
Similarly, the role of increased education, in particular, in
Europe, is not clear probably because 'the simple increase of
educational participation and attainment is too broad a concept
for a clear answer to be given' (Ballarino et al. 2014: 144).

The high inequality of wealth is due to demographic reasons
(wealth is higher for older people, who represent a higher share
of the population) and the inclusion in wealth of debt as a
negative component. This enlarges the scale of wealth inequality simply because some people's wealth can be negative. The

---

[31] As discussed earlier, the role of technology and globalisation is disputed.
For example, a recent paper (Jaumotte, Lall and Papageorgiou 2013) has
derived from a panel of fifty-one countries over a twenty-three-year period
from 1981 to 2003 that the rise in income inequality derives from an impact
of technological progress greater than that of globalisation.

[32] Atkinson (2013: 10), echoing some of his previous work on the factors
influencing the distribution of earnings, concludes his historical and
analytical survey of rising inequality by saying that 'ever-increasing
income inequality is not inevitable. The recent rise is not only due to
technology and globalization, but reflects the institutions and policies
adopted in the labour and capital markets.' National governments and
international institutions (in particular, European ones) are not power-
less in taking measures to reduce excessive inequality.

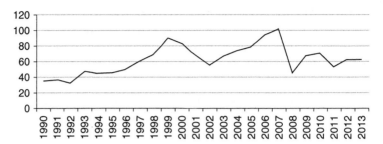

Figure 5.10 *Financialisation. Average value of market capitalisation in the stock exchange (per cent of GDP) in thirty-four OECD countries, 1990–2013.*
(Source: Tridico 2017)

ratio of wealth to income has increased in the last thirty years as an effect of soaring financial wealth and asset values, but it has declined a little after the financial crisis. This has been accompanied by increasing polarisation of wealth, as both the number of families having zero or negative wealth and the top wealthy families have grown. This growth depended on the increased importance of capital income, diminishing taxation and the allocation of capital to offshore centres. A notable change is also the increasing correlation between capital and labour income.[33] Finally, wealth inequality varies highly between countries, being higher in the United Kingdom, the United States, France and the Scandinavian countries,[34] while East Asian countries, Spain, Ireland and Italy have lower inequality levels (Maestri, Bogliacino and Salverda 2014).

[33] Milanovic (2016: fig. 4.6, p. 187) notes a rising correlation in the last thirty years in the United States between these two sources of income, from an initial value of almost zero to about 0.12 in 2000 and the following years until 2013. Obviously, the value in the new millennium is not particularly high, as the correlation is mainly due to capital investment of very rich workers, but is still important because it denotes the rise of a new type of capitalism with no rigid class separation.

[34] The contrast between the high inequality of wealth and the low inequality of income in these countries, which may appear puzzling, is really simple to explain, being due to the high provisions of the welfare state, which can make accumulation of wealth unnecessary to low-income earners.

Personal inequality of both income and wealth is linked to worsening factor inequality and, to a large extent, also depends on it. The distribution of income within the labour share has also worsened. Wages of the top 1 per cent of the income distribution have generally risen, more than doubling in the United States and the United Kingdom, whereas labour income for poorer workers has declined (Franzini and Pianta 2016: fig. 2). The decline has derived from lower pay for workers at the low end of skills due to 'non-standard' forms of employment (i.e. temporary and precarious jobs), less employment during the Great Recession (ILO 2015) and polarisation between the rates of growth of income and capital.

On the latter factor, Piketty (2013) has dug deeply as a determinant of the distribution of income, referred to all income earners. He shows that the trend in personal inequality has taken a *U*-form in the last century or so due to the main factor that has accompanied the rise in the average income, i.e. a value of the interest rate that is higher than the rate of growth (see Figure 5.11). This has benefitted wealth owners to the detriment of other income earners.

This is certainly only one of the factors behind the distribution of income. In addition, one should dig further in the determinants of the polarisation between income and capital growth, which have certainly to do with institutional and political factors that are largely country dependent. This point of view is emphasised by Acemoglu and Robinson (2015a), who point out that common stimuli to change have different effects according to the historical, political, institutional and contingent features of each country in a certain epoch. We have indeed shown above that Piketty is certainly aware of the different trends of inequality in different countries.

5.6.4 Policies for Inequality

Among the policies that can be implemented to reduce inequality, some derive from various sources and act on

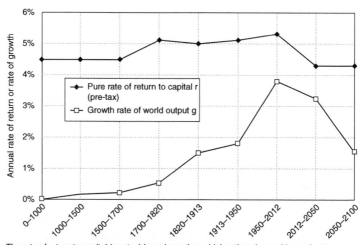

The rate of return to capital (pre-tax) has always been higher than the world growth rate, but the gap was reduced during the 20th century, and might widen again in the 21st century. sources and series: see piketty.pse.ens.fr/capital21c

Figure 5.11 *Rate of return versus growth rate at the world level, from antiquity until 2100.*
(Source: Piketty 2013)

the primary distribution; others derive from the public budget and contribute to the secondary (or net) distribution. The former include both direct actions influencing wages (e.g. minimum wage regulation, collective bargaining and promotion of equal pay across subgroups) and indirect policies acting on employment (e.g. policies aimed at expanding education through equal access to it, policies tending to increase the skills of the labour force and to promote employment, particularly of those at the bottom of the distribution,[35] and actions to improve matching of labour skill demand and supply, including tax and expenditures scaled for different incomes in order to encourage lower-income individuals to move into employment). As noted by Ravallion (2016), some

---

[35] On the need to back improvement in human capital formation by direct and effective redistributive efforts, see Marx (2013).

authors criticise direct policy interventions because of their interference with markets, which should be left free to operate to ensure efficiency. The government should limit the redistribution of the outcomes of free markets. This position, which amounts to anti-poverty policymaking being 'shy' – as Ravallion says (2016: 477) – about influencing the working of markets, cannot be held, as we also know of market failures in terms of efficiency and, more generally, because efficiency cannot be separated from equity.

Policies acting on the secondary distribution include taxes and public expenditures. In order not to produce negative incentives on one of the factors influencing the primary distribution (employment, as different from its remuneration), taxes and subsidies should be designed in a proper way. They should help or encourage lower-income individuals to move into employment, as already seen in discussing indirect policies acting on the primary distribution (active employment policies such as support for job search, training, childcare expenses, transportation, etc.; ILO 2015). Piketty (2013) suggests a number of actions to fight inequality. In particular, in order to hit what he thinks to be its principal cause – i.e. the high level of the real interest rate – a highly progressive tax on capital at a global scale (or, more pragmatically, at least at a regional or continental scale) should be implemented, together with enhanced financial transparency, which would add in exposing wealth to democratic scrutiny. This proposal is certainly difficulty to implement. It is true that the proper level for doing so is the world level, but the possibility of agreeing on such a deep and incisive decision is very low, also due to fierce opposition of rich people and, more generally, of those who would loose from the change. Possibly, a more feasible route is to proceed by steps, not only trying to enforce it to a more limited geographic scale (as proposed by Piketty himself) but also trying to solve some issues that facilitate tax evasion or elusion, such as existence of tax holidays.

As a whole, redistributive efforts matter, even if it is difficult to disentangle the effect of the different measures (Marx and Van Rie 2014).

5.7   Dealing with Secular Stagnation

This topic has again come to the forefront in recent years. In fact (despite the recent recovery from the Great Recession), especially Japan and the Euro zone – but also some other countries, as an effect of the international links – will probably experience low growth for a number of years, facing lasting low demand and low real interest rates and potential growth. Stagnation is not a new phenomenon. Concern with it emerged at the beginning of the twentieth century (and most classical economists were concerned about the possible advent of a 'stationary state' as a negative prospect[36]); in the 1930s and again in the 1970s, in this case associated to inflation; and in 1990s, this time mainly in Japan and Europe. Now, however, the problem is deeper and more widespread, and economists have begun to talk again of a global secular stagnation.[37] Larry Summers, in particular, has insisted on the reality of this

---

[36] J. S. Mill was an exception among them. He was not critical of this prospect as other classical economists were and wrote: 'I cannot, therefore, regard the stationary state of capital and wealth with the unaffected aversion so generally manifested towards it by political economists of the old school. I am inclined to believe that it would be, on the whole, a very considerable improvement on our present condition. I confess I am not charmed with the ideal of life held out by those who think that the normal state of human beings is that of struggling to get on; that the trampling, crushing, elbowing, and treading on each other's heels, which form the existing type of social life, are the most desirable lot of human kind, or anything but the disagreeable symptoms of one of the phases of industrial progress. It may be a necessary stage in the progress of civilization' for already developed countries (Mill 1848: books IV–VI).

[37] An index of this is offered by Backhouse and Boianovsky (2015), who have traced the number of economics articles using the phrase 'secular stagnation' in *JSTOR* from 1934 to 2011.

prospect (Summers 2014a, 2014b), even if his arguments have been questioned by Bernanke (2015) and others.[38]

Eichengreen (2015) suggests discussing four possible causes of stagnation, which he defines as a downward tendency of real interest rates, reflecting an excess of savings over investment: a rise in savings rates due to the higher propensity to save of emerging markets, a decline in attractive investment opportunities or in the relative price of investment goods and a decline in the rate of population growth. This implies that both the demand- and the supply-side perspectives are relevant.[39]

The Great Recession has raised the issue of a prospect of stagnation through its hysteresis effects, which makes falling GDP have a negatively influence on potential output (Krugman 2014a; Fatás and Summers 2016a).[40] In fact, the median loss in potential output in 2014 among the nineteen OECD countries experiencing a bank crisis over the period 2007–11 has been estimated to be 3.75 per cent, which is to be contrasted with an estimated loss across all OECD countries of about 2.75 per cent in the same year (Ollivaud and Turner 2015).

However, Ollivaud and Turner argue that the most adverse effects derive from a lower productivity trend. Thus, technological progress – the main source of this trend – should also be taken into account, but its role is difficult to assess. Some authors are critical about the possibility of continuing to have high rates of productivity growth in the future. Data are difficult to collect, as indicators such as research and development

---

[38] One of Bernanke's argument against Summers' fear of stagnation is based on the consideration that with a persistently negative (or zero) real interest rate, there will always be 'a permanent dearth of profitable investment projects'. However, he recognises that there are counterarguments for this (see, in fact, Eggertsson and Mehrotra 2014).

[39] This explains why Krugman (2014a) and Gordon (2014), who represent these two points of view, largely agree on the determinants of stagnation. On the supply-side perspective, see also Gordon (2012).

[40] As this negative effect of the recession on potential output begins to materialise, while the recession is fading out (thus raising the current growth rate), the gap between the two tends to disappear. This fact could be an explanation alternative to Gordon's (2014) argument, according to which the reduction in the gap shows that the hysteresis effect is of scarce relevance.

(R&D) expenditures and patent registrations can be biased and misguiding, and some other measures of productivity growth may be illusory, concerning largely tertiary sectors, where productivity is difficult to be assessed due to absence of material content (Cowen 2011). According to Gordon (2014), productivity growth in the next decades is predicted to be as high as it was in the five previous decades. However, to some extent, the effects of technological progress may appear less relevant in some countries, namely, the innovation leaders, due to the geographic distribution of its implementation in a globalised world. In fact, innovations devised in one country – such as those derived from information technology – can be implemented in other countries due to decentralisation of production. In addition, technological progress appears to be more relevant for investment than for consumption goods, where the weight of services tends to grow, which is consistent with the secular decline in the price of investment goods (Eichengreen 2015).

Also demographics can have an impact on the secular stagnation that, according to some authors, can be even more important than that of technology. Ageing and the increased life expectancy have been shown to be the main demographic trends in many countries, especially in Europe, the United States, Japan and China. They have an uncertain effect on net aggregate demand and on real interest rates. As a matter of fact, these factors have decreased to very low levels in the last three decades. However, the a priori impact of demographic trends is complex; on the one hand, increased savings can derive from the section of the population having a higher propensity to it, due to the increase in longevity; on the other hand, the larger share of older people – having a lower propensity, consistent with the life-cycle theory (Modigliani and Brumberg 1954) – will act in the opposite direction. The net effect on real interest rates is therefore uncertain (Favero and Galasso 2015), the more so – we can add – as account should be taken of possible changes in the retirement age, some of which are already being implemented. A final effect of demographic trends is to be noted: reduction in the working cohorts of the population lowers their direct contribution to growth, unless the retirement age is prolonged. Intuition thus suggests that an ageing population can reduce growth. However, in practice, this is not so, as the positive effect of higher automation – in response to the demographic trend – can counteract this effect (Acemoglu and Restrepo 2017).

Rising inequality in both developed and less developed countries (even if inequality between them has decreased) has reinforced these negative effects. In fact, the increasing concentration of wealth and income in the hands of the top 1 per cent has led to under-consumption, and/or over-saving (Piketty 2013).[41] The rise of financialisation and monopoly capitalism has also been suggested as a factor underlying both rising inequality and under-consumption (Foster and McChesney 2012). The negative impact of inequality on growth mentioned earlier is an additional cause of stagnation.

Overall, with respect to the debate about the causes of secular stagnation, institutional aspects and political mistakes are also to be considered. Secular stagnation was surfacing in some regions such as Europe and Japan in the last couple of decades. In the former case, it was mainly an effect of the deflationary design of institutions and to some extent of wrong policies (De Grauwe 2013, 2015). Crafts (2014) emphasises that the risks of stagnation are greater for Europe than for the US hypochondria, due to a number of factors, among which institutional factors such as the burden of fiscal consolidation and the ECB's focus on low inflation. More recently, Ferrero, Gross and Neri (2017) have shown the impact of demographic factors in Europe. In Japan, wrong policies as well as the effects of ageing population prevailed.[42]

---

[41] The negative effects on growth of economic concentration – causing under-consumption – were initially underlined by Hobson (1909).

[42] There are many suggestions for the relevant type of inappropriate policies implemented in Japan. Krugman refers first to a liquidity trap and then to a

Other barriers to growth can be education, increasing government debt, energy shortages and the environment.[43] In particular, as to education, Gordon (2014) complains about the rising number of dropouts in the United States.[44] Education and productivity growth are the focus of Mokyr (2014). As in the past centuries, progress in science and technology will have indirect beneficial effects on productivity that can outpace the direct effects in the long run.[45] However, this will polarise labour markets and require proper education to deal with the rise of new jobs and the loss of previous qualifications.

We can add that many countries have limited their public deficits, in particular, in order to comply with institutional limits, just by curbing public investment and, within it, the items that are more sensible for productivity growth, such as educational expenditures, due to the relatively larger flexibility in their management with respect to almost fixed current expenditures. From this perspective, Fatás and Summers (2016b) underline the permanent effects deriving from fiscal consolidation.

Gordon (2012) has made an exercise of considering the effects on the supply side of most of the factors that did support growth of the US economy in the two decades after

number of wrong monetary and fiscal policies but underlines that these were minor mistakes compared to those committed in the United States and Europe (Krugman 2000, 2014b). Other authors stress in addition to the ageing demographic, over-reliance by local governments on transfers from the central government and capital requirements. These made Japanese banks reluctant to lend money to start-up businesses and small and medium-sized enterprises, which discouraged Japanese innovation and technological progress (e.g. Yoshino and Taghizadeh-Hesary 2015), possibly the most important cause of Japanese stagnation (Tyers 2012).

[43] From the point of view of a specific country such as the United States, the interaction of globalisation and the ICT technology also can be of a problem, as it has caused or facilitated outsourcing.

[44] In this perspective, we can recall what we noticed earlier about the increasing number of NEETs in OECD countries after the crisis.

[45] If this is the case, hysteresis of supply could produce a situation of prolonged deflation and reduction in employment when aggregate demand does not keep pace with increasing supply (Buiter, Rahbari and Seydl 2015).

1987 and should no longer apply in the future. This allowed him to foresee a prospective future annual rate of growth of consumption per head for the 99 per cent of lower-income earners, which drops from 1.8 to.2 per cent (see Figure 5.12).

Some changes in these determinants may be possible, but, as we will see, this mainly depends on political 'winds' and the policies that will be implemented. Possibly, some pressing – derived from international coordination – on countries with low debt and current account surpluses to raise demand could be useful, as indicated in international forums (Bernanke 2015), but we agree with Buiter, Rahbari and Seydl (2015) that international coordination is a difficult task on these matters.

With reference to monetary policy, recent experience suggests that the ZLB matters more than previously thought, following the secular decline in real interest rates (Laubach and Williams 2016).[46] All this implies that 'it could be a very long time before "normal" monetary policy resumes' (Krugman 2014a: 66). Only a credible promise of a high enough inflation rate that reduces real interest rates would produce an economic boom, which would yield the target inflation. As Krugman says, the promise of a high inflation rate should be credible, as to involve 'a strong element of self-fulfilling prophecy'.

Some authors (Buiter, Rahbari and Seydl 2015) are sceptical about a rise in inflation rates as a way to go beyond the ZLB and suggest instead lowering the policy rate below zero. However, the difficulties of implementing the policy of a negative interest rate are high. Apart from their being 'stupid' for shrinking bank's capital, with all the consequences that can be imagined (Stiglitz 2016), the resistance of some sections of the finance

---

[46] One must be aware, however, that these estimates – and their possible consequences for secular stagnation – are characterised by a considerable degree of uncertainty, even if they use the same methodology developed by Laubach and Williams in a previous paper, as shown by Holston, Laubach and Williams (2017) with reference to the United States, Canada, Europe and the United Kingdom and Belke and Klose (2017) with reference to the Euro zone countries only.

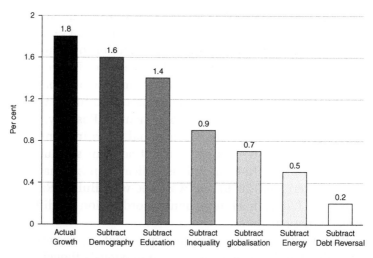

Figure 5.12 *Components of growth in per-capita real GDP, 1987–2007.*
(Source: Gordon 2012)

sector and the population may be very powerful – especially in countries having a high propensity to save and/or an ageing population. In addition, one of the reactions to such policy could be hoarding of cash balances with possible bubbles under certain conditions. Finally, a negative interest rate would lower lending to firms and the government.

A policy on a target rate of inflation that is higher than that hitherto chosen by policymakers should be different from simply temporarily tilting people's expectations of a higher inflation rate when the ZLB is reached, to be achieved through forward guidance or a policy framework based on history dependence, as indicated by Woodford (2013) and others (Bayoumi et al. 2014). It should involve a longer period of time and would either face less resistance, if the rate promised is not too high (being more subtle to be understood by many sections of the population), or generate self-fulfilling expectations of a high enough inflation, as suggested by Krugman (2014a).[47] In addition, it would have a number of advantages. The promise to implement a very expansionary monetary policy, consistent with this policy, could better fight contractionary factors still at work in the short run and the associated hysteresis. This would not be because a more expansionary monetary policy and a higher inflation target would reduce the probability of future real policy rates not to be low enough to give an incentive to investment.[48] In fact, a negative policy rate could do the same. A higher inflation rate would instead help to release the burden on fiscal policy and the extant public debt (see Chapter 3), avoiding the need of making recourse to consolidation, which would certainly cause negative short-run effects and activate the loop crisis stagnation. At the same time, a higher target inflation rate would unlock fiscal policy for short-term use. This would be very useful at least for deep recessions, when fiscal policy is most effective and should largely be self-financing. It would also facilitate the task of monetary policy, which has limited effectiveness or can result in incentives to asset bubbles, especially if prolonged (Rawdanowicz, Bouis and Watanabe 2013).[49]

On the side of demand, both conventional and unconventional monetary policies should be implemented, in addition to fiscal policy. From this point of view, their coordination, which also could take the form of helicopter money, seems to be ideal (see also Buiter, Rahbari and Seydl 2015).

Structural reforms are also needed. Public-sector efficiency should be raised. Improving material and immaterial infrastructures is another field of action (Buiter, Rahbari and

---

[47] Obviously, these are opposite requirements to be balanced.

[48] This could be due, on the one hand, to the ZLB and, on the other, to the secular decline in the real interest rate (Blanchard, Dell'Ariccia and Mauro 2010; Ball 2014; Krugman 2014a).

[49] We know from Section 3.5 that some costs and risks of permanently rising target inflation rates exist, but they seem to be of a lower order of magnitude.

Seydl 2015). A necessary reform is also restructuring of public debt, which can reduce its overhang. As to fiscal consolidation, Ostry, Loungani and Furceri (2016: 40) say that 'the short-run costs in terms of lower output and welfare and higher unemployment have been underplayed, and the desirability for countries with ample fiscal space of simply living with high debt and allowing debt ratios to decline organically through growth is underappreciated'. In the field of distribution, all the instruments directed at reducing inequality should be implemented (see Section 5.5). Gottfries and Teulings (2015) suggest extending retirement age and pay-as-you-go benefit systems.

Structural reforms take time to materialise but in some cases can entail immediate positive demand effects (Bouis et al. 2012) and can boost potential output in the longer term. Some structural reforms have different effects according to other circumstances, such as the cyclical contingency or the level of protection in other markets. This can be the case when reducing unemployment support or the difference in provisions for permanent and temporary workers, which could have negative short-run effects in 'bad times'. Product market reforms can reduce employment under weak job protection. This finding points to substitutability between product and labour market reforms; i.e. a combination of reforms would yield smaller long-term gains than the sum of the effects of each of them taken in isolation.

Policies towards secular stagnation also must be assessed from an international perspective. In fact, stagnation in a country also spreads its effects to other countries, through a higher real exchange rate that reduces net exports and thus shifts the AD curve inward in the country first experiencing it. A similar contractionary effect derives from capital inflows, possibly associated to a net trade surplus abroad (Eggertsson, Mehrotra and Summers 2016).

A general issue then arises: whether alternative policies and international institutions can be conceived of that reduce the prospect of stagnation while avoiding the risk of financial imbalances and new financial crises. This also calls for some kind of regulation. Both aspects – rapid growth in some countries and regulation issues – are relevant for a new design of world governance. The latter is the object of the next section.

5.8 Finding an International Equilibrium in Times of Globalisation and Redesign of International Institutions

5.8.1 Data on Globalisation and Its Implications

A further channel through which the financial crisis can have an impact on stagnation is globalisation.[50] In fact, globalisation is a powerful way of transmitting shocks, crises and the tendency to stagnation from the countries or regions initially more affected to other countries or regions. The financial crisis has shown that industrialised countries are not immune from contagion and that international imbalances can have a high cost for all countries. Regional agreements, such as the EMU, do not isolate countries from shocks but, on the contrary, may exacerbate them if they are not dealt with by appropriate institutions and policies.

As largely shown by Table 5.4 (but see also Ortiz-Ospina and Roser 2016), international trade has grown remarkably since the nineteenth century. Over the course of the second half of the nineteenth century, what is commonly called the 'first wave of globalisation' occurred, with a marked growth in world trade and foreign investment. It was fostered by technological advance and free trade policies. A halt to

---

[50] In turn, globalisation has magnified the effects of secular stagnation (Eggertsson, Mehrotra and Summers 2016).

globalisation occurred in the period between the two world wars (not shown in the table), but after World War II, 'international trade and investment started growing again, and in the last decades before the crisis trade expansion has been faster than ever before. Today, the sum of exports and imports across nations is higher than 50% of global production.' At the turn of the nineteenth century this ratio was below 10 per cent. After World War II, the share of exports rose very rapidly from 10 per cent in 1960 to a little more than 30 per cent in 2014, even if it suffered a drop of around 4 per cent as an effect of the global recession (UNCTAD 2016).

In the twentieth century, the stock of foreign capital with respect to the world's GDP moved from almost 20 per cent in 1900 to almost 80 per cent a century after (Ortiz-Ospina and Roser 2016: 1). In most recent decades, the high dynamics of foreign direct investment has continued and also has involved developing economies (see Figure 5.13).

Globalisation has also had a large impact on single economies, influencing the competitive position of each country (with effects on wage policy, content of production and domestic governance of social relations), changing their relative positions and then the balance of power for international governance. Globalisation represents a challenge for policymakers. It brings new opportunities but also new problems. There is no doubt that the globalisation observed in the last three decades, like the wave of globalisation around the turn of the nineteenth century, has contributed – together with technical progress – to an increase in world growth rates as a whole.[51] It has supported growth in many ways; among them, allowing information on people, available resources and knowledge to move internationally. Many developing

---

[51] See e.g. Denis, McMorrow and Röger (2006), according to whom about 20 per cent of the increase in EU15 living standards over 1950–2002 can be attributed to the European Union's growing integration into the world's economy.

Table 5.4 *globalisation waves in the nineteenth and twentieth Centuries (percentage change unless indicated otherwise)*

World	1850–1913	1950–2007	1950–1973	1974–2007
Population growth	0.8[a]	1.7	1.9	1.6
GDP growth (real)	2.1[a]	3.8	5.1	2.9
Per capita	1.3[a]	2.0	3.1	1.2
Trade growth (real)	3.8	6.2	8.2	5.0
Migration (net), million				
United States, Canada, Australia, New Zealand (cumulative)	17.9[a]	50.1	12.7	37.4
United States, Canada, Australia, New Zealand (annual)	0.42[a]	0.90	0.55	1.17
Global FDI outward stock, year			1982	2006
FDI as % of GDP (world)	–	–	5.2	25.3

[a] Refers to period 1870–1913.
Source: WTO 2008.

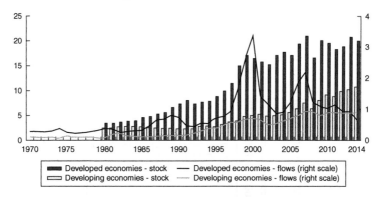

Figure 5.13 *Stock and flows of inward foreign direct investment as a share of global output by country group (per cent), 1970–2014.* (Source: UNCTAD, 2016).

countries have in fact grown fast as an effect of catching up to the frontier of technology. This effect can be seen in Table 5.5, which shows the relative increase in income growth in the more recent decades along the progress of globalisation.

At the same time, the kind of globalisation we have experienced so far has created new risks. A risk has arisen in particular with reference to jobs, due to sudden changes in the competitive position of a given country and to the conduct of transnational corporations, which has made it difficult for the nation-state to protect labour (Beck 2015). These risks often materialise in specific sectors of more developed countries and entire less develop economies. The need for compensating losers should be stressed. In fact, 'trickle-down of gross benefits spilling over the losers cannot be taken for granted, a reverse trickle-up is just as likely' (Nuti 2017: 4). Compensation can take a form such as that implemented by the United States with the Trade Act of 1974, establishing a Trade Adjustment Assistance Program that provided $1 billion of federal spending in 2010. This should be generalised to other countries, regions or world organisations and agreements.

Moreover, risks derive from global imbalances of various kinds, fuelled by countries pursuing different growth strategies. External imbalances – associated with financial liberalisation and the fragility of the international financial system – represent one of the fundamental causes of the global financial crisis. Their rising dynamics, in particular, in the last fifteen years is shown in Figure 5.14.

One notable example is the sovereign debt crisis in the Euro zone, which has derived from previously unchecked capital account imbalances (Acocella 2016b). Cross-border capital movements and financialisation of the economies have indeed increased, rather than decreased, risk. Lasting increases in imbalances of the balance of payments, favoured by other imbalances internal to each economy and also by the liberalisation of capital movements, have led to concentration of wealth, unequal distribution and crises, as discussed earlier. These, in turn, have largely come to the detriment of the welfare state (on this, see also Atkinson 2002).

Drawing a balance of the benefits and costs of globalisation is a difficult task. Dollar (2007) examines case studies of several developing countries with high growth records and makes them partly depend on the growth of their populations but also on their openness and international integration. Dissenting views are also diffuse, however. Pogge (2007) emphasises the role of global institutions, which deter abatement of inequality. Thompson (2007) notes that trade and capital movements still take place mainly among developed countries – i.e. instead of globalisation, we should speak of 'sub-globalisation'. Wade (2007) questions the correctness of the pro-market orientation of economists who hold that globalisation has led to benefits in terms of both growth and reduced inequality. In fact, he says, growth rates have slowed down, the distance between developed and less developed countries in terms of per-capita income has not reduced and most of the apparent benefits derive from the performance of China. Most likely, globalisation generates mixed outcomes,

Table 5.5 *Growth of real GDP per capita at purchasing power parity, selected regions and economies, 1951–2015*

	1951–1980	1981–2015	1951–1960	1961–1970	1971–1980	1981–1990	1991–2000	2001–2010	2011–2015
Developed economies	3.5	1.8	3.1	4.2	2.6	2.5	2.1	1.2	1.1
United States	2.3	1.8	1.3	3.4	2.2	2.6	2.4	0.9	1.4
Developing economies	2.7	3.8	2.7	2.6	3.0	2.1	3.2	5.8	4.0
Africa	1.8	1.2	1.5	1.9	1.2	−0.4	0.7	3.0	1.8
America	2.6	1.3	2.4	2.4	3.0	−0.4	1.6	2.4	1.1
Asia	2.8	5.0	2.8	2.7	3.3	3.6	4.2	7.0	4.9
East Asia	3.0	7.1	4.2	3.4	4.1	6.7	5.8	9.6	6.5
China	2.3	7.7	4.1	2.7	3.1	6.5	6.2	11.1	7.2
Southeast Asia	2.6	3.5	2.3	1.6	4.0	2.6	3.0	4.2	4.0
South Asia	1.4	4.1	1.5	1.5	1.2	3.1	3.7	5.7	4.1
West Asia	4.4	1.4	3.2	4.9	3.4	−1.6	1.6	3.3	−0.1
Transition economies	3.2	0.5	3.7	3.7	2.0	0.5	−4.9	6.2	2.1
World	2.7	2.1	2.6	3.1	2.0	1.5	1.7	3.1	2.5
Memo Items:									
Developing economies, excluding China	2.7	2.4	2.4	2.5	2.9	1.1	2.3	3.6	2.3

Developing economies, excluding East Asia	2.6	2.3	2.3	2.4	2.7	0.6	2.1	3.7	2.4
Developing economies, excluding East and Southeast Asia	2.6	2.0	2.3	2.5	2.5	0.2	2.0	3.6	2.0
Developing economies, excluding East, Southeast and South Asia	2.8	1.1	2.4	2.8	2.7	−0.8	1.2	2.5	0.6

Note: The Islamic Republic of Iran is included in West Asia. Real GDP corresponds to Geary-Khamis PPP (See United Nations, 1992).

Source: UNCTAD 2016.

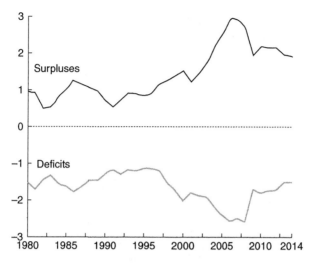

Figure 5.14 *Global current account surpluses and deficits as a share of world output (per cent), 1980–2014.*
(Source: UNCTAD, 2016).

and the balance much depends on at least three factors: (1) the period of reference, (2) the nature of the international operations considered and (3) the value judgments and preference function on which the balance is drawn.

A picture of the world economy's blocs that have emerged parallel to globalisation can be useful because it summarises existing imbalances and the recent trends prevailing in the different countries. Some played the role of net importers of both raw materials and manufactured goods (e.g. the United Kingdom and the United States); others were net exporters of manufactures (e.g. Germany, Japan, China, Southeast Asia and Brazil) or of raw materials (Russia, Saudi Arabia and many other developing countries). Growth in each bloc was supported by different factors. It was finance-led growth for net importers tout court and export led in the net exporters of manufactures. Growth of these two blocs, in turn, benefitted raw materials exporters.

In the last two decades, countries in the above-mentioned blocs had experienced different, but positive, rates of growth. These were very low in most of Europe and Japan but very high elsewhere. In general, countries in all groups experienced a rather good performance. Some countries, however, for various reasons, suffered from low or even negative growth until recently as an effect of the Great Recession. As we know from Section 5.1, this has transmitted in waves from the United States to Europe and later hit Brazil, Russia, India, China and South Africa (BRICS). More recently, positive signs of recovery have emerged in the countries that were initially hit by the crisis.

This picture of the world economy in blocs can explain why countries have suffered differently from the prospect of stagnation. In fact, some of them devised export strategies to cope with low domestic growth of demand to the benefit or detriment of other countries. Countries receiving a benefit were raw materials exporters, mostly developing countries. Others suffered as an effect of beggar-thy-neighbour strategies.

After 2008, the growth of the world as a whole did fall, but no bloc changed its role, and there were a few changes in their relative roles. The financial crisis has reduced growth in the net importers. Exporters of raw materials, in turn, have been hit by lower growth than net importers. Again, net exporters of manufactures performed better as an effect of their beggar-thy-neighbour strategies; however, they suffered from the growth slowdown too.

5.8.2   Policies to Deal with Globalisation

The strategies of some specific countries parallel to globalisation has already been considered. Whether the policies they implemented were the best possible ones is certainly an issue worth digging into further and difficult to answer, as this would involve knowledge of the specific situation of each. Instead of doing this, we prefer to investigate the reaction to globalisation by international institutions. How these institutions have and will cope with the developments of globalisation is, in fact, an intriguing point. As to the past, on the one hand, we should first note that a century of evolution of the international payment system represents a good guide to understanding the ability of international institutions to adapt to changes; a notable example is the IMF after introduction of a floating exchange-rate system, which, from a historical perspective, is a recent innovation. On the other hand, international institutions have been directed to a large extent to pursue not only the interests of some industrial countries in general but also, in particular, the commercial and financial interests in those countries (Stiglitz 2002).[52] This raises issues involving the equilibrium of the international system and the orientation of its governance.

Here we aim to offer some more technical reflections on how to devise a new and fair design of international institutions to cope with these and other issues arising from globalisation. These reflections refer to: arrangements to favour equilibrium, check of the correctness of existing institutions, the nature of positive and negative international spill-overs and the need to internalise them in a number of areas; progress achieved and desirable in order to pursue international policy coordination.

The need for discussing the arrangements to favour equilibrium arises, in particular, for the case of the public goods existing in a global space, i.e. global public goods, such as the environment, financial stability and the like. The traditional theory of public goods, in fact, can be recast in terms of the new theory of economic policy in a strategic context where some of the players share common targets (having either

---

[52] His critiques refer in particular to the policies imposed by the Washington Consensus.

equal or different target values) that can be thought of as public goods by reason of their commonality.

In general, as mentioned earlier, from the point of view of the theory of economic policy, difficulties in finding a unique equilibrium or an equilibrium at all can arise. We recall that even when target values coincide, such as between countries, multiple equilibria arise in the instrument space because the number of instruments is higher than that of targets. Different target values, instead, imply the non-existence of an equilibrium in the target space (see Chapter 4).

Global public goods raise a coordination problem among policymakers on how to settle conflicts or how to converge to the commonly preferred solution. A decentralised solution is difficult to implement because the level of the public goods desired by the various countries is usually different. When that level is common to all countries, decentralisation leads to indeterminacy and destabilisation (if not collapse) of the system if the players randomise their policies in response, unless specific circumstances occur or can be imposed that make it possible to reach a decentralised equilibrium.

The necessary circumstances include the case where some players voluntarily abstain from making use of their instruments (Acocella and Di Bartolomeo 2011), as with the Bretton Woods system. In fact, the arrangements established at Bretton Woods did so for more than a couple of decades, since the United States acted as a hegemon, abstaining from controlling its balance-of-payments deficit. The arrangements that followed have not ensured equilibrium for a number of reasons: a notable one – in addition to the well-known Triffin dilemma – was the lifting of limits to capital mobility and the features taken by globalisation, which have added to the problems to be faced; or the players were forbidden to use their instruments for some reason. As opposed to these situations, the tendency to ensure an equilibrium was facilitated by introduction of some additional (possibly common) targets that changed the nature and contents of the game, creation of a mechanism for announcing the strategies to be played (as in international forums) or the existence of situations in which politics, history, conventions and path dependence act as the constraints that provide for a 'smooth' solution.

A centralised solution always exists from an abstract point of view, as the exceeding instruments could freely be set and the distributive problems (deriving from the conflict) solved. However, such a solution would be difficult to obtain in an international context like the current one, as there is no such thing as a superstate to deal with conflicts, and resistance to the devolution of powers to an external authority is extreme, unless very specific situations and issues occur.

Moving on now to consideration of the suitability of existing international institutions, we can say that the correctness of current institutions – and the theoretical assumptions on which they are based – can be questioned from a number of points of view. First, current institutions are unable to reallocate demand across economies in order to generate growth. Moreover, freely floating exchange rates cannot support demand and act as a shock absorber. Finally, free international capital movement cannot improve the global allocation of capital and make international adjustment smoother. All three assumptions have been questioned by the experience of the last decades as well as recent research.

In particular, as to the first point, the capacity of the global economy to sustain an appropriate pace of global growth has been questioned because of the export-led strategies implemented by some countries, generating high savings and a low interest-rate trap.[53] As to the second point, global

---

[53] The need also arises of limiting current account deficits that correspond to structural inefficiencies. On this, Blanchard and Milesi-Ferretti (2012: 11) note that spill-over effects, either from deficits or from surpluses,

interconnections seem to have altered the shock-absorbing role of floating exchange rates. The third point is tied to the first one (due to the symmetry between the current and capital accounts of the balance of payments), but we dealt with it earlier (for all three points, see Cœuré 2015).

As for spill-overs, they can be either negative or positive. Tax havens – which largely continue to act in a number of places, not only in underdeveloped but also in European countries – generate issues of the former type, as they reduce the tax base and the tax proceeds for other countries and sometimes also divert investment, while feeding, and adding to, other sources of unstable (and sometimes illegal) capital movement. This is particularly to the benefit of corporations, which can elude taxes by manipulating transfer prices relative to their intracorporate transactions.

Spill-overs of a positive kind can, instead, derive from fiscal expansion in one country. Especially in a situation such as the current one, characterised by low demand and interest rates, such an expansion can have a beneficial expansionary effect in other countries. Certainly, the open-economy multipliers are lower than those for a closed economy, but this should favour simultaneous expansion by many countries. International coordination thus could add to the expansionary outcomes in a remarkable way (see Eggertsson, Mehrotra and Summers 2016; Gaspar, Obstfeld and Sahay 2016).

A redesign of international institutions should take place to realise the potential for good of globalisation while reducing or eliminating its shortcoming and the distortion of its current governance. Both authors and policymakers have become aware of the numerous holes in the current

suggest a direct role for multilateral surveillance. 'This process can play two potentially useful roles; first, as a discussion of the differences in assessments; second, as a potentially useful commitment device for countries to implement some of the required but politically unpalatable fiscal or structural adjustments.'

governance, but policy responses show some inertia. For example, concern for the free mobility of capital has arisen. The need for limitations has been urged (among others, see Cœuré 2015; Stiglitz 2015a) via the use of instruments (such as regulation tending to avoid volatile capital flows and taxation) reducing negative externalities and increasing the effectiveness of domestic policies (in particular, monetary policy). A similar position is shared by the IMF, which has recently altered its previous position in favour of full capital market liberalisation and fiscal consolidation towards a more cautious, or even negative, attitude. The new position is justified especially in view of the negative effect of these policies on inequality, which also hurts the growth rate and its sustainability (Ostry, Loungani and Furceri 2016).

By contrast to the free mobility of capital, take the limited mobility of persons. In some areas (such as the European countries that are members of the 'area of Schengen'), mobility of persons has been put in check recently by the wave of immigrants from developing countries, in particular, those hit by war and repression, and lack of a common attitude. Immigration is the single most relevant and hot issue – even more prominent than that of free capital movement – that should be the object of international coordination. It could be allowed to some extent in advanced countries, which should also act on its economic and political roots, in particular, by aid to development in order to contain or reduce it.

Apart from action for immigration, international coordination can indeed be initially limited to the areas where it is most needed, such as central bank policy (Claessens, Stracca and Warnock 2015; Engel 2015),[54] tax harmonisation in particular within regional institutions (Keen and Konrad 2012; Karakosta, Kotsogiannis and Lopez-Garcia 2014; Bénassy-Quéré, Trannoy and Wolff 2014), financial

---

[54] However, one should consider the possibility that international coordination of monetary policies can lower the credibility of central banks vis-à-vis the private sector at the domestic level (Rogoff 1985b).

regulation (Davies and Green 2013; Schenk 2016), environmental issues (United Nations Environment Programme 2015), anti-monopoly action and, as said, freedom of capital movement (Ostry and Ghosh 2013).To face and solve these and other problems, at least three points must be discussed that have a practical relevance: (1) whether limited amendments to the existing institutional architecture are sufficient or a new architecture needs to be designed, (2) whether a change in the rules of the game and the relative roles of different countries will be required and (3) how to devise institutions that can ensure both fairness and progress in a stable context.

The answer to the first two issues, as far as monetary institutions are concerned, is that much depends on whether China and other BRICS countries will continue to push towards a new balance of power within the existing institutions. From this point of view, the Renminbi (RMB or yuan), the Chinese currency, has been recognised as a new reserve currency. Any prospect of rivalry with the dollar is certainly premature. However, in due time, an uneasy duopoly between the dollar and the RMB could arise. This prospect appears to be rather new in the world economy[55] and may require changes in the rules of the game. In the past, equilibrium and stability depended on the dominance of only one currency and its hegemony. Big issues arise having to do with volatility, trade imbalances and the new rules that, in turn, have an influence on political stability. Issues of a more limited nature arise with reference to coordination in specific sectors. Other issues arise

---

[55] A situation of duopoly also arose in the interwar period, with the US leadership emerging in a world that was still largely dominated by the British hegemony. The relative affinity of the two countries and other circumstances – the economic difficulties of the United Kingdom trying to return to gold, the Great Depression and the ascent of Nazism in Germany – avoided a clash between them, which together chose the lines of the new international order after World War II in relative harmony. With reference to the rising duopoly between the United States and China, the reasons for a clash are more founded, and a real problem of escaping Thucydide's trap arises (Allison 2017).

about the way to facilitate the transition and the reforms of national policies and regional or international institutions such as the IMF needed for achieving this.[56]

As to the third issue, the actual development of international institutions, it seems to have disregarded the need for more fairness, stability and steady growth. Principles for devising a new order are therefore needed at various levels. Most discussions and the limited changes made so far (even after the crisis) have aimed only at constraining member countries to act in a way that is not detrimental to others in certain areas, as in the case of tax havens or environmental protection, with very limited achievements in both areas.[57] Some progress has been made for coordination of anti-monopolistic policies through the International Competition Network, established at the WTO Doha Round of negotiations. The participants of these negotiations agreed on a guidance document on investigative process that reflects key tools and

---

[56] These issues are investigated, among others, by Eichengreen (2015b).

[57] In April 2009, the London G20 meeting agreed to define a blacklist for tax havens, to be segmented according to a four-tier system based on compliance with an 'internationally agreed tax standard'. In November 2016, the European Council reached an agreement on the criteria and the process for the establishment of a EU list of non-cooperative jurisdictions in taxation matters. This list will be determined by the Council in 2017. The screening of third-world countries should have been completed by the end of September 2017 so as to enable the Council to endorse the full list by the end of the year. In order to be considered compliant on tax transparency, a jurisdiction will need to have, *inter alia*, arrangements to automatically exchange tax information with all EU Member States and have agreed on the OECD Multilateral Convention on Mutual Administrative Assistance in Tax Matters. Having said this does not dispense us from noting that tax havens, such as Luxembourg and the Netherlands, operate within the European Union.

The Paris Agreement, an agreement within the United Nations Framework Convention on Climate Change, was reached in 2015. It aims, in particular, to 'holding the increase in the global average temperature to well below 2°C above pre-industrial levels and to pursue efforts to limit the temperature increase to 1.5°C above pre-industrial levels, recognizing that this would significantly reduce the risks and impacts of climate change' (from article 2). The new US president has announced withdrawal of his country from the agreement, but this cannot be effective until 2020.

procedural fairness principles. To some extent – i.e. apart from the influence of vested interests – the limitation in international agreements seems to derive from absence of a clear and shared concept of fairness, consistent over time, when the institutions were founded or reformed.

The existing asymmetries have become codified. Principles of responsible behaviour that take account both of the initial position of a country and the policies implemented by that country appear to be lacking. They should involve not only deficit countries but also those running surpluses. Symmetric adjustment would avoid the risk, on the one hand, of lasting inefficiencies and, on the other, of surplus countries regarding global institutions simply as an insurance mechanism that allows them to devise export-led strategies in a way that is less reactive to negative shocks and avoids taking the expansionary adjustments that would be needed to reduce their international imbalance. As to the specific imbalances of developing countries and, more generally, to the need to ensure a higher world liquidity and international regulation coordination of policies, the Stiglitz Commission established by the United Nations has recently suggested a number of solutions (see United Nations 2009).

This raises a more general issue, that of ensuring a number of requirements, beyond the targets and target values expressed by the policymakers of each country and referred to their relations or to issues relative to each country that derive from theories of justice. These may consist, first, in helping to boost living standards and ensuring democracy. In particular, as far as the first such target is concerned, the relative positions of less developed countries deserve specific attention not only for reasons of fairness but – as mentioned earlier – because aid to development also could help more developed countries to face some problems, such as that of the excessive flows of immigrants.

To the targets already indicated, i.e. boosting standards and ensuring democracy, self-determination within the nation-state could be added. However, Rodrik (2000, 2002, 2011) has shown that a trilemma of the global economy would then arise, as nation-state self-determination, democratic politics and full economic integration are mutually incompatible. If we deem the latter two requirements to be basic, the first one should be abandoned: global markets need global governance. A larger role of the nation-state requires a kind of 'Bretton Woods compromise', with some limits to integration (Rodrik 2000, 2002, 2011).[58] Full integration would require dropping either democratic choices within nation-states or stronger world governance. Insisting on self-determination of people and countries would add to this prospect.

---

[58] On this, see also Bibow (2010), De Cecco (2013) and Carabelli and Cedrini (2014). Bibow (2013) suggests application of the trilemma to the European Union.

6

One Step Forward towards Realism in Theories Relevant to Effective and Accountable Policymaking

In this chapter we first discuss some policy solutions necessary to ensure proper working of a capitalist system. We also have a closer look at the issues to tackle for building a democratic society. In particular, we are concerned with two basic issues: (1) information, in terms of the signals built into market institutions or as offered by the policymakers, together with the possibility of moral hazard or adverse selection arising in the system, and (2) incentives for both private agents and policymakers to engage in opportunistic behaviour deriving from self-interest. The question of proper incentives for both private agents and policymakers to a large extent is tied to the existing signals. Proper signals offered by policymakers lead to both greater effectiveness of their policies and their better accountability and thus can guarantee the democratic government of market outcomes.

The issue of proper incentives of private agents being necessary to ensure policy effectiveness is self-evident. As to policymakers, if they have an incentive to behave as announced or promised, private agents too will have an incentive to accept the signal, which will then be effective. However, announcements and promises will also ensure the accountability of policymakers, the more so the clearer the signals are. This latter aspect of signals involves extensive analysis of a political economy nature. The first section of this chapter deals with the signals issued by markets. This

253

section also introduces the question of the relationship between signals and incentives for private agents. The signals issued by policymakers about their actions and how to make policymakers accountable are the objects of Section 6.2. Section 6.3 investigates a related aspect of the relations between private and public agents, the asymmetry of information between private agents and policymakers about the workings of the economy. Section 6.4 discusses how our discipline can be enriched by incorporating some political economics and other more realistic features of policy action. The final section deals with various ways to refine the abstract theory of policymaking developed in previous chapters.

6.1   Searching for the Right Signals in a Market Economy to Prevent Crises and to Manage Them

6.1.1   Why Can Wrong Signals or Difficulties of Signal Extraction Arise in a Market Economy?

The components of signals, which must be intended as preconditions for their effectiveness, are two: information provision – together with the ability of agents to process it – and incentives (or disincentives) deriving from this provision. We deal with the first in this subsection and with the second in the next subsection. The final subsection refers in particular to the ability of policymakers to steer the economy when private agents are assumed to exploit all the available information.

The ability of private and public agents to perceive the right information for their conduct can be debated in a market economy. From this point of view, the issue emerges as to whether markets can send the right signals to policymakers and private agents and, if so, under what conditions. Symmetrically, what are the difficulties of accurate signal extraction in market economies?

One can say that information could be drawn by private agents from market trends and the constraints those trends impose on their conduct. However, there are a number of reasons why difficulties in signal extraction arise. Some refer to markets and political institutions in general. First, signals coming out of market trends can be noisy, depending on the existence of multiple equilibria. In this case, they could also direct agents towards a 'bad' equilibrium (in the case of equilibria that can be ranked in a univocal way). In addition, myopia of people and policymakers, populism and national specificities (including home bias) can lead agents to misinterpret information.[1] Short-sightedness is particularly acute with reference to financial market trends and certainly has been seen in the European Monetary Union (EMU; De Grauwe and Ji 2013). More generally, capital markets can send signals, and policymakers and private agents may correctly interpret them. However, these markets are plagued by issues such as 'beauty contests' and, as seen, can overreact and create bubbles. The increase in the size and role of financial markets in the last decades has implied a rise in the possibility of misinterpreting the relevant underlying factors and trends. Issues then can be complicated by the different speeds of adjustment in the different markets.[2] Moreover, the procedures followed by public and private agents in extracting the right signals are imperfect because such agents may not know the right model. In the end, only

---

[1] This could also be true when there is a unique equilibrium.

[2] Let us take the case of the EMU as an example. The very manner in which a monetary union operates, with structural differences among the different countries and free capital movements, with low labour mobility, no fiscal union, no lender of last resort for governments, absence of other common policies, would expose (and has exposed) the EMU to the risk of breakup (Krugman 2013). In this case, the nature of the existing institutions and their inability to allow for a correct extraction of signals from market trends emerge with clarity. One example is Balassa's 'border effect', which underlines the incompleteness of a monetary union when policies other than monetary policy are under control of individual member countries, as in the EMU (Balassa 1973).

a few people may be able to apply the correct methods of signal extraction. Most private agents perceive signals and adapt their expectations mainly on the basis of the specific market where they operate. Their ability to perceive imbalances looming elsewhere and ultimately affecting the market where they operate is often weak. Usually agents ignore signals from other, related markets because they are specifically interested in the evolution of their own market, as either this is better known and more pressing or interrelations between markets are difficult to assess.

Difficulties of private agents in discerning signals deriving from market trends can be remedied by proper supplementary information supplied by policymakers (e.g. by announcements) and their policies. As to policies, excessive capital inflows and current account imbalances can be regulated by taxes or proper direct control. In the case of a current account imbalance due to competitiveness, wages could be lowered or raised according to the nature of the imbalance; correction also could be achieved by means of price and income policies. Imbalances in the current account not due to competitiveness could be faced by boosting or contracting aggregate demand.

Some authors are against similar proposals and raise objections, especially addressed to using direct policy instruments. These are considered to be 'naive and dangerous, because, by attempting to mimic through controls the outcome of market discipline, they are bound to confuse symptoms with causes and direct the attention to policy tools that are entirely inappropriate as remedies against long-term structural deficiencies of market economies' (European Economic Advisory Group 2011: 82, referring to the EMU). Both these considerations are debatable. It is true that causes rather than pure symptoms should be removed. However, this requires time, as the causes are often difficult to tackle, the more so when this must be done at the country level, due – in the case of a monetary union – to the absence of suitable common labour and industrial policies. Arguments against the position expressed by the European Economic Advisory Group (EEAG) also derive from the critique of the theoretical foundations of EMU institutions and the need to reform them (Acocella 2014a). From this point of view, direct instruments are a way to immediately respond to some urgencies, in anticipation of suitable structural changes, which require time to be implemented.

6.1.2   Incentives, Signals, Moral Hazard and Adverse Selection

As noted earlier, signals can induce proper actions by the private and public-sector agents only if some information is coupled with suitable incentives or disincentives. The case of a monetary union can help us to make the point. A number of requirements were prescribed for being admitted to the EMU. In the third and final phase of progress to the union, conditions of low inflation rates, low long-term interest rates, stable exchange rates and limits to public deficit and debt were required. Many countries were impressed by the prospective gains from being part of the EMU (the prize), and many private agents and the public sector behaved accordingly.

This outcome conflicts with what happened after admission. The important signals of the balance of payments and the exchange rate were lost, not because of lack of information but because of a lack of proper, clear signals. For any country, relaxing the external constraint by means of free capital movements implied the possibility that a loss in competitiveness could be compensated by those movements. In fact, a rather high – but unsustainable – rate of growth in those countries could derive from the asset bubbles created out of easy credit conditions fed by capital that deficit countries borrowed from abroad. In a currency union, the balance of payments, the current account and some indicators of competitiveness can still be calculated. However, absence of a true constraint on the action of policymakers and mixed signals could be wrongly reassuring to them. As a consequence, policymakers have few incentives to implement long-needed structural changes. Similarly, for private agents, the reduction in the foreign component of aggregate demand and at least partial substitution of the domestic to foreign markets (made possible to some extent by the looming bubble) meant that signals of lost competitiveness were noisy and hard to see. Moreover, reliance on temporary jobs and on the opportunity to relocate some industrial production lines abroad implied that many firms could cope with reduced exports, the inability to resort to nominal currency devaluation and inefficiencies and rents without suffering a substantive loss in their competiveness, at least in the short to medium run.

Constraints similar to those in existence before admission – such as the limits to public deficit and debt – were inherited by the EMU and are still in force for its member countries. However, they have often been violated. The 3 per cent limit on annual public-sector deficit has been ineffective after admission, since the incentives to comply are now lower than before admission, as shown by the case of violation of the rule by France, Germany and Portugal in 2003–4, not to mention later violations by others due mainly to the crisis and the inappropriate policies asked from member countries. This failure might have to do with the expected value of the benefit before entry compared to the cost after. Other factors that have probably acted at least in the case of France and Germany could be a calculation that they were in a position to avoid sanctions because of their dominant role in the EMU.

Other requirements, such as those implying sufficient competitiveness or limited current account imbalances, were not prescribed after admission. Ex post, member countries had an apparent interest to respect them, apart from the negative spill-over effects mentioned earlier, since they were a cause of the financial crisis and its duration. But those requirements were ignored. Only in 2012 was a formal requirement introduced, the Macroeconomic Imbalances Procedure (MIP), which set limits – though imperfect and asymmetric – to current account imbalances (see Section 3.9).

Absence of clear signals and of a proper system of incentives or disincentives thus reduced the value of information and condemned the residual constraints to failure. To sum up from earlier, this absence could simply imply that some other signals let member countries think that the environment in which they acted had lasting positive features, which induced public and private agents to believe that their current conduct was profitable to them and immune from risks, independently of their actions. In this case, signals would have been noisy. Alternatively, agents were unable to correctly infer the consequences of their action or inaction. In any case, absence of signals and incentives would not imply moral hazard per se in the conduct of the agents. That would also require the existence of asymmetric information and conduct by agents that is irrational (detrimental to the principal). Moral hazard then arises because an agent does not take into consideration the full consequences and responsibilities of his or her actions, thus acting less carefully than he or she otherwise would and leaving the principal to bear some negative effects.

Let us look at the different markets where moral hazard might have played a role. The main markets are those for goods, labour and financial assets. There is no immediate way of devising some kind of asymmetric information relevant for our issues in the first two markets. However, the change in institutions can act on the incentives usually existing in those markets. Take the case of the Hartz IV reforms in Germany: the situation of public deficit induced the government to enact a series of reforms related to the labour market that had a positive impact on workers' incentive to accept a job and possibly also to change the terms of wage bargaining in a way that increased competitiveness and growth. An even more manifest type of moral hazard could have interested financial operators with respect to the government but, most likely, after the start of the crisis, when some kind of aid or bailout was expected.

The bubbles that were created in deficit countries can act not only on the incentives of agents in general but also on the adverse selection of politicians and managers. As a matter of fact, they can add noise to the information available to voters and shareholders by making all the mistakes of politicians and managers 'largely imperceptible', thus hiding mistakes and lowering the level and quality of both public and private accountability during the boom (Fernandez-Villaverde, Garicano and Santos 2013: 164).

Leaving issues of partisanship aside, when we introduce asymmetric information, separating bad from good politicians is very difficult, as the programme of future policy declared by each candidate before the election is always incomplete and may not correspond to his or her real intentions and choices. This is especially important for the case already made of some countries after their admission to the EMU. In fact, after 1999, the process of restructuring the economy of 'peripheral' countries still had to be completed, but the prospects of continuing relatively high growth rates and the benefits from participation in the EMU were so diffuse. As a result, voters were more inclined to opt for candidates – even the less able and/or those having a special private interest in taking office – promising some relaxation of the tight policy experienced until then (Le Borgne and Lockwood 2002). Promises of soft budget constraint to the 'core' constituency were appealing and appeared credible and thus increased the probability of success at the polls or political survival of the ruling government (Robinson and Torvik 2009).

6.1.3   *Signalling and Economic Policy after the Crisis: The Role of Rational Expectations*

An additional issue arises when one assumes rational expectations (REs). On the one hand, this assumption takes for granted the ability of agents to correctly infer the outcomes of some facts or information. On the other, they are relevant for the incentive to cheat of policymakers. Since the work of Barro (1974), Sargent and Wallace (1975), Lucas (1976) and Kydland and Prescott (1977), forward-looking expectations have been regarded as placing severe limits on what policymakers can achieve in a world of policy conflicts and for requiring strong policy commitments to get even that far. The Lucas critique and time inconsistency are often said to imply that announcements and loose commitments cannot be considered credible and will inevitably lead to policy failure. In the context of a recession, this would mean, in the immediate, difficulties in achieving a recovery path, creation of unsustainable debt or excessive costs for debt financing and future inflation caused by delaying the exit strategy or allowing the debt to be monetised.

These arguments, however, do not consider two possibilities. First, the theory we developed in Chapter 4 (in particular, recall Section 4.5.5) has shown that REs do not impair policy controllability if certain conditions are met. In fact, even with REs, static controllability is guaranteed if the number of instruments equals that of targets. The true threat to controllability could arise when this condition cannot be satisfied in real life, e.g. when use of some instrument is prevented or constrained by institutions, such as for fiscal policy (see Section 5.1). Even so, dynamic controllability could be ensured if the time horizon is sufficiently long. An additional possibility to control the system is offered in the case where policymakers actively engage in managing expectations by policy announcements, along with direct policy interventions, for the express purpose of shifting the expectations path itself. In this case, REs can indeed help policymakers in succeeding in their attempts to control the economy.

One thus can clearly understand that this idea is also in the minds of the policymakers. In fact, the cases previously cited with reference to the US government, the Federal Reserve, the European Central Bank (ECB) and other important central banks have shown that policymakers do attempt to influence current economic conditions. They do so by outlining the future path of interest rates and announcing future monetary actions, new fiscal stimulus and credit guarantee packages, new bank regulations and future exit strategies and the instruments to be used. In all these cases they trust that REs by the private sector ensure the effectiveness of the announced policies.

The literature also has often used this idea in debates over the feasibility and desirability of trying to anchor inflation expectations for monetary policy changes or in arguments over the desirability of publishing interest-rate forecasts (Soderlind 1999; Woodford 2003, 2005; Blinder et al. 2008; Rudebusch and Williams 2008).

6.2   Signals, Transparency and Forward Guidance

6.2.1   Transparency As a Precondition for the Effectiveness of Signals

In the preceding section we introduced a discussion of signals. The problem there was whether institutions and policies can lay down the right signals or system of signals for a proper conduct of both private agents and the policymakers, in particular, to prevent the start of a crisis. In this section we first refer specifically to the content of signals issued by policymakers from the point of view of their transparency. Forward guidance, the object of Section 6.2.2, introduces novelties from this point of view. The information

provided by signals is important not only for the working of
the system but also for the accountability of policymakers
and their incentives to pursue their declared intentions, an
issue relevant from a political point of view. This is the object
of Section 6.2.3.

The information provided by signals relates to the transparency of actions and goals of the various agents. By the
term 'transparency' we mean visibility of the information
referred to one's action (especially policymakers) and its
inferability, i.e. the potential for other agents to understand
its implications (Michener and Bersch 2013). These aspects –
or preconditions for transparency – have numerous requirements, in particular, the issuance of proper signals by some
agents and the ability of other agents to rationally deduce
their implications.

Reciprocal transparency of signals issued by private and
public agents would be useful. However, on the one hand,
the private agents' conduct is easier to foresee. On the other,
even if – and to the extent to which – it is not, in a market
system policymakers cannot require transparency on the
side of private agents for most of their choices, even if exceptions are diffuse, such as in the case of antitrust legislation or
tax compliance and entitlement to subsidies.

As for public agents, transparency has been referred in
particular to monetary policy, for a number of reasons, especially in connection with independence of central banks,
which raises the additional issue of their accountability.
Transparency can refer to at least four different aspects of
monetary policy: objectives and strategies, motives behind
certain policy decisions, economic outlook of the economy
and future monetary policy decisions (Blinder et al. 2008).[3]
Actually, until not long ago, monetary policy was conceived

---

[3] Communication is just as much a crucial factor in fiscal policy as in
monetary policy. Obviously, what is said in the text as to the content of
transparency in relation to monetary policy can be repeated also for fiscal
policy.

as an art, almost an arcane matter. After the 1960s, the mystique of central banks gradually disappeared to full disclosure of the various objects of transparency along an increasing trend.

The literature on the effects of transparency about the action of the central bank trying to influence inflation and output has grown in the last fifteen years, parallel to its growing implementation. The conclusions derived have changed through time. In the 1980s, it was common to ask for a high degree of opacity, mostly under the influence of the argument that the 'surprise effect' was a necessary element. Rather recently, Blinder et al. (2008) have concluded that higher transparency positively affects macroeconomic outcomes. Indeed, higher transparency confers greater credibility to the actions of the central bank, as this can explain to the public the details of the actions and how they can affect the economy. It influences inferability and expectations, thus enabling agents in the private sector to plan their decisions (especially those that need long-term projections, such as investment) and to coordinate their plans. In fact, they can base their plans on firm and reliable expectations about future short-term interest rates, as the long-term rate – which influences investment – depends on them.

To be more specific, up to the crisis, the literature on transparency predicated an optimal degree of transparency intermediate between the two extremes of complete opacity and complete transparency, with various accents on the two extremes according to the models used. Ciccarone, Marchetti and Di Bartolomeo (2007) held that bank transparency has two opposite effects on wages whose relative strength determines macroeconomic performance. This depends on the orientation of the central bank: higher opacity has positive effects in the case of a populist bank; if this is instead sufficiently conservative, transparency has positive effects on macroeconomic performance but at the cost of higher volatility. Lack of transparency always implies, at least as a direct effect, an increase in uncertainty and thus a variability cost (Demertzis and Hughes Hallett 2007) – as long as agents aim for smooth and predictable dynamics. Indirect effects are uncertain, since the associated changes in private-sector expectations may sometimes offset or partially offset this effect.

In more recent work, Demertzis and Hughes Hallett (2015) have concluded that transparency does not much affect macroeconomic averages but lowers inflation variability (the opposite may occur for output, which justifies a limited degree of ambiguity). Another argument for this position is offered by Friedman (2015: 16), who is still sceptical about the ability of central banks to supply the optimal degree of transparency, since 'the market will inevitably want to know more than what policymakers can possibly disclose'.

The orientation in favour of some ambiguity has changed to a large extent as an effect of the practical implementation of forward guidance. In fact, as far as theoretical analysis is concerned, REs may even reinforce the policymaker's ability to pursue his or her targets when he or she provides suitable information about his or her future actions through forward guidance, the object of the next subsection. Before passing to it, we must add that one aspect of the optimal level of transparency has specifically to do with its inferability. It has been shown that there is a trade-off between the level of information provided and its possibility of being acquired and used by the public, due to the risk of overwhelming communication and the inability of the private sector to choose among the various signals and correctly process the right ones. There is thus a limit to the optimal level of information provided by central banks. Moreover, any signal should be clear and precise, exactly to the end of properly influencing the public (Chahrour 2014).

6.2.2 Transparency and Forward Guidance

Forward guidance has introduced novelties into the topic of transparency. In fact, transparency has risen to prominence recently with specific reference to the targets of central banks and their future actions, in an attempt to help the economies recover from the crisis or stabilise them in a crisis. The issue is whether this is limited to the current situation of zero lower bound (ZLB), which requires some kind of engagement for future policy (Williams 2013).

In the abstract case where not only the conditions for dynamic controllability are satisfied but also perfect knowledge of both the model and of the policymaker's preferences is ensured, forward-looking expectations actually enhance the ability of the policymaker to reach his or her targets and guarantees controllability in a shorter time. In this case, knowledge of the policymaker's preferred target values becomes crucial to form 'correct' and thus 'useful' expectations by the private sector. This knowledge can be spread directly by providing information about the policy targets or indirectly via other announcements that offer information about future policies. According to this view, in the case where expectations reinforce policy actions, a good communication system becomes an essential prerequisite for good policy.

In order to be able to consider policy announcements as an instrument of economic policy for supplementing or extending the impact of conventional policy instruments, some circumstances must be clarified. In fact, even if real policy interventions show the multiplicity of practical cases where intentions of future policy are announced, until now, the literature has failed to identify (1) the conditions under which the expectations deriving from policy announcements (and also real policy interventions) can be managed, (2) their effect on the scope for policymaking (as distinct from the possibility of managing expectations) and (3) how and when unconventional policy instruments will be necessary.

Only after giving a satisfactory answer to these questions can the conditions under which policy announcements may be used as policy tools be stated. If these conditions are met, announcements can be added as new policy tools to those already in existence. This can allow policymakers to satisfy conditions for controlling the economic system even in the absence of other instruments, in particular, fiscal ones, thus getting rid of the conditions under which an impasse develops that impairs policy control.

If, by contrast, announcements are ineffective, REs could make the whole policymaking action ineffective, unless other solutions of the kind indicated in Chapter 5 can be found. In particular, in order to overcome a crisis situation – such as the one that has recently developed – mutually supporting combinations of fiscal and monetary policy would be needed.

Forward guidance should be seen from the perspective of transparency and signals on policy action. From this perspective, policy announcements, if communicated properly, can be used to supplement or extend the impact of conventional policy instruments. Specifically, within a general RE framework, policy invariance can only arise in specific cases of parameter values. In all other cases, policy announcements can be used by policymakers to help steer economic behaviour, and as a result, certain targets can be reached in reduced time. Thus, expectations typically enhance the power to control the economy over time. The rationale for this result can be understood by using the concept of controllability from the theory of economic policy and its dynamic extensions (see Chapter 4). Put differently, if a policymaker can achieve any desired vector of targets given exogenous expectations, then he or she will also be able to do so with endogenous expectations, i.e. with expectations generated by its announcements. If nothing else, the policymaker can attempt to steer the endogenous expectations to achieve specific targets in a shorter time. A detailed explanation of this result is given in Hughes Hallett and Acocella (2017).

To make use of this property of REs, however, another ingredient should be added. The policymakers must be able to communicate, in a clear and effective manner, the intent and purpose of their policies and how exactly those policies can be expected to produce the desired result. This will be necessary to convince the private sector that the promised policy measures will in fact be undertaken when they become due and that the intended outcomes can reasonably be expected to be achieved. Otherwise, there are no grounds to suppose that the private sector would shift, or anchor, its expectations in a way that adds to the policymakers' ability to reach their desired goals, such as recovery, smooth exit, debt reduction and low inflation.

The crucial element is to reaffirm the targets and why the policies chosen can be expected to reach them. Woodford (2003) observed that policy trade-offs will be eased when expectations fall in line. And Libich (2009: 685) underlines that '[s]everal recent empirical papers contributed to this debate by showing that in countries with an explicit (i.e., legislated) inflation target expectations are better anchored'.

Astute policymakers will therefore realise that good communication lies at the heart of the policy problem if they want to reach their policy targets in the early periods or at lower cost. This is a fact that has not been lost by central bank policymakers in their attempts to control or anchor private-sector expectations of future inflation in such a way as to make interest-rate policies more effective (Woodford 2005; Blinder et al. 2008; Rudebusch and Williams 2008).

Thus, forward-looking expectations are a powerful mechanism, in combination with the chosen policy values, for influencing the natural dynamics of the economy. The proposition on announcement-based controllability stated earlier (Chapter 5) shows how communication and policy announcements can be exploited to supplement and extend the impact of conventional policy instruments. This gives a formal justification for using policies designed to manage expectations, such as publishing interest-rate forecasts, or a future exit strategy, or the details of a programme of quantitative easing (QE), as well as defining the circumstances in which expectations cannot be anchored or steered (known as cases of policy impotence, instances in which it would be wiser for central banks not to act). Recent research on the effects of US unconventional policies on the economy show that an important factor has been the gradual change in policy expectations by the public, which thought that the pace of recovery would be much faster, anticipating a rapid rebound of the economy and cancellation of the policies. The novelty of the situation could have contributed to this (Engen, Laubach and Reifschneider 2015).

A key implication of forward guidance is that the quality and credibility of communication by policymakers are key issues (Acocella, Di Bartolomeo and Hughes Hallett 2013). Examining the conditions that permit effective signalling and commitment is important.[4] But equally important is to recognise that there is a large class of problems for which effective signalling and commitment are neither necessary nor relevant. However, clear communication is still required in practice for a large class of policy problems in order to allow the agents to check the consistency of the announced policies and target values with their own information. This is relevant from a number of points of view: in particular, for ensuring time consistency and to allow for policymakers' accountability. The latter issue is dealt with in the next subsection.

---

[4] Let us take a couple of examples of the relevance of communication for policy effectiveness. On a number of occasions, the ECB has expressed its concern that long-term policies introduced to combat the financial crisis (greater transparency, new regulation, reduced pro-cyclicality, planned liquidity withdrawals) should have their effects when they are announced. Equally, the announcement of new fiscal stimulus or credit guarantee packages has proved to be effective for fast exit from the financial crisis in the United States.

6.2.3 Rules, Incentives, Degree of Centralisation for the Accountability of Policymakers

This subsection is organised as follows: (1) We first discuss the issue of constraints on the actions of policymakers as a way to ensure certain results; (2) we show that they can be insufficient to get such results and that it is advisable to follow the other path to avoid moral hazard, i.e. the one of incentives (and punishments); (3) we then deal with the nature of rewards, whether economic or of a different kind; (4) within non-economic incentives we discuss the interactions between formal incentives and social norms, the accountability of policymakers and the relevance of partisanship; and (5) we finally discuss the issue of the optimal organisation and accountability of the government from the point of view of its degree of centralisation.

As to the incentives deriving from constraints imposed on the action of policymakers, one could think that institutions should establish a regime of fiscal and monetary discipline and reforms, as these would enhance efficiency and reduce moral hazard by politicians. Strict policy rules as well as market liberalisation, privatisation and so on are often thought to constrain private agents to act in an efficient way and public agents not to pursue their personal or partisan interests. In the EMU, a regime of discipline was enforced both in the way to the common currency (to constrain the countries with higher inflation and public deficit and/or debt, for which fulfilling the Maastricht requirements was more problematic) and afterwards (as the ECB had to establish a reputation of conservativeness and the Stability and Growth Pact (SGP) was in effect). Also in the United States and certain other countries, public debt and/or deficit caps are set. Market liberalisation and similar constraining policies have often inspired international institutions, e.g. the IMF and the World Bank (as an expression of the Washington Consensus) when providing lending or aid.

The literature on the usefulness of constraints to public action is on the whole rather sceptical about the effectiveness of a disciplinary regime. In Coricelli, Cukierman and Dalmazzo (2006), a stricter monetary policy has positive effects on both inflation and unemployment, as it imposes a discipline on trade unions. Fatás and Mihov (2006) find that, in the United States, of the two possible effects of budgetary restrictions – reducing policy discretion and limiting the fiscal responsiveness to shocks – the first effect prevails, and fiscal policy restrictions lead to less volatility.

On the opposite side, according to Dalmazzo, 'commitment to price-stability may allow governments to persist in "bad" fiscal policies and tolerance for low competition, as governments can trade part of the social gains deriving from it for distortionary taxation, redistribution, patronage and the like' (Dalmazzo 2014: 4). Hence, a more conservative central bank tends to produce the effect of a rise in the tax rate, thus questioning the desirability of this type of monetary authority claimed by Coricelli, Cukierman and Dalmazzo (2006). In addition, monetary discipline reduces market deregulation. Acemoglu et al. (2008) have presented a model in which reforms of the kind advocated by the Washington Consensus can be detrimental. In their opinion, such reforms induce politicians to adopt other instruments for furthering their redistributive actions, patronage and so on, thus originating a kind of 'seesaw' effect. These results cast doubts on the validity of the argument in favour of resorting to an external constraint in the form of a conservative central bank or other constraint in order to reform countries characterised by lax fiscal policies and scarcely competitive goods markets. As a conclusion on this point, discipline per se is not a way to get efficient conduct from policymakers and private agents if rules and signals do not contain proper incentives.

A problem to some extent related to that of disciplinary rules but indeed more general is that of obedience to rules.

According to Lawrence Write, reported by Vanberg (2014: 219), 'if everyone knows that the rule of law will be followed, such that nobody will be bailed out, the incentive for imprudence disappears ... [and at least] there won't be system-wide mal-incentives producing an epidemic of imprudence'. In order to discourage imprudence, there should also be rules to follow in case of emergency situations.

The problem arising from this position is that rules cannot foresee all possible contingencies. To face situations not included in the rule, some discretionary attitude must be necessary. An alternative to this way of avoiding malincentives could be that of providing positive incentives, which might lead to better results.

Then let us consider incentives rather than 'disincentives'. Tirole (1994) underlined that economic theory has developed a theory of organisations that has been applied for devising effective incentives in private institutions. This theory is based on three ingredients, i.e. adverse selection, moral hazard and incomplete contracting. Difficulties arise in governments making use of the tools that have been devised for firms, as the field of public organisations is rather different. In fact, both the type of maximand and the number of specific targets are different. The unity of goals in private organisations (maximisation of profits) must be replaced by multiple targets for the government, and maximisation is not required or is difficult or impossible to pursue. The existence of multiple principals, such as when realisation of some goals is entrusted to different departments, can also complicate the effectiveness of control. Finally, asymmetric information can compound troubles in the case of public organisations, because of the possible capture of public officials by lobbies and interest groups. In any case, incentives also can be laid down for public institutions.

Then discussion is open on the proper ways to lay down incentives for effective policymaking. To do this, there are institutional (constitutional) rules that can provide an incentive to policymakers not to act in their interest and to be respectful of their constituencies. However, sometimes these rules are double edged and can have undesired effects, which implies that they should be designed with extreme accuracy.

As to the issue of the kinds of incentives to implement, the literature on the economics of organisations and employee compensation, which mainly refers to the organisation of private firms, provides a foil both for economic and for other, non-economic motivations (Prendergast 1999). Drawing on works from the corporate culture literature (e.g. Kreps 1990), we can refer to four kinds of incentives: work inputs; formal incentives such as pay, bonuses and so on; career incentives; and non-economic kinds of incentives. Work inputs refer mainly to employees. This is the simplest way of checking whether workers comply with their duties, and extra work is usually given an incentive. The ineffectiveness of such inputs is largely demonstrated, and we disregard them. We concentrate here on non-economic incentives and leave the issue of career incentives to later.

Akerlof and Kranton (2005) emphasise the pitfalls of monetary rewards and punishments to motivate workers to work in a firm's interest. They show that identity can act as a substitute for monetary incentives. Also, according to other authors, pecuniary incentives can crowd out workers' motivations to cooperate in the workplace (see e.g. Prendergast 2008; Berdud, Cabasés and Nieto Vázquez 2014). More generally, Bénabou and Tirole (2006) show that people's actions reflect a mix of altruistic motivation, material self-interest and social or self-image concerns. This mix varies across individuals and situations. Sometimes, altering the weights of the three components changes the outcome, thus leading to pro-social (or antisocial) behaviour.

A parallel issue involves the assessment of government performance. This is an awkward object of analysis because, in a world of partisan politics, performance can be differently judged according to the very different preferences of the electorate. In addition, partisan governments can issue signals apparently contradictory to their real preferences in order to gain a larger support (Chatagny 2015).

An analysis of how the accountability of politicians affects public choices is necessary. Political accountability is, in fact, a fundamental feature for evaluating democracy and the performance of governments (Powell 2000). Different institutional arrangements provide differential incentives for politicians to behave in a correct way and to respect their engagements and promises. However, accountability requires a number of conditions to be satisfied for fulfilling this role and, if these are not met, entails some drawbacks.[5] Along this route, Maskin and Tirole (2004) set out a two-period model. In each period, a homogeneous electorate must decide between two possible actions. The electorate believes one action to be optimal and can decide itself (direct democracy) or delegate some official, who will judge which action is optimal. Maskin and Tirole conclude that accountability has both benefits (removal of officials whose conduct appears to be non-congruent with the electorate's will) and drawbacks (as it encourages cheating by officials or pandering). It is desirable when (1) the electorate is informed about the optimal action, (2) acquiring information about the decision is not costly, which is not the case with technical decisions and (3) feedback about the quality of decisions is fast, as the electorate can easily understand the optimality of the politician's decision.

Partly along this route, one can ask whether rules devising the possibility of reappointment can serve as a way to reduce

---

[5] Acemoglu and Jackson (2017) underline the relevance of social accountability, as law-abiding agents have an interest in asking compliance to the law by other agents.

moral hazard and have policymakers acting in the 'public interest'. Again, the issue returns to information and the cost and time for acquiring it in order to refute false claims. In fact, Lambert-Mogiliansky (2015) shows that reappointment of public officials based on 'cheap talk' complaints and their public defence of previous actions can be very useful.

The real issue is whether these conditions can be met in practice. From the point of view of transparency and costs to citizens for the accountability of policymakers, one of the most important issues, raised especially in more recent times, is distrust of citizens. A system for increasing accountability and confidence and 'bring[ing] government back to the people' might consist in a larger degree of decentralisation of policymaking. We discuss this topic below and in Chapter 7.

Decentralisation and federalism – as opposed to centralised governance – have numerous supporters and detractors and can have mixed outcomes. The theoretical literature on federalism and decentralisation is vast and concerns in particular (1) competition among sub-national governments, (2) fiscal federalism, (3) veto players and points, (4) accountability and (5) the size of government. We discuss here only the aspects related to accountability. Other issues will be discussed in Chapter 7.

Decentralisation was initially supported on the argument that it can help in the taking of better decisions and ensure allocation efficiency. Local governments would be more responsive and accountable because of their proximity to interested citizens and their better information than the national government about local conditions and preferences (Hayek 1945). On this, Oates (1972) added that in the absence of spill-overs from one jurisdiction to the others – which would call for centralisation – fiscal responsibilities should be decentralised, as local governments are responsive to preference heterogeneity and needs (Oates' theorem of decentralisation). An argument pointing in the same direction stated that public goods should be provided by the jurisdiction of the minimum geographic area necessary for internalising the benefits and costs of such provision. The local government's malfunctioning would be subject to the threat posed by citizens' 'voting with their feet' due to competition among jurisdictions (Tiebout 1956; Oates 1972). A variant of this argument is that federalism can ensure better information – due to decentralisation – and competition among jurisdictions, thus providing a credible commitment of the engagements taken at the lower levels of government (Qian and Weingast 1997).

However, decentralised solutions would ensure self-interested decision-making while disregarding the existence of positive or negative externalities and interrelationships between issues in the various jurisdictions. Apart from this issue, a regime ensuring these characteristics 'does not come about spontaneously, but depends crucially upon a number of minimum political and social conditions', such as an open, fair political system with binding rules, low barriers to accountability and, thus, transparency, social cohesion and organisation, with 'central government as [a] neutral administrator and referee' (Faguet 1997: 16).

Public-choice theorists insist on the necessity of binding rules in decentralised settings. Rules should limit politicians' discretionary power and force them to serve the public interest (Buchanan 1995; Inman and Rubinfeld 1997). Rules, however, are not a 'panacea' for solving issues of accountability, policy effectiveness and trust in government.[6] Decentralisation works better if there is local democracy and self-governance, which are easier in a community that is homogeneous from economic and social points of view (Azfar et al. 1999), an issue that we will discuss further in Chapter 7. Dissemination of information is also relevant,

---

[6] Suggestions for improving citizens' trust in their government are offered by OECD (2017b). There are quasi-objective ways to measure – or check – citizens' trust, such as the functioning of public services.

since information heterogeneity favours centralisation to reduce rent extraction, while preferences hetereogeneity pushes towards decentralisation (Boffa, Piolatto and Ponzetto 2016).

From an empirical point of view, results have been mixed. First, lobbies and vested interests can 'capture' local government bodies and impair competition among local constituencies (Shah 2008). In addition, in some cases, poor analysis of the characteristics of local communities, inexperience and the weak capacity of local government (especially in less developed countries), as well as an excess of controls by central governments, together with the multiplication of veto players, have impaired the results of decentralisation. In order to succeed, decentralisation should take place in a manner that adds to the accountability of local governments, e.g. by increasing representation of women and other vulnerable groups and allowing for recalls of elected officials from public office (Ylmaz et al. 2008). However, as mentioned earlier, decentralisation would ensure the self-interested decision-making of communities at the cost of disregarding the existence of positive or negative externalities.[7] It should then be avoided when these are relevant, unless a federal government can provide effective solutions to account for such interrelationships. We will also return to this issue in Chapter 7.

Quite different conclusions are reached by authors advocating anarchist solutions, who hold that a society could be governed by free and equal people directly or through their

[7] The definition of externalities as a market failure made by Bator (1958) was too extensive. Baumol and Oates (1975: 17) offer a more precise definition: they exist 'whenever some individual's utility or production relationships include real ... variables whose values are chosen by others (persons, corporations, governments) without particular attention to the effects on ... (their) welfare'. Thus, their definition explicitly includes the case of decentralised governments within or even outside a given country. On this concept, see also Papandreou (1994). Eggertsson, Mehrotra and Summers (2016) deal with this problem in an international environment, concluding on the need to limit international capital mobility.

delegates (in a representative democracy) as an outcome of a convergence of interests (Candela 2014).

6.3   The Issue of Knowledge Sharing of Models and Policy Effectiveness

Information available to the private sector and the government can differ, involving not only the actions of the agents and their nature but also the working of the entire economic system.[8] Our interest here is not on the whole issue of the information available to the various agents but only on a specific part of it, involving the information that the private sector can get through government announcements (forward guidance) about the model and its policy intentions. There are two extreme ways of modelling the information possessed by the private sector in a condition of uncertainty. The assumption of REs is a way to solve the problem of asymmetric information (Grossman 1981). It ensures that the private sector knows how the economy works and/or the preference function of government. Learning is an alternative tool to deal with the issue, finally converging, possibly slowly, to RE solutions under certain conditions.[9] We choose an intermediate one, consisting in announcements by the government, which may or may not be trusted by the private sector. This is indeed a simpler way than the alternative of learning from the policymakers' actions but also a way to avoid the opposite assumption of full REs of the model and the intentions of the government.

More specifically, policymakers can provide their private information (also in terms of projections) to the private sector about the parameters and errors of the model as well as its future actions. Obviously, the private sector should gain

---

[8] This section draws on Acocella and Hughes Hallett (2016).
[9] The literature on the topic is very wide. For the conditions under which learning can lead to RE solutions, in particular, with respect to convergence of monetary policy rules, see Woodford (2003).

from this if two assumptions are made: the policymaker has better knowledge about the workings of the economy and his or her announced actions are credible. Both assumptions are debatable, but conditions under which they – in particular, the latter – are met can be easily satisfied.

In a game between the two sectors of the economy, where the reaction function of private agents is expressed in terms of REs, whereas that of the government may be the object of forward guidance, the model of the economy can be as follows:

(6.1) $\quad y_t = Ay_{t-1} + Bu_t + Cy_{t+1|t} + v_t$

for $t = 1,\ldots,T$, given values for y_0 and y_{T+1}, where $y \in R^S$ is the vector of the states of the system reflecting the policymaker's target variables, $y_{t+1|t} = E[y_{t+1}|\Omega_t]$ denotes the mathematical expectation of y_{t+1} conditional on Ω_t (the common information set available to all the agents at t) and u_t is the vector of control variables in the hands of the policymaker. Matrices A, B and C are constant, of order S, Sxm and S, respectively, and have at least some nonzero elements. In this representation, y_0 is a known initial condition, and y_{T+1} is some known, assumed or expected terminal condition, which is part of the common information set Ω_t. Finally, v_t is a vector of exogenous shocks or other exogenous influences on y_t; it has a known mean but comes from an unspecified probability distribution.

The final form of this model can be derived as

(6.2) $\quad y = Ru + b$

where R and b are appropriate values of the parameters in (6.1). We can use this model for a number of applications. In particular, the effects of forward guidance in terms of pursuit of the policymaker's goals can be assessed. In other words, the contribution of forward guidance to narrowing the gap between the government's target values and the expected outcomes can be calculated in both its deterministic and stochastic parts.

Converting model (6.2) to a 'matching deviations from desired targets' format, we have

(6.3) $\tilde{y} = Ru + c$ where $c = b - \bar{y}$

The additive error term can be decomposed into deterministic and stochastic components:

(6.4) $E_1(\tilde{y}) = RE_1(u) + E_1(c)$ and $\eta = R\xi + \sigma$

where $\eta = y - E_1(y)$, $\xi = u - E_1(u)$, and $\sigma = c - E_1(c)$, and $E_1(\cdot) = E(\cdot|\Omega_1)$ is a convenient shorthand.

With respect to this model, the differences between the information of the two sectors of the economy may occur for at least the following reasons:

1. The policymakers' private information or projections of the errors in the term b in (6.4) differ from the common information or, more likely, from the default position of certainty equivalence. If this forward guidance is accepted by the private sector, we subtract $\Delta b = T_T^{-1}\{v_p - v_g\}$ from the variable c. If, however, the private sector disregards the forward guidance offered completely, only the parts involving the stochastic term σ change.
2. The private information from forward-guidance figures for the announced or expected forward policy variables differ from the private sector's expectations. In this case, where private information differs from forward-guidance figures for the policy variables, $\Delta b = T_T^{-1}(B \otimes I)\{u_p - u_g\}$ must be added to c or σ in (6.4), where u_g contains the forward-guidance elements and u_p contains what the private sector might have expected before the announcement.
3. Differences in understanding how the economy works, which involves differences in the matrices in (6.4).

In this case, if forward guidance is offered on that point, $\Delta b = \{R_p - R_g\}u_g$ from c and/or σ must be subtracted in (6.4).

6.4 How to Enrich the Classical Conception of Economic Policy As a Discipline

In this section we deal with three essential ingredients necessary to enrich economic policy as a discipline along the lines indicated in the previous analysis. The first such ingredient refers to the reliability of analytical propositions. This has to do with economic analysis more than with economic policy properly. However, economic policy is involved, as it should take such analytical propositions into account when prescribing effective policy actions. The second ingredient concerns welfare and social-choice theory, as well as the normative theory of economic policy, which can both be enriched by incorporating political economy concepts. These take account of empirically grounded socioeconomic relations and personal or group interests. Also, the third ingredient refers to both the first and second pillars of economic policy as a discipline in considering realistic possibilities to devise democratic institutions.

The three subsections of this section deal, respectively, with these three ingredients. The resulting implications for institutions are drawn in Section 6.5.

6.4.1 *More Realistic Assumptions for Effective Policy Action*

The need for more realistic assumptions about policymaking in order to improve guidance for persons charged with policy responsibilities has recently been reaffirmed by Duflo (2017). Realism refers to the need to avoid scanty propositions derived from drastic analytical assumptions and too narrow empirical analyses; incorporating analysis of the implied institutions; making clear the political targets to pursue and distinguishing the consequences of the various instruments on each of them.

The first point has to do with the frequent case where policy prescriptions are derived from very 'heroic' and partial theoretical assumptions or are backed by limited or lacking empirical checking. This happened with the theory of 'expansionary austerity' mentioned in Section 3.8., but there have been a number of other similar cases. This shortcoming is common where policy prescriptions are derived directly from analytical propositions, outside the realm indicated by the discipline of economic policy, as indicated in the previous pages. In particular, this would be the case when the complexity of an economic plan (with the interrelationships between the effects of the different instruments) is not considered. Neglect of the whole institutional setting of reference and coexistence of other situations and measures can lead to similar invalid conclusions or suggestions about policy actions. In fact, one of the basic assumptions behind econometric testing is the existence of stable causal relations between variables. This makes it impossible to refer to the values of the parameters estimated in a specific spatiotemporal context in a totally different context. The assumption is easily violated when the initial test is referred to a limited number of countries and the outcomes are not controlled with other possible 'determinants' of the endogenous variable.

In addition, the political targets to pursue must be indicated. For example, one can judge abatement of the interest rate in the United Kingdom after the results of the referendum on Brexit only when the targets pursued by monetary authorities have been clarified. The action by the Bank of England in 2016 was criticised on the ground that it could damage protecting savings, but the bank's governor, Mark Carney, clarified that the goal was instead to protect employment. Similarly, when the Bundesbank authorities protest the near-ZLB interest rates introduced by the ECB as damaging bankers and German savers, they seem to forget that two other targets have been pursued by the ECB through its policy of low interest rates: saving the euro and providing an incentive for recovery. The impossibility of using expansionary fiscal policy, due to the SGP and the 'fiscal compact', compelled the ECB to try to substitute it in the role of pushing the European economy towards recovery.

6.4.2   Incorporating Political Economy Concepts

The theory of economic policy being traditionally part of the discipline of economic policy is normative. It prescribes the course of action to be taken by policymakers trying to pursue their goals, someway derived from the preferences of their constituency. This theory, while a benchmark for policy action, does not always (or often) take account of sociopolitical relations and interests, including those leading to government failures. Incorporating these in workable analyses of policy actions (needed in particular for applications) implies a number of logical or realistic difficulties and additions or changes that are the object of 'political economy'.

To be sure, this term has been used with different meanings. In the first contributions to economic science, from Smith to Marx and Mill, 'political economy' implied attention to the social and political issues underlying the economic process. Later, it has meant study of the interrelationships between economics and politics. There are two basic orientations:

1. That of the mainstream literature, going under the names of political economics or political economy, which we can group together (also by using the terms interchangeably), even if some authors conceive the content and methodology of each as competitive (see e.g. Persson and Tabellini 2000; Mueller 2003); it

applies analytical economics to the political issues of a market system;

2. That of radical political economy, which expresses a methodological attitude contrary to mainstream economics.[10]

We deal with these two trends in the order, describing their content and methodology.

As Glaeser (2005: 2) puts it, 'the insight that economics impacts politics as much as politics impacts economics lies at the heart of political economy'. A number of fields have been affected by political economics.

A recent line of analysis tends to clarify the means whereby a politician or the government in charge can pursue election or reelection. Alonso and Câmara (2016) build a voting model tending to provide information for heterogeneous voters in such a way as to influence their behaviour. They issue a strategic signal that influences the voters in a way that targets different winning coalitions. If the politician and voters share the same preferences, the signal benefits the voters, but this is not the case for conflicting interests between the politician and voters. A simple-majority rule would make a majority of voters always weakly worse off. This can be avoided by requiring a supermajority voting rule, inducing the politician to supply more information.

A more general analytical issue explored by political economics is the explanation of the preferences of voters and the results of elections, as well as the divergences between real policy actions and the social optimum deriving from specific incentive-constraints of policymakers. We begin with these divergences. They can be due to political opportunism or ideology, political competition between candidates with differentiated identity or between government

---

[10] To take account of both sociological and political concepts, in addition to the basic insights from economics, the discipline of economic sociology has been developed (see Swedberg 2008).

parties (divided government), pressure from interest groups (with the related theory of group formation) and lobbying, voting behaviour, political accountability, non-democratic politics and models of bureaucracy. An enquiry reported by Graziano (2001) referring to the United States has noted a prevalence of profit-sector groups interested in public policy, especially on issues related to the economy, with respect to non-profit groups and citizen groups. Public-interest groups – i.e. groups that do not serve the exclusive interests of their members such as environmentalists, pacifists and consumers – are numerous but represent the weak link of the relation between communities and policy authorities. Limits to the action of these groups derive from underrepresentation of minorities, such as African Americans, as well as excessive workload, low pay and little social recognition of people working for these groups, which creates frustration and finally leads them to leave the groups (Graziano 2001).

Grossman and Helpman (2001) have devoted an entire book to the issue of vested interests, dealing not only with the political interests of candidates, partisanship, lobbies and campaign contributions, competition for influencing politicians and legislatures but also with ways to increase communication and educate voters. One of their most important conclusions is that lobbies can add cheap or costly information (the former by speaking to politicians or their staff, the latter by advertising campaigns or similar initiatives influencing the politicians and the public). The influence on politicians depends on the credibility of the information. Politicians will 'accept at face value only those assertions that a lobbyist has reason to make truthfully; otherwise, they discount the claims appropriately in recognition of the (interest) group's bias' (Grossman and Helpman 2001: 23). Lobbyists are credible to politicians having preferences sufficiently similar to theirs or if information can be easily verified or, paradoxically, if it is costly. Grossman and

Helpman (2005), instead, deal with 'pork barrel' as a motivation for ignoring electoral promises by parties.[11]

Most works on vested interests refer to the American case. An important result of empirical research in the United States is that apart from the stricter attitude towards lobbyists of Democrats with respect to Republicans, overall, both representatives and senators are lenient towards them. In fact, they are against further restrictions to lobbyists as unfair or unconstitutional and think that lobbying practices are not abusive (Graziano 2001). The case of Europe also has been the object of analysis (e.g. Bouwen 2002; Coen and Richardson 2009). More recently, a number of other important contributions have been added. Klüver (2013) has inquired not only about isolated interest groups' activity but also about their coalitions, reaching optimistic conclusions about the relevance of business interests and public pressures on EU decisions, with no systematic bias in favour of the former, a result shared by Dür, Bernhagen and Marshall (2015). Dür and Mateo González (2013) and Dür and Mateo (2014) inquire not only about the different means of furthering groups' interests (gaining access or going public) but also about the area covered by groups' pressures (the European Union, as preferred by business groups, or the country level).

Some studies depart from the main current of the literature that depicts lobbying as a distortion of politics. Hall and Deardorff (2006) model lobbying not as vote buying or persuasion but as a type of legislative subsidy in terms of policy information, political intelligence and legislative labour. However, results from empirical analyses indicate that information is mainly a tactic for getting access to decision-makers, in particular, with reference to both the United

---

[11] On the effects of lobbying on policy action, see also Baumgartner et al. (2009).

States and the European Union (e.g. respectively for the two, Hrebenar and Morgan 2009 and Chalmers 2013).

Berry (2015), instead, inquires about lobbying in favour of common people. As mentioned earlier, this tends to protect the environment or other public interests such as creating open and accountable government, promoting equal rights and opportunities and making people's voices heard in the political process.

The opportunism of policymakers has negative consequences in macroeconomic terms, as it generates excess expenditure, debt accumulation and tax distortions. Inefficiencies arise at the level of the system, contrary to what should happen if the Coase theorem could be extended to politics, since inefficiencies serve the interests of politicians and social groups holding political power (Acemoglu 2003).

At a normative level, proper institutions and a constitutional design based on rules rather than policymakers' discretionary conduct are suggested to ensure accountability and commitment of policymakers and reduce the above-mentioned divergences between public and private interests. For reasons of space, we cannot deal with any of them here, even if in general these suggestions can enrich both pillars of economic policy in their practical applications. In fact, on the one hand, they influence procedures for the election of politicians and the relationships between different levels of government; on the other, they can impose limits to the government policy or at least influence it. However, we must note that certain specific conclusions of this strand of literature have been rejected by our analysis in previous chapters or appear as problematic in the light of our theory, such as in the case of the supposed superiority of rules in order to limit the inefficient conduct of policymakers. In other cases, however, political economy contributions do really enrich the theory we have developed so far.

Another important issue examined by the political economy literature is the preferences of governments having different political orientations. The current political debate holds that left-wing governments are less fiscally responsible, Recent empirical analyses have disproved this belief and have shown that left-wing governments give rise to lower public debt accumulation than right-wing ones (Müller, Storesletten and Zilibotti 2016).

As discussed earlier, the second analytical trend under the name of radical political economy is based on a critique of the capitalist system. It intends to combine economic analysis with political activism in an attempt to practically gain better standards of life for individuals and communities. In some cases, the conclusions of this strand of analysis do not lead to significant practical applications, and the critical aspects of the existing order prevail over constructive suggestions of institutional reforms and political changes. Other works are, instead, more constructive and useful.

We will enrich our analysis of the previous chapters with political economy considerations of both lines of research. In the next subsection as well as in Chapter 7 we will refer to institutions inherited from history – notably, democracy – and analyse the possibility to change or amend them as well as current policies in such a way as to increase their effectiveness. To accomplish this task, we exploit political economy considerations in a manner that highlights obstacles to the implementation of economic policy as we have developed it in previous chapters. However, we must make it clear that our value premise is that the capitalist system can be reformed in a way to better satisfy citizens' interest, at least in its present stage. We are conscious that this is not an easy task, as there are powerful vested interests acting against reforms. The potential to overcome these interests largely depends on the existence of a democratic government, which is the object of the next subsection. Obviously enough, this government should first remove the determinants of 'distorted' voter preferences. The possibility of success of this action much depends on reduction of the inequalities that feed the action of lobbyists. It also depends on the education of citizens and the emergence of new ideas about fading outdated theories that still have an influence on current conduct (Keynes 1936: 383).

6.4.3   The Political Issues of a Democratic Government

A number of issues arise when one wants to ensure a democratic government. The very idea of democracy should indeed be critically discussed. As Graham (1986: 1) puts it, '[c]rudely speaking, up to the eighteenth century everyone had a clear idea what democracy was and hardly anyone was in favour of it. Now the position is reversed. Everyone is in favour of it but no one has a clear idea any longer what it is.'

In our context, two critical issues need deeper analysis. They are strictly intertwined, and both pertain to the first pillar of the core but also have implications for the second pillar. The first issue has to do with the logical (and procedural) possibility of finding a government's maximand representing the citizen's – usually conflicting – preferences. The second refers to the possibility that in practice the various interests in the society and the government are composed in a non-conflicting way, enabling us to reach that maximand or to get close to it. Democracy should ensure this. We accept the idea that people can pursue goals concerning not their strict interests but other people's as an effect of 'sympathy' (in Sen's (1977) words). More difficult is adhering to the idea that other people's interests can be imposed on some agent, who should be committed to pursue them and really does so. In this case, the agent will always try to pursue his or her personal goals, to the detriment of others', thus disobeying or eluding commitment (Sen 1987), unless he or she tacitly accepts other people's goal as his or her own, as in the case of group behaviour (Cudd 2014). When conflicts cannot be resolved, either non-democratic governance or separation of conflicting parts takes place. In the former case, only some people's interests are satisfied, whereas in the latter, all of them tend to be, at least in principle, satisfied by each separate community. However, as we will see, to some extent, separation can be avoided by adopting suitable procedural rules.

In the remaining part of this subsection we deal with the influence of inequalities on the construction of a democratic order. In Chapter 7 we investigate the issues that arise in an attempt to resolve conflicts among the various sections of a community.

There can be obstacles in ensuring representation of all citizens' preferences in a democratic society, the first such obstacle being inequalities among citizens. According to some, this would not be a problem in a democratic setting, since rising inequalities should lead the median voter to vote in favour of redistribution, which would re-establish equality (Meltzer and Richard 1981; Bolton and Roland 1997). This outcome could, however, be hindered by a number of factors. These range from the impact of redistribution on labour supply, deadweight losses, low turnout of the poor or impediments to their voting – e.g. for immigrants – ideological orientation and ethnic differences. Finally, as we know from the preceding subsection, the rich can introduce a bias in the orientation of the popular vote. In fact, they can impose their interests and visions via lobbying, campaign contributions and other more or less acceptable ways (Bénabou 2000; McCarty, Poole and Rosenthal 2006; Bonica et al. 2013). In general, uneven distribution enables the rich to push for economic and political institutions that are favourable to maintaining inequality (Acemoglu, Johnson and Robinson 2005). However, in practice, the issue is even more complex, as a more intricate pattern of the initial distribution determines the outcome for institutions and post-voting inequality. In fact, post-tax inequality is higher if the gap between the middle class and the poor is small and when land inequality is high (Acemoglu et al. 2015).

Some authors minimise the democratic failures that could be introduced in the 'political market' as an effect of unequal distribution of income and wealth (e.g. Wittman 1995). By contrast, Louis Brandeis, US Supreme Court judge in the first half of the last century, is reported by Gilens (2012) as saying that wealth concentration and democracy are two conflicting situations. There is indeed empirical evidence in favour of this position. Marshall and Jaggers (2000) show that 95 per cent of the more equal countries in terms of Gini indices can be classified as democracies, whereas only 75 per cent of the less equal societies can be considered as democracies.

However, this relation between democracy and distribution should be considered in deeper detail, which we can do if we do not just look at the surface of people's apparent preferences but also take account of the forces modelling them. Gilens (2012: 2) finds that policy actions in the United States correspond to the preferences of the society but are strongly tilted towards the most affluent citizens, especially when opinions differ. In general, the preferences of the majority of Americans do seem to have no influence on policy decisions, at least for those having a strong impact on distributive issues. Gradstein (2007) finds that in cases of very unequal distribution, the rich do not relinquish their power in favour of a democratic setting. In other cases, they prefer to exert their influence for building a democratic society on the presumption that this will ensure protection of their property rights in the future. The uneven responsiveness of political representatives and citizens' preferences has also been revealed in the case of Europe, differing, however, in intensity over the different countries (see Lefkofridi, Giger and Kissau 2012 and other papers published in the same issue of the journal[12]). These authors also find that there is poor knowledge about the mechanism by which economic and social inequalities transfer into uneven political representation and political inequalities because the preferences of some groups are systematically neglected by the political elites.

At least a part of this mechanism is explained by Przeworski (2006: 316) in convincing terms. In a democracy, starting from some assumptions, one can say that 'the result of the election is accepted by everyone ... if [it] ... leaves both the poor and the wealthy at least as well off as they expect to be were they to seek to establish their respective dictatorships'. The underlying assumptions 'imply that when a country is poor, either the electoral winner or the loser may opt for dictatorship, while when a country is wealthy, the winner pushes the loser to indifference, but not further'. This could explain why a negative correlation can be found between inequality and democracy and justify Przeworski's words (2006: 313) when he says that 'if the degree of income redistribution is insufficient for the poor or excessive for the wealthy, they may turn against democracy'. This implies, on the one hand, that in less developed contries there is no room for redistribution and also that 'the probability that a democracy survives rises steeply in per capita income' (Przeworski 2006: 316). However, redistribution can never be too large because not only the rich have powerful tools to ensure this outcome but also the size of redistribution must leave the incentive for the rich to live in a democratic setting, also hoping that this will ensure protection of their property rights in the future.

This reasoning might be thought as drawing unwarranted conclusions from a simple correlation, but in addition to the

---

[12] An important comparative analysis with reference to Europe is offered by Rosset, Giger and Bernauer (2013), who show that system inequality, as measured by the Gini coefficient, reinforces the political underrepresentation of the poor. Possible explanations are the different political weight tied to the economic position and/or economic cleavage and self-interest.

theoretical motivations offered by Przeworski, there are historical analyses showing that the direction of causality should run from inequality to the degree of democratic government. In fact, from a comparative investigation on the American colonies, Engerman and Sokoloff (2002) found historical evidence that more initial inequality tended to deter democracy.

As a manner of conclusion, we can say that economic inequalities are likely to be the most important obstacle to democratic representation and non-conflicting harmonisation of interests, more important than divisions of race, religion and the like. This validates Graham's (1986) and Arblaster's (2002) idea that in order to implement the basic idea of democracy as self-rule, the role of both political liberty and equality should be emphasised.

6.5   Complementing and Refining the Abstract Theory of Policymaking

This chapter has accomplished a number of tasks. After the first four chapters sketched an abstract theory of policymaking and a fifth chapter applied our conception of economic policy to the main current issues, in this chapter we have tried to refine the theory and application of the previous chapters. We have done so from three points of view. The first refers to suitable institutions disciplining and directing both the private and public agents for correct decisions through signals and incentives. In addition, we have raised the issue of the model used for policymaking and its congruence with the private sector's model. Finally, we have discussed the need for more realistic assumptions about effective policymaking, notably with reference to the incorporation of political economy concepts and the need of ensuring conditions for a democratic government in systems with economic inequality. When noting the need for realism in devising institutions and policy, one should not forget that some degree of abstract and even utopian thinking is useful and needed in order not to become prisoners of compromises and special interests.[13] In a number of points, we have dealt with the issue of a proper institutional setting, which is the object of Chapter 7 as a unifying concept of economic policy as a discipline.

---

[13] The great probabilistic mathematician Bruno de Finetti encouraged moving away from a vision of society constrained by what is seen as realistic. As Ietto-Gillies (2008: 119) notes in recalling de Finetti's thought, 'this often means a view which is in line with the interests of the existing establishment and the status quo. Instead we should think of the ultimate aims we want for society and then on the means to achieve them.' In fact, de Finetti (1976: 8–9, my translation) clarifies that his 'Utopia' is not to be taken as 'something absurd and unrealizable, [but] rather as a preliminary and idealized description of a future to be constructed as far as possible in line with such a model'.

7

Why Can Economic Policy Be a Useful Discipline?

7.1 Institutions As the Ring Connecting the Three Parts of Economic Policy

Until now we have used the term 'institution' in a rather loose sense, generally as long-term rules set by the government but also as an organisation, public or private. At this point, the precise meaning of the term needs some clarification. The term has indeed been given a variety of meanings in social sciences. However, these can be reduced essentially to the following two, which offer a more formal definition of the concept. First, the term may indicate a set of 'rules' that regulate in a lasting manner economic and social relationships within a group of agents; in this sense, for example, marriage, private property and the market are all institutions.[1] A second meaning extends the previous definition to include the organised agents involved in implementing the rules and allocating the resources necessary to do so; in this second sense, the

---

[1] North (1991: 97) has a concept of institutions that appears to be similar to this: institutions are formal and informal constraints structuring political, economic and social interactions. They define the choice set, provide the incentive structure of an economy, evolve incrementally and tend to create order and reduce uncertainty.

   According to Swedberg (2008: 946), 'an institution may be conceptualized as a dominant system of interrelated informal and formal elements – customs, shared beliefs, norms, and rules – which actors orient their actions to, when they pursue their interests'.

295

firm, the government, the family and the Mafia are all institutions. Henceforth, we will use the term in both senses.

Institutions are largely inherited from history (Iversen 2006), and there are institutional complementarities. Both these features make it difficult to reform institutions, starting anew, and sometimes even to partially reform them. There are, however, ways to change them partially. Policymakers should take account of some of the existing rules and organisations as constraints while planning to reform others over time, gradually.

The role of institutions is relevant to our discussion from many points of view. They permeate the whole discipline of economic policy,[2] being of the utmost relevance when identifying – or weighing – the goals that should direct public policy according to citizens' preferences or because they affect the general nature of the performance of the system and condition current policies and their effects (Acocella 1994: 1–2, English edn).[3] Institutions are a necessary ingredient for all three parts of economic policy as a discipline. In fact, they are behind both its pillars and the logic and theory of economic policy, as well as their practical implementation, applied economic policy, which can be defined only in a given historical and institutional context.

Thus, institutions hold together the discipline and characterise it with respect to other branches of the economic science, economic analysis – which largely but not completely neglects them – and public finance, which focuses on certain specific rules and activities of public bodies.

---

[2] Not to mention the relevant role of institutions in shaping economic behaviour and structure underlined by the old institutional school, born with Veblen's seminal contribution (e.g. Veblen 1898).

[3] Colander and Kupers (2016) correctly speak of institutions as an 'ecostructure' in which individuals can operate and of institutional policy as 'metapolicy'. Examples of 'ecostructural' interventions are offered in the fields of educational, entrepreneurship, intellectual property and climate change.

To be true, institutions play a role in both economic analysis and policy, but in the former their range is much more limited, and they are not often explicitly discussed or compared as such. However, one should consider that this statement strictly holds true only for highly theoretical analysis. In real life, institutions are 'embedded' in economic relations, as they influence the action of rational men (Granovetter 1985, who develops and corrects Polanyi's (1957) position).

The purpose of the following sections is to show in greater detail why institutions are the glue that holds together the two pillars of economic policy and the whole discipline. Concisely, the line of our argument is as follows: we are convinced that any social discipline is value laden.[4] Then, values are behind any discipline, in particular, social sciences. In the realm of economic policy, values are behind its pillars, as they determine social choice and welfare and direct the goals of policymakers and other social institutions (as well as their interactions). Institutions are, in some sense, the reverse side of value judgments. In fact, on the one hand, they define the procedures – which reflect values – needed for both ensuring the possibility of devising social choices out of individuals' preferences and determining any desired goal (Sections 7.2. to 7.4). On the other hand, they set the frame within which these goals are implemented through policy action, taking account also of the historical setting of each country. Institutions are then needed for ensuring the effectiveness of policy action directed at social goals

---

[4] We cannot – nor would we want to – deny the role of value judgments in economic analysis. Also in this discipline, they direct the researcher to the object and field of his or her inquiry as well as to the methodology he or she employs. They thus mix with 'objective' findings. In this we agree with Myrdal (1953) and, more recently, with Reiss (2013). Reiss also underlines the value-laden nature of even such basic statistical measurements as the construction of a consumer price index. *A fortiori*, this applies to econometric estimation. Nevertheless, the role of value judgments and theories of justice in economic policy is much deeper and more extensive, as they are the basis of the preference function of policymakers.

(Sections 7.5 and 7.6). Section 7.7 concludes by underlining the central role of institutions as the glue connecting the two pillars of economic policy (and, indeed, the three parts of economic policy) and restating its role as a unitary discipline.

7.2   Social Choice and Institutions for Building a Fair Society

In Section 3.1 we showed that value judgments – or, better, a theory of justice – are necessary to define a social ordering out of individual preferences and how institutions shaping the desired social rules can be properly implemented. In Section 6.4.3 we also inquired into how the performance of the economy can be shaped by the practical impacts of theories of justice, in terms of distribution of income and wealth. In this section we return to the strict implications of theories of justice and investigate more deeply their connection with institutions. The concepts of justice and institutions are strictly intertwined, almost as two sides of the same coin (at least as far as economic disciplines and social sciences are considered). In order to see this, one can think of the procedural counterpart of the axiomatic theory of social choice, which emphasises the different value judgments underlying construction of a social order.

For example, consider that the various types of democracy (as well as other voting procedures or, more generally, canons of social relations) have different consequences for the social order in terms of distribution. We read the link between theory of justice and the related institutions through Sen's analysis of the different types of institutions implied by the different requirements of theories of justice. Then we focus on the types of institutions that are closer to practical applications of some theories of justice and issues, specifically as far as inequality and redistribution are concerned.

Sen (2009) sees two types of institutions, 'transcendental-focused institutions' and 'realisation-focused institutions'. The former aim at devising a unique set of principles that can ideally define just institutions. The latter aim equally at the fundamental goal of any theory of justice, attainment of a better world. However – differently from transcendental-focused institutions – they do not try to pursue the same demanding goal and judge the relative merits of different practical institutions on the basis on their possible outcomes and in the light of some social-choice principle. We discuss both in turn.

The transcendental theories aim to identify an ideal of a perfectly just society. These theories want to devise a unique set of principles to select specific institutions that satisfy these principles and are then *perfectly* just. Their most recent and forceful expression is offered by Rawls (1971). Before Rawls, there were other attempts in Western philosophy to pursue the same end of stating propositions that define the archetype of a perfectly ideal society, starting with the Greek philosophers, mainly Plato and Aristotle, moving to modern social thinkers such as Hobbes, Locke, Rousseau and Kant and, finally, to contemporaries such as Dworkin, Gauthier and Nozick. However, as an outcome of an even unitary enterprise for defining a perfect social contract, the bricks and architecture for describing the features of an ideal society differ among these authors depending on the different foundations or postulates that support their analysis.

To exemplify, Plato in his 'Form of the Good' identifies this as the superlative to guide philosopher-kings in ruling the Republic. For Aristotle's *Metaphysics*, the concepts transcending the categories are 'being', 'unity', 'truth' and 'goodness', but he discusses unity ('One') alone in an explicit way because this is the only transcendental intrinsically related to being, whereas truth and goodness relate to rational creatures. In the *Nicomachean Ethics*, Aristotle offers possibly the first version of justice as fairness, with a requirement of correction of what is inequitable ('corrective' justice). Jumping to modern times, Hobbes (1651) starts from the postulate of the negative aspects of the situation that is likely to be an alternative to any kind of government, the 'war of all against all'. This and the underlying nature of men justify a *pactum unionis* that is also a *pactum subiectionis*, whereby individuals decide to live together and to cede some rights to a sovereign authority for the sake of their protection. According to Kant (1797), justice must first respect the sole 'innate' (as distinct from 'acquired') right of men, i.e. freedom of their action, with the only limitation of not violating others' rights.

Among contemporaries, Rawls prefers to speak, instead of utilities, of 'expectations' of individuals as members of a society with shared values. His yardstick for inequality is the quantity of 'primary' social goods available to individuals: rights and liberties, opportunities and powers, income and wealth (Rawls 1971: 90*ff*).

In his theory, a given distribution is just when it is fair, in the sense that it offers everyone the same opportunities. Rawls arrives at this position by way of a thought experiment in which individuals find themselves in an 'original' position in which they decide as free and equal persons the structure (rules) of a just society (in other words, the basis of their social contract). Each individual ignores how the various alternatives can influence himself or herself and decides on the basis of general considerations only, since he or she is covered by a veil of ignorance with regard to

1. His or her current and future position in society, particularly his or her class and social status;
2. The distribution of endowments, natural abilities such as strength, intelligence and so on;
3. His or her personal preferences, especially aversion to risk; and
4. Other circumstances such as the political and economic situation, his or her age group and so on.

In such conditions, the members of this society would unanimously accept the following two principles of justice:

1. 'Each person is to have an equal right to the most extensive total system of equal basic liberties compatible with a similar system of liberty for all.'
2. 'Social and economic inequalities are to be arranged so that they are: a) to be of the greatest benefit of the least advantaged ... and b) attached to offices and positions open to all under conditions of fair equality of opportunity' (Rawls 1971: 302).

The second of these could be of particular importance to our discussion, as Rawls's position differs from the one that would result from other theories of justice, in being markedly – if not perfectly – egalitarian or egalitarian in a space different from that of utilities. The reasons for this conclusion lie in the underlying assumption that people share values with the other members of their society. This results in the need to ensure availability of primary goods for all people to become a rule, and this rule turns into an institutional trait of the society (Schiattarella 2013).

By contrast, Nozick (1974), starting from the Kantian idea that people should be treated as individual ends (because of 'separateness of persons'), argues in favour of a 'minimal state' designed only to protect them against force, theft and fraud and provide the norms to enforce contracts in order not to violate people's rights. Nozick (1974) develops the so-called entitlement theory, which has numerous forebears (among the most recent ones, see von Hayek 1960). His theory assesses distributive justice with regard not to results (e.g. the quantity of goods available to individuals or the utility each enjoys) but rather to procedures. Any distribution is considered just if individuals' fundamental rights have been respected. Regardless of levels and differences in individual utilities, these rights include the right to life and to enjoy the products of one's labour and freedom of choice.

They are inalienable rights, being independent of, and antecedent to, all forms of social organisation. They are also absolute, in that they are not subject to any constraint other than the duty to respect the fundamental rights of others.

This sort of theory of justice aims only to guarantee liberty and the exercise of rights, not to satisfy preferences. The yardstick of justice is not individual utility, i.e. the consequences of a certain social state for an individual, but rather the exercise and respect of rights. For Nozick, individual utilities are not the appropriate yardstick for assessing whether the justice criterion (safeguarding rights) has been satisfied. Thus, apart from the common reference to a space different from that of utility, Nozick challenges the principles of justice derived by Rawls (1971), setting himself almost at the opposite end of the spectrum.

Realisation-focused institutions have been suggested by a number of authors, mainly economists and philosophers, starting with Smith, the Marquis de Condorcet, Bentham, Marx and John Stuart Mill to Sen and Nussbaum. Most of these authors have different ideas of how a just society should look and of the ways of making social comparisons. However, in referring to them, Sen says:

> They were all involved in comparisons of societies that exist or could emerge, rather than confining their analyses to transcendental searches for a perfectly just society. Based on realization-focused comparisons, they were often primarily interested in the removal of manifest injustices they saw in the world, such as slavery, or policy-induced poverty, or cruel and counterproductive penal codes, or rampant exploitation, or the subjugation of women. (Sen 2010: 58)

According to Sen, to design the contour of a perfectly just society is neither necessary nor sufficient to advance justice in the real world, where hunger, illiteracy, torture, arbitrary incarceration and medical exclusion are sources of iniquities and injustice. For getting rid of these, we just need to make comparative judgments of justice across different social systems. This would avoid being engaged in a more difficult exercise also because – as discussed earlier – very different conceptions of the perfectly just society emerge from different postulates. The issues of 'redundancy' and 'feasibility' when searching for a transcendental solution would then emerge (see e.g. Sen 2009: 9).

Some authors are inclined to think that Sen's distinction has some flaws, since realisation-oriented comparisons need some idea of transcendental superiority (Valentini 2011; Ege, Igersheim and Le Chapelain 2012). However, Sen (2009) illustrates the reasons why transcendental theories are neither necessary nor sufficient for comparative judgments of justice.

The relative merits of each type of institution could be beyond our interest, as both positions would imply a relationship between social-choice theory and institutions. However, reference to realisation-focused institutions seems to be more pregnant to us, as this concept insists on the implementation of institutions and their effects. In addition, it is simpler for people to accept its conclusions, since it is not based on an ultimate conception of what justice is. It thus can offer us a practical counterpart to social goals.[5]

Think in particular of the procedural counterpart of the axiomatic approach to social welfare and choice followed by Arrow (1950, 1951). If we take an example of this approach, we easily understand why a realisation-focused theory of justice can better assess institutions. Let us take some form of democratic voting. This would be both a social-choice procedure and a (fundamental) institution of a society, tightly connected with social justice. Sen (1999a) insists on this tight connection, as democracy would enhance capabilities for both its instrumental value in supporting people's

---

[5] Again, as for the applications examined in Chapters 5 and 6, reference to reality can help the theory to be more pregnant and fruitful.

claims and rights and its constructive value for participation to public life ('democracy as public reason'). These conclusions can be easily accepted by any other theory of justice, either realisation focused or transcendental focused, as all could share the ability to support people's claims and rights and the dynamic value of democracy as a way of enlarging the potential for participation in public life and thus achievement of 'democracy as public reason'.

The central task of a theory of social justice should be – at least from our point of view – to suggest policy changes to the social and institutional setting of some country. Suggestions should be useful and feasible. From the former point of view, they should start from the social situation existing in the country in question and the most basic or urgent needs to be satisfied there; reference to the best possible solution – as derived from an ideal optimum – may not be useful and can even be dangerous. From the latter, from a dynamic perspective, suggestions of changes should account for the potential improvements that can be derived from their implementation, given each country's initial historical and institutional situation. Transcendental-focused theories, aiming at the best possible institutions, disregard both suggestions of these requirements. For this reason, it is easier and more useful to start from realisation-focused theories. The following sections will articulate the issues arising in democratic institutions and their possible content.

7.3 Conflicts and Coordination in a Democratic Society

This section attempts to assess whether democracy as an institution can implement social choice and ensure some kind of equality, hopefully in a peaceful way, in a situation with different preferences and interests among citizens. It is important at this point to qualify our notion of democracy. This is an institutional arrangement ensuring competition for political power between citizens and parties, participation in the selection of leaders and policies, at least under the form of free and fair elections (but, possibly, also through various forms of people's involvement in policy decisions), and finally, the potential for citizens to enjoy political and civil liberties (Diamond, Linz and Lipset 1995).

An important objection to democracy can arise from the requirement that we possess knowledge for deciding. According to Plato's 'Republic', policy decisions should follow the lead of those who know, specifically philosophers. Democracy would then be inefficient as a means for determining the right thing to do, as everybody's opinions would be treated equally, disregarding one's knowledge. The implication is that, if – as a group – we want to go to some place, it is not reasonable to assume that everyone has an equally valid opinion of how to get to that place.

This argument is easy to counter. Several assumptions that one can find difficult to accept underlie it. Apart from the notation that philosophers may lack the practical wisdom that can orient policy action, there are certainly areas where technical knowledge is necessary. However, in any case, policy decisions should be the responsibility of the majority of people. The argument of being informed before deciding is relevant, but this is one of the reasons why democracy should be supported by education and discussion in a way that citizens can discover the best course of action.[6] The process of social choice needs to be dynamic, having this opportunity for the whole people of discovering the way to arrive at better decisions. We will devote the next section to a discussion of education.

Sen develops and clarifies his notion of democracy as public reasoning and emphasises the relevance of issues such as the informational role of democracy, tolerant values, the inescapable plurality of principles and the necessity to

---

[6] Dukes (1996) also argues in a similar way.

connect opportunity freedom and process freedom. The former type of freedom represents the real opportunity to achieve functionings, whereas for the latter what matters is the opportunity to achieve and thus to belong to institutions and to practice democracy. According to Sen (2009: 113), it is through public reasoning, education, especially of women, and demand for participation – as required by social-choice theory – that democracy can advance.[7] This is also a way for 'basing an adequately articulated idea of social justice on the demands of the social theory of justice and fairness'.[8]

The issue arising from this conception is whether public reasoning can cope not only with informational differences but also with other sources of conflicts. In our societies, a number of conflicts arise, as in the past, because of different interests or religion or race. Sometimes they are resolved in a peaceful way. Often conflicts lead to some kind of violence or separation of states. Conflicts also can take a violent expression in advanced countries. As to separation, which recurred especially in the 1970s and 1980s, the number of democratic governments has increased threefold in the world, and transition to democracy has witnessed a rise in violent struggles and has led to the oppression of some over other citizens (Reilly 2001 and the references therein).These consequences are not an inevitable characteristic of politics in divided societies but often a reaction to the institutional "rules of the game" under which the democratic competition of the electoral process takes place' (Reilly 2001: 2).

---

[7] This echoes Frisch (1970), who said, 'I want a society which is a living democracy, not only a formal one with free elections, so-called freedom of speech, a so-called free press and so on, but a democracy that is living in the sense of actually engaging as many as possible of the citizens to take an active part in the affairs of the small community where they are living, and also to take an active part in the affairs of the nation as a whole.'

[8] On this, Sen evokes J. S. Mill, who wrote that 'for practical purposes, Political Economy is inseparably intertwined with many other branches of Social Philosophy' (Mill 1848: 3).

Such rules should not favour the tendency to politicise ethnic demands because politicians in divided societies would have an incentive to play the 'ethnic card'. By changing these rules, conflicts can be eliminated or, at least, reduced. Candidates for election should be given an incentive to cooperate across different ethnicities, by encouraging, for example, 'reciprocal vote transfer between candidates representing antagonistic social groups' (Reilly 2001: 8).

The argument has also been proposed that extreme conflicts can be avoided by democracy through accountability, as this should temper them. However, accountability also weakens actions for repressing conflicts and maintaining security. The net effect is uncertain. Collier and Rohner (2008) have examined the topic from an empirical point of view and conclude that the positive effect of accountability tends to become more potent as income rises. A democratic regime would thus be suitable only for developed countries.

Acemoglu et al. (2008) suggest that the correlation between income level and democracy is apparent rather than real. Studies that find such a correlation do not control for factors that simultaneously affect both variables. Survival of dictatorships is indeed independent of income. By contrast, democratisation has a positive effect on growth. It is true that clientelism, the strength of powerful groups, negative exogenous shocks and other factors can have an influence on the outcome of democratisation. However, when the effects of democratisation are controlled for these factors, empirical estimates show that a country switching from autocracy to democracy achieves about 20 per cent higher gross domestic product (GDP) per capita (in addition to the positive effects on the tax-to-GDP ratio and primary school enrolment rates) over roughly thirty years (Acemoglu et al. 2014). Against these possible gains are, however, obstacles to the implementation of democracy. In particular, we should remember that obstacles arise, especially in less developed countries, to removing one of most important determinants of interest groups' action aiming at distorting citizens' preferences, i.e. income and wealth inequality (see Section 6.4).

Sen (2009: chap. 15) contends that democracy can be implemented only in Western societies or – better – in countries with a higher average income level. On the one hand, he argues that the ideals of 'political participation, dialogue and public interaction' underlying it have a universal value (2009: 326). On the other hand, one should not assume that a satisfactory level of democracy has been achieved in those countries. Sen's notation seems to be highly remarkable, as in apparently democratic countries subtle ways can be used to create consensus for the dominant groups, as we have seen in Chapter 6.

As to less developed countries – more generally, countries with deep conflicts – a number of suggestions can improve social relations. For this reason, deliberative democracy should be adopted.[9] This is a form of democracy – whose roots can be traced back to Aristotle and J. S. Mill – recently advocated by Habermas (1984) in terms of communicative rationality, which differs from mere voting in that it associates elements of consensus to some majority rule.[10]

In implementing democracy, one could exploit actions and institutions that can avoid or reduce conflicts. Take concertation among workers, firms and the government, which has proved to be an effective way to avoid conflicts in developed countries. With specific reference to Europe, De Leonardis, Negrelli and Salais (2012) show why and how in a democracy where pluralism is ensured and citizens participate in collective bargaining, public decision is crucial for its future. Another way to reduce conflicts is by compensating the losers from some policy actions by those who are

---

[9] See Horowitz (1993), Sisk (2003) and Dryzek and List (2003).
[10] Mill (1848) had warned about the risk of authoritarian distortions deriving from strict democratic rules, not respecting the rights of minorities.

advantaged. As a matter of fact, welfare-state provisions are an instrument for compensating the losers in the social race.

The issue of the relationships between democracy and justice should be further clarified at this point as a way to introduce the central role of education in a democratic society. Democracy and justice are two rather clearly different concepts (Goodin 2004). The former emphasises procedures, whereas the latter is interested in outcomes. The difficulty is to ensure both at the same time.

According to some authors, the process of freedom advocated by Sen can be of detriment to opportunity freedom, i.e. social justice. In this situation, only those active would enjoy full benefits (hence the objection of 'athleticism' referred to in Sen's theory). Critics say that in addition to activism, or a specific kind of it, some other conditions need to be guaranteed in order to ensure democracy in unequal societies. In particular, the outcomes of democratic procedures can be distorted for a number of reasons: not only misinformation and ignorance will hit some specific sections of the population but mainly the power of the rich, who impose distortions.[11] In his *The Idea of Justice*, Sen seeks to answer this criticism: he develops and clarifies his notion of democracy as public reasoning and emphasises the relevance of issues such as the informational role of democracy, tolerant values, the inescapable plurality of principles and the necessity to connect opportunity freedom and process freedom (Bonvin 2005). Education can be a powerful means to this end.

7.4 The Central Role of Education for Democracy

An important – and preliminary – issue to discuss involves the goal of education, in particular, whether this should be

---

[11] The close connection between education (and other non-income dimensions of welfare) and inequality is stressed by Ravallion (2016). A number of ways to avoid capture of policymakers by vested interests are suggested by OECD (2017c).

directed towards enhancing economic growth or democracy. Education is certainly important for growth[12] – and we focused on this objective in a number of points earlier – but this is not its only possible relevant effect.

Remaining within this objective of education, it must be realised that a whole range of institutions can perform the role of enhancing growth. To be sure, Lucas' explanation of comparative growth focuses on differential patterns of learning by doing and human capital accumulation together with openness of the country (Lucas 1993). However, comparing the growth paths of Korea and the Philippines in the last fifty years, as initially done by Lucas, Acemoglu and Robinson (2015b), shows that education should be complemented by cohesive social relations and an effective role of the state. In any event, education can play an important role (Acemoglu, Johnson and Robinson 2005).[13]

With reference to the more general issue of the goals of education, growth or other ends, Lauder (1991) has criticised the diffusion of education concerned with providing notions that ensure economic efficiency as opposed to an education system tending to offer the grid references of a democratic (while economically sophisticated) society. The Bologna Declaration on higher education, dated 1999, tends to pursue as its main end an objective suitable for the Lisbon Strategy of making Europe the most competitive area in the world, which was launched the year after. This contradicts the Universal Declaration of Human Rights of 1948 (see United Nations General Assembly 1948) as well as the UNESCO Declaration of 1998 (UNESCO 1998) and the project launched by the European Council itself in 1999 for making the universities sites of citizenship with the aim to educate

---

[12] One of the positive roles that education can play in this respect refers to enhancing the competencies and skills needed for a well-performing civil service (see OECD 2017a).

[13] Aghion et al. (2009) find a noticeable effect only of four-year type higher education, not of two-year college education for the United States.

for democracy and to promote citizenship (Council of Europe, Committee of Ministers 1999).

Contrary to the pragmatic orientation of the Bologna Declaration, some authors underline the need to consider a more general target for education. Zgaga (2009) asks for recognition of the full range of the educational purposes. Attention for less-endowed pupils in basic education and other features of the education system can be important for innovation and growth, as well as for the democratic development of a society. From this point of view, the Finnish public comprehensive system is exemplary. It is able not only to offer high-quality education that can be used by firms and other organisations for innovation and growth (Finland is at the top of innovative systems) but also to increase the development of human capabilities and the flexibility of the society (Miettinen 2013).

Englund (2002), Rajapakse (2016) and many other authors emphasise the democratic potential of the university system. From this point of view, one should first reflect on the fact that the true limit of democracy is the initial inequality in the distribution of income and wealth and, more generally, in the status of different persons. These can shape people's orientation in political attitudes, limit their aspirations and make the poor and other disadvantaged groups accept their status and limit their aspirations. In this way, the dominant sections of the population ensure continuation of injustices and inequalities, even in an apparently 'democratic' environment.

Education can play an important role in the process of breaking the perpetuation of the initial state and empowering the democratic process. In fact, according to Sen, it is central to the capability approach, being crucial to well-being. As Walker and Unterhalter (2007) underline, Nussbaum – whose interest in education dates back at least to 1997 – identifies three key capabilities associated with education: critical thinking, the ideal of world citizenship and the development of narrative imagination.

Nussbaum (2010) is clear on the role that education can play in forming students as responsible citizens, able to think and choose with respect to issues relevant to the country they live in and the entire world. In particular, they should be able to understand the motivation of power groups and contrast them in a way that democracy can prevail over hierarchy. In order to do this, the roots of the struggle – inner to each person – between respect, compassion and the need for equity across different people, gender, religion and race, on the one hand, and greed and aggressiveness, on the other, should be understood. Thus, education, far from being some kind of indoctrination, should instead open people's minds towards both their inner qualities and inclinations and respect for other people.[14]

This requires nourishing the ability of students to look at different points of view to develop their sense of responsibility as well as their sensitivity to others, together with critical knowledge, the more so the more open and composite the society is. In order to accomplish this task, educating the population to reason is essential, not superfluous, as if the mission of education was to maximise economic growth. The latter, in fact, could require a completely different approach, of a pragmatic type.

There is a long tradition in both Western and Oriental philosophy that argues in favour of education promoting critical learning by students and respect for others. In the Western tradition, it can be dated back first to Socrates, then to Rousseau and, more recently, to Dewey and many other philosophers and pedagogues. In the Indian tradition, Tagore's school has been famous for following a very similar track.

Walker (2003) supports Nussbaum's position but favours an approach where the reality of today's education is taken

---

[14] From this point of view, education can improve accountability of policy-making and avoidance of vested interest in it.

into account. The theory of desirable changes as suggested by the capability approach should enlighten the changes to introduce in due time almost as an effect of a dialectic 'rolling' of theory and practice. The outcomes of empirical research are not univocal on the relationship between education and democracy. However, in most cases, a positive correlation has been found.

7.5   Institutions for Building a Well-Functioning Society

There are two main ingredients in the choice of institutions that are strictly interconnected. One is offered by the suggestions deriving from the theory of social choice and the theory of justice, as well as the theory of macroeconomic market failures together with the analysis of political economy and the effectiveness of policy action. The former can indicate the shortcomings of markets – and of different market forms – in terms of some social-choice criterion taken as a yardstick. This ingredient alone cannot be sufficient for substituting the government to the market, as this requires the supposed shortcoming of markets to be weighed against the possibility for governments to ensure an efficient action or, by contrast, to show failures similar to those of markets. Thus, the other ingredient is the idea that the community has in terms of the different abilities of the basic institutional forms of government to cope with a number of economic (as well as non-economic) issues that arise.[15] This requires knowledge deriving from both the normative and the positive theories of economic policy.

Considering both the ingredients, philosophical and economic ideas are required whose reciprocal influences can

---

[15]   Bruno de Finetti (2015: 41, my translation) suggests devising, in a utopian conception of economic science, 'forms of social organisation tending to lead to the desired situations, after checking their comparative attitude to work in a simple and efficient way and to ensure stability'.

vary according to a number of circumstances. These ideas lie at the root of the constitution of a country. With reference to a mixed economy, which is common to all developed countries, the choice involves public intervention in different fields to correct for distortions in the markets. This can be either discretionary and/or derived from rules that impose differing degrees of constraints on public action and shape its organisation. In any case, the role and effectiveness of public action must be ensured, having in mind the need for solving problems of conflicts and problems of equilibrium in the system, which is certainly not a likely result of market functioning.

Before ending this section, we must also take note of the fact that in addition to the issue of searching a proper and effective way to regulate markets by public action, another issue to discuss is how to find a solution for conflicts not only between different sections of the population but also between different public bodies.[16] The nature and depth of the conflicts that might arise are illustrated by the possibility that endogenous governments may arise from the populist preferences of a public resentful of the establishment of an independent and conservative central bank. This would likely lead to conflicts between government and monetary authorities and to the ineffectiveness of both monetary and fiscal policy (Demertzis, Hughes Hallett and Viegi 2004). In general, the action of different public institutions should be coordinated.

To fulfil all these requirements, the degree of centralisation of public choices must be carefully designed. It should take account of the need to find an acceptable (partly) decentralised equilibrium and the need to control the economy and avoid short- or long-run instability and multiple equilibria

---

[16] We have already dealt with this at least with reference to the relations between an independent and conservative central bank and a populist government.

while ensuring transparency, information and accountability for both the effectiveness of public action and the exercise of democratic control. We deal with both sets of issues in the next section.

7.6   The Many Reasons Why the Theory of Economic Policy Has an Impact on Institutions

A number of institutional issues arise in organising an economic and social system, on which the strategic theory of economic planning can throw light, in particular, because the theory of economic policy set up in Chapter 4 states conditions for (1) target controllability, (2) equilibrium existence and (3) multiplicity of equilibria.[17] These issues involve choosing the optimal institutional mix in terms of market and government, providing for proper signals to be issued by markets and policymakers, searching for a variety of effective policy instruments and their coordination, solving conflicts between groups and ensuring equilibrium for the system as a whole.[18]

Each of these issues is strictly interconnected with the others. We will start with the issue of the institutional mix of market and government and then all the issues (including this) under the heading of centralised versus decentralised solutions. As to the optimal mix of markets and government, it is important, first, to restate the importance of the 'ecostructure', which should not only establish the role of both but also allow their possible evolution according to their performance and/or in a way to create virtuous feedbacks

---

[17] Some passages in this section draw on Acocella, Di Bartolomeo and Hughes Hallett (2013: chap. 13).

[18] This is not the right place to discuss a number of other aspects of the institutional regime, such as the system of checks and balances necessary for avoiding totalitarianism, which more specifically pertain to the political science. Suffice it to mention the need to complete the institutional setting with this and other needs.

(Colander and Kupers 2016).[19] In discussing the optimal mix, the issue of effective and coordinated policy actions should be taken into account, together with that of the equilibrium of the system.

Economic systems are characterised by instability, which can derive from either short-run fluctuations and/or the existence of multiple long-run equilibria. In the former case, given an equilibrium path, instability takes the form of short-run fluctuations around that path. In order to reduce their size, control of the system by public discretionary action would be required, but this is possible only when a sufficient number of instruments is available. If no enough instruments can be found, at least government rules could ensure that fluctuations are reduced and not exacerbated. It is then important that correct constraints and signals are built into the system in order for the various players to find a proper way to correct their decisions.

In the case of multiple long-run equilibria, the economy might be trapped in a suboptimal equilibrium for a long time with high welfare losses or may switch between different equilibria, thus causing instability. Multiple equilibria do indeed depend on a number of situations. Generally speaking, they derive from uncoordinated actions set at a decentralised level and, more precisely, from the absence of mechanisms to coordinate the expectations of the players, even when their

---

[19] These authors also advocate overcoming the distinction between market (as an expression indicating institutions tending to earn a 'profit') and non-profit organisations. They hold that a change in the eco-structure can lead to 'for-benefit enterprises', which, on the one hand, guarantee more freedom for individuals and, on the other, are conducive to social goals. This would be particularly necessary if one conceives of social systems as complex evolving entities rather than mechanical entities. This conception is of some relevance at least in so far as the need to create institutions that can allow a self-regulating conduct of private institutions is concerned. It seems more utopian as to the possibility that only policy interventions in terms of eco-structure can ensure social goals without other policy interventions to correct the conduct of private institutions or its outcomes due to the emergence of bottom-up policy solutions.

target values do no conflict.[20] This is especially so in the case where the market is more relevant. The case of no conflict is, however, very difficult to find because conflicts over goals predominate. To some extent, conflicts can be at least partially reduced by implementing a decentralised setting with proper limits to freedom of action. The opportunities deriving from decentralised solutions and their limitations will now be discussed.

7.6.1   Decentralised Conflicts

Decentralisation is a dominant political trend of our time as a key to good governance. This needs some justification and clarification. In Chapter 6, we have already dealt with the issue of accountability, finding mixed arguments in favour of or contrary to decentralisation. Possibly, the main determinants for practical cases of decentralisation are the 'third wave' of democratisation and the explosion of centrifugal forces due in particular to inter-communal ethnic groups (Reilly 2001)[21] tending to the formation of communities that are homogeneous from the point of view of race and religion. However, scarcity of employment opportunities and defence from immigration have been other important determinants – not exclusive of those already indicated. Here we do not deal with all these determinants and limit our discussion to more technical matters tied mainly to the necessity of finding an equilibrium,[22] given conflicting goals of single agents or coalitions of agents.

[20] We recall again that the theory of economic policy in a strategic context has shown that one instance of this case derives from control over the system of the various players having equal target values. A unique equilibrium in the target space exists for the economy, but agents are not able to reach it, as there are multiple paths towards it (see Chapter 4).

[21] An ethnic group is here broadly defined as a collectivity identified by its 'color, appearance, language, religion, some other indicator of common origin, or some combination thereof' (Horowitz 1985: 17–18).

[22] We often used the term 'equilibrium' with a different meaning, but in this section it mainly indicates a solution for settling conflicting targets of people.

As discussed in Chapter 4, in a decentralised setting where there are multiple equilibria that differently influence agents having different goals, announcements can help all players to converge on a certain equilibrium, possibly mediating between their conflicting goals. When, instead of single agents, subsets of agents operate having identical goals – and thus implicit or explicit coalitions exist – conflicts can be overcome, possibly to the benefit of some specific coalition. In fact, as an extension of the concept of controllability by a single agent, the theory of economic policy in a strategic context has considered the related possibility of coalitions or implicit coalitions between agents or policymakers. In this case, these continue to act non-cooperatively but appear to operate as if they were in a coalition and thereby benefit by appropriating the coalition gains over the fully non-cooperative solution. For the system as a whole, this produces an intermediate position – partly cooperative and partly non-cooperative or partly centralised and partly decentralised. This is an important case to look at because the gains to the implicit coalition partners will be larger than those they could achieve in a fully cooperative solution, if the coalition is powerful enough to expropriate some of the gains that would otherwise go to the coalition's non-members.[23]

In short, the implicit coalition approach has studied common-interest games for some of the agents or policymakers, discovering that there might be no equilibrium if more than one controlling coalition exists having conflicting interests with other coalitions, similarly to what happens in a two-player game. More generally, unique or multiple Nash equilibria or no equilibrium will exist. The concept of implicit coalitions may be generalised. In fact, an implicit

---

[23] However, expropriation cannot be beyond certain limits, in order not to cause reactions by non-members. Taking these into consideration in a long-term perspective, full cooperation may even be a superior alternative.

coordination can emerge even without players sharing the same target values. As said in Chapter 4, this case requires the concept of Tinbergen controllability to be substituted by that of decisiveness, which implies a degree of control of some variables by a group of players; but not necessarily the achievement of any desired targets. However, the institutional conditions needed to exploit and realise coalition gains are different from those for the standard centralisation case.[24]

Since the coalition outcomes, either implicit or not, will make each participant better off than under purely non-cooperative decision making, and may produce an equilibrium when unfettered non-cooperative decisions do not, we need an institutional framework that allows coalition members to agree on target values. That is largely a matter of trading and agreeing information on the policy targets and expected outcomes for each player, and then modifying those target values as a step necessary to make it possible to realise the gains of the agreed coalition policies for each participant.

In a broader perspective, implicit coalitions may thus be viewed as the credible operating mechanism to implement societal cooperation based on bargaining on the objectives and reinforced by a commitment technology. Policymakers – or people – with different conflicting objectives can agree to pursue sets or subsets of common goals that will be bound by the conditions of implicit coalition. These conditions, together with the technologies of commitment on the target, will ensure the credibility of the policy. They will agree if the cost of such a policy is lower than the cost associated with

[24] Implicit coalitions are rather different from explicit coalitions, although the institutional implications are the same, since all players continue to play non-cooperatively, even if they end up behaving as if they were in an explicit coalition and benefit from the absence of internal conflicts. The conditions for existence or multiplicity of equilibria are thus the same as for any examples of a non-cooperative policy game, and the institutional requirements are the same as for explicit coalitions.

the creation of a 'common institution' or self-government to manage their policy and internalise the externalities from the non-cooperative solution. The institutional lesson here is that agreeing on target values, not policy rules, may be the key to achieving better overall outcomes.

7.6.2   Centralised Solutions

There are a number of scenarios where centralised decision-making is needed together with some kind of institution to support and promote it rather than to leave the field free for decentralised (and possibly self-interested) institutions. This provides a rationale for why such institutions are necessary in a number of rather common cases.

One set of situations where institutions are needed to support centralised or coordinated decisions will involve an institutional framework directed by a hegemon or desig-nated leader, aiming at (one hopes) of the *common good* or a common institution jointly run by the participants as a social planning device. This will be the case when extern-alities or other kinds of interrelationships exist between dif-ferent communities. The need for centralised institutions or coordinated decisions may arise both when there is no defined equilibrium and when there are multiple equilibria: in the former case where we have to pick out a sequence of policy positions that are acceptable (the hegemon/desig-nated leader case) and in the latter where we need to choose one equilibrium that maximises the joint gains to all on a Pareto-optimal or optimal bargaining basis (the social-planner case). A social planner would have no problem coordinating his or her action as he or she would determine all the instruments at the same time on behalf of the common good.

A second set of situations emerges when a coordinating institution is needed to oversee a sequence of policy announcements intended to act as an equilibrium selection device. In this case, the institution coordinates all the information sets that players need in order to establish the credibility of the announcements. The need for institutions regulating this type of situation derives from cases where there are multiple (and not necessarily equally good) equilibria or where there is no defined equilibrium and where there are multiple equilibria and where the equilibrium is not optimal.

A centralised solution has many practical problems of implementation, in the case of both common-interest games and conflicts. In the former, for instance, centralisation may have high costs in collecting the information needed or can be subject to costly delays. There are also issues of moral hazard in the transmission of preferences from the members of the community to the social planner. In the latter case, which involves conflicting goals between the members, centralisation also has to solve the problem of which equilibrium the social planner should converge to. Conflicts between the players do not guarantee a clear answer to this question.

In fact, mediation of conflicting targets and target values of the various players, in order to suggest a final acceptable compromise, implies a hard task for a centralised institution. In some cases, some players may facilitate the equilibrium of the system as a whole in a way that satisfies the goals of the other players. In others, some players can exploit to their advantage either centralised or decentralised institutions. A further issue relevant to deciding on the degree of centralisation refers to the extent of the conflict of interests between the government levels. Dreher et al. (2016) show that the extent of misaligned interests and the relative importance of local and central government knowledge affect the optimal choice of policy decision schemes.

In practical life, examples of centralised institutions abound both at a domestic and at an international level, even if they do not perfectly correspond to the ideal types featured earlier. And many of those characteristics may be represented by one real institution.

At a domestic level, practically all the cases where a government performs tasks beyond those of the minimal state to avoid microeconomic and macroeconomic failures will end up coordinating private decisions and, possibly, mediating between the different interests of agents. At an international level, some of the more obvious institutions deal with trade policy, especially where tariff or non-tariff barrier reductions are concerned or international monetary arrangements and the management of exchange-rate regimes (especially with respect to the choice of exchange-rate target values for joint stability). Another example would be institutions for protecting the environment.

Examples of coordinating institutions to jointly manage policy (in the sense of a social planner) are the World Trade Organization (WTO) for trade policy and the International Monetary Fund (IMF) for international monetary arrangements or the European Commission to oversee Europe's Stability and Growth Pact (SGP), the Fiscal Compact and other common rules. Some of these institutions allow a hegemon or designated leader to act as a coordinated focal point. Among them, the exchange-rate system instituted at Bretton Woods, which allowed the United States to act as hegemon, or the European Monetary Committee (as it was) to oversee the European Monetary System of exchange rates that allowed Germany to act as designated leader for EU monetary policies.

More controversially, perhaps, one could argue that the iterative process of national budget plans being monitored and then adjusted in the light of anticipated changes in European Central Bank (ECB) monetary policies, under the European Commission's convergence and medium-term objectives programme, is an instance of a sequence of policy announcements leading (if everyone keeps to the rules) to a selected equilibrium point. The same argument could be used more generally for cases where fiscal and monetary policies adjust to each other in a series of policy changes, where the fiscal authorities and central bank both have instrument independence (as in the United States and the United Kingdom, for example).

The lesson here is that we often need some form of centralised policymaking to devise policies or to get to a policy equilibrium or a stable point where the economic system is over-determined or under-determined since either multiple equilibria or no equilibrium would otherwise prevail as a result of policy conflicts. Policies in these circumstances will break down unless suitable institutions are brought into play. This is not an issue of whether the policies are effective or not but of what to do when there are multiple or no under-lying equilibria. In this case, strong centralised policy insti-tutions are unavoidable. However, they should not be to the benefit of some countries and the specific interest groups therein (or the interest groups of institutions spanning the borders of countries, such as transnational corporations). In other words, we should aim at a system that is different from the current system and ensures 'global governance without global government', as Stiglitz (2002: 21) says. In fact, Stiglitz suggests that proper government requires representation of all the interests at stake and transparency and accountability of leaders.[25] Stiglitz (2006: chap. 10) adds at least two other requirements for a proper government: better judicial procedures and better enforcement of the international rule of law.

---

[25] A notable example refers to the IMF, where representation of the bankers is ensured (through finance ministers and the governors of central banks), but this is not the case for the workers who can be affected by its bailout programmes. The problems indicated for the IMF are not exclusive to this international organisation, however. Many other organisations lack transparency because decisions and the motivations supporting them are kept secret (Stiglitz 2002: chap. 9).

7.7 For a Democratic, Fair and Efficient Society: A Restatement of the Need for a Unitary Discipline of Economic Policy

Agreeing on these goals implies referring to a discipline of economic policy that must be unitary in its conception. A democratic society can only be built by deriving some social-choice rule out of the preferences of citizens. In order to do this, value judgments – or more generally, a theory of justice – must be accepted and used. By definition, a theory of justice specifies criteria of fairness. Proper institutions should ensure not only the procedures for deriving social preferences out of any kind of individuals' preferences but also that the latter are not influenced by vested interests and the power of some agents, which can establish interest groups, lobbies, etc. to protect them due to their income and wealth. Proper institutions should also be devised in order to ensure the essence of democracy, which implies not only a democratic election but also democratic government, i.e. a government that requires continuous forms of control by citizens (see e.g. the recent contribution by Rosanvallon 2015).

Education plays an essential role in this conception, as it can inoculate the seeds of change as well as social cohesion and cooperation, protecting from concentrations of power and the actions of vested interests, which would destroy democracy or make it only apparent, as is the case in many – or most – countries.

Once social goals are derived, proper institutions should organise available instruments or devise new ones in a coordinated way that makes them effective with respect to those goals. From this point of view, a combination of market and non-market institutions can preserve personal freedom in the economic realm, microeconomic and macroeconomic efficiency as well as equity and pursuit of the common good.

Solving incentive problems and carefully programming public actions – consistently with this design – are two essential steps. 'Implementation theory' and both the 'positive' and the 'normative theory' of economic policy are essential ingredients to this end that have institutional counterparts. Finally, any practical suggestion of policy action should refer to a given institutional – and historical – environment.

Thus, institutions are the glue connecting the three parts of a discipline – economic policy – that must be unitary and differentiate itself from other economic disciplines, which either largely leave institutions aside, such as economic analysis, or focus on a limited set of institutions, such as public finance.

References

Aaberge R., A. Brandolini (2014), Multidimensional poverty and inequality, Bank of Italy, Temi di discussione (economic working paper) no. 976

Acemoglu D. (2003), Why not political Coase theorem? Social conflict, commitment, and politics, *Journal of Comparative Economics* **3**(1): 620–52

Acemoglu D., M. O. Jackson (2017), Social norms and the enforcement of laws, *Journal of the European Economic Association* **15**(2): 245–95

Acemoglu D., J. A. Robinson (2015a), The rise and decline of general laws of capitalism, *Journal of Economic Perspectives* **29**(1): 3–28

Acemoglu D., J. A. Robinson (2015b), Political institutions and comparative development, National Bureau of Economic Research (NBER) Reporter: Research Summary no. 2, available at www.nber.org/reporter/2015number2/acemoglu.html

Acemoglu D., P. Restrepo (2017), Secular stagnation? The effect of aging on economic growth in the age of automation, MIT Department of Economics working paper no. 17-02, January 12

Acemoglu D., S. Johnson, J. A. Robinson (2001), The colonial origins of comparative development: an empirical investigation, *American Economic Review* **91**(5): 1369–401

Acemoglu D., S. Johnson, J. A. Robinson (2005), Institutions as a fundamental cause of long-run growth, in P. Aghion, S. Durlauf, eds., *Handbook of Economic Growth*, vol. **1**, chap. 6, pp. 385–472. Amsterdam: Elsevier

Acemoglu D., S. Johnson, P. Querubin, J. A. Robinson (2008), When does policy reform work? The case of Central Bank independence, *Brooking Papers on Economic Activity* (Spring): 351–418

Acemoglu D., S. Johnson, J. A. Robinson, P. Yared (2008), Income and democracy, *American Economic Review* **98**(3): 808–42

Acemoglu D., S. Naidu, P. Restrepo, J. A. Robinson (2014), Democracy does cause growth, NBER working paper no. 20004, March

Acemoglu D., S. Naidu, P. Restrepo, J. A. Robinson (2015), Democracy, redistribution and inequality, in A. B. Atkinson, F. Bourguignon, eds., *Handbook of Income Distribution*, vol. **2**, pp. 1885–966. Amsterdam: Elsevier

Acocella N. (1994), *Fondamenti di politica economica. Valori e tecniche*. Rome: Nuova Italia Scientifica (English trans., *Foundations of Economic Policy: Values and Techniques*. Cambridge: Cambridge University Press, 1998)

Acocella N. (1999), *Politica economica e strategie aziendali*. Rome: Carocci (English trans., *Economic Policy in the Age of Globalisation*. Cambridge: Cambridge University Press, 2005)

Acocella N. (2011), The deflationary bias of exit strategies in the EMU countries, *Review of Economic Conditions in Italy* **2**–3: 471–93

Acocella N. (2013), Teoria e pratica della politica economica: l'eredità del recente passato (Economic theory and policies: the inheritance of the recent past), *Rivista di Storia Economica* **29**(2): 223–48

Acocella N. (2014a), The theoretical roots of EMU institutions and policies during the crisis, *Fondazione Einaudi. Annali* **2013**: 3–36

Acocella N. (2014b), Federico Caffè and economic policy as a discipline, *Global and Local Economies Review* **18**(2): 7–46

Acocella N. (2015), A tale of two cities: the evolution of the crisis and exit policies in Washington and Frankfurt, in B. Dallago, J. McGowan, eds., *Crises in Europe in the Transatlantic Context: Economic and Political Appraisals*. London: Routledge

Acocella N. (2016a), Signalling imbalances in the EMU, in B. Dallago, G. Guri, J. McGowan, eds., *A Global Perspective on the European Economic Crisis*. London: Routledge

Acocella N. (2016b), The European monetary union: an institution at a crossroad, mimeo

Acocella N. (2016c), Federico Caffè e i problemi concreti della politica economica, allora ed oggi, in G. M. Rey, C. Romagnoli, eds., *Federico Caffè a cento anni dalla nascita*. Rome: F. Angeli

Acocella N. (2017), Rise and decline of economic policy as an autonomous discipline: a critical survey, *Journal of Economic Surveys* **31**(3): 661–902

Acocella N., G. Di Bartolomeo (2004), Non-neutrality of monetary policy in policy games, *European Journal of Political Economy* **20**(3): 695–707

Acocella N., G. Di Bartolomeo (2005), Non-neutrality of economic policy: an application of the Tinbergen-Theil approach to a strategic context, Department of Public Economics, University of Rome 'La Sapienza', working paper no. 82, May

Acocella N., G. Di Bartolomeo (2006), Tinbergen and Theil meet Nash: controllability in policy games, *Economics Letters* **90**(2): 213–18

Acocella N., G. Di Bartolomeo (2011), Organisational issues in the provision of global public goods, in N. Acocella, ed., *Governance and Distributional Issues in Global Public Goods*. Rome: University La Sapienza Press

Acocella N., A. Hughes Hallett (2016), Forward guidance policy announcements: how effective are they?, mimeo

Acocella N., G. Di Bartolomeo, D. A. Hibbs (2008), Labor market regimes and the effects of monetary policy, *Journal of Macroeconomics* **30**(1): 134–56

Acocella N., G. Di Bartolomeo, A. Hughes Hallett (2013), *The Theory of Economic Policy in a Strategic Context*. Cambridge: Cambridge University Press

Acocella N., G. Di Bartolomeo, A. Hughes Hallett (2016), *Macroeconomic Paradigms and Economic Policy: From the Great Depression to the Great Recession*. Cambridge: Cambridge University Press

Acocella N., G. Di Bartolomeo, P. G. Piacquadio (2009), Conflict of interest, (implicit) coalitions and Nash policy games, *Economics Letters* **105**(3): 303–5

Acocella N., G. Di Bartolomeo, P. Tirelli (2007), Fiscal leadership and coordination in the EMU, *Open Economies Review* **18**(3): 281–89

Acocella N., G. Di Bartolomeo, A. Hughes Hallett, P. G. Piacquadio (2014), Announcement wars as an equilibrium selection device, *Oxford Economic Papers* **66**(1): 325–47

Aghion P., L. Boustan, C. Hoxby, J. Vandenbussche (2009), The causal impact of education on economic growth: evidence from US, mimeo, March

Aghion, P., E. Caroli, C. Garcia-Peñalosa (1999), Inequality and economic growth: the perspective of the new growth theories, *Journal of Economic Literature* **37**(4): 1615–60

Akerlof G. (1970), The market for lemons. Uncertainty and the market mechanism, *Quarterly Journal of Economics* **84**(3): 488–500

Akerlof G. A., R. E. Kranton (2005), Identity and the economics of organizations, *Journal of Economic Perspectives* **19**(1): 9–32

Akerlof G. A., W. T. Dickens, G. L. Perry (1996), The macroeconomics of low inflation, *Brookings Papers on Economic Activity* **1**: 1–59

Akerlof G. A., W. T. Dickens, G. L. Perry (2000), Near-rational wage and price setting and the long run Phillips curve, *Brookings Papers on Economic Activity* **1**: 1–60

Akerlof G. A., O. Blanchard, D. Romer, J. E. Stiglitz, eds. (2014), *What Have We Learned? Macroeconomic Policy after the Crisis.* Cambridge, MA: MIT Press

Aizenman J., N. Marion (2011), Using inflation to erode the U.S. public debt, *Journal of Macroeconomics* **33**(4): 524–41

Aizenman J., G. K. Pasricha (2010), On the ease of overstating the fiscal stimulus in the US, 2008–9, NBER working paper no. 15748, available at www.nber.org/papers/w15784

Akhtar M. A. (1995), Monetary policy goals and central bank independence, *BNL Quarterly Review* **48**(195): 423–39

Albanesi S. (2007), Inflation and inequality, *Journal of Monetary Economics* **54**(4): 1088–114

Albanesi S., V. V. Chari, L. J. Christiano (2002), Expectation traps and monetary policy, *Review of Economic Studies* **70**(4): 715–41

Alcidi C., G. Thirion (2016), The interaction between fiscal and monetary policy: before and after the financial crisis, FIRSTRUN (Fiscal Rules and Strategies under Externalities and Uncertainties), mimeo

330   References

Alesina A. (1987), Macroeconomic policy in a two-party system as a repeated game, *Quarterly Journal of Economics* **102**(3): 651–78

Alesina A. (1988), Macroeconomics and politics, in S. Fischer, ed., *NBER Macroeconomics Annual 1988*. Cambridge, MA: MIT Press

Alesina A., R. Perotti (1995), Fiscal expansions and fiscal adjustments in OECD countries, NBER working paper no. 5214

Alesina A., R. Perotti (1996), Fiscal discipline and the budget process, *American Economic Review* **86**(2): 401–7

Alesina A., R. Perotti (1997), The welfare state and competitiveness, *American Economic Review* **87**(5): 921–39

Alesina A., G. Tabellini (1990), A positive theory of fiscal deficits and government debt, *Review of Economic Studies* **57**(3): 403–14.

Alesina A., L. H. Summers (1993), Central bank independence and macroeconomic performance: some comparative evidence, *Journal of Money, Credit and Banking* **25**(May): 151–62

Allen F., D. Gale (1994), Liquidity preference, market participation and asset price volatility, *American Economic Review* **84**(4): 933–55.

Allen F., D. Gale (2000), Financial contagion, *Journal of Political Economy* **108**(1): 1–33

Allison G. T. (2017), *Destined for War: Can America and China Escape Thucydides's Trap?* Boston: Houghton Mifflin Harcourt

Alonso R., O. Câmara (2016), Persuading voters, *American Economic Review* **106**(11): 3590–605

Altavilla C., U. Marani (2005), European economic policies at work: the costs of price stability and budget consolidation, *European Journal of Comparative Economics* **2**(1): 111–36

Alvaredo F., A. B. Atkinson, T. Piketty, E. Saez (2013), The top 1 percent in international and historical perspective, *Journal of Economic Perspectives* **27**(3): 3–20

Amari G., N. Rocchi, eds. (2007), *Federico Caffè. Un economista per gli uomini comuni*. Rome: Ediesse

Amari G., N. Rocchi, eds. (2009), *Federico Caffè. Un economista per il nostro tempo*. Rome: Ediesse

Anand P., G. Hunter, R. Smith (2005), Capabilities and well-being: evidence based on the Sen-Nussbaum approach to welfare, *Social Indicators Research* **74**(1): 9–55

Ando A., C. Palash (1976), Some stabilization problems of 1971–75, with an application of optimal control algorithms, *American Economic Review* **66**(2): 346–48

Angelini P., S. Neri, F. Panetta (2011), Monetary and macroprudential policies, Bank of Italy working papers no. 801, March

Anundsen A. K., R. Nymoen, T. S. Krogh, J. Vislie (2014), Overdeterminacy and endogenous cycles: Trygve Haavelmo's business cycle model, *Metroeconomica* **65**(3): 460–86

Arblaster A. (2002), *Democracy*, 3rd edn. Buckingham: Open University Press

Arestis P. (2009), Fiscal policy within the 'New Consensus Macroeconomics' framework, in J. Creel, M. Sawyer, eds., *Current Thinking on Fiscal Policy*. Basingstoke: Palgrave Macmillan, pp. 6–27

Arestis P. (2015), Coordination of fiscal with monetary and financial stability policies can better cure unemployment, *Review of Keynesian Economics* **3**(1): 233–47

Armstrong C. S., J. E. Core, W. R. Guay (2014), Do independent directors cause improvements in firm transparency? *Journal of Financial Economics* **113**(3): 383–403

Armstrong A., F. Caselli, J. Chadha, W. Den Haan (2015), Risk-sharing and the effectiveness of the ECB's quantitative easing programme, chap. 27 in W. den Haan, ed., *Quantitative Easing: Evolution of Economic Thinking As It Happened*. Washington, DC: Center for Economic and Policy Research (CEPR) Press, pp. 221–28

Arnone M., B. Laurens, J. Segalotto, M. Sommer (2007), Central bank autonomy: lessons from global trends, IMF working paper 07/88

Arrow K. J. (1950), A difficulty in the concept of social welfare, *Journal of Political Economy* **58**(4): 328–46 (Italian trans. in Caffè 1956b)

Arrow K. J. (1951), *Social Choice and Individual Values*. New York: Wiley

Arrow K. J., A. K. Sen, K. Suzumura, eds. (1997), *Social Choice Re-examined*, 2 vols. New York, NY: St Martin's Press

Arrow K. J., A. K. Sen, K. Suzumura, eds. (2011), *Handbook of Social Choice and Welfare*, vol. **2**. Amsterdam: Elsevier–North Holland

Arrow K. J., A. K. Sen, K. Suzumura, eds. (2002, 2011), *Handbook of Social Choice and Welfare*, 2 vols. Amsterdam: Elsevier–North Holland

Ascari G. (2000), Optimising agents, staggered wages and persistence in the real effects of monetary shocks, *Economic Journal* **110**: 664–86

Ascari G. (2003), Staggered price and trend inflation: some nuisances, *Review of Economic Dynamics* **7**, 642–67

Asso P. (1990), *The Keynesian Revolution in Historical Perspective*. Rome: Ente Einaudi

Atkinson A. B. (2002), Globalization and the European welfare state at the opening and the closing of the Twentieth Century, in H. Kierzkowski, ed., *Europe and Globalisation*. London: Palgrave Macmillan, chap. 12, pp. 249–73

Atkinson A. B. (2013), Reducing income inequality in Europe, *IZA Journal of European Labor Studies*, **2**: 12, available at www .izajoels.com/content/2/1/12

Auerbach A. J., Y. Gorodnichenko (2012), Fiscal multipliers in recession and expansion, mimeo, University of California, Berkeley

Azfar O., S. Kähkönen, A. Lanyi, P. Meagher, D. Rutherford (1999), *Decentralization, Governance and Public Services: The Impact of Institutional Arrangements – A Review of the Literature*. College Park, MD: University of Maryland

Backhouse R. E., M. Boianovsky (2015), Secular stagnation: the history of a macroeconomic heresy, Blanqui Lecture, 19th Annual Conference of the European Society for the History of Economic Thought, Rome, 14–16 May

Bade R., M. Parkin (1978), Central bank laws and monetary policies: a preliminary investigation, in M. Porter, ed., *The Australian Monetary System in the 1970s*. Clayton, Victoria, Australia: Monash University Press

Balassa B. (1973), Comment on R. Mundell (1973), a plan for a European currency, in H. Johnson, A. Swoboda, eds., *The Economics of Common Currencies*, Cambridge, MA: Harvard University Press, pp. 143–77

Balducci R., G. Candela (1991), *Teoria della politica economica*, 2 vols. Rome: La Nuova Italia Scientifica

Balducci R., G. Candela, A. E. Scorcu (2001), *Introduzione alla politica economica.* Bologna: Zanichelli

Balducci R., G. Candela, A. E. Scorcu (2002), *Teoria della politica economica: Modelli dinamici e stocastici.* Bologna: Zanichelli

Ball L. (2014), The case for a long-run inflation target of four percent, IMF working paper no. 14/92

Ball R. J., ed. (1978), *Committee on Policy Optimisation Report.* London: Her Majesty's Stationery Office

Ballarino G., M. Bratti, A. Filippin et al. (2014), Increasing educational inequalities?, Chap. 5 in W. Salverda, B. Nolan, D. Checchi et al., eds., *Changing Inequalities in Rich Countries: Analytical and Comparative Perspectives.* Oxford: Oxford University Press

Banerjee A. V., E. Duflo (2003), Inequality and growth: what can the data say?, *Journal of Economic Growth* **8**(3): 267–99

Bank for International Settlements (BIS) (2016), Macroprudential policy, BIS paper no. 86, September

Barone E. (1908), Il ministro della produzione nello stato collettivista, *Giornale degli economisti*, September: 267–93; October: 391–414 (English trans. as an appendix to Hayek F. A., ed., *Collectivist Economic Planning.* London: Routledge, 1935)

Barro R. J. (1974), Are government bonds net wealth? *Journal of Political Economy* **82**(6): 1095–118

Barro R. J. (2000), Inequality and growth in a panel of countries, *Journal of Economic Growth* **5**(1): 5–32

Barro R. J., D. Gordon (1983), Rules, discretion and reputation in a model of monetary policy, *Journal of Monetary Economics* **12**(1): 101–21

Basco S., D. Lopez-Rodriguez, E. Moral-Benito (2017), Housing bubbles and misallocation: evidence from Spain, mimeo, April

Başkaya Y. S., J. di Giovanni, S. Kalemli-Ozcan, J.-L. Peydro, M. F. Ulu (2016a), Capital flows, credit cycles and macroprudential policy, in Bank for International Settlements (BIS), Macroprudential policy, BIS paper no. 86, September, pp. 63–68; available at www.bis.org

Başkaya Y. S., T. Kenç, I. Shim, P. Turner (2016b), Financial development and the effectiveness of macroprudential measures, in Bank for International Settlements (BIS), Macroprudential policy, BIS paper no. 86, September, pp. 102–15; available at www.bis.org

Bastiat F. (1850), *Harmonies économiques*. Paris: Guillaumin

Batini N., G. Callegari, G. Melina (2012), Successful austerity in the United States, Europe and Japan, IMF working paper no. 190

Bator F. (1958), The anatomy of market failure, *Quarterly Journal of Economics* **72**(3): 351–79

Baumgartner F. R., J. M. Berry, M. Hojnacki, D. C. Kimball, B. L. Leech (2009), *Lobbying and Policy Change: Who Wins, Who Loses, and Why*. Chicago, IL: University of Chicago Press

Baumol W. J., W. E. Oates (1975), *The Theory of Environment Policy: Externalities, Public Outlays, and the Quality of Life*. Englewood Cliffs, NJ: Prentice Hall

Baxter M., R. King (1993), Fiscal policy in general equilibrium, *American Economic Review* **83**(3): 315–34

Bayoumi T., G. Dell'Ariccia, K. Habermeier, T. Mancini-Griffoli, F. Valencia, and IMF Staff Team (2014), Monetary policy in the new normal, IMF working paper SDN 14/13

Beck U. (2015), *What Is Globalization?* New York, NY: Wiley

Beetsma R. M. W. J., A. L. Bovenberg (1998), Monetary union without fiscal coordination may discipline policymakers, *Journal of International Economics* **45**(2): 239–58 (first published as discussion paper no. 1955–59, Tilburg University, Center for Economic Research, 1955)

Beetsma R. M. W. J., M. Giuliodori (2011), The effects of government purchases shocks: review and estimates for the EU, *Economic Journal* **121**(550): F4–F32

Beetsma R. M. W. J., H. Uhlig (1999), An analysis of the Stability and Growth Pact, *Economic Journal* **109**(458): 546–71 (first published as CEPR discussion paper no. 1669, 1997)

Beetsma R. M. W. J., X. Debrun, F. Klaassen (2001), Is fiscal policy coordination in EMU desirable? *Swedish Economic Policy Review* **8**(1): 57–98

Beetsma R. M. W. J., M. Giuliodori, F. Klaassen (2006), Trade spillovers of fiscal policy in the European Union: a panel analysis, *Economic Policy* **21**(48): 639–87

Beetsma R. M. W. J., M. Giuliodori, F. Klaassen (2008), The effects of public spending shocks on trade balances and budget deficits in the EU, *Journal of the European Economic Association* **6**(2–3): 414–23

Belke A., J. Klose (2017), Equilibrium real interest rates and secular stagnation: an empirical analysis for Euro-area member countries, 5 May, DOI:http://10.1111/jcms.12552

Bénabou R. (2000), Unequal societies: income distribution and the social contract, *American Economic Review* **90**(1): 96–129

Bénabou R., J. Tirole (2006), Incentives and prosocial behavior, *American Economic Review* **96**(5): 1652–78

Bénassy-Quéré A., A. Trannoy, G. Wolff (2014), Tax harmonization in Europe: moving forward, French Council of Economic Analysis, Les notes du Conseil d'analyse économique no. 14, July

Benhabib J. (2003), The trade-off between inequality and growth, *Annals of Economics and Finance* **4**(2): 329–45

Benigno P. (2002), A simple approach to international monetary policy coordination, *Journal of International Economics* **57**(1): 177–96

Benigno P., S. Nisticò (2015), Quantitative easing: who's backing currency?, chap. 18 in W. den Haan, ed., *Quantitative Easing: Evolution of Economic Thinking As It Happened*. Washington, DC: Center for Economic and Policy Research (CEPR) Press, pp. 149–52

Benigno P., L. A. Ricci (2011), The inflation-output trade-off with downward wage rigidities, *American Economic Review* **101**(4): 1436–66

Benigno P., M. Woodford (2004), Optimal monetary and fiscal policy: a linear-quadratic approach, in M. Gertler, K. Rogoff, eds., *NBER Macroeconomic Annual 2003*. Cambridge, MA: MIT Press, pp. 271–364B

Berdud M., J. M. Cabasés, J. Nieto Vázquez (2014), Identity, incentives and motivational capital in public organizations, Public University of Navarra, Department of Economics, March 6

Berger H., J. den Haan, S. C. W. Eijffinger (2001), Central bank independence: an update of theory and evidence, *Journal of Economic Surveys* **15**(1): 3–40

Bergson A. (1938), A reformulation of some aspects of welfare economics, *Quarterly Journal of Economics* **52**(2): 310–34 (published under the pseudonym of A. Burk) (Italian trans. in Caffè 1956b)

Bernanke B. S. (2010), Testimony before the Joint Economic Committee of Congress, 14 April

Bernanke B. S. (2015), Why are interest rates so low: 2. Secular stagnation, March 31, available at www.brookings.edu/blog /ben-bernanke/2015/03/31/why-are-interest-rates-so-low-part -2-secular-stagnation/

Bernanke B. S. (2016), *What Tools Does the Fed Have Left? 3. Helicopter Money*. Washington, DC: Brookings Institution

Bernanke B., J. Boivin, P. S. Eliasz (2005), Measuring the effects of monetary policy: a factor-augmented vector autoregressive (FAVAR) approach, *Quarterly Journal of Economics* **120**(1): 387–442.

Berry J. M. (2015), *Lobbying for the People: The Political Behavior of Public Interest Groups*, Princeton, NJ: Princeton University Press

Bibow J. (2010), Bretton Woods 2 is dead, long live Bretton Woods 3?, Levy Economics Institute of Bard College working paper no. 597

Bibow J. (2013), The Euroland crisis and Germany's euro trilemma, *International Review of Applied Economics* **27**(3): 360–85

Bilbiie F., T. Monacelli, R. Perotti (2012), Tax cuts vs. spending increases: welfare at the zero lower bound, mimeo

Bilbiie F., T. Monacelli, R. Perotti (2014), Is government spending at the zero lower bound desirable?, CEPR discussion paper no. 10210, October

Bini Smaghi L. (2014), Monetary policy, the only game in town, in G. Akerlof, O. Blanchard, D. Romer, J. Stiglitz, eds., (2014), *What Have We Learned? Macroeconomic Policy after the Crisis*. Cambridge, MA: MIT Press

Bjerkholt O. (1998), Interaction between model builders and policy makers in the Norwegian tradition, *Economic Modelling* **15**(3): 317–39

Bjerkholt O. (2005), Markets, models and planning: the Norwegian experience, Department of Economics, University of Oslo, Memorandum no. 14

Bjerkholt O. (2008), Ragnar Frisch on scientific economics, paper prepared for seminar in the Research Department of Banca d'Italia, 3 November

Bjerkholt O. (2014), Ragnar Frisch and the postwar Norwegian economy: a critical comment on Sæther and Eriksen, *Econ Journal Watch* **11**(3): 297–312

Bjerkholt O., J. F. Qvigstad (2007), Introduction to Ragnar Frisch's 1933 pamphlet, Saving and circulation regulation, *Rivista di Storia Economica* **33**(2): 209–32

Blanchard O. (2016a), The Phillips curve: back to the '60s? Peterson Institute for International Economics, Policy brief 16-1 January, also in *American Economic Review* **106**(5): 31–34

Blanchard O. (2016b), Currency wars, coordination, and capital controls, NBER working paper no. 22388, July

Blanchard O., S. Fischer (1989), *Lectures on Macroeconomics*, Cambridge, MA: MIT Press

Blanchard O. J., D. Leigh (2013a), Growth forecast errors and fiscal multipliers, IMF working paper no. 13/1, January, also in *American Economic Review* **103**(3): 117–20,DOI http://10.1257/aer.103.3.117

Blanchard O. J., D. Leigh (2013b), Fiscal consolidation: at what speed?, CEPR Policy Portal, 3 May

Blanchard O., G. Milesi-Ferretti (2012), (Why) should current account balances be reduced?, *IMF Economic Review* **60**(1): 139–50

Blanchard O., R. Perotti (2002), An empirical characterization of the dynamic effects of changes in government spending and taxes on output, *Quarterly Journal of Economics* **117**(4): 1329–68

Blanchard O. J., G. Dell'Ariccia, P. Mauro (2010), Rethinking macroeconomic policy, IMF Staff Position Note no. 2010/03

Blanchard O. J., G. Dell'Ariccia, P. Mauro (2014), Introduction: rethinking macro policy II – Getting granular, in G. A. Akerlof, O. Blanchard, D. Romer, J. E. Stiglitz, eds. (2014), *What Have We Learned? Macroeconomic Policy after the Crisis.* Cambridge, MA: MIT Press

Bleaney M. (1996), Central bank independence, wage-bargaining structure, and macroeconomic performance in OECD countries, *Oxford Economic Papers* **48**(1): 20–38

Blinder A. S. (1982a), Issues in the coordination of monetary and fiscal policy, NBER working paper no. 982, September

Blinder A. S. (1982b), The anatomy of double-digit inflation in the 1970s, in R. E. Hall, ed., *Inflation: Causes and Effects.* Chicago, IL: University of Chicago Press, pp. 261–82

Blinder A. S. (2004), The case against the case against discretionary fiscal policy, Centre for European Policy Studies (CEPS) working paper no. 100

Blinder A. S., M. Ehrmann, M. Fratzscher, J. de Haan, D.-J. Jansen (2008), Central bank communication and monetary policy: a survey of theory and evidence, NBER working paper no. 13932, April

Boeckx J., P. Ilbas, M. Kasongo Kashama, M. de Sola Perea, Ch. Van Nieuwenhuyze (2015), Interactions between monetary and macroprudential policies, National Bank of Belgium, September, pp. 7–27, available at www.nbb.be/doc/oc/repec/ecrart/ecore vii2015_h1.pdf

Boffa F., A. Piolatto, G. A. M. Ponzetto (2016), Political centralization and government accountability, *Quarterly Journal of Economics* **131**(1): 381–422

Bogliacino F., V. Maestri (2014), Increasing income inequalities?, chap. 2 in W. Salverda, B. Nolan, D. Checchi et al., eds., *Changing Inequalities in Rich Countries: Analytical and Comparative Perspectives*. Oxford: Oxford University Press

Bogliacino F., V. Maestri (2016), Wealth inequality and the Great Recession, *Intereconomics, Review of European Economic Policy* **51**(2): 61–66

Bolton P., G. Roland (1997), The breakup of nations: a political economy analysis, *Quarterly Journal of Economics* **112**: 1057–90

Bomfim A., G. D. Rudebusch (2000), Opportunistic and deliberate disinflation under imperfect credibility, *Journal of Money, Credit and Banking* **32**(4): 707–21

Bonica A., N. McCarty, K. T. Poole, H. Rosenthal (2013), Why hasn't democracy slowed rising inequality?, *Journal of Economic Perspectives* **27**(3):103–24

Bonvin J.-M. (2005), La démocratie dans l'approche d'Amartya Sen, *L'Économie Politique* **3**(27): 24–37

Bonvin J.-M. (2008), Capacités et démocratie, in J. de Munck B. Zimmermann, eds., *La liberté au prisme des capacités. Amartya Sen au-delà du libéralisme*, vol. **18**. Paris: Éditions de l'École des Hautes Études, pp. 237–61

Bossert W., J. A. Weymark (2008), Social choice (new developments), in S. N. Durlauf, L. E. Blume, eds., *The New Palgrave*

Dictionary of Economics, 2nd edn. Basingstoke: Palgrave Macmillan

Bossone B. (2016), Unconventional monetary policies revisited (parts I and II), chaps. 12 and 13 in W. den Haan, ed., *Quantitative Easing: Evolution of Economic Thinking As It Happened*. Washington, DC: Center for Economic and Policy Research (CEPR) Press, pp. 101–18

Bouis R., O. Causa, L. Demmou, R. Duval, A. Zdzienicka (2012), The short-term effects of structural reforms: an empirical analysis, OECD Economics Department working paper no. 949, available at http://dx.doi.org/10.1787/5k9csvk4d56d-en

Boulding K. E. (1958), *Principles of Economic Policy*. Englewood Cliffs, NJ: Prentice Hall

Bouwen P. (2002), Corporate lobbying in the European Union: the logic of access, *Journal of European Public Policy* 9(3): 365–90, DOI:http://10.1080/13501760210138796

Brandsma A., A. Hughes Hallett (1984), The structure of rational expectations behaviour: an empirical view, in J. P. Ancot, ed., *The Structural Analysis of Economic Models*. Dordrecht: Nijhoff Academic Publishers

Bray J. (1975), Optimal control of a noisy economy with the UK as an example, *Journal of the Royal Statistical Society, Series A (General)* **138**(3): 339–73

Bray J. (1977), The logic of scientific method in economics, *Journal of Economic Studies* 4(1): 1–28, available at http://dx.doi.org/10.1108/eb002463

Brennan G., J. M. Buchanan (1980), *The Power to Tax: Analytical Foundations of a Fiscal Constitution*, Indianapolis, IN: Liberty Fund.

Brzoza-Brzezina M., M. Kolasa, K. Makarski (2013), Macroprudential policy instruments and economic imbalances in the Euro area, European Central Bank (ECB) working paper no. 1589, September

Buchanan J. M. (1960), La scienza delle finanze. The Italian tradition in fiscal theory, in J. M. Buchanan, ed., *Fiscal Theory and Political Economy: Selected Essays*. Chapel Hill, NC: University of North Carolina Press, pp. 24–74.

Buchanan J. M. (1975), *The Limits of Liberty: Between Anarchy and Leviathan.* Chicago, IL: University of Chicago Press

Buchanan J. M. (1995), Federalism as an ideal political order and an objective for constitutional reform, *Publius: The Journal of Federalism* 25(2): 19–27

Buchanan J. M., G. Brennan (1981), *Reasons of Rules.* Cambridge: Cambridge University Press

Buchanan J. M., G. Tullock (1962), *The Calculus of Consent: Logical Foundations of Constitutional Democracy.* Ann Arbor, MI: University of Michigan Press

Buiter W. H. (2004), Helicopter money: irredeemable fiat money and the liquidity trap. Or: is money net wealth after all?, mimeo

Buiter W., E. Rahbari, J. Seydl (2015), Secular stagnation: the time for one-armed policy is over, Vox CEPR's Policy Portal, 5 June

Bundesverfassungsgerich, BvR 2728/13 of 14 January 2014 (OMT Ruling), para. 70

Burlon L., A. Gerali, A. Notarpietro, M. Pisani (2016a), Macroeconomic effectiveness of non-standard monetary policy and early exit: a model-based evaluation, Bank of Italy working paper no. 1074, July

Burlon L., A. Gerali, A. Notarpietro, M. Pisani (2016b), Non-standard monetary policy, asset prices and macroprudential policy in a monetary union, Bank of Italy working paper no. 1089, October

Butlin N. G., R. G. Gregory (1989), Trevor Winchester Swan 1918–1989, *Economic Record* 65(4):369–77

Cabral R., R. G. Díaza (2015), Is fiscal policy coordination desirable for a monetary union? An assessment from the perspective of a small open economy, *Investigación Económica* 74(294): 3–72

Caffè F. (1942), *Risparmio spontaneo e risparmio forzato nel finanziamento della guerra.* Rome: Nuove Grafiche

Caffè F. (1943a), Compiti e limiti della politica economica in recenti pubblicazioni, Giurisprudenza e Dottrina Bancaria, in Caffè (1953b), reprinted in Amari G., N. Rocchi, eds., *Federico Caffè. Un economista per il nostro tempo* (2009). Rome: Ediesse

Caffè F. (1943b), Pianificazione democratica, in Caffè (1945), reprinted in Amari G., N. Rocchi, eds., *Federico Caffè. Un economista per gli uomini comuni* (2007). Rome: Ediesse

Caffè F. (1945), E' evitabile la pianificazione?, in F. Caffè (1945), *Aspetti di un'economia di transizione*. Rome, October, reprinted in Amari and Rocchi (2009)

Caffè F. (1946a), First Memorandum on the Central Economic Plan 1946 and National Budget 1947, 'Critica economica' no. 4, December, La politica delle priorità ed il pensiero degli economisti inglesi, in Caffè (1953b), reprinted in Amari and Rocchi (2009)

Caffè F. (1946b), Nuove esperienze in fatto di pianificazione, in Caffè (1953b).

Caffè F. (1947), Consiglio Economico Nazionale e problemi di pianificazione, Cronache sociali no. 8, 15 September, reprinted in Amari and Rocchi (2009)

Caffè F. (1948a), La politica delle priorità ed il pensiero degli economisti inglesi, in Caffè (1953b), reprinted in Amari and Rocchi (2009)

Caffè F. (1948b), 'Bilancio economico' e 'contabilità sociale' nell'economia britannica, in F. Caffè, *Annotazioni sulla politica economica britannica in un 'anno di ansia'*. Rome: Tecnica Grafica, 1948, reprinted in Amari and Rocchi (2009)

Caffè F. (1949a), Bilancio di una politica (II), Cronache sociali no. 18, October, reprinted in Amari and Rocchi (2007)

Caffè F. (1949b), Bilancio di una politica (III), Cronache sociali no. 19, October, reprinte in Amari and Rocchi (2007)

Caffè F. (1953a), *Vecchi e nuovi indirizzi nelle indagini sull'economia del benessere*. Rome: Tecnica Grafica

Caffè F. (1953b), *Orientamenti nella letteratura economica contemporanea*. Rome: Contributi bibliografici, Edizioni dell'Ateneo

Caffè F. (1954a), Considerazioni sulla formazione del capitale nelle aree economicamente arretrate, in *Teoria e politica dello sviluppo*. Milan: Giuffrè

Caffè F. (1954b), *Politiche dell'interesse e degli investimenti*. Rome: Tecnica Grafica

342   References

Caffè F. (1956a), Economia del benessere, in C. Napoleoni, ed., *Dizionario di economia politica*. Milan: Edizioni di Comunità

Caffè F., ed. (1956b), *Saggi sulla moderna economia del benessere*, Torino: Boringhieri

Caffè F. (1957), Sguardi su un mondo economico in trasformazione, in *Rivista trimestrale di diritto e procedura civile*, reprinted in F. Caffè, *Saggi critici di economia* (1958). Rome: De Luca

Caffè F. (1958), Considerazioni intorno al settore pubblico dell'economia, in *Rivista trimestrale di diritto e procedura civile*, reprinted in F. Caffè, *Saggi critici di economia* (1958). Rome: De Luca

Caffè F. (1962), La politica economica nel sistema degli economisti classici, *Giornale degli Economisti*, May–June

Caffè F. (1964a), La politica economica nei sistemi di analisi 'al livello soggettivo', in *Contributi in omaggio di G.U. Papi*, Milan: Giuffrè

Caffè F. (1964b), *Appunti introduttivi alla politica economica*. Rome: Edizioni Ricerche

Caffè F. (1965), *Sistematica e tecniche della politica economica*, vol. 1: *Parte introduttiva*. Rome: Edizioni Ricerche

Caffè F. (1966a), *Politica economica: Sistematica e tecniche di analisi*, vol. I. Torino: Boringhieri

Caffè F. (1966b), Vecchi e nuovi trasferimenti anormali di capitali, in *Studi in onore di Marco Fanno*. Padova: Cedam, reprinted in G. Amari, ed., *Attualità del pensiero di Federico Caffè nella crisi odierna* (2010). Rome: Ediesse

Caffè F. (1970), *Politica economica: Problemi economici interni*, vol. II. Torino: Boringhieri

Caffè F. (1972), La strategia dell'allarmismo economico, *Giornale degli economisti e annali di economia*, September–October, pp. 693–99, reprinted in F. Caffè (1976), *Un'economia in ritardo*, Torino: Boringhieri, and in Amari and Rocchi (2007)

Caffè F. (1977), *Economia senza profeti*. Rome: Edizioni Studium

Caffè F. (1978a), *Lezioni di politica economica*. Torino: Boringhieri (4th edn 1984)

Caffè F. (1978b), Su alcune trasformazioni recenti del Fondo Monetario Internazionale, *La Comunità internazionale* no. 4, reprinted in Amari and Rocchi (2009)

Caffè F. (1985), *Politica economica della CEE, Novissimo Digesto Italiano, Appendix*. Torino: Utet

Cagliozzi R. (1994), *Profili delle lezioni di politica economica*. Naples: Liguori

Calmfors L. (2012), The Swedish Fiscal Policy Council: watchdog with a broad remit, CESifo working paper no. 3725, CES Institute, University of Munich

Calmfors L., S. Wren-Lewis (2011), What should fiscal councils do?, CESifo working paper no. 3382, Fiscal Policy, Macroeconomics and Growth

Candela G. (2014), *Economia, Stato, Anarchia: Regole, Proprietà e Produzione fra Dominio e Libertà*. Milan: Elèuthera

Canova F., G. De Nicoló (2002), Monetary disturbances matter for business fluctuations in the G-7, *Journal of Monetary Economics* **49**(6): 1131–59

Cantillon R. (1755), *An Essay on Economic Theory*. Auburn: Ludwig von Mises Institute (2010)

Carabelli A., M. Cedrini (2014), *Secondo Keynes. Il disordine del neoliberismo e le speranze di una nuova Bretton Woods*. Rome: Castelvecchi

Cargill T. F, G. P. O'Driscoll (2012), Measuring central bank independence, policy implications, and federal reserve independence, mimeo

Carli G. (1996), *Cinquant'anni di vita italiana*. Bari: Laterza

Carlson B., L. Jonung (2006), Knut Wicksell, Gustav Cassel, Eli Heckscher, Bertil Ohlin and Gunnar Myrdal on the role of the economist in public debate, *Econ Journal Watch* **3**(3): 511–50

Carlson B., L. Jonung (2013), Ohlin on the Great Depression, Knut Wicksell working paper no. 9

Carpenter S., J. Ihrig, E. Klee, D. Quinn, A. Boote (2013), The Federal Reserve's balance sheet and earnings: a primer and projections, Finance and Economics Discussion Series no. 2013-01

Casella A. (1989), Letter to the Editor, *The Economist*, 22–28 July, p.6

Cecchetti S. G., P. M. W. Tucker (2015), Is there macroprudential policy without international cooperation?, presented at for the 2015 biennial Asia Economic Policy Conference (AEPC) on Policy Challenges in a Diverging Global Economy at the Federal Reserve Bank of San Francisco, 19–20 November 2015

344   References

Cecioni M., G. Ferrero, A. Secchi (2011), Unconventional monetary policy in theory and in practice, Bank of Italy occasional paper no. 102

Cerutti E., S. Claessens, L. Laeven (2017), The use and effectiveness of macroprudential policies: new evidence, *Journal of Financial Stability* **28**: 203–24

Chahrour R. (2014), Public communication and information acquisition, *American Economic Journal: Macroeconomics* **6**(3): 73–101

Chalmers A. W. (2013), Trading information for access: informational lobbying strategies and interest group access to the European Union, *Journal of European Public Policy* **20**(1): 39–58

Chatagny F. (2015), Incentive effects of fiscal rules on the finance minister's behaviour: evidence from revenue projections in Swiss Cantons, *European Journal of Political Economy* **39**(C): 184–200

Checherita-Westphal C., P. Rother (2010), The impact of high and growing government debt on economic growth an empirical investigation for the Euro area, ECB working paper no. 1237

Checherita-Westphal C., A. Hughes Hallett, P. Rother (2014), Fiscal sustainability using growth-maximising debt targets, *Applied Economics* **46**(6): 638–47

Chen Q., A. Filardo, D. He, F. Zhu (2016), Financial crisis, US unconventional monetary policy and international spillovers, *Journal of International Money and Finance* **67**(C): 62–81

Chiarella C., P. Flaschel, W. Semmler (2001), The macrodynamics of debt deflation, in R. Bellofiore, P. Ferri, eds., *Financial Fragility and Investment in the Capitalist Economy: The Economic Legacy of Hyman Minsky*, vol. II, chap. 7. Basingstoke: Palgrave Macmillan

Chichilnisky G., G. M. Heal (1983), Necessary and sufficient conditions for a resolution of the social choice paradox, *Journal of Economic Theory* **31**(1): 68–87

Chichilnisky G., G. M. Heal (1997), Social choice with infinite populations: construction of a rule and impossibility results, *Social Choice and Welfare* **14**(2): 303–18

Chow G. C. (1973), Problems of economic policy from the viewpoint of optimal control, *American Economic Review* **63**(5): 825–37

Chow G. C. (1976), Control methods for macroeconomic policy analysis, *American Economic Review* **66**(2): 340–45

Christiano L. J., M. Eichenbaum, C. L. Evans (2005), Nominal rigidities and the dynamic effects of a shock to monetary policy, *Journal of Political Economy* **113**(1): 1–45

Christiano L. J., M. Eichenbaum, S. Rebelo (2011), When is the government spending multiplier large?, *Journal of Political Economy* **119**(1): 78–121

Ciccarone G., E. Marchetti, G. Di Bartolomeo (2007), Unions, fiscal policy and central bank transparency, *Manchester School* **75**(5): 617–33

Cingano F. (2014), Trends in income inequality and its impact on economic growth, OECD Social, Employment and Migration working paper no. 163, available at http://dx.doi.org/10.1787 /5jxrjncwxv6j-en

Ciocca P. (1995), Per il tramite dei grandi economisti, in A. Esposto, M. Tiberi, eds., *Federico Caffè. Realtà e critica del capitalismo storico*. Rome: Donzelli

Claessens S., L. Stracca, F. E. Warnock (2015), International dimensions of conventional and unconventional monetary policy, *Journal of International Money and Finance*, June, DOI http://10 .1016/j.jimonfin.2015.06.006

Coase R. H. (1960), The problem of social cost, *Journal of Law and Economics* **3**(1): 1–44

Cochrane J. H. (1998), What do the VARs mean? Measuring the output effects of monetary policy, *Journal of Monetary Economics* **41**(2): 277–300.

Coen D., J. Richardson (2009), *Lobbying the European Union: Institutions, Actors, and Issues*, Oxford: Oxford University Press

Coenen G., V. Wieland (2002), Inflation dynamics and international linkages: a model of the United States, the Euro area and Japan, Board of Governors of the Federal Reserve System International Finance discussion paper no. 745, July

Coenen G., C. G. Erceg, C. Freedman et al. (2012), Effects of fiscal stimulus in structural models, *American Economic Journal: Macroeconomics* **4**(1): 22–68

Cœuré B. (2013), The usefulness of forward guidance, speech before the Money Marketeers Club of New York, 26 September, available at www.ecb.europa.eu/press/key/date/2013/html /sp130926_1.en.html

Cœuré B. (2015), Paradigm lost: rethinking international adjustments, Egon and Joan von Kashnitz Lecture at the Clausen Center for International Business and Policy, Berkeley, CA, 21 November

Cœuré B. (2016), The internationalisation of monetary policy, *Journal of International Money and Finance* **67**: 8–12

Cogley T., A. M. Sbordone (2008), Trend inflation, indexation, and inflation persistence in the New Keynesian Phillips curve, *American Economic Review* **98**(5): 2101–26

Coibion O., Y. Gorodnichenko, J. Wieland (2012), The optimal inflation rate in New Keynesian models: should central banks raise their inflation targets in light of the zero lower bound?, *Review of Economic Studies* **79**(4): 1371–406

Colander D., R. Kupers (2016), *Complexity and the Art of Public Policy: Solving Society's Problems from the Bottom Up.* Princeton, NJ: Princeton University Press

Collier P., D. Rohner (2008), Democracy, development, and conflict, *Journal of the European Economic Association* **6**(2–3): 531–40

Cook D., M. B. Devereux (2013), Sharing the burden: monetary and fiscal responses to a world liquidity trap, *American Economic Journal: Macroeconomics* **5**(3): 190–228

Coombs H. C. (1994), From Curtin to Keating: the 1945 and 1994 white papers on employment, discussion paper, North Australia Research Unit, Australian National University

Cooper R. N. (1969), Macroeconomic policy adjustment in interdependent economics, *Quarterly Journal of Economics* **83**(1): 1–24

Cooper R., A. John (1988), Coordinating coordination failures in Keynesian models, *Quarterly Journal of Economics* **103**(3): 441–63

Corak M. (2013), Income inequality, equality of opportunity, and intergenerational mobility, *Journal of Economic Perspectives* **27**(3): 79–102

Coricelli F., A. Cukierman, A. Dalmazzo (2006), Monetary institutions, monopolistic competition, unionized labour markets and economic performance, *Scandinavian Journal of Economics* **108**(1): 39–63

Corsetti G., L. Dedola (2016), The mystery of the printing press: monetary policy and self-fulfilling debt crises, *Journal of the European Economic Association* **14**(6): 1329–71

Corsetti G., P. Pesenti (2001), Welfare and macroeconomic interdependence, *Quarterly Journal of Economics* **116**(2): 421–46

Council of Europe, Committee of Ministers (1999), Declaration and programme on education for democratic citizenship, based on the rights and responsibilities of citizens, 7 May

Cova P., P. Pagano, M. Pisani (2016), Global macroeconomic effects of exiting from unconventional monetary policy, Bank of Italy Temi di Discussione (working paper) no. 1078, September

Cowen T., (2011), *The Great Stagnation*. New York, NY: Dutton

Crafts N. (2014), Secular stagnation: US hypochondria, European disease?, in C. Teulings, R. Baldwin, eds., *Secular Stagnation: Facts, Causes and Cures* (2014). Washington, DC: Center for Economic and Policy Research (CEPR)

Creel J., P. Monperrus-Veroni, F. Saraceno (2007), Has the golden rule of public finance made a difference in the UK?, OFCE Documents de Travail no. 2007/13, Avril

Crowe C., E. Meade (2008), Central bank independence and transparency: evolution and effectiveness, *European Journal of Political Economy* **24**(4): 763–77

Cudd A. E. (2014), Commitment as motivation: Amartya Sen's theory of agency and the explanation of behaviour, *Economics and Philosophy* **30**(1): 35–56

Cukierman A. (1992), *Central Bank Strategy, Credibility, and Independence: Theory and Evidence*. Cambridge, MA: MIT Press

Cukierman A. (1994), Commitment through delegation, political influence and central bank independence, in: W. J. O. De Beaufort, S. C. W. Eijffinger, L. H. Hoogduin, eds., *A Framework for Monetary Stability*. Dordrecht: Kluwer, pp. 55–74

Dalmazzo A. (2014), Monetary discipline as a substitute for fiscal reforms and market liberalizations, *Economic Notes* **43**(3): 193–210

D'Antonio M., A. Graziani, S. Vinci (1972), *Problemi e metodi di politica economica*. Naples: Liguori; 2nd edn, *Cooperativa editrice Economia e commercio*. Naples: Liguori, 1974; 3rd edn, vol. 1: *Aspetti di metodo, Gli interventi di breve period*. Naples: Liguori, 1979

Darvas Z. (2010), Fiscal federalism in crisis: lessons for Europe from the US, Bruegel Policy contribution, July

Darvas Z., A. Simon (2015), Filling the gap: open economy considerations for more reliable potential output estimates, Bruegel working paper no. 11

Davies H., D. Green (2013), *Global Financial Regulation: The Essential Guide*. Cambridge: Polity

Debelle G., S. Fischer (1994), How independent should a central bank be?, in J. Fuhrer, ed., *Goals, Guidelines and Constraints Facing Monetary Policymakers*. Boston: Federal Reserve Bank of Boston, pp. 195–221

Debortoli D., J. Kim, J. Lindé, R. Nunes (2017), Designing a simple loss function for central banks: does a dual mandate make sense?, Universitat Pompeu Fabra Economics Working Paper Series, working paper no. 1560, March

De Cecco M. (2013), Global imbalances: past, present and future, *Contributions to Political Economy* **31**(1): 29–50

de Finetti B. (1938), Ai margini del dominio della matematica nei problemi dell'assicurazione, *Assicurazioni* **5**: 365–82

de Finetti B. (1976), *Dall'utopia all'alternativa*. Milan: F. Angeli

de Finetti B. (2015), L'utopia come presupposto necessario per ogni impostazione significativa della scienza economica, in B. de Finetti, ed., *Requisiti per un Sistema Economico Accettabile in Relazione alle Esigenze della Collettività*. Milan: F. Angeli, 1973; reprinted in *Un Matematico tra Utopia e Riformismo*, ed. with an Introduction by G. Amari and F. de Finetti. Rome: Ediesse

De Grauwe P. (2011), A less punishing, more forgiving approach to the debt crisis in the Eurozone, CEPS policy brief no. 230

De Grauwe P. (2012), *Lectures on Behavioral Macroeconomics*, Princeton, NJ: Princeton University Press

De Grauwe P. (2013), Design failures in the Eurozone: can they be fixed?, Euroforum KU Leuven policy paper no. 1, April

De Grauwe P. (2015), Secular stagnation in the Eurozone, Vox, CEPR's Policy Portal, 30 January 2015

De Grauwe P., Y. Ji (2013), Fiscal implications of the ECB's bond-buying programme, Vox, CEPR's Policy Portal, 14 June, available at http://voxeu.org/article/quantitative-easing-eurozone-its-possible-without-fiscal-transfers

De Grauwe P., Y. Ji (2015), Quantitative easing in the Eurozone: it's possible without fiscal transfers, Vox, CEPR's Policy Portal, 15 January

de Haan J., J. Sturm (1992), The case for central bank independence, *BNL Quarterly Review* **45**(182): 305–27

De Leonardis O., S. Negrelli, R. Salais, eds. (2012), *Democracy and Capabilities for Voice, Welfare, Work and Public Deliberation in Europe*. New York, NY: Peter Lang

DeLong B., L. H. Summers (2012), Fiscal policy in a depressed economy, *Brookings Papers on Economic Activity*, Spring: 233–74

Del Negro M., M. Giannoni, C. Patterson (2015), The forward guidance puzzle, Federal Reserve Bank of New York staff reports no. 574, December

Demertzis M., A. Hughes Hallett (2007), Central bank transparency in theory and practice, *Journal of Macroeconomics* **29**(4): 760–89.

Demertzis M., A. Hughes Hallett (2015), Three different approaches to transparency in monetary policy, *Economia Politica: Journal of Analytical and Institutional Economics* **32**(3): 277–300

Demertzis M., A. Hughes Hallett, N. Viegi (2004), An independent central bank faced with elected governments, *European Journal of Political Economy* **20**(4): 907–22

Denes M., G. B. Eggertsson, S. Gilbukh (2013), Deficits, public debt dynamics and tax and spending multipliers, *Economic Journal* **123**(566): F133–63

Den Haan W. J., ed. (2016), *Quantitative Easing: Evolution of Economic Thinking As It Happened*. Washington, DC: Center for Economic and Policy Research (CEPR) Press

De Nicolò G., G. Favara, L. Ratnovski (2012), Externalities and macroprudential policy, IMF Staff discussion note 12/05, June 7

Denis C., K. Mc Morrow, W. Röger (2006), Globalisation: trends, issues and macro implications for the EU, European Economy, economic papers no. 254, July

Desai M. (1991), Human development: concepts and measurement, *European Economic Review* **35**(2–3): 350–57

Deutsche Bundesbank (2012), Stellungnahme gegenüber dem Bundesverfassungsgericht zu den Verfahren mit den Az. 2 BvR 1390/12, 2 BvR 1421/12, 2 BvR 1439/12, 2 BvR 1824/12, 2 BvE 6/

12 (Statement to the Federal German Constitutional Court in the Proceedings with Reference Nos. 2 BvR 1390/12, 2 BvR 1421/12, 2 BvR 1439/12, 2 BvR 1824/12, 2 BvE 6/12)

De Viti De Marco A. (1888), *Il carattere teorico dell'economia finanziaria*. Rome: Pasqualucci

De Viti De Marco A. (1934), *Principi di economia finanziaria*. Torino: Einaudi (English trans.: *First Principles of Public Finance*. New York, NY: Jonathan Cape-Harcourt Brace & Co., 1936)

Diamond L., J. J. Linz, S. M. Lipset (1995), What makes for democracy, in L. Diamond, J. J. Linz, S. M. Lipset, eds., *Politics in Developing Countries: Comparing Experiences with Democracy*. Boulder, CO: Lynne Rienner

Diamond P. A. (1965), National debt in a neoclassical growth model, *American Economic Review* 55(5): 1126–50

Di Bartolomeo G., L. Rossi, M. Tancioni (2011), Monetary policy, rule-of-thumb consumers and external habits: a G7 comparison, *Applied Economics* 43(21): 2721–38

Di Bartolomeo G., P. Tirelli, N. Acocella (2014), Trend inflation, the labor market wedge, and the non-vertical Phillips curve, *Journal of Policy Modeling* 36(6): 1022–35

Di Bartolomeo G., P. Tirelli, N. Acocella (2015), The comeback of inflation as an optimal public finance tool, *International Journal of Central Banking* 11(1): 43–70

Dickinson H. D. (1933), Price formation in a socialist community, *Economic Journal* 43(170): 237–50

Di Fenizio F. (various years), *Le leggi dell'economia,* vol. 1: *Il metodo dell'economia politica e della politica economica*. Milan: L'industria, 1957; vol. 2: *Il sistema economico, i grandi attori e i flussi di reddito*. Milan: L'industria, 1958; vol. 3: *La funzione del consumo*. Milan: L'industria, 1958; vol. 4: *Diagnosi, previsioni, politiche congiunturali in Italia*. Rome: Isco, 1958; vol. 5: *La programmazione globale in Italia*. Rome: Isco, 1962

Dincer N. N., B. Eichengreen (2014), Central bank transparency and independence: updates and new measures, *International Journal of Central Banking* 10(1): 189–259

Di Tella R., R. MacCulloch (2004), Unemployment benefits as a substitute for a conservative central banker, *Review of Economics and Statistics* 86(4): 911–22

Dixit A. (1996), *The Making of Economic Policy: A Transaction-Cost Politics Perspective*. Cambridge, MA: MIT Press

Dixit A., L. Lambertini (2001), Monetary-fiscal policy interactions and commitment versus discretion in a monetary union, *European Economic Review* **45**(4–6): 977–87

Dixit A. K., S. Honkapohja, R. M. Solow (1992), Swedish economics in the 1980s, in L. Engwall, ed., *Economics in Sweden: An Evaluation of Swedish Research in Economics*. London: Routledge

Dollar D. (2007), Globalisation, poverty and inequality since 1980, in D. Held, A. Kaya, A. Downs, eds., *An Economic Theory of Good Decision-Making in Democracy* (1957). New York: Harper & Row

Draghi M. (2016), Helicopter money is a very interesting concept, 10 March, available at www.youtube.com/watch?v=Zbb–KxTjWc

Dreher A., K. Gehring, C. Kotsogiannis, S. Marchesi (2016), Information transmission within federal fiscal architectures: theory and evidence, CEPR discussion paper no. 11344

Dryzek J. S., C. List (2003), Social choice theory and deliberative democracy: a reconciliation, *British Journal of Political Science* **33**(1): 1–28

Du Caju P., E. Gautier, D. Momferatou, M. Ward-Warmedinger (2008), Institutional features of wage bargaining in 22 EU countries, the US and Japan, ECB working paper no. 974

Duesenberry J. (1949), *Income, Saving and the Theory of Consumer Behaviour*. Cambridge, MA: Harvard University Press

Duflo E. (2017), The economist as plumber, MIT Department of Economics working paper no. 17-03, 23 January

Duménil G., D. Lévy (2014), The crisis of the early 21st century: general interpretation, recent developments, and perspectives, chap. 2 in R. Bellofiore, G. Vertova, eds., *The Great Recession and the Contradictions of Contemporary Capitalism*. Cheltenham: Edward Elgar

Dukes E. F. 1996, *Resolving Public Conflict: Transforming Community and Governance*. Manchester: Manchester University Press

Dür A., G. Mateo (2014), The Europeanization of interest groups: group type, resources and policy area. *European Union Politics* **15**(4): 572–94

Dür A., G. Mateo González (2013), Gaining access or going public? Interest group strategies in five European countries, *European Journal of Political Research*, 52(5): 660-686, available at https://papers.ssrn.com/sol3/papers.cfm?abstract_id=2125812

Dür A., P. Bernhagen, D. Marshall (2015), Interest group success in the European Union: when (and why) does business lose? *Comparative Political Studies* 48(8): 951–83

Ege R., H. Igersheim, C. Le Chapelain (2012), Transcendental vs. comparative approaches to justice: a reappraisal of Sen's dichotomy, BETA working paper no. 2012–15

Eggertsson G., P. Krugman (2013), Debt, deleveraging, and the liquidity trap: a Fisher-Minsky-Koo approach, *Quarterly Journal of Economics* 127(3): 1469–513

Eggertsson G. B., N. R. Mehrotra (2014), A model of secular stagnation, NBER working paper no. 20574, October

Eggertsson G., M. Woodford (2003), The zero bound on interest rates and optimal monetary policy, NBER working paper no. 11535, 26 June

Eggertsson G. B., N. R. Mehrotra, L. H. Summers (2016), Secular stagnation in the open economy, *American Economic Review* 106(5): 503–7

Eichengreen B. (2015a), Secular stagnation: the long view, *American Economic Review: Papers & Proceedings*, 105(5): 66–70, available at http://dx.doi.org/10.1257/aer.p20151104

Eichengreen B. (2015b), The International Monetary System after the financial crisis, in B. J. Eichengreen, B. Park, eds., *The World Economy after the Global Crisis: A New Economic Order for the 21th Century*. London: World Scientific Studies in International Economics, chap. 4

Eijffinger S. C. W., M. Hoeberichts (1998), The trade off between central bank independence and conservativeness, *Oxford Economics Papers* 50(3): 397

Eijffinger S. C. W., M. Hoeberichts (2008), The trade off between central bank independence and conservativeness in a New Keynesian framework, *European Journal of Political Economy* 24(4): 742–47

Eijffinger S., E. Schaling, M. Hoeberichts (1998), Central bank independence: a sensitivity analysis, *European Journal of Political Economy* **14**(1): 73–88

Einaudi L. (1934), Preface, in De Viti De Marco A., *Principi di economia finanziaria*. Torino: Einaudi (English trans.: *First Principles of Public Finance*. New York, NY: Jonathan Cape-Harcourt Brace & Co., 1936)

Engel C. (2015), International coordination of central bank policy, *Journal of International Money and Finance*, available at www.sciencedirect.com/science/article/pii/S0261560615001096

Engen E. M., T. Laubach, D. Reifschneider (2015), *The Macroeconomic Effects of the Federal Reserve's Unconventional Monetary Policies* (Finance and Economics Discussion Series 2015-005). Washington, DC: Board of Governors of the Federal Reserve System, available at http://dx.doi.org/10.17016/FEDS.2015.005

Engerman S. L., K. L. Sokoloff (2002), Factor endowments, inequality, and paths of development among New World economies, NBER working paper no. 9259, October

Englund T. (2002), Higher education, democracy and citizenship: the democratic potential of the university?, *Studies in Philosophy and Education* **21**(4): 281–87

Erceg C., C. Gust D. Lopez Salido (2007), The transmission of domestic shocks in the open economy, chap. 2 in NBER, *International Dimensions of Monetary Policy*, Cambridge, MA: NBER, pp. 89–148

Eriksen I., T. J. Hanisch, A. Sæther (2007), The rise and fall of the Oslo school, *Nordic Journal of Political Economy* **33**: 1–31

Erixon L. (2011), Formalizing a new approach to economic policy: Bent Hansen, Gosta Rehn and the Swedish model, mimeo

Etzioni A. (1985), Opening the preferences: a socio-economic research agenda, *Journal of Behavioral Economics* **14**(1): 183–205

European Economic Advisory Group (EEAG) (2011), *The EEAG Report on the European Economy*. Munich: CESifo

Eurostat (various years), Unemployment statistics, available at http://ec.europa.eu/eurostat/statisticsexplained/index.php/Unemployment_statistics

Faguet J.-P. (1997), Decentralization and local government performance, London School of Economics, Centre for Economic Performance and Development Studies Institute, 4 December

Fair R. C. (1999), Estimated inflation costs had European unemployment been reduced in the 1980s by macro policies, *Journal of Macroeconomics* **21**(1): 11–28

Farrell J. (1988), Communication, coordination and Nash equilibrium, *Economics Letters* **27**(3): 209–14

Fatás A., L. H. Summers (2016a), Hysteresis and fiscal policy during the Global Crisis, CEPR Vox, 12 October

Fatás A., L. H. Summers (2016b), The permanent effects of fiscal consolidations, NBER working paper no. 22374, June

Fatás A., J. von Hagen, A. Hughes Hallett, R. R. Strauch, A. Sibert (2003), Stability and growth in Europe: towards a better pact, in *Monitoring European Integration*, vol. **13**. London: CEPR

Fatás A., I. Mihov (2006), Restricting fiscal policy discretion: the case of U.S. states, *Journal of Public Economics* **90**(1–2): 101–17

Faucci, R. (2002), L'economia per frammenti di Federico Caffè, *Rivista Italiana degli Economisti* **7**(3): 363–410

Favero C. A., V. Galasso (2015), Demographics and the secular stagnation hypothesis in Europe, CEPR discussion paper no. 10887, October

Fernandez-Villaverde J., L. Garicano, T. Santos (2013), Political credit cycles: the case of the Euro zone, *Journal of Economic Perspectives* **27**(3): 145–66

Ferrara F. (1859), Prefazione a C. Dunoyer, in *Opere complete di Francesco Ferrara*, vol. **5**. Rome: De Luca (1961)

Ferrero G., M. Gross, S. Neri (2017), On secular stagnation and low interest rates: demography matters, ECB working paper no. 2088, July

Filardo A. (2001), Should monetary policy respond to asset price bubbles? Some experimental results, in G. Kaufman, ed., *Asset Price Bubbles: Implications for Monetary and Regulatory Policies*. Amsterdam: Elsevier Science

Filardo A., B. Hofmann (2014), Forward guidance at the zero lower bound, *BIS Quarterly Review*, March: 37–53

Fisher I. (1933), The debt-deflation theory of the Great Depression, *Econometrica* **1**(4): 337–57

Fitoussi J.-P., J. Camassi, G. Di Giorgio et al. (2010), *After the Crisis: The Way Ahead*. Rome: Luiss University Press

Flaschel P., R. Franke, W. Semmler (1997), *Dynamic Macroeconomics: Instability, Fluctuation, and Growth in Monetary Economics*. Cambridge, MA: MIT Press

Fratzscher M., M. Lo Duca, R. Straub (2013), On the international spillovers of US quantitative easing, ECB working paper no. 1557

Fleurbaey M., F. Maniquet (2011), *A Theory of Fairness and Social Welfare*. Cambridge: Cambridge University Press

Fontana Russo L. (1902), *I trattati di commercio e l'economia nazionale*. Rome: Soc. ed. Dante Alighieri

Fontana Russo L. (1935), *Corso di politica economica generale e corporative*. Rome: Cremonese

Forbes K., D. Reinhardt, T. Wieladek (2016), Banking de-globalisation: a consequence of monetary and regulatory policies?, Bank for International Settlements (BIS), Macroprudential policy, BIS paper no. 86, September, pp. 49–56; available at www.bis.org

Foster J. B., R. McChesney (2012), *The Endless Crisis: How Monopoly-Finance Capital Produces Stagnation and Upheaval from the USA to China*. New York, NY: Monthly Review Press

Franchini Stappo A. (1955), *Studi sulla teoria macroeconomica della congiuntura*. Firenze: Società editrice universitaria

Frankel J. (2014), Considering QE, Mario? Buy US bonds, not Eurobonds, in W. den Haan, ed., *Quantitative Easing: Evolution of Economic Thinking As It Happened*. Washington, DC: Center for Economic and Policy Research (CEPR) Press

Franzini M., M. Pianta (2016), The engines of inequality, Centre for European Policy Studies, *Intereconomics: Review of European Economic Policy* 51(2): 49–55, available at www.ceps.eu/sys tem/files/IEForum22016_1.pdf

Franzini M., M. Raitano (2016), Economic inequality and its impact on intergenerational mobility, *Intereconomics: Review of European Economic Policy* 51(2): 331–35

Franzini M., M. Pianta, J. K. Galbraith et al. (2016), Wealth and income inequality in Europe: Forum, *Intereconomics: Review of European Economic Policy* 51(2): 331–56

Friedman M. (1962), *Capitalism and Freedom*. Chicago, IL: University of Chicago Press

Friedman M. (1968), The role of monetary policy, *American Economic Review* **58**(1): 1–17

Friedman M. (1969), *The Optimum Quantity of Money*. London: Macmillan

Friedman B. M. (2015), Has the financial crisis permanently changed the practice of monetary policy?, *Manchester School* **83**(S1): 5–19

Frisch R. (1933), Sparing of circulasjons reguletering, *Fabritius & Sønners Forlag* (English trans.: Saving and circulation control, *Rivista di Storia Economica* **23**(2): 233–48)

Frisch R. (1934), Circulation planning: proposal for a national organisation of a commodity and service, *Econometrica* **2**(3): 258–336

Frisch R. (1949), A memorandum on price-wage-tax subsidy policies as instruments in maintaining optimal employment, UN Document E (CN1/Dub 2), New York, reprinted as Memorandum fra Universitets Sosialøkonomiske Institutt, Oslo, 1953

Frisch R. (1950), L'emploi des modèles pour l'élaboration d'une politique économique rationnelle, *Revue d'Économie Politique* **60**: 474–98, 601–34

Frisch R. (1957), Numerical determination of a quadratic preference function for use in macroeconomic programming, memorandum fra Universitets Sosialøkonomiske Institutt, Oslo, no. 14, reprinted in Studies in honour of Gustavo Del Vecchio, *Giornale degli Economisti e Annali di Economia* **20**(1–2): 43–83 (1961)

Frisch R. (1961), Economic planning and the growth problem in developing countries, *Øst-økonomi* **1**(1): 51–74

Frisch R. (1970), From utopian theory to practical applications: the case of econometrics (Lecture to the memory of Alfred Nobel, June 17), in A. Lindbeck, ed., *Nobel Lectures, Economics 1969–1980*. Singapore: World Scientific Publishing (1992), also available at www.nobelprize.org/nobel_prizes/economic-sciences/laureates/1969/frisch-lecture.pdf

Fry M., D. Julius, L. Mahadeva, S. Roger, G. Sterne (2000), Key issues in the choice of monetary policy framework, in L. Mahadeva, G. Sterne, eds., *Monetary Policy Frameworks in a Global Context*. London: Routledge, pp. 1–216

Fuà G., P. Sylos-Labini (1963), *Idee per la programmazione economica*. Bari: Laterza

Fujita S., I. Fujiwara (2016), Declining trends in the real interest rate and inflation: the role of aging, Federal Reserve Bank of Philadelphia working paper no. 16/29, October

Furman J. (2016), The New View of fiscal policy and its application, paper presented at the Conference on Global Implications of Europe's Redesign, New York, 5 October

Galati G., R. Moessner (2013), Macroprudential policy: a literature review, *Journal of Economic Surveys* **27**(5): 846–78

Galbraith J. K. (1987), *Economics in Perspective: A Critical History*. Boston: Houghton Mifflin

Galbraith J. K. (2016a), Causes of changing inequality in the world, in Franzini, Pianta, Galbraith, Bogliacino, Maestri, Raitano, Bosch, Kalina, eds., pp. 55–60

Galbraith J. K. (2016b), *Welcome to the Poisoned Chalice: The Destruction of Greece and the Future of Europe*. New Haven, CT: Yale University Press

Galí J. (2005), Modern perspectives on fiscal stabilization policies, *CESifo Economic Studies* **51**(4): 587–99

Galí J., J. D. López-Salido, J. Vallés (2007), Understanding the effects of government spending on consumption, *Journal of the European Economic Association* **5**(1): 227–70

Galor O., O. Moav (2004) From physical to human capital accumulation: inequality and the process of development, *Review of Economic Studies* **71**(4): 1001–26

Gaspar V., M. Obstfeld, R. Sahay (2016), Macroeconomic management when policy space is constrained: a comprehensive, consistent and coordinated approach to economic policy, IMF staff discussion note no. 16/09

Gechert S. (2015), What fiscal policy is most effective? A meta-regression analysis, *Oxford Economic Papers*, DOI:http://10.1093/oep/gpv027

Gechert S., R. Mentges (2013), What drives fiscal multipliers? The role of private wealth and debt, IMK working paper no. 124-2013, IMK at the Hans Boeckler Foundation, Macroeconomic Policy Institute

Gechert S., A. Rannenberg (2014), Are fiscal multipliers regime-dependent? A meta regression analysis, Macroeconomic Policy Institute (IMK) working paper no. 139, 18 September

Gechert S., A. Rannenberg (2015), The costs of Greece's fiscal consolidation, Macroeconomic Policy Institute (IMK) policy brief, March

Gechert S., A. Hughes Hallett, A. Rannenberg (2015), Fiscal multipliers in downturns and the effects of Eurozone consolidation, CEPR policy insight no. 79, 26 February

Giannoni M., M. Woodford (2005), Optimal inflation targeting rules, in B. S. Bernanke, M. Woodford, eds., *Inflation Targeting*. Chicago, IL: University of Chicago Press

Giavazzi F., M. Pagano (1988), Capital controls in the EMS, in D. E. Fair C. de Boissieu eds., *International Monetary and Financial Integration: The European Dimension*. Dordrecht: Martinus Nijhoff

Giavazzi F., M. Pagano (1990), Can severe fiscal contractions be expansionary? Tales of two small European countries, in *NBER Macroeconomics Annual*, vol. **5**. Cambridge, MA: MIT Press, pp. 75–122

Giavazzi F., M. Pagano (1996), Non-Keynesian effects of fiscal policy changes: international evidence and the Swedish experience, *Swedish Economic Policy Review* **3**(1): 67–112

Gilens M. (2012), *Affluence and Influence: Economic Inequality and Political Power in America*. Princeton, NJ: Princeton University Press

Glaeser E. L. (2005), Inequality, NBER working paper no.11511, June

Goodfriend M., R. G. King (1997), The new neoclassical synthesis, in B. S. Bernanke, J. Rotemberg, eds., *NBER Macroeconomics Annual*, vol. **12**. Cambridge, MA: MIT Press, pp. 231–96

Goodin R. (2004), Democracy, justice and impartiality, chap. 6 in K. Dowding, R. E. Goodin, C. Pateman, eds., *Justice and Democracy: Essays for Brian Barry*. Cambridge: Cambridge University Press, pp. 97–126

Gordon R. J. (1976), Recent developments in the theory of inflation and unemployment, *Journal of Monetary Economics* **2**(2): 185–219

Gordon R. J. (2012), Is U.S. economic growth over? Faltering innovation confronts the six headwinds, NBER working paper no. 18315, August

Gordon R. J. (2014), The turtle's progress: secular stagnation meets the headwinds in C. Teulings, R. Baldwin, eds. (2014), *Secular Stagnation: Facts, Causes and Cures.* Washington, DC: CEPR

Gottfries A., C. Teulings (2015), Can demography explain secular stagnation?, CEPR Vox, 30 January

Gradstein M. (2007), Inequality, democracy and the protection of property rights, *Economic Journal* **117**(516): 252–69

Graham K. (1986), *The Battle of Democracy: Conflict, Consensus and the Individual.* Brighton: Wheatsheaf Books

Graham L., D. J. Snower (2008), Hyperbolic discounting and the Phillips curve, *Journal of Money, Credit and Banking* **40**(2–3): 427–48

Grampp W. D. (2000), What did Smith mean by the invisible hand?, *Journal of Political Economy* **108**(3): 441–65

Granovetter M. (1985), Economic action and social structure: the problem of embeddedness, *Anerican Journal of Sociology* **91**(3): 481–510

Graziano L. (2001), *Lobbying, Pluralism and Democracy.* Basingstoke: Palgrave

Gregory M., D. Weiserbs (1998), Changing objectives in national policymaking, in J. Forder, A. Menon, eds., *European Union and National Macroeconomic Policy.* London: Routledge

Grilli V., D. Masciandaro, G. Tabellini (1991), Institutions and policies, *Economic Policy* **6**(13): 341–92

Gros D., C. Hefeker (2002), One size must fit all national divergences in a monetary union, *German Economic Review* **3**: 247–62

Grossman G. M., E. Helpman (2001), *Special Interest Politics.* Cambridge, MA: MIT Press

Grossman G. M., E. Helpman (2005), Party discipline and pork-barrel politics, NBER working paper no. 11396

Grossman S. J. (1981), An introduction to the theory of rational expectations under asymmetric information, *Review of Economic Studies* **48**(4): 541–59

Guglielminetti E. (2016), The labor market channel of macroeconomic uncertainty, Bank of Italy working paper no. 1068, June

Guibourg G., M. Jonsson, B. Lagerwall, C. Nilsson (2015), Macroprudential policy: effects on the economy and the interaction with monetary policy, *Sveriges Riksbank Economic Review* 2: 29–46

Guzzo V., A. Velasco (2002), Revisiting the case for a populist central banker: a comment, *European Economic Review* 46(3): 613–21

Guzzo V., A. Velasco (1999), The case for a populist central banker, *European Economic Review* 43(7): 1317–44

Haavelmo T. (1966), Orientering i makroøkonomisk teori (Orientation on macroeconomic theory), Memorandum from the Institute of Economics, University of Oslo, 15 December

Haavelmo T. (1965), Some observations on countercyclical fiscal policy and its effects on economic growth; comments made by Leontief, Isard, Allais, Fisher, Malinvaud, Koopmans, Wold, and Haavelmo's responses, in *Semaine d'Etude sur le Rôle de l'Analyse économetrique dans la Formulation de Plans de Développement* Rome: Pontificiae Academiae Scientiarum Scripta Varia, 28: 503–27

Haberler G. (1952), The Pigou effect once more, *Journal of Political Economy* 60(3): 240–46

Habermas J. (1984), *Theory of Communicative Action: Reason and the Rationalization of Society*, vol. I. Boston: Beacon Press

Hagemann R. P. (2010), Improving fiscal performance through fiscal councils, OECD Economics Department working paper no. 829, available at http://dx.doi.org/10.1787/5km33sqsqq9v-en

Hall R. L., A. V. Deardorff (2006), Lobbying as legislative subsidy, *American Political Science Review* 100(1): 69–84

Hansen B. (1955), *The Economic Theory of Fiscal Policy*. London: Allen & Unwin (1958) (English edn of the first edn published in Swedish in 1955 as a report to Penningvärdeundersökningen)

Hansen B. (1968), Lectures in Economic Theory II: The Theory of Economic Policy and Planning, Lund: Studentlitteratur

Harashima T. (2007), Why should central banks be independent?, MPRA working paper no. 1838, February

Harrod R. F. (1938), Scope and method of economics, *Economic Journal* 48(191): 383–412

Hayek, F. A., ed. (1935), *Collectivist Economic Planning*. London: Routledge

Hayek F. A. (1945), The use of knowledge in society, *American Economic Review* 35(4): 519–30

Hayek F. A. (1960), *The Constitution of Liberty.* Chicago, IL: University of Chicago Press

Hayo B. (1998), Inflation culture, central bank independence and price stability, *European Journal of Political Economy* **14**(2): 241–63

Hayo B., C. Hefeker (2002), Reconsidering central bank independence, *European Journal of Political Economy* **18**(4): 653–74

Hayo B., C. Hefeker (2007), Does central bank independence cause low inflation? A sceptical view, mimeo, May

Heal G. M. (1969), Planning without prices, *Review of Economic Studies* **36**, 347–62, reprinted in M. J. Farrell, ed., *Readings from the Review of Economic Studies in Welfare Economics.* London: Macmillian (1973).

Heal G. M. (1971), Planning, prices and increasing returns, *Review of Economic Studies* **38**(3): 281–94.

Heal G. M. (1972), The theory of voting: Robin Farquharson, *Journal of Public Economics* **1**(2): 277–80

Heal G. M. (1973), *The Theory of Economic Planning.* Amsterdam: North Holland

Heal G. M. (1987), Some analytical issues in long-run planning, *International Journal of Development Planning* **2**(1): 14–28, also in I. Adelman, J. E. Taylor, eds., *The Design of Alternative Development Strategies.* Rohtak: Jan Tinbergen Institute of Development Planning

Heal G. M. (1997), Social choice and resource allocation: a topological perspective, *Social Choice and Welfare* **14**(2): 147–60

Heal G. M. (2005), Planning, chap. 29 in K. J. Arrow, M. D. Intriligator, eds., *Handbook of Mathematical Economics*, 2nd edn, **2** vols. 3. Amsterdam: Elsevier, pp. 1483–1510

Hebous S. (2010), The effects of discretionary fiscal policy on macroeconomic aggregates: a reappraisal, Goethe University Frankfurt, July 2009, Munich, archive paper no. 23300, available at http://mpra.ub.uni-muenchen.de/23300/

Hefeker C., Zimmer B. (2011), Central bank independence and conservatism under uncertainty: substitutes or complements?, CESifo working paper no. 3344

Held D., A. Kaya, eds. (2007), *Global Inequality.* Cambridge: Polity Press

Herndon T, M. Ash, R. Pollin (2013), Does high public debt consistently stifle economic growth? A critique of Reinhart and Rogoff, *Cambridge Journal of Economics* **38**(2): 257–79

Henning C. R., M. Kessler (2012), Fiscal federalism: US history for architects of Europe's fiscal union, Bruegel Essay and Lecture Series

Hetzel R. L. (1998), Arthur Burns and inflation, *Federal Reserve Bank of Richmond Economic Quarterly* **84**(1): 21–44

Hibbs D. A. (1977), Political parties and macroeconomic policy, *American Political Science Review* **71**(4): 1467–87

Hicks J. R. (1939), The foundations of welfare economics, *Economic Journal* **49**(196): 696–712 (Italian trans. in Caffè 1956b)

Hobbes T. (1651), *Leviathan*, critical edition by N. Malcolm in three volumes. Oxford: Oxford University Press (2012)

Hobson J. (1909), *The Industrial System: An Inquiry into Earned and Unearned Income*. London: Longmans

Holden S. (2003), Wage-setting under different monetary regimes, *Economica* **70**(278): 251–65

Holly S. (1987), Non-cooperative dynamic games with rational observers, *Journal of Economic Dynamics and Control* **11**(2): 159–61

Holly S., A. Hughes Hallett (1989), *Optimal Control, Expectations and Uncertainty*. Cambridge: Cambridge University Press

Holston K, T. Laubach, J. C. Williams (2017), Measuring the natural rate of interest: international trends and determinants, *Journal of International Economics* **108**(S1): S59–S75

Hoover K. D., O. Jorda (2001), Measuring systematic monetary policy, *Federal Reserve Bank of St. Louis Review*, July–August: 113–44

Horowitz D. L. (1985), *Ethnic Groups in Conflict*. Berkeley, CA: University of California Press

Horowitz D. L. (1993), Democracy in divided societies, *Journal of Democracy* **4**(4): 18–38

Horváth B., W. Wagner (2013), The disturbing interaction between countercyclical capital requirements and systemic risk, 29 November, mimeo, available at http://ssrn.com/abstract=2187020

Horváth B., W. Wagner (2016), Macroprudential policies and the Lucas critique, in Bank for International Settlements (BIS),

Macroprudential policy, BIS paper no. 86, September, pp. 39–44; available at www.bis.org

Hotelling H. (1938), The general welfare in relation to problems of taxation and of railways and utility rates, *Econometrica* **6**(3): 242–69 (Italian trans. in Caffè 1956b)

Hrebenar R., B. Morgan (2009), *Lobbying in America*. Santa Barbara, CA: ABC-Clio, Inc.

Hughes Hallett A. (1986), International policy design and the sustainability of policy bargains, *Journal of Economic Dynamics and Control* **10**(4): 457–94

Hughes Hallett A. (1989), Econometrics and the theory of economic policy: the Tinbergen-Theil contributions 40 years on, *Oxford Economic Papers* **41**(3): 189–214

Hughes Hallett A. (2000), Aggregate Phillips curves are not always vertical: heterogeneity and mismatch in multiregion or multisector economies, *Macroeconomic Dynamics* **4**(4): 534–46

Hughes Hallett A. (2008), Sustainable fiscal policies and budgetary risk under alternative monetary policy arrangements, *Economic Change and Restructuring* **41**(1): 1–28, DOI http://10.1007 /s10644-008-9036-6

Hughes Hallett A., N. Acocella (2016), Forward guidance: stabilization and stabilizability under endogenous policy rules at the zero lower bound, University of Rome and St Andrews University

Hughes Hallett A., N. Acocella (2017), Stabilization and expanded commitment: a theory of forward guidance for economies with rational expectations, Sapienza University of Rome, Memotef, working paper no. 132/2014, forthcoming in *Macroeconomic Dynamics*

Hughes Hallett A., H. J. B. Rees (1983), *Quantitative Economic Policies and Interactive Planning*. Cambridge: Cambridge University Press

Hughes Hallett A., D. N. Weymark (2005), Independence before conservatism: transparency, *Politics and Central Bank Design* **6**(1): 1–21

Hughes Hallett A., G. Di Bartolomeo, N. Acocella (2012a), Expectations dynamics: policy, announcements and limits to dynamic inconsistency, *Studies in Nonlinear Dynamics &*

Econometrics **16**(2), available at www.degruyter.com/view/j/snde.16.issue-2/1558–3708.1918/1558–3708.1918.xml

Hughes Hallett A., G. Di Bartolomeo, N. Acocella (2012b), A general theory of controllability and expectations anchoring for small-open economies, *Journal of International Money and Finance* 31(2): 397–411

Hughes Hallett A., J. Libich, P. Stehlík (2014), Monetary and fiscal policy interaction with various degrees of commitment, *Czech Journal of Economics and Finance* **64**(1): 2–29

Ietto-Gillies G. (2008), Why de Finetti critique of economics is today more relevant than ever, chap. 9 in M. C. Galavotti, ed., *Bruno de Finetti, Radical Probabilist.* London: College Publications, pp. 115–27

IMF (2010), Recovery, risk, and rebalancing, world economic and financial surveys, *World Economic Outlook*, October

IMF (2013), The functions and impact of fiscal councils, policy papers, July 16

IMF (2015), Chapter 4: Private investment: what's the holdup?, chap. 4 in *World Economic Outlook*, April

IMF (2016), Fiscal policies for innovation and growth, chap. 4 in *Fiscal Monitor*, April

Ingberman D. E., R. P. Inman (1988), The political economy of fiscal policy, in P. G. Hare, ed., *Surveys in Public Sector Economics.* Oxford: Blackwell

Inman R. P. (1996), Do balanced budget rules work? U.S. experience and possible lessons for the EMU, NBER working paper no. 5838, February

Inman R. P., D., L. Rubinfeld (1997), The political economy of federalism, in D. C. Mueller, ed., *Perspectives on Public Choice: A Handbook.* Cambridge: Cambridge University Press

Ireland P. N. (2007), Changes in the Federal Reserve's inflation target: causes and consequences, *Journal of Money, Credit and Banking* **39**(8): 1851–2110

Iversen T. (2006), Capitalism and democracy, chap. 33 in B. Weingast, D. Wittman, eds., *The Oxford Handbook of Political Economy.* Oxford: Oxford University Press, pp. 601–23

Jaumotte F., S. Lall, C. Papageorgiou (2013), Rising income inequality: technology, or trade and financial globalization?, *IMF Economic Review* **61**(2): 271–309

Jesperson J. (2015), John Maynard Keynes, in B. Amoroso, ed., *Un manifesto per la buona vita e la buona società*. Rome: Castelvecchi

Jevons W. S. (1871), *The Theory of Political Economy*. London: Macmillan

Johansen L. (1977, 1978), *Lectures on Macroeconomic Planning*, 2 vols. Amsterdam: North Holland

Johnson H. G. (1971), The Keynesian revolution and the monetarist counter-revolution, *American Economic Review* **61**(2): 1–14

Jonung L., ed. (1991), *The Stockholm School of Economics Revisited*. Cambridge: Cambridge University Press

Jonung L. (2013), What can we learn from the Swedish approach to the crisis in the 1930s?, dinner speech at the conference 'Towards a sustainable financial system', organized by the Swedish House of Finance, Global Utmaning and the Financial Market Group at the London School of Economics, Stockholm, 12–13 September

Jordan A., R. Wurzel, A. Zito (2005), The rise of 'new' policy instruments in comparative perspective, *Political Studies* **53**(3): 477–96

Kærgård N., B. Sandelin, A. Sæther (2008), Scandinavian economics, in S. N. Durlauf, L. E. Blume, eds., *The New Palgrave Dictionary of Economics*, 2nd edn. London: Palgrave Macmillan

Kaldor N. (1939), Welfare propositions and interpersonal comparison of utility, *Economic Journal* **49**(195): 549–52 (Italian trans. in Caffè 1956b)

Kaldor N. (1957), A model of economic growth, *Economic Journal* **67**(268): 591–624

Kaldor N. (1971), Conflicts in national economic objectives, *Economic Journal* **81**(321): 1–16.

Kalecki M. (1933), Próba teorii koniunktury, Warsaw Institute of Research on Business Cycles and Prices

Kalecki M. (1935a), Essai d'une theorie du mouvement cyclique des affaires, *Revue d'economie politique* **49**(2): 285–305

Kalecki M. (1935b), A macrodynamic theory of business cycles, *Econometrica* **3**(3): 327–44, in M. Kalecki (1966), *Studies in the*

Theory of Business Cycles, 1933–1939. Oxford: Blackwell, chap. 1, and in M. Kalecki (1971) *Selected Essays on the Dynamics of the Capitalist Economy, 1933–1970.* Cambridge: Cambridge University Press

Kant I. (1797), The Metaphysics of Morals, trans. Mary J. Gregor. Cambridge: Cambridge University Press (1991)

Kapp K. W. (1950), *The Social Costs of Private Enterprise.* Cambridge, MA: Harvard University Press

Karakosta O., C. Kotsogiannis, M.-A. Lopez-Garcia (2014), Indirect tax harmonization and global public goods, *International Tax and Public Finance* 21(1): 29–49

Keen M., K. A. Konrad (2012), The theory of international tax competition and coordination, Max Planck Institute for Tax Law and Public Finance working paper, 6 July

Kelly N. J., P. K. Enns (2010), Inequality and the dynamics of public opinion: the self-reinforcing link between economic inequality and mass preferences, *American Journal of Political Science* 54(4): 855–70

Kendrick D. (1976), Applications of control theory to macroeconomics, in NBER, Annals of Economic and Social Measurement, vol. 5. Cambridge, MA:National Bureau of Economic Research, pp. 171–90.

Kendrick D. (2000), Control theory with applications to economics, chap. 4 in K. J. Arrow, M. D. Intriligator, eds., *Handbook of Mathematical Economics*, vol. 4. Amsterdam: Elsevier, pp. 111–58

Keynes J. M. (1930), *A Treatise on Money.* London: Macmillan, reprinted in *The Collected Writings*, vols. 5 and 6. London: Macmillan, 1978

Keynes J. M. (1936), *The General Theory of Employment, Interest and Money.* London: Macmillan, reprinted in *The Collected Writings*, vol. 7. London: Macmillan, 1973

Khan A., R. G. King, A. L. Wolman (2003), Optimal monetary policy, *Review of Economic Studies* 70(4): 825–60

King M. (2014), Monetary policy during the crisis: from the depths to the heights, in G. A. Akerlof, O. Blanchard, D. Romer, J. E. Stiglitz, eds. (2014), *What Have We Learned? Macroeconomic Policy after the Crisis.* Cambridge, MA: MIT Press

Klein L. R. (1998), Ragnar Frisch's conception of the business cycle, chap. 15 in S. Strom, ed., *Econometrics and Economic Theory in the 20th Century* (The Ragnar Frisch Centennial Symposium). Cambridge: Cambridge University Press, pp. 483–98

Klüver H. (2013), *Lobbying in the European Union: Interest Groups, Lobbying Coalitions, and Policy Change.* Oxford: Oxford University Press

Knight F. (1952), Institutionalism and empiricism in economics, *American Economic Review* **42**(2): 45–55

Kok C., M. Darracq Pariès, E. Rancoita (2015), Quantifying the policy mix in a monetary union with national macroprudential policies, *Financial Stability Review*, November: 158–70

Kollman R. (2010),Government purchases and the real exchange rate, *Open Economies Review* **21**(1): 49–64

Kreps D. (1990), *Game Theory and Economic Modeling.* Oxford: Oxford University Press

Krugman P. (2000), Thinking about the liquidity trap, *Journal of the Japanese and International Economies* **14**(4): 221–37

Krugman P. (2013), Revenge of the optimum currency area, in *NBER Macroeconomics Annual.* Chicago: University of Chicago Press

Krugman P. (2014a), Four observations on secular stagnation, in C. Teulings, R. Baldwin, eds., *Secular Stagnation: Facts, Causes and Cures.* Washington, DC: CEPR

Krugman P. (2014b), Apologizing to Japan, *New York Times*, October 31

Kumar M. S., J. Woo (2010), Public debt and growth, IMF working paper no. 10/174

Kydland F. E., E. C. Prescott (1977), Rules rather than discretion: the inconsistency of optimal plans, *Journal of Political Economy* **85** (3): 473–92

ILO (2015), *Global Wage Report 2014/15: Wages and Income Inequality.* Geneva: International Labour Office

Lambert-Mogiliansky A. (2015), Social accountability to contain corruption, *Journal of Development Economics* **116**(C): 158–68

Lange O. (1936), On the economic theory of socialism, part 1, *Review of Economic Studies* **4**(1): 53–71

Lange O. (1937), On the economic theory of socialism, part 2, *Review of Economic Studies* **4**(2): 123–42

Lansing K. J. (2002), Learning about a shift in trend output: Implications for monetary policy and inflation, Federal Reserve Bank of San Francisco working paper series 2000-16

Laubach T., J. C. Williams (2016), Measuring the natural rate of interest redux, *Business Economics* **51**(2): 257–67

Lauder H. (1991), Education, democracy and the economy, *British Journal of Sociology of Education* **12**(4): 417–31

Lazear E. P., S. Rosen (1981), Rank-order tournaments as optimum labor contracts, *Journal of Political Economy* **89**(5): 841–64

Le Borgne E., B. Lockwood (2002), Candidate entry, screening, and the political budget cycle, IMF working paper no. 02/48.

Lefkofridi Z., N. Giger, K. Kissau (2012), Inequality and representation in Europe, *Representation: Journal of Representative Democracy* **48**(1): 1–11

Leibenstein H. (1950), Bandwagon, snob and Veblen effects in the theory of consumers' demand, *Quarterly Journal of Economics* **64**(2): 183–207

Leibenstein H. (1962), Notes on welfare economics and the theory of democracy, *Economic Journal* **72**(286): 299–319

Leitemo K. (2004), A game between the fiscal and the monetary authorities under inflation targeting, *European Journal of Political Economy* **20**(3): 709–24

Leith C. S., Wren-Lewis S. (2011), Discretionary policy in a monetary union with sovereign debt, *European Economic Review* **55**(1): 57–74

Leontief W. (1941), *The Structure of American Economy, 1919–1929*. Cambridge, MA: Harvard University Press

Lerner A. P. (1934), Economic theory and socialist economy, *Review of Economic Studies* **2**(1): 51–61

Libich J. (2009), A note on the anchoring effect of explicit inflation targets, *Macroeconomic Dynamics* **13**(5): 685–97

Lim C., F. Columba, A. Costa et al. (2011), Macroprudential policy: what instruments and how to use them? Lessons from country experiences, IMF working paper no. WP/11/238, October

Lindahl E. (1919), Die Gerechtigkeit der Besteuerung, Lund (partial English trans., Just taxation: a positive solution, in R. A. Musgrave, A. T. Peacock, eds., *Classics in the Theory of Public Finance*. London: Macmillan (1958), pp. 168–76

Linnemann L., A. Schabert (2003), Fiscal policy in the new neoclassical synthesis, *Journal of Money, Credit and Banking* **35**(6): 911–29

Little I. M. D. (1949), The foundations of welfare economics, *Oxford Economic Papers* **1**(2): 227–46 (Italian trans. in Caffè 1956b)

Lombardini S. (1954), *Fondamenti e problemi dell'economia del benessere*. Milan: Giuffré

Lucas R. E. (1976), Econometric policy evaluation: a critique, in K. Brunner, A. Meltzer, eds., *The Phillips Curve and Labor Markets* (Carnegie-Rochester Conference Series on Public Policy), vol. I. Amsterdam: North Holland

Lucas R. E. (1987), *Models of Business Cycles*. Oxford: Blackwell

Lucas R. E. (1993), Making a miracle, *Econometrica* **61**(2): 251–72

Lucas R. E. (1996), Nobel lecture: monetary neutrality, *Journal of Political Economy* **104**(4): 661–82

Lucas R. E. (2003), Macroeconomic priorities, *American Economic Review* **93**(1): 1–14

Maestri V., F. Bogliacino, W. Salverda (2014), Wealth inequality and the accumulation of debt, chap. 4 in W. Salverda, B. Nolan, D. Checchi et al., eds., *Changing Inequalities in Rich Countries: Analytical and Comparative Perspectives*. Oxford: Oxford University Press

Malthus T. R. (1820), *Principles of Political Economy, Considered with a View to Their Practical Application*. London: W. Pickering

Marglin S. (2008), *The Dismal Science: How Thinking Like an Economist Undermines Community*. Cambridge, MA: Harvard University Press

Marrama V. (1948), *Teoria e politica della piena occupazione*. Rome: Edizioni italiane

Marrama V. (1962), *Problemi e tecniche di programmazione economica*. Rocca S. Casciano: Cappelli

Marshall A. (1890), *Principles of Economics*. London: Macmillan

Marshall M. G., K. Jaggers (2000), *Political Regime Characteristics and Transitions, 1800–2002: Dataset Users' Manual*. Polity IV Project, Integrated Network for Societal Conflict Research (INSCR) Program, Center for International Development and Conflict Management (CIDCM), University of Maryland, available at www.cidcm.umd.edu/inscr/polity

Marx I. (2013), Why direct income redistribution matters if we are really concerned with reducing poverty, *Intereconomics: Review of European Economic Policy* **48**(6): 350–56

Marx I., T. Van Rie (2014), The policy response to inequality: redistributing income, chap. 10 in W. Salverda, B. Nolan, D. Checchi et al., eds., *Changing Inequalities in Rich Countries: Analytical and Comparative Perspectives*. Oxford: Oxford University Press

Maskin E., T. Sjostrom (2002), Implementation theory, chap. 5 in K. J. Arrow, A. K. Sen, K. Suzumura, eds. (2011), *Handbook of Social Choice and Welfare*, vol. **2**. Amsterdam: Elsevier–North Holland, pp. 237–88

Maskin E., J. Tirole (2004), The politician and the judge: accountability in government, *American Economic Review* **94**(4): 1034–54

Mayer T. (1999), *Monetary policy and the Great Inflation in the United States: The Federal Reserve and the Failure of Macroeconomic Policy, 1965–1979*. Cheltenham: Edward Elgar

Majone G. (1994), The European Community: an 'independent fourth branch of government?', in G. Brüggemeier, ed., *Verfassungen für ein ziviles Europa*. Baden-Baden: Nomos

Majone G. (1996), *Regulating Europe*. London: Routledge

Masciandaro D., M. Quintyn (2016), The governance of financial supervision: recent developments, *Journal of Economic Surveys* **30**(5): 982–1006

Mazzola U. (1890), *I dati scientifici della finanza pubblica*. Rome: Loescher e C. (English trans. In R. A. Musgrave, A. T. Peacock, eds., *Classics in the Theory of Public Finance*. London: Macmillan (1958) (2nd edn, 1994))

McCarty N., T. K. Poole, H. Rosenthal (2006), *Polarized America: The Dance of Ideology and Unequal Riches*. Cambridge, MA: MIT Press

McCarty N., T. K. Poole, H. Rosenthal (2013), *Political Bubbles: Financial Crises and the Failure of American Democracy*. Princeton, NJ: Princeton University Press

McKay A., E. Nakamura, J. Steinsson (2016), The power of forward guidance revisited, *American Economic Review* **106**(10): 3133–58

Meade J. E. (1951), *The Theory on International Economic Policy*, vol. 1: *The Balance of Payments*. Oxford: Oxford University Press

Meade J. E. (1955), *The Theory on International Economic Policy*, vol. 2: *Trade and Welfare*. Oxford: Oxford University Press

Meade J. E. (1971), *Principles of Political Economy: The Controlled Economy*, vol. III. London: Allen & Unwin

Meltzer A. H., S. F. Richard (1981), A rational theory of the size of government, *Journal of Political Economy* **89**(5): 914–27

Menna L. (2016), Optimal fiscal and monetary policies under limited asset market participation, *Italian Economic Journal* **2**(3): 363–83

Menna L., P. Tirelli (2017), Optimal inflation to reduce inequality, *Review of Economic Dynamics* **24**: 79–94

Michener G., K. Bersch (2013), Identifying transparency, *Information Polity* **18**(3): 233–42

Miettinen R. (2013), *Innovation, Human Capabilities, and Democracy: Towards an Enabling Welfare State*. Oxford: Oxford University Press

Milani F., J. Treadwell (2012), The effects of monetary policy 'news' and 'surprises', *Journal of Money, Credit and Banking* **44**(8) 1667–92

Milanovic B. (2013), Global income inequality in numbers: in history and now, *Global Policy* **4**(2): 199–207

Milanovic B. (2016), *Global Inequality: A New Approach for the Age of Globalization*. Cambridge, MA: Harvard University Press

Mill J. S. (1848), *Principles of Political Economy with Some of Their Applications to Social Philosophy*. London: John Parker (abridged edn, Indianapolis/Cambridge: Hackett Publishing Company, 2004)

Minsky H. P. (1993), The financial instability hypothesis, in P. Arestis, M. Sawyer, eds., *Handbook of Radical Political Economy*. Aldershot: Edward Elgar

Mishkin F. S. (1982), Does anticipated monetary policy matter? An econometric investigation, *Journal of Political Economy* **90**(1): 22–51

Mishkin F. S. (2011), Monetary policy strategy: lessons from the crisis, NBER working paper no. 16755, February

Mishkin F., K. Schmidt-Hebbel (2007), Monetary policy under infla-
tion targeting: an introduction, in F. Mishkin, K. Schmidt-
Hebbel, eds., *Monetary Policy under Inflation Targeting*.
Santiago: Central Bank of Chile

Mittnik S., W. Semmler (2012), Regime dependence of the fiscal
multiplier, *Journal of Economic Behavior & Organization* **83**(3)
502–22

Modigliani F. (1961), Long-run implications of alternative fiscal
policies and the burden of the national debt, *Economic Journal*
71: 730–55

Modigliani F. (1977), The monetarist controversy or, should we
forsake stabilization policies?, *American Economic Review*
67(2): 1–19

Modigliani F., R. Brumberg (1954), Utility analysis and the con-
sumption function: an interpretation of cross-section data, in
K. Kurihara, ed., *Post-Keynesian Economics*. New Brunswick,
NJ: Rutgers University Press, pp. 388–436

Mokyr J. (2014), Secular stagnation? Not in your life, in C. Teulings,
R. Baldwin, eds., *Secular Stagnation: Facts, Causes and Cures*.
Washington, DC: CEPR

Mueller D. C. (1989), *Public Choice II*. Cambridge: Cambridge
University Press

Mueller D. C. (2003), *Public Choice III*. Cambridge: Cambridge
University Press

Müller A., K. Storesletten, F. Zilibotti (2016), The political color of
fiscal responsibility, *Journal of the European Economic
Association* **14**(1): 252–302.

Mundell R. A. (1962), The appropriate use of monetary and fiscal
policy under fixed exchange rates, *IMF Staff Papers* **9**(1): 70–79
(reproduced in Mundell 1968)

Mundell R. A. (1968), *International Economics*. London: Macmillan

Murphy R. (no date), *Fiscal-Multiplier-Workbook: Econometric
Estimations of the Spending Multiplier*, available at www.google
.it/url?sa=t&rct=j&q=&esrc=s&source=web&cd=1&ved=0ahUKE
wizwNyLmJnQAhUD7BQKHf_jDMUQFggdMAA&url=http per
cent3A per cent2F per cent2Fwww.govtmultiplier.com
per cent2Fwp-content per cent2Fuploads per cent2F2013 per
cent2F10 per cent2Ffiscal-multiplier-workbook.xlsx&usg=AFQj
CNGF5lIJrkG60uWUpvM7cYzDhkCiKQ

Musgrave R. A., A. T. Peacock (1958), eds., *Classics in the Theory of Public Finance*. London: Macmillan (2nd edn, 1994)

Myrdal, G. (1953), *The Political Element in the Development of Economic Theory*. London: Routledge & Kegan Paul

Nash J. E. (1950), The bargaining problem, *Econometrica* **18**(2): 155–62

Neck R. (1976), Der Beitrag kontrolltheoretischer Methoden zur Analyse der Stabilisationspolitik, *Zeitschrift fuer Nationaloekonomie/Journal of Economics* **36**(1–2): 121–51

Neck R., E. Dockner (1987), Conflict and cooperation in a model of stabilization policies: a differential game approach, *Journal of Economic Dynamics and Control* **11**(2): 153–58

Neck R., E. Dockner (1995), Commitment and coordination in a dynamic game model of international economic policy-making, *Open Economies Review* **6**(1): 5–28

Neri S., A. Notarpietro (2014), Inflation, debt and the zero lower bound, Bank of Italy Questioni di Economia e Finanza (occasional paper) no. 242, October

Niemann S., J. von Hagen (2008), Coordination of monetary and fiscal policies: a fresh look at the issue, *Swedish Economic Policy Review* **15**(1): 89–124

Niskanen W. (1971), *Bureaucracy and Representative Government*. Chicago, IL: Aldine

Nocciola L., D. Żochowski (2016), Cross-border spillovers from macroprudential policy in the Euro area, in Bank for International Settlements (BIS), Macroprudential policy, BIS paper no. 86, September, pp. 45–48; available at www.bis.org

Nordhaus W. D. (1975), The political business cycle, *Review of Economic Studies* **42**(2): 169–90

North D. C. (1981), *Structure and Change in Economic History*. New York, NY: W.W. Norton

North D. C. (1991), Institutions, *Journal of Economic Perspectives* **5**(1): 97–112

Norton H. S. (1966), *Economic Policy: Government and Business*. Columbus, OH: Charles E. Merrill Books

Nozick R. (1974), *Anarchy, State and Utopia*. New York, NY: Basic Books

Nussbaum M. C. (1999), *Sex and Social Justice*. Oxford: Oxford University Press

Nussbaum M. C. (2010), *Not for Profit: Why Democracy Needs the Humanities*. Princeton, NJ: Princeton University Press

Nussbaum M. C. (2011), *Creating Capabilities: The Human Development Approach*. Cambridge, MA: Harvard University Press

Nuti D. M. (2017), Seismic faults in the European Union, paper presented at the Conference in Honour of Francesco Forte, Sapienza University of Rome, 2–3 December 2016

Oates W. (1972), *Fiscal Federalism*. New York, NY: Harcourt Brace

OECD (2012), *General Government Revenue*. Paris: OECD Publishing

OECD (2015), Lifting investment for higher sustainable growth, chap. 3 in *OECD Economic Outlook*. Paris: OECD Publishing

OECD (2016), *OECD Employment Outlook 2016*. Paris: OECD Publishing, available at http://dx.doi.org/10.1787/empl_out look-2016-en

OECD (2017a), *National Schools of Government: Building Civil Service Capacity* (OECD Public Governance Reviews). Paris: OECD, available at http://dx.doi.org/10.1787/9789264268906-en

OECD (2017b), *Trust and Public Policy: How Better Governance Can Help Rebuild Public Trust* (OECD Public Governance Reviews). Paris: OECD, available at http://dx.doi.org/10.1787/978926 4268920-en

OECD (2017c), *Preventing Policy Capture: Integrity in Public Decision Making* (OECD Public Governance Reviews). Paris: OECD, available at http://dx.doi.org/10.1787/9789264065239-en

Ohlin B. (1937), Some notes on the Stockholm theory of savings and investment I & II, *Economic Journal*, **47**(185): 53–69, reprinted in *Readings in Business Cycle Theory*, London: Allen & Unwin, 1950

Ollivaud P., D. Turner (2015), The effect of the global financial crisis on OECD potential output, OECD Economics Department working paper no. 1166, also in *OECD Journal: Economic Studies* **2014**: 41–60

Olson M. (1965), *The Logic of Collective Action: Public Goods and Theory of Groups*. Cambridge, MA: Harvard University Press

Onorante L. (2006), Interaction of fiscal policies on the Euro area: how much pressure on the ECB?, European University Institute working paper no. 2006/9

Orphanides A., D. W. Wilcox (2002), The opportunistic approach to disinflation, *International Finance* **5**(1): 47–71

Orphanides A., R. M. Solow (1990), Money, inflation and growth, in B. M. Friedman, F. H. Hahn, eds., *Handbook of Monetary Economics*. Amsterdam: North Holland

Ortiz-Ospina E., M. Roser (2016), International trade, our world in data, available at https://ourworldindata.org/international-trade

Ostry J. D., A. R. Ghosh (2013), Obstacles to international policy coordination, and how to overcome them, IMF Staff discussion notes 13/11

Ostry J. D., A. Berg, C. G. Tsangarides (2014), Redistribution, inequality, and growth, IMF SDN 14/02

Ostry J. D., P. Loungani, D. Furceri (2016), Neoliberalism: Oversold?, *Finance and Development* **3**(2), available at www .imf.org/external/pubs/ft/fandd/2016/06/ostry.htm

Ozkan F. G., D. F. Unsal (2014), On the use of monetary and macroprudential policies for small open economies, IMF working paper no. 14/112, June

Pagano P. (2004), An empirical investigation of the relationship between inequality and growth, Bank of Italy working paper no. No 536, December

Palsson Syll L., B. Sandelin (2001), The spread of Italian economic thought in Sweden 1750–1950, in P. F. Asso, ed., *From Economists to Economists: The International Spread of Italian Economic Thought*. Firenze: Polistampa

Pantaleoni M. (1883), Contributo alla teoria del riparto delle spese pubbliche, *La rassegna italiana*, October: 25–60; reprinted in M. Pantaleoni, *Scritti varii di economia*. Palermo: Sandron, 1904, and in F. Volpe, ed., *Teorie della finanza pubblica*. Milan, 1975 (selected parts are translated into English in R. A. Musgrave, A. T. Peacock, eds., *Classics in the Theory of Public Finance*. London: Macmillan (1958), pp. 16–27)

Papandreou A. A. (1994), *Externality and Institutions*. Oxford: Clarendon Press

376   References

Papi G. U., ed. (1953), *Studi keynesiani*. Milan: Giuffrè

Pappa E. (2004), Do the ECB and the Fed really need to cooperate? Optimal monetary policy in a two-country world, *Journal of Monetary Economics* **51**(4): 753–79

Pareto V. (1896–97), *Cours d'économie politique*. Lausanne: F. Rouge

Pareto V. (1906), *Manuale di economia politica*. Milan: Società editrice libraria (reprinted by *Nuova grafica Bizzarri*. Rome, 1965); the English edition is *Manual of Political Economy*. New York: A. M. Kelley, 1971, trans. from the French edition of 1927 (first French edn, 1909)

Peck H. W. (1921), Review of 'Die Gerechtigkeit der Besteuerung' by Erik Lindahl, *Political Science Quarterly* **36**(3): 700–2

Pedone A. (2015), Il destino della progressività tributaria, *il Mulino* **65**(4): 760–68

Pekkarinen J. (1988), Keynesianism and the Scandinavian models of economic policy, World Institute for Development Economics Research of the United Nations University, working paper no. 35, February

Perotti R. (1996), Growth, income distribution, and democracy, *Journal of Economic Growth* **1**(2): 149–87

Perotti R. (2013), The 'austerity myth': gain without pain?, in A. Alesina, F. Giavazzi, eds., *Fiscal Policy after the Financial Crisis*. Chicago, IL: University of Chicago Press

Perotti R. (2014), Fiscal policies in recession, in G. Akerlof, O. Blanchard, D. Romer, J. Stiglitz, eds., (2014), *What Have We Learned? Macroeconomic Policy after the Crisis*. Cambridge, MA: MIT Press

Persson T., G. Tabellini (1990), *Macroeconomic Policy, Credibility and Politics*. Newark, NJ: Harwood Academic Publishers (Italian trans. *Politica macroeconomica. Le nuove teorie*. Rome: Nuova Italia Scientifica, 1996)

Persson T., G. Tabellini (2000), *Political Economics: Explaining Economic Policy*. Cambridge, MA: MIT Press

Peters B. G. (2002) The politics of tools choice, chap. 19 in L. Salamon, ed., *Tools of Government*. Oxford: Oxford University Press, pp. 552–64

Petit M. L. (1990), *Control Theory and Dynamic Games in Economic Policy Analysis*. Cambridge: Cambridge University Press

Phelps E. S. (1967), Phillips curves, expectations of inflation and optimal unemployment over time, *Economica* **34**(3): 254–81

Phelps E. S. (1973), Inflation in the theory of public finance, *Swedish Journal of Economics* **75**: 67–82.

Phillips A. W. (1958), The relation between unemployment and the rate of change of money wage rates in the United Kingdom, 1861–1957, *Economica* **25**(100): 283–99

Pigou A. C. (1912), *Wealth and Welfare*. London: Macmillan

Pigou A. C. (1920), *The Economics of Welfare*, 1st edn (4th edn, 1932). London: Macmillan

Piketty T. (2013), *Le Capital au XXIe siècle*. Paris: Éditions du Seuil (English trans. *Capital in the Twenty-First Century*. Cambridge, MA: Harvard University Press, 2014)

Pogge T. W. (2007), Why inequality matters, in D. Held, A. Kaya, eds. (2007), *Global Inequality*. Cambridge: Polity Press

Plasmans J., J. Engwerda, B. van Aarle, G. Di Bartolomeo, T. Michalak (2006), *Dynamic Modeling of Monetary and Fiscal Cooperation among Nations*. Berlin: Springer-Verlag

Polanyi, K. (1957), The economy as instituted process, in K. Polanyi, C. Arenburg, H. Pearson, eds., *Trade and Markets in the Early Empires*. Glencoe, IL: Free Press, pp. 243–70

Pomini M. (2015), L'economia del benessere e il problema della fondazione scientifica della politica economica in Federico Caffè, *Il pensiero economico italiano* **23**(2): 113–26

Posen A. (1995), Declarations are not enough: financial sector sources of central bank independence, in B. Bernanke J. Rotemberg, eds., *NBER Macroeconomic Annual 1995*. Cambridge, MA: MIT Press

Posen A. (1998), Central bank independence and disinflationary credibility: a missing link? *Oxford Economic Papers* **50**(3): 335–59

Powell G. B. (2000), *Elections as Instruments of Democracy: Majoritarian and Proportional Visions*. New Haven, CT: Yale University Press

Prendergast C. (1999), The provision of incentives in firms, *Journal of Economic Literature* **37**(1): 7–63

Prendergast C. (2008), Intrinsic motivation and incentives, *American Economic Review* **98**(2): 201–5

Preston A. J. (1974), A dynamic generalization of Tinbergen's theory, *Review of Economic Studies* **41**(1): 65–74

Preston A. J., A. R. Pagan (1982), The Theory of Economic Policy. Cambridge: Cambridge University Press

Przeworski A. (2006), Self-enforcing democracy, chap. 17 in B. Weingast, D. Wittman, eds., *The Oxford Handbook of Political Economy*. Oxford: Oxford University Press, pp. 312–28

Qian Y., B. Weingast (1997), Federalism as a commitment to market incentives, *Journal of Economic Perspectives* **11**(4): 83–92

Quint D., P. Rabanal (2014), Monetary and macroprudential policy in an estimated dsge model of the Euro area, *International Journal of Central Banking* **10**(2): 169–236

Raitano M., F. Vona (2015), Measuring the link between intergenerational occupational mobility and earnings: evidence from eight European countries, *Journal of Economic Inequality* **13**(1):83–102

Rajan R. (2013), A step in the dark: unconventional monetary policy after the crisis, Andrew Crockett Memorial Lecture, delivered at the Bank for International Settlements, 23 June

Rajapakse N. (2016), Amartya Sen's capability approach and education: enhancing social justice, *Revue LISA/LISA e-journal* **14**(1), DOI:http://10.4000/lisa.8913

Rannenberg A., C. Schoder, J. Strasky (2015), The macroeconomic effects of the Eurozone's fiscal consolidation 2011–2013: a simulation-based approach, Central Bank of Ireland research technical paper no. 3

Ravallion M. (2016), *The Economics of Poverty: History, Management and Policy*. New York, NY: Oxford University Press

Ravn M., S. Schmitt-Grohé, M. Uribe (2007), Explaining the effects of government spending shocks on consumption and the real exchange rate, mimeo, EUI Florence and Duke University

Rawdanowicz Ł., R. Bouis, S. Watanabe (2013), The benefits and costs of highly expansionary monetary policy, OECD Economics Department working paper no. 1082

Rawls J. (1971), *A Theory of Justice*. Cambridge, MA: Harvard University Press (revised edn, 1999)

Reichlin L., A. Turner, M. Woodford (2013), Helicopter money as a policy option, VoxEU.org, May

Reilly B. (2001), *Democracy in Divided Societies: Electoral Engineering for Conflict Management*. Cambridge: Cambridge University Press

Reinhart C., K. Rogoff (2010), Growth in a time of debt, *American Economic Review* **100**(2): 573–78

Reiss J. (2013), *Philosophy of Economics: A Contemporary Introduction*. London: Routledge

Rey G. M. (1967), *Regole ottimali per la politica economica*. Milan: Giuffrè

Ricardo D. (1817), *On the Principles of Political Economy and Taxation*, ed. P. Sraffa, Cambridge: Cambridge University Press (1951)

Robbins L. (1932), *An Essay on the Nature and Significance of Economic Science*, 1st edn (2nd edn, 1935). London: Macmillan

Robinson J. A., R. Torvik (2009), A political economy theory of the soft budget constraint, *European Economic Review* **53**(7): 786–79

Rodrik D. (1999), Where did all the growth go? External shocks, social conflict, and growth collapses, *Journal of Economic Growth* **4**(4): 385–412

Rodrik D. (2000), Governance and economic globalization, chap. 16 in J. S. Nye, J. D. Donahue, eds., *Governance in a Globalizing World*; chap. 7 in D. Rodrik, eds., *One Economics, Many Recipes: Global Institutions and Economic Growth*. Princeton, NJ: Princeton University Press, 2007

Rodrik D. (2002), Feasible globalizations, NBER working paper no. 9129, July

Rodrik D. (2011), *The Globalization Paradox: Democracy and the Future of the World Economy*. New York, NY: W.W. Norton

Rogoff K. (1985a), The optimal degree of commitment to an intermediate monetary target, *Quarterly Journal of Economics* **100**: 1169–89

Rogoff K. (1985b), Can international monetary policy coordination be counterproductive?, *Journal of International Economics* **18**(3–4): 199–217

Rogoff K. S. (2010), Why America isn't working, Project Syndicate, available at www.project-syndicate.org/

Rogoff K. (2017), Dealing with monetary paralysis at the zero bound, *Journal of Economic Perspectives* **31**(3): 47–66

Romani R. (2015), Minimal state theories and democracy in Europe: from the 1880s to Hayek, *History of European Ideas* **41**(2): 241–63, available at http://dx.doi.org/10.1080/01916599.2014.914313

Roncaglia A. (2005), *Il mito della mano invisibile*. Bari: Laterza

Rosanvallon P. (2015), *Le Bon Gouvernement*. Paris: Éditions du Seuil

Rosset J., N. Giger, J. Bernauer (2013), More money, fewer problems? Cross-level effects of economic deprivation on political representation, *West European Politics* **36**(4): 817–35, available at www.tandfonline.com/doi/abs/10.1080/01402382.2013.783353?journalCode=fwep20

Rothschild E. (2001), *Economic Sentiments: Adam Smith, Condorcet, and the Enlightenment*. Cambridge, MA: Harvard University Press

Rudebusch G. D., J. C. Williams (2008), Forecasting recessions: the puzzle of the enduring power of the yield curve, Federal Reserve Bank of San Francisco working paper no. 2007-16, July, available at www.frbsf.org/publications/economics/papers/2007/wp07-16bk.pdf

Sachs, J., X. Sala-i-Martin (1992), Fiscal federalism and optimum currency areas: evidence for Europe from the United States, in M. B. Canzoneri, V. Grilli, P. R. Masson, eds., *Establishing a Central Bank: Issues in Europe and Lessons from the U.S.* Cambridge: Cambridge University Press

Sæther A., I. E. Eriksen (2014a), Ragnar Frisch and the postwar Norwegian economy, *Econ Journal Watch* **11**(1): 46–80

Sæther A., I. E. Eriksen (2014b), A reply to Olav Bjerkholt on the postwar Norwegian economy, *Econ Journal Watch* **11**(3): 313

Saint-Paul G. (1992), Fiscal policy in an endogenous growth model, *Quarterly Journal of Economics* **107**(4): 1243–59

Salamon L. M. (2000), The new governance and the tools of public action: an introduction, *Fordham Urban Law Journal* **28**(5): 1611–74

Salverda W., B. Nolan, D. Checchi et al. (2014), *Changing Inequalities in Rich Countries: Analytical and Comparative Perspectives*. Oxford: Oxford University Press

Samuelson P. A. (1947), *Foundations of Economic Analysis.* Cambridge, MA: Harvard University Press

Samuelson P. A., R. M. Solow (1960), Problems of achieving and maintaining a stable price level: analytical aspects of anti-inflation policy, *American Economic Review, Papers and Proceedings* **50**(2): 177–94

Santoni G. J. (1986), The Employment Act of 1946: some history notes, *Federal Reserve Bank of St. Louis Review*, November: 5–16

Santor E., L. Suchanek (2013), Unconventional monetary policies: evolving practices, their effects and potential costs, *Bank of Canada Economic Review* **2013**(Spring): 1–15

Sardoni C. (2015), Is a Marxist explanation of the current crisis possible?, *Review of Keynesian Economics* **3**(1): 143–57

Sargent T. J., N. Wallace (1975), Rational expectations, the optimal monetary instrument, and the optimal money supply rule, *Journal of Political Economy* **83**(2): 241–54

Sargent T. J., N. Wallace (1981), Some unpleasant monetarist arithmetic, *Federal Reserve Bank of Minneapolis Quarterly Review*, Fall: 1–17

Schelling T. C. (1958), The strategy of conflict: prospectus for a reorientation of game theory, *Journal of Conflict Resolution* **2**(3): 203–64

Schelling T. C. (1960), *The Strategy of Conflict.* Cambridge, MA: Harvard University Press

Schenk C. (2016), International financial regulation and supervision, in Baten, J., ed., *A History of the Global Economy: 1500 to the Present.* Cambridge: Cambridge University Press, pp. 40–42

Schiattarella R. (2013), Le teorie delle scelte pubbliche, Camerino University, mimeo

Schmitt-Grohé S., M. Uribe (2004), Optimal fiscal and monetary policy under sticky prices, *Journal of Economic Theory* **114**(2): 198–230

Schmitt-Grohé S., M. Uribe (2011), The optimal rate of inflation, in B.M. Friedman, M. Woodford, eds., *Handbook of Monetary Economics.* Amsterdam: Elsevier, pp. 723–828

Schneider E. (1959), Frederik Zeuthen in memoriam 1888–1959, *Weltwirtschaftliches Archiv* **82**(1): 147–49

382   References

Schoenmaker D., P. Wierts (2015), Macroprudential supervision: from theory to policy, Bruegel working paper no. 2015/15, November

Schumpeter J. A. (1954), *History of Economic Analysis*. New York, NY: Oxford University Press

Scitovsky T. (1941), A note on welfare propositions in economics, *Review of Economic Studies* 9(1): 77–88

Screpanti E., S. Zamagni (1989), *Profilo di storia del pensiero economic*. Rome: La Nuova Italia Scientifica (English trans: *An Outline of the History of Economic Thought*. Oxford: Clarendon Press, 1993)

Šehović D. (2013), General aspects of monetary and fiscal policy coordination, *Journal of Central Banking Theory and Practice* 2(2): 5–27

Semmler W., A. Haider (2015), The perils of debt deflation in the euro area: a multiregime model, ZEW discussion paper no. 15-071, available at http://ftp.zew.de/pub/zew-docs/dp/dp15071.pdf

Semmler W., A. Semmler (2013), The macroeconomics of the fiscal consolidation in the European Union, mimeo, 15 June

Sen A. K. (1970a), *Collective Choice and Social Welfare*. Edinburgh: Oliver & Boyd (new enlarged edition: Cambridge, MA: Harvard University Press, 2017)

Sen A. K. (1970b), The impossibility of a Paretian liberal, *Journal of Political Economy* 78(1): 152–57

Sen A. K. (1977), Rational fools: a critique of the behavioral assumptions of economic theory, *Philosophy & Public Affairs* 6(4): 317–44, reprinted in F. Hahn, M. Hollis, eds., *Philosophy and Economic Theory*. Oxford: Oxford University Press, pp. 87–109

Sen A. K. (1980), Description as a choice, *Oxford Economic Papers* 32(3):353–69 (reprinted in Sen 1982)

Sen A. K. (1982), *Choice, Welfare and Measurement*. Oxford: Blackwell

Sen A. K. (1985), *Commodities and Capabilities*. Amsterdam: North Holland

Sen A. K. (1987), *On Ethics and Economics*. Oxford: Blackwell

Sen A. K. (1992), *Inequality Re-examined*. Oxford: Clarendon Press

Sen A. K. (1999a), Democracy as a universal value, *Journal of Democracy* **10**(3): 3–17

Sen A. K. (1999b), The possibility of social choice, *American Economic Review* **89**(3): 349–78

Sen A. K. (2009), *The Idea of Justice*. Cambridge, MA: Harvard University Press

Sen A. K. (2010), Adam Smith and the contemporary world, *Erasmus Journal for Philosophy and Economics* **3**(1): 50–67

Shah A. (2008), Interregional competition and federal cooperation: to compete or to cooperate? That's not the question, in A. Shah, ed., *Macrofederalism and Local Finances*. Washington, DC: World Bank

Shapiro C., J. E. Stiglitz (1984), Equilibrium unemployment as a worker discipline device, *American Economic Review* **74**(3): 433–44

Sibert A. (1999), Monetary integration and economic reform, *Economic Journal* **109**(452): 78–92

Sidgwick H. (1874), *The Methods of Ethics*. London: Macmillan (7th edn, 1907)

Sidgwick H. (1883), *Principles of Political Economy*. London: Macmillan

Sims C. A. (1980), Macroeconomics and reality, *Econometrica* **48**(1): 1–48

Sinn H.-W. (2013), Verantwortung der Staaten und Notenbanken in der Eurokrise (Responsibilities of governments and central banks in the Euro crisis), *Ifo Schnelldienst* **66**(Special Issue, June): 3–33 (also published in *Wirtschaftsdienst* 93(7): 451–54)

Sisk T. D. (2003), Democracy and conflict management, beyond intractability, August, available at www.beyondintractability .org/essay/democ-con-manag

Siven C.-H. (1985), The end of the Stockholm school, *Scandinavian Journal of Economics* **87**(4): 577–93

Smerilli A. (2007), 'We-rationality': per una teoria non individualistica della cooperazione, *Economia Politica* **24**(3): 407–26

Smith A. (1759), *The Theory of Moral Sentiments and Essays on Philosophical Subjects*. London: Alex Murray (1869)

Smith A. (1776), *An Inquiry into the Nature and Causes of the Wealth of Nations*. London: Straham & Cadell

Soderlind P. (1999), Solution and estimation of RE macromodels with optimal policy, *European Economic Review* **43**(4–6): 813–23

Spencer H. (1850), *Social statics*. London: Williams & Norgate

Spilimbergo A., S. Symansky, M. Schindler (2009), Fiscal multipliers, IMF Staff Position Note SPN/09/11

Sraffa P. (1926), The laws of returns under competitive conditions, *Economic Journal* **36**(144): 535–50

Sraffa P. (1960), *Production of Commodities by Means of Commodities: Prelude to a Critique of Economic Theory.* Cambridge: Cambridge University Press

Steinmo S. (1993), *Taxation and Democracy*. New Haven, CT: Yale University Press

Stiglitz J. E. (1986), *Economics of the Public Sector*. New York, NY: W.W. Norton

Stiglitz J. E. (2002), *Globalization and Its Discontents*. London: Allen Lane Penguin

Stiglitz J. E. (2006), *Making Globalization Work*. New York: W.W. Norton

Stiglitz J. E. (2015a), Monetary policy in a multi-polar world, in J. E. Stiglitz, R. Gurkaynak, eds., *Taming Capital Flows: Capital Account Management in an Era of Globalization*. Basingstoke: Palgrave Macmillan

Stiglitz J. E. (2015b), *The Great Divide*. London: Allan Lane

Stiglitz J. E. (2016), Globalisation and its new discontents, Project Syndicate, 5 August

Stockhammer E., D. P. Sotiropoulos (2014), The costs of internal devaluation, *Review of Political Economy* **26**(2): 210–33

Stone R., G. Croft-Murray (1959), *Social Accounting and Economic Models*. London: Bowes & Bowes

Summers L. H. (2014a), Reflections on the 'New Secular Stagnation Hypothesis', in C. Teuilings, R. Baldwin, eds., *Secular Stagnation: Facts, Causes, and Cures* (a VoxEU.org eBook). London: CEPR Press

Summers L. H. (2014b), U.S. economic prospects: secular stagnation, hysteresis, and the zero lower bound, *Business Economics* **49**(2): 65–73

Svensson L. E. O. (1997), Optimal inflation targets, 'conservative' central banks and linear inflation contracts, *American Economic Review* **87**(1): 98–114

Svensson L. (2012), Comment on Michael Woodford, 'Inflation Targeting and Financial Stability', *Penning-och valutapolitik* 1: 33–39

Swan T. W. (1960), Economic control in a dependent economy, *Economic Record* 36(73): 1–178

Swedberg R. (2008), The toolkit of economic sociology, in B. Weingast, D. Wittman, eds., *The Oxford Handbook of Political Economy*. Oxford: Oxford University Press, pp. 937–50

Tabellini G. (2016), Building common fiscal policy in the Eurozone, in R. Baldwin, F. Giavazzi, eds., *How to Fix Europe's Monetary Union: Views of Leading Economists*. A VoxEU.org eBook, pp. 117–31

Tagliacozzo G. (1933), *Economia e massimo edonistico collettivo*. Padova: Cedam

Tereanu E., A. Tuladhar, A. Simone (2014), Structural balance targeting and output gap uncertainty, IMF working paper no. 14/107

Teulings C., R. Baldwin, eds. (2014), *Secular Stagnation: Facts, Causes and Cures*. Washington, DC: CEPR

Theil H. (1956), On the theory of economic policy, *American Economic Review* 46(2): 360–66

Theil H. (1958), *Economic Forecasts and Policy*. Amsterdam: North Holland

Theil H. (1964), *Optimal Decision Rules for Government and Industry*. Amsterdam: North Holland

Thomas J.-P. (1994), *Les politiques économiques au XXe siècle*. Paris: Armand Colin

Thompson G. F. (2007), Global inequality, the 'Great divergence' and supranational regionalization, in D. Held, A. Kaya, eds., *Global Inequality*. Cambridge: Polity Press

Tiebout C, (1956), A pure theory of local expenditures, *Journal of Political Economy* 64(5): 416–24

Tinbergen J. (1935), Suggestions on quantitative business cycle theory, *Econometrica* 3(3): 241–51

Tinbergen J. (1949), Du système de Pareto aux modèles modernes, *Revue d'économie politique* 59: 642–52

Tinbergen J. (1952), *On the Theory of Economic Policy*. Amsterdam: North Holland (Italian trans. and ed. by F. Di Fenizio, *Sulla teoria della politica economica*. Milan: L'industria, 1955)

Tinbergen J. (1956), *Economic Policies: Principles and Design.* Amsterdam: North Holland

Tirelli P., G. Di Bartolomeo, N. Acocella (2015), US trend inflation reinterpreted: the role of fiscal policies and time-varying nominal rigidities, *Macroeconomic in Dynamics* **19**(6): 1294–308

Tirole J. (1994), The internal organization of government, *Oxford Economic Papers* **46**(1): 1–29

Tridico P. (2012), Financial crisis and global imbalances: its labour market origins and the aftermath, *Cambridge Journal of Economics* **36**(1): 17–42, DOI:http://:10.1093/cje/ber031

Tridico P. (2015), The rise of income inequality in OECD countries, Università degli studi Roma Tre, Dipartimento di Economia working paper no. 201

Tullock G. (1976), *The Vote Motive.* London: Institute of Economic Affairs (2nd edn, 2006)

Tullock, G. (1965), *The Politics of Bureaucracy.* Washington, DC: Public Affairs Press

Tyers R. (2012), Japanese economic stagnation: causes and global implications, *Economic Record*, **88**(283): 517–36

UNCTAD (2016), *Trade and Development Report, 2016.* New York, NY: United Nations

UNESCO (1998), Higher education in the twenty-first century: vision and action, World Conference on Higher Education, Paris, 5–9 October

United Nations (1992), *Handbook of the International Comparison Programme*, Studies in Methods, series F, no. 62: *Glossary.* New York, NY: Department of Economic and Social Development, Statistical Division

United Nations (2009), Report of the Commission of Experts of the President of the United Nations General Assembly on Reforms of the International Monetary and Financial System, Washington, 21 September, available at www.un.org/ga/econcrisissummit /docs/FinalReport_CoE.pdf

United Nations Environment Programme (2015), Climate change: time for action for people and planet, UNEP

United Nations General Assembly (1948), The Universal Declaration of Human Rights, General Assembly Resolution 217 A, Paris, 10 December

Unterhalter E., M. Walker, R. Vaughan (2007), The capability approach and education, Prospero, November, available at www .capabilityapproach.com/

van den End J. W. (2014), The breakdown of the money multiplier at the zero lower bound, *Applied Economics Letters* **21** (13): 875–77

van Eijk C. J., J. Sandee (1959), Quantitative determination of an optimum economic policy, *Econometrica* **27**(1): 1–13

Vanberg V. J. (2014), Ordnungspolitik, the Freiburg School and the reason of rules, in *i-lex*, **21**, pp. 205–20 (www.i-lex.it)

Valentini L. (2011), A paradigm shift in theorizing about justice? A critique of Sen, *Economics and Philosophy* **27**(3): 297–315

Veblen T. (1898), Why is economics not an evolutionary science?, *Quarterly Journal of Economics* **12**(4): 373–97

Visco I. (2014), Lawrence R. Klein: macroeconomics, econometrics and economic policy, *Journal of Policy Modeling* **36**(4): 605–28

Visco I. (2015), Eurozone challenges and risks, London, Wharton, University of Pennsylvania, Second Annual Meeting of the Zell/ Lurie Real Estate Center, 6 May

Voitchovsky S. (2009), Inequality and economic growth, in W. Salverda, B. Nolan, D. Checchi et al., eds., *Changing Inequalities in Rich Countries: Analytical and Comparative Perspectives.* Oxford: Oxford University Press

Von Hagen J. (2013), Scope and limits of independent fiscal institutions, in G. Kopits, ed., *Restoring Public Debt Sustainability: The Role of Independent Fiscal Institutions.* Oxford: Oxford University Press

von Mises L. (1920), Die Wirtschaftsrechnung im sozialistischen Gemeinwesen Archiv für Sozialwissenschaften **47**: 86–121 (Economic calculation in the Socialist Commonwealth), reprinted in F. A. Hayek, ed., *Collectivist Economic Planning.* London: Routledge (1935)

von Neumann Whitman M. (1969), Comment, in R. A. Mundell, A. K. Swoboda, eds., *Monetary Problems of the International Economy.* Chicago, IL: University of Chicago Press

Wade R. H. (2007), Should we worry about income inequality?, in D. Held, A. Kaya, eds., *Global Inequality.* Cambridge: Polity Press

Walker M. (2003), Framing social justice in education: what does the 'capabilities' approach offer?, *British Journal of Educational Studies* **51**(2): 168–87

Walker M., E. Unterhalter, eds. (2007), *Amartya Sen's Capability Approach and Social Justice in Education.* Houndmills: Palgrave Macmillan

Walras L. (1874–77), Eléments d'économie politique pure ou théorie de la richesse sociale, in A. and L. Walras, *Oeuvres économiques complètes*, vol. **VIII**. Paris: Economica (1999)

Walras L. (1898, 1936), *Etudes d'économie politique appliquée* (Théorie de la richesse sociale, final edn). Paris: Pichon & Durand, 1936 in A. and L. Walras, *Oeuvres économiques complètes*, vol. X,. Paris: Economica (1992)

Walsh C. E. (1995), Optimal contracts or central bankers, *American Economic Review* **85**(1): 150–67

Watson D. S. (1960), *Economic Policy: Business and Government.* Boston: Houghton Mifflin,

Weale M., T. Wieladek (2014), What are the macroeconomic effects of asset purchases?, chap. 4 in W. den Haan, ed., *Quantitative Easing: Evolution of Economic Thinking As It Happened.* Washington, DC: CEPR Press, pp. 45–49

Weber A. (2010), Kaufprogramm birgt erhebliche Risiken (Bond Program Carries Substantial Risks), *Börsen-Zeitung* **89**(1)

Weingast B., D. Wittman, eds. (2006), *The Oxford Handbook of Political Economy.* Oxford: Oxford University Press

Wicksell K. (1896), *Finanztheoretische Untersuchungen.* Jena: Gustav Fischer (English trans. A new principle of just taxation, in R. Musgrave, A. T. Peacock, eds., *Classics in the Theory of Public Finance.* New York: St. Martin's Press, pp. 72–118)

Wicksell K. (1898), *Geldzins und Güterpreise.* Jena: Gustav Fischer (English trans. by R. F. Kahn, *Interest and Prices.* London: Macmillan (1936))

Wicksell K. (1934, 1935), *Lectures on Political Economy* (English trans. **2** vols. originally published in 1900, 1901), London: George Routledge and Sons, 1946

Wilkinson R., K. Pickett (2009), *The Spirit Level: Why More Equal Societies Almost Always Perform Better.* London: Allen Lane

Williams J. C. (2013), Lessons from the financial crisis for unconventional monetary policy, panel discussion at the Boston NBER Conference, mimeo, available at http://citeseerx.ist.psu.edu /viewdoc/download?doi=10.1.1.406.7506&rep=rep1&type=pdf

Wittman D. (1977), Platforms with policy preferences: a dynamic model, *Journal of Economic Theory* **14**(1): 180–89

Wittman D. (1995), *The Myth of Democratic Failure: Why Political Institutions Are Efficient.* Chicago, IL: University of Chicago Press

Wolff G. B. (2014), Monetary policy cannot solve secular stagnation alone, in C. Teulings, R. Baldwin, eds., *Secular Stagnation: Facts, Causes and Cures.* Washington, DC: CEPR

Woodford M. (1996), Control of public debt: a requirement for price stability?, NBER working paper no. 5684, July

Woodford M. (2000), Interest and Prices, Princeton University, mimeo

Woodford M. (2003), *Interest Rate and Prices.* Princeton, NJ: Princeton University Press

Woodford M. (2005), Central bank communication and policy effectiveness, paper presented at FRB Kansas City Symposium on the Greenspan Era: lessons for the Future, Jackson Hole, Wyoming, 25–27 August

Woodford M. (2009), Comment on Williams, *Brookings Papers on Economic Activity* **2**: 38–45

Woodford M. (2011), Simple analytics of the government expenditure multiplier, *American Economic Journal: Macroeconomics* **3**(1): 1–35

Woodford M. (2013), Monetary policy targets after the crisis, presented at the Conference on 'Rethinking Macro Policy II', IMF, April 16–17

Wren-Lewis S. (2003), Changing the rules, *New Economy* **10**(2): 73–78

Wruuck P., K. Wiemer (2016), Better budgeting in Europe: what can fiscal councils contribute?, Deutsche Bank Research, EU Monitor, 7 June

WTO (2008), Trade in a globalizing world, in *World Trade Report 2008.* Geneva: WTO

Yellen (2014), Many targets, many instruments: where do we stand?, in G. Akerlof, O. Blanchard, D. Romer, J. Stiglitz, eds.,

What Have We Learned? Macroeconomic Policy after the Crisis. Cambridge, MA: MIT Press

Yilmaz S., Y. Beris, R. Serrano-Berthet (2008), Local government discretion and accountability: a diagnostic framework for local governance, World Bank, Local Governance & Accountability Series, working paper no. 113/July

Yoshino N., F. Taghizadeh-Hesary (2015), Japan's lost decade: lessons for other economies, Asian Development Bank Institute, working paper no. 521, April

Zeuthen F. (1958), *Videnskab og Velfaerd I okonomisk Politik, Gads Forlag, Copenaghen* (Italian trans. and ed. by F. Caffè, *Scienza e benessere nella politica economica – Science and welfare in economic policy*). Torino: Boringhieri (1961)

Zeuthen F. (1959), Science and welfare in economic policy, *Quarterly Journal of Economics* **73**(4): 513–21

Zgaga P. (2009), Higher education and citizenship: 'the full range of purposes', *European Educational Research Journal* **8**(2): 175–88

Author Index

Subject Index